DOUBLE CHARACTER

DOUBLE CHARACTER

SLAVERY AND MASTERY IN THE ANTEBELLUM SOUTHERN COURTROOM

Ariela J. Gross

PRINCETON UNIVERSITY PRESS · PRINCETON AND OXFORD

PUBLISHED BY PRINCETON UNIVERSITY PRESS, 41 WILLIAM STREET,
PRINCETON, NEW JERSEY 08540
IN THE UNITED KINGDOM: PRINCETON UNIVERSITY PRESS,
3 MARKET PLACE, WOODSTOCK, OXFORDSHIRE OX20 1SY

LIBRARY OF CONGRESS CATALOGING-IN-PUBLICATION DATA

GROSS, ARIELA JULIE.
DOUBLE CHARACTER: SLAVERY AND MASTERY IN THE ANTEBELLUM
SOUTHERN COURTROOM / ARIELA J. GROSS.
P. CM.
INCLUDES BIBLIOGRAPHICAL REFERENCES AND INDEX.
ISBN 0-691-05957-8
1. SLAVES—LEGAL STATUS, LAWS, ETC.—SOUTHERN STATES—HISTORY—
19TH CENTURY. 2. SLAVERY—LAW AND LEGISLATION—SOUTHERN STATES—
HISTORY—19TH CENTURY. 3. COURTS—SOUTHERN STATES—HISTORY—
19TH CENTURY. I. TITLE.
KF482.G76 2000   342.75′087—dc21   00-035395

THIS BOOK HAS BEEN COMPOSED IN SABON BOOK MODIFIED TYPEFACE

THE PAPER USED IN THIS PUBLICATION MEETS THE MINIMUM REQUIREMENTS
OF ANSI/NISO Z39.48-1992 (R1997) *PERMANENCE OF PAPER*
WWW.PUP.PRINCETON.EDU

PRINTED IN THE UNITED STATES OF AMERICA

1   3   5   7   9   10   8   6   4   2

For Jon

CONTENTS

ACKNOWLEDGMENTS

I HAVE incurred many debts, both intellectual and personal, in the preparation of this book. A number of wonderful teachers in graduate and law school at Stanford University helped me in the first years of this project. I offer my deepest thanks to George Fredrickson, who directed my dissertation, for his encouragement, his insights, and his example. Rarely is a brilliant scholar and thinker such a humane teacher and thoroughly decent human being. Robert Gordon's wit, erudition, generosity, and critical sensibility have made him an invaluable mentor, reader, and adviser. Janet Halley's probing questions and keen perceptions helped me to clarify muddy thinking at every stage in this process. Jack Rakove read the dissertation with a sharp critical eye. Al Camarillo, Estelle Freedman, Tom Grey, Mark Kelman, Deborah Rhode, Kathleen Sullivan, and Bob Weisberg were challenging and inspiring teachers.

For unfailing good fellowship and rare intellectual and personal support, as well as for their readings of countless drafts, I thank Karen Dunn-Haley, Leslie Harris, Wendy Lynch, Renee Romano, Wendy Wall, and Alice Yang-Murray. Several eminent scholars gave me crucial advice and encouragement at an early stage in the project and continued to be supportive throughout: Carl Degler, Terry Fisher, Winthrop Jordan, and Patricia Williams. I also owe thanks to a number of generous colleagues who have shared ideas, read chapters in draft, or helped me with research: Scott Altman, Michelle Aronowitz, Sharon Block, David Cruz, Pete Daniel, Ron Davis, Mary Dudziak, Harry Elam, Paul Finkelman, Catherine Fisk, Ron Garet, Howard Gillman, Tom Green, Tom Grey, Sam Gross, Dirk Hartog, Walter Johnson, Tony Kaye, Andrew Kull, Tom Lyon, Chris Morris, Nell Painter, Jeannie Rhee, Tom Russell, Elyn Saks, Clyde Spillenger, Steven Stowe, Chris Waldrep, and colleagues who participated in faculty workshops at USC Law School, Yale Law School, and Princeton University. Laura Edwards, Leslie Harris, Hilary Schor, and Nomi Stolzenberg read and commented insightfully on the entire manuscript. I would also like to thank Peter Bardaglio, Kathleen Brown, Jonathan Bush, Gwendolyn Hall, Rachel Moran, the late Armstead Robinson, and Mark Tushnet, whose comments on presentations at several conferences provoked me to think harder about my project. Kenneth Greenberg and an anonymous reviewer for Princeton University Press read the manuscript and offered many cogent and helpful criticisms. Brigitta van Rheinberg and Lauren Lepow of Princeton University Press also deserve thanks for their advice and editing.

During the research for this book, I had a second home in Natchez, Mississippi. My greatest debt is to Mimi and Ron Miller, the powerhouses who run the Historic Natchez Foundation. Besides being a fount of knowledge about Natchez and Southern history in general, they make the phrase "Southern hospitality" a living, breathing reality. Mike Willey generously photographed documents for me, and entertained my daughter at the same time. Thanks also to Ethel Banta, Alma Carpenter, Ron Davis, and Joyce Broussard-Hogan. Dallas Clement, Gwen Hall, John Hammond Moore, and Mike Wall shared their homes with me during my research trips, and Peter Caron, Gwen Hall, and Tony Kaye shared data and leads in the archives.

Archivists have gone out of their way to help me locate the things I needed. I am especially grateful to Marie Windell at the University of New Orleans, Ann Webster at the Mississippi Department of Archives and History, Norwood Kerr at the Alabama Department of Archives and History, and Carolyn Hamby at the South Carolina Department of Archives and History, all of whom were generous with their time and advice on tracking down hard-to-find cases.

I would like to thank the following institutions for research funds and financial support: the American Historical Association, for the Littleton-Griswold Research Grant; the Center for Research on Legal Institutions at Stanford Law School, and the Stanford Humanities Center for research fellowships; and the University of Southern California Law School and the Zumberge Research and Innovation Fund of the University of Southern California for generous financial support. The tuition and stipend provided by the Foreign Language Area Studies Fellowship of the Department of Education and the University Fellowship of Stanford History Department made my graduate studies possible. The Stanford Humanities Center gave me something that allowed me to begin the writing of this study in the midst of law school: a room of my own. The University of Southern California Law School has given me every kind of assistance necessary to complete this project. I would like to thank in particular Dean Scott Bice and Associate Dean Scott Altman for their unfailing encouragement, generous research leaves, and accommodation of every request. Michelle Jones provided excellent secretarial services, and David Alverson, Jason Hamm, and Laura Premi contributed crucial research assistance. Thanks also to Eric Siemens for brilliant jacket design work.

An earlier version of chapter 3 was published under the title "Pandora's Box: Slave Character on Trial in the Antebellum Deep South" in *Yale Journal of Law and the Humanities* 7 (1995): 267–317; another incarnation of it appears in *Slavery and the Law*, ed. Paul Finkelman (Madison, Wis.: Madison House, 1997). A version of chapter 4 appeared in *Cardozo Law Review* 18 (1996): 263–99, under the title " 'Like Master, Like

Man': Constructing Whiteness in the Commercial Law of Slavery, 1800–1861." My thanks to the editors for permissions to reprint.

I owe a special thanks to my mother, Shulamith Gross, who furthered this project in two important ways that go far beyond the typical maternal support. In the winter of 1995, she accompanied me to the Deep South for two weeks to care for her seven-week-old granddaughter while I worked in the archives. The following summer, she spent nearly a month working with the data I collected from Adams County, running statistical tests to explain the outcomes in the cases I studied. David Gross, Sheva Gross, and my late grandfather, Bertram Gross, lent me support and encouragement. Raphaela and Sophia Gross Goldman, both of whom were born during the course of writing, gave me a reason to hurry up and finish. Finally, Jon Goldman made this book possible through his unfailing good humor, coparenting, critical reading, and difficult questions. In more ways than I can say, I am so lucky.

DOUBLE CHARACTER

INTRODUCTION

THOMAS READE COBB, the young reporter for the Georgia Supreme Court, managed to complete only one volume of his projected two-volume treatise on the law of slavery before he met an untimely death in the Confederate Army. In the preface to that volume, he explained that slaves in the American South had the "double character" of person and property under the law; therefore, the first part of his work would be devoted to slaves "as persons," and the second to slaves "as property."[1] Modern historians have also made use of this dichotomy as an organizing principle. The leading work on the history of Southern slavery and law is divided into sections on "slaves as property" and "slaves as persons" as well, roughly corresponding to a split between civil and criminal law.[2] By implication, slaves under Southern law had the character of persons in criminal cases and that of property all the rest of the time.[3] But there are other ways to understand the "doubleness" of slaves' character than in terms of a fissure in Southern law. By looking at the moment when slaves were *most* property-like to white Southerners—at the moment of sale or hire—this study will explore the paradoxes that arose from slaves' double identity as human subjects and the objects of property relations *at one and the same time.*

In a variety of civil disputes, courts attempted to treat slaves as they treated horses or machines. When slave buyers felt their newly acquired human property to be "defective" physically or morally, they sued the seller for breach of warranty—just as they would over a horse or a piece of machinery. Similarly, slave owners sued hirers, overseers, and other white men for damage to their slave property when they beat or neglected slaves, and slaveholders disputed over possession of slaves as they would over other chattel. Yet in these mundane civil cases, the parties in the courtroom brought into question, and gave legal meaning to, the "character" as well as the resistant behavior of enslaved people who persisted in acting as people. I do not mean to suggest a naive belief that Southern judges, or other white participants in the courtroom, suffered moral qualms at treating people as things, nor even that contests over character meant a recognition of slaves' personhood in its moral dimensions, but rather that the very logic and structure of disputes about property claims pushed forward and made white Southerners confront the character of slaves in challenging ways.

Of course, horses too could run away or be recalcitrant, leading one historian to suggest that slaves influenced the law merely the way horses influence the law.[4] Some legal historians have explained all contradictions in slavery law by slaveholders' efforts to shape the law instrumentally to serve their own economic interests, or by the tendency of the common law to approach economic efficiency.[5] Yet in civil disputes such as warranty suits, slaves themselves both directly and indirectly influenced the law far more than horses ever could, for two reasons. First, putting slave character on trial allowed slaves' moral agency to intrude into the courtroom, which raised difficulties for legal transactions dealing with slaves in the same manner as other forms of property. "Double character" suggests deceit, trickery, the presentation of a false face. Deceit was one of the few tools available to slaves in the effort to manipulate their worlds and their fates, and many of these legal disputes were shaped by whites' fear of slaves' trickery. Second, these disputes, by forcing "the law" to consider slaves' character, also challenged slaveholders' self-conception as honorable masters. Thus "double character" took on another dimension in trials involving slaves: the double character of masters and slaves. These cases mattered to white Southerners because their self-understandings as white masters depended on their relationships to black slaves; putting black character on trial called white character into question as well.

Southern culture also had a "double character." On the one hand, the plantation South was a world governed by conceptions of honor. White men of the Deep South understood their own place in society and that of others according to their ability to participate in an honor culture. They prized their reputation as honorable men, and they vowed to defend their honor against all slights. Yet, simultaneously, increasing numbers of men, and some women, participated in a vigorous commercial market, whose values seem at first glance contradictory to those of the honor culture. Despite their apparent incompatibility, both commercial and honorific practices and values were sustained and knitted together by slavery, the central institution of the Deep South. Indeed, slaves themselves saw commerce and the honor culture as inextricably linked, with the marketplace providing the arena for many of the rituals of white honor and black dishonor that most deeply defined slavery. Going to the core of what slavery meant to them, upon freedom, many sang,

> Tain't no mo' sellin' today,
> Tain't no mo' hirin' today,
> Tain't no pullin' off shirts today,
> It's stomp down freedom today.[6]

In celebrating the end of the demeaning practices of the market, newly freed slaves suggested that the essence of slavery's dishonor was making people into objects of commerce. This study travels into the courtrooms of Deep Southern counties, where disputes over the bodies, minds, and character of enslaved people implicated *both* commerce and honor.

Most historians who have written about the "private" law of slavery—disputes involving slaves as property—have focused on the opinions of appellate courts and have discussed the relationship between legal doctrine and the Southern economy, rather than local trials and local culture.[7] These studies have called attention to the dilemmas antebellum Southern high court judges faced in applying legal rules first developed by Northern and English courts to cases involving slaves.[8]

Local trials, however, reveal another sense of the "double character" of the law: the conjunction of rules handed down by high courts with legal understandings developed by ordinary people. Rules of evidence and the language of legal argument shaped local disputes, but so did community norms. The stories of trials involving slaves could be read as the triumph of custom over law, in which social practices overwhelmed formal legal rules. Yet such a view depends on an overly narrow definition of "law." The litigation of commercial disputes involving slaves also demonstrates that law as it is actually experienced is created by a variety of lawmakers: not only by judges and legislators, but by the litigants, witnesses, and jurors in the courtroom.[9]

Trials also illuminate the double character of white Southerners' racial ideology. At the day-to-day working level, slave masters had no choice but to deal with slaves as people in some respects; to acknowledge that they had preferences, volition, personality, relationships, families—whether or not their masters chose to override all of these by force.[10] Thus in witnesses' testimony as in private slave lists, descriptions of slaves went far beyond the simple "Sambo" and "Nat Turner" stereotypes; while they may not have recognized the full range of human personality, they did include comments on slaves' intelligence, playfulness, and pride. On the other hand, the second quarter of the nineteenth century saw the development of a highly articulated, stylized racial ideology used in the defense of slavery as a positive good. As legal historians have shown, appellate opinions were part of this highly articulate, outward-looking proslavery defense; judges knew that abolitionists in the North scoured the published reports to find damning evidence of the inhumanity of slavery.[11] It was quite possible for these two discourses of racial ideology to coexist: a white slaveholder could believe on one level that all black people were children; at the same time in his daily life he could expect his slave blacksmith to complete very skilled work, and he could get angry when the work was not completed. What is remarkable about trials of civil disputes is that they represent the moment of confrontation between these two discourses. These disputes arose from ordinary incidents in daily life, where white people were dealing with a fuller dimension of their slaves' personalities. In the courtroom, however, they came up against the highly stylized discourse of the color line. Trials, then, were an important arena for the discovery of the double character of both racial ideology and law in the antebellum South.

This study attempts to draw on the insights and methods of several disciplinary approaches to legal history. Like traditional intellectual historians of legal thought, I am centrally concerned with questions of ideology and, in particular, with the relationship between law and racial ideology. I have also followed the lead of critical legal historians who have focused attention on the constitutive role of law in culture.[12] From social history and law-and-society studies, I inherited a commitment to archival research and quantitative analysis of trial-level data. In addition to readings of all the available local trial records of cases appealed to the state supreme courts of the Deep South, this study is based on a very large sample of unappealed trials from Adams County, Mississippi.[13] These cases, as well as all the participants for whom I was able to locate information in manuscript census records, personal tax rolls, and land deed records, formed two large databases for analysis. Finally, legal anthropology taught me to approach the courtroom as an arena in which ordinary people experienced and shaped legal meanings, and to view law as "one of the great cultural formations of human life."[14] Diaries, letters, travelers' accounts, newspapers, ex-slave narratives, and other documents allowed me to open a window on the trial as an important cultural event in people's daily lives.

The five states surveyed constitute the region known today as the "Deep South," or the "Black Belt." These states were united by the culture and economy of the cotton plantation. They held the largest slave populations by the second quarter of the nineteenth century; the Deep Southern states were the greatest slave importers in the domestic trade. By focusing on the states with large numbers of slaves and slave buyers, as well as large plantations, not only do we find vigorous litigation over slave sales, but we observe a relatively coherent planter culture and ideology. At the same time, these states encompass both the "Old South" of South Carolina, and the newer areas of the Southwest, such as Mississippi. The trials were widely distributed: from thirty-four counties in Georgia, thirty in Alabama, twenty-five in South Carolina, and eighteen in Mississippi, approximately mirroring the distribution of slaveholding.

The study also includes both common law regimes and the civil law system of Louisiana. Of the five states, Louisiana had by far the most litigation on these subjects at the Supreme Court level; 237 out of 503 cases came from Louisiana. Because of Louisiana's codified consumer protections for slave buyers, warranty litigation was extremely common and generated many of the examples in this study.[15] However, despite Louisiana's unusual Roman law heritage and its Civil Code, its cases exhibit struggles over the character of slaves and masters remarkably similar to those in common law states.[16]

Cases appealed to high courts were more representative of the typical trial than one might imagine today. All five state supreme courts were required to hear every appeal that came before them, unlike today, when only a small fraction of appeals are accepted for a hearing. There were no intermediate courts of appeal to filter cases out. A comparison of the five-state sample with the Adams County sample of unappealed cases revealed no important differences; appealed suits did not even involve larger amounts of money, nor were the appellants who took cases to a higher court themselves wealthier than other plaintiffs.[17] Furthermore, a small sample from two rural South Carolina counties suggests that Adams County was not an unrepresentative county despite its significant population of wealthy planters.[18]

· · · · ·

This study opens in Adams County, Mississippi, on St. Catherine's Road into Natchez, which ran past the slave market to the courthouse. Using Adams County as an example, but drawing on research from throughout the Deep South, chapter 1 describes "Court Week," the local and legal culture of circuit courts, and the slave economy in which lawsuits originated. Then, entering the courtroom itself, it follows a typical trial from beginning to end, with a discussion of juries, witnesses, and litigants, based on quantitative data from Adams County. The chapter closes with a discussion of the silent subjects of trials, the slaves themselves, their awareness of the role of law in their lives, and their ability to influence its outcomes.

Chapter 2 argues that we can best understand civil disputes over slaves by viewing them within the context of a culture of honor. The chapter explores the relationship among honor, commerce, and law in Southern society. An in-depth discussion of one case from Adams County reveals the way legal disputes became affairs of honor between white men, and vice versa. Then the chapter turns to the *dis*honoring of slaves in litigation: both the treatment of their bodies and the disrespect of their words through the ban on slave testimony. Another case study from Adams County demonstrates the dishonor of slaves and free blacks through the erasure of their stories from the legal and historical record. The chapter concludes by discussing the difficulties courts faced in silencing slaves completely, and the ways that slaves' agency intruded into the courtroom, throwing their masters' honor into question, when slaves' words were repeated in the courtroom.

Chapters 3 and 4 examine the portrayal of slaves' and masters' character in the courtroom. Civil disputes brought forth many of the racial theories that characterized Southern culture, and helped to define which images of black men and women would prevail in the legal arena. Parties came into the courtroom telling various stories about slaves' character, but the courtroom process favored certain stories over others. For example, when the slave at issue was a woman, the range of acceptable stories narrowed dramatically. By privileging particular slave personae for both men and women, the law established racial meanings, not only through specific stereotypes of black people, but by painting a picture of black moral character development that differed from Southern white accounts of white moral character development. Chapter 3 considers how legal actors sought to erase slaves' moral agency from their explanations of slaves' behavior. But, despite these efforts, witnesses continued to report on slaves who thought and acted for themselves, even deceiving whites.

Chapter 4 explores the ramifications for masters and mastery of litigating slave character. Because the most common theories of black character emphasized its mutability and dependence on the influence of white men, these cases inevitably shone a spotlight on the character of white "masters"—including owners, hirers, and other supervisors of slaves. Furthermore, tort cases set judicial standards for the care of slaves by parties other than the slave owner. These disputes took on significance in a culture imbued with notions of honor that depended on white gentlemen's mastery of social inferiors. Commercial trials became an arena for proving mastery and honor, as well as denying the market basis for those values.

Chapter 5 extends the argument about slaves' and masters' character to the most routine conflicts involving slaves, those that concerned illness—whether a slave was "sound in body and mind" at the time of sale or hire. Despite the mundane nature of these cases, they, too, put white and black character on trial. Buyers, sellers, and hirers read slaves' bodies for signs of character; at the same time, their own characters were judged on the basis of their ability to read slaves' bodies. Doctors established themselves as intermediaries between master and slave, and between "the law" and both master and slave, by asserting their expertise in all matters concerning slaves' bodies. Historians have chronicled the role of physicians in creating Southern discourses of biological racism; in the courtroom, medical and legal discourses merged to brand slaves as racially distinct, "other," and inferior to whites. Yet efforts to "medicalize" the character traits of slaves, and to assert professional control over their bodies, were not wholly successful. For doctors, in their diagnosis and treatment of slaves, and hence in their testimony about diagnosis and treatment, relied on slaves' own words and actions. Thus warranty suits over sick slaves forced courts to consider slaves' own constructions of their conditions, and allowed slaves to influence the process by "feigning" illness.

The book concludes with a brief discussion of post–Civil War legal proceedings of two sorts. Commercial disputes involving slaves continued to be litigated and appealed throughout the 1860s and 1870s, some of them with novel legal arguments invoking emancipation as grounds for the cancellation of debts owed by slave purchasers. Despite the efforts of Republicans in state constitutional conventions to relieve debts based on "slave consideration," most courts declared that commerce demanded these cases be decided on exactly the same terms they had been in the decades before. In a very different legal forum, ex-slaves speaking before the Southern Claims Commission and the U.S. Court of Claims used their first opportunity to have their voices heard in legal testimony to cast aspersions on the loyalty claims of their former masters.

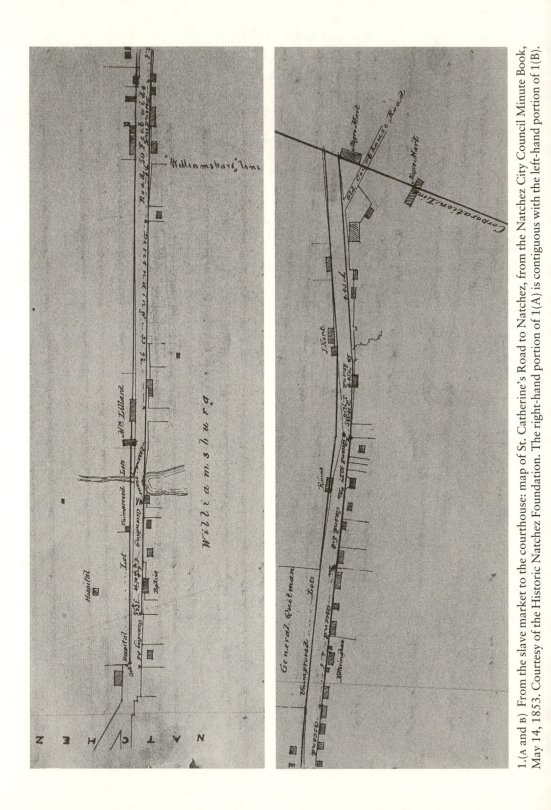

1. (A and B) From the slave market to the courthouse: map of St. Catherine's Road to Natchez, from the Natchez City Council Minute Book, May 14, 1853. Courtesy of the Historic Natchez Foundation. The right-hand portion of 1(A) is contiguous with the left-hand portion of 1(B).

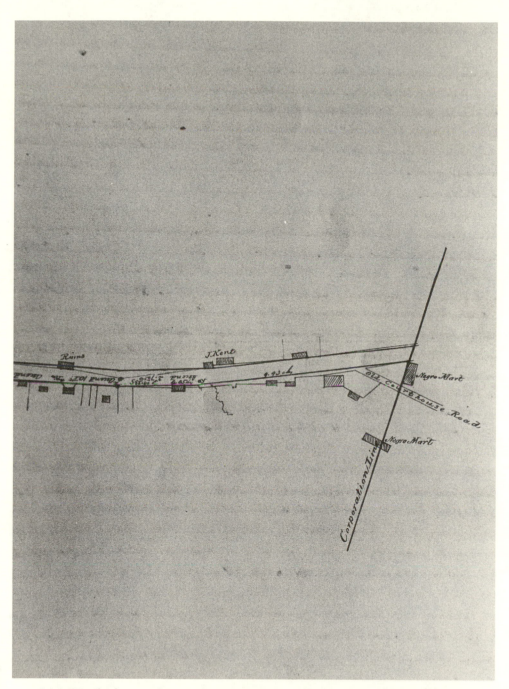

1.(c) Detail of map of St. Catherine's Road to Natchez, from the Natchez City Council Minute Book, May 14, 1853. Courtesy of the Historic Natchez Foundation.

2. Natchez, 1835. Charles Risso and William R. Browne, after James Tooley. I. N. Phelps Stokes Collection, Miriam and Ira D. Wallach Division of Arts, Prints, and Photographs, The New York Public Library.

3. Slaves in the shadow of the courthouse, Montgomery, Alabama. Wood engraving in *Harper's Weekly* 5 (1861). Library of Congress, Z62-33653.

4. "Selling Females by the Pound." Library of Congress, Z62-30823.

5. "The Slave Market." Courtesy of the Amistad Research Library, Tulane University.<lt>

6. "Judges, Lawyers, and Their Clients Going to Court." From *The Romance and Tragedy of Pioneer Life*, by Augustus L. Mason, 1884. Library of Congress, Z62-13605.

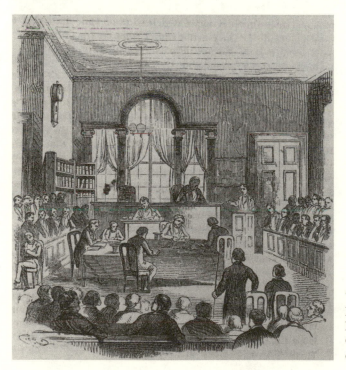

7. "The Court Room." 1852. Library of Congress, Z62-67562.

8. Bills of sale and warranties for the slave Mary Jane, from L. D. Collins to H. Geo. Doyle, March 17, 1834; from H. Geo. Doyle to Emanuel Rogillio, November 21, 1834; and from Emanuel Rogillio to Samuel Cotton, January 2, 1835. Courtesy of the Historic Natchez Foundation.

9. Record of the trial in Adams Circuit Court of *Cotton v. Rogolio*, December Term, 1835. Courtesy of the Historic Natchez Foundation.

10. List of court costs in *Cotton v. Rogolio*. Courtesy of the Historic Natchez Foundation.

11. Witness subpoena in *Cotton v. Rogolio*, March 4, 1837. Courtesy of the Historic Natchez Foundation.

KNOW ALL MEN BY THESE PRESENTS, THAT WE, BALLARD, FRANKLIN

& Co. have for and in consideration of the sum of *Thirteen Thousand*

Seven Hundred and fifty Dollars

to us in hand paid by *H & F L Turner*

the receipt and payment of which is hereby acknowledged, we have this day bargained, sold and delivered unto the said

H & F L Turner his heirs and assigns, the following described Slaves, viz:

NAME	AGE	FEET	INCHES	COMPLEXION	PRICE	AMOUNT
Reuben Gray				Black	1300	
Fleming Page				Bro	1300	
Nitt Hammons	18	5	3½	Bro	1000	
Elizabeth Degges	19	5	8½	Bro	1000	
Eliza Ann Smith	16	5	2	Bro	900	
Amelia West				Bro	850	
Matilda Parker				Bro	900	
Fanny Allen				Bro	1000	
Mary Ann Dickerson				Bro	800	
Lucy Ann Taylor				Bro	850	
Eveline Austin				Br	800	
Hannah Greene				Bro	800	
Hannah Williams				Bro	1000	
Delaware Gray				Bro	1250	$13,750.00

Which said Negroes, all and each of them we do warrant Slaves for life; clear and free from any habitual or constitutional disease, to the best of our knowledge and belief. And the right and title we do warrant and will forever defend
against the lawful claim and demand of all and every person or persons. For which we bind ourselves, our heirs, execu-
tors, &c. unto the aforesaid purchaser, his heirs and assigns.
In testimony whereof we have hereunto set our hands and seals.

Ballard Franklin & Co.

pr Jno R Guys

12. Form bill of sale from Ballard & Franklin. Quitman Papers, #616, Southern
Historical Collection, Wilson Library, The University of North Carolina at Chapel Hill.

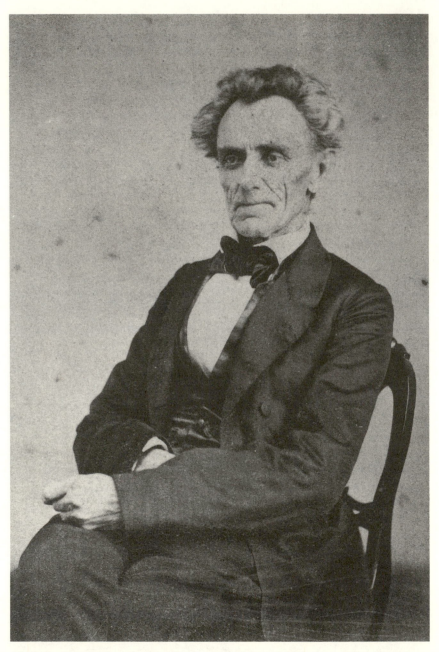

13. John T. McMurran, Natchez lawyer. Edward Turner and Family Papers, Louisiana and Lower Mississippi Valley Collections, Louisiana State University Libraries.

14. Judges Edward Turner and George Winchester, Natchez, Mississippi. Courtesy of the Historic New Orleans Collection, Acc. No. 1986.110.1.

ONE

COURT AND MARKET

TRAVELING to Natchez, Mississippi, from the east by horse-drawn carriage in 1830, as did the "Yankee" Joseph Ingraham, one's first sight would have been "a cluster of rough wooden buildings, in the angle of two roads, in front of which several saddle-horses, either tied or held by servants, indicated a place of popular resort." This was the slave market, known as "Forks-of-the-Road" or "niggerville," the busiest slave market in the South after Algiers, in New Orleans.[1] Slave buyers entered a gate into a courtyard, where "a line of negroes, commencing at the entrance with the tallest . . . down to a little fellow about ten years of age, extended in a semicircle around the right side of the yard."[2]

The journey to Forks-of-the-Road seemed different to one who approached the pen from the other entrance. William Wells Brown remembered arriving at Natchez as the hired slave of a "soul-driver," probably Isaac Franklin, who had built the marketplace there. The slaves landed at night and were driven to the pen in the morning; as soon as they arrived in the pen, "swarms of planters [were] seen in and about them." Brown wrote about the ordeal of sale from the perspective of the trader's helper, dressing the slaves and driving them into the yard. "Some were set to dancing, some to jumping some to singing, and some to playing cards . . . I have often set them to dancing when their cheeks were wet with tears."[3] Isaac Stier, an Adams County slave whose father had been sold at Forks-of-the-Road, remembered his father's stories of being "fed an' washed an' rubbed down lak race horses," then "dressed up an' put through de paces that would show off dey muscles." Stier's father "was sol' as a twelve year old, but he always said he was nigher twenty."[4]

The traveler continuing along St. Catherine's Road would soon have reached the town of Natchez. Towering above the town, on a hill over-looking the Mississippi River, loomed the Adams County Courthouse.[5] Like most antebellum courthouses, it was built in the Greek Revival style, with Ionic columns in front and a tall clock-tower. Its imposing architecture, and its centrality in the town, made it not only the primary meeting place but also the chief symbol of government authority in the environs. If the traveler arrived at Natchez in May or November, he would have found crowds of people gathered in the courthouse square for Court Week. People came to court for many reasons, but often, what brought them there began at Forks-of-the-Road. At the courthouse, neighbors and strangers came together to work out the disputes that arose in the daily business of the slave-and-cotton economy. The market for slaves, land, and cotton spilled over into the courtroom in battles about unpaid debts, failed crops, and sick and recalcitrant slaves.

These two institutions, the courthouse and the slave market, were central to Southern culture, but they have often been seen as quite separate and distant from one another. Cultural historians of the nineteenth-century South have not paused long on the courthouse steps. Most have assumed that for whites, rituals of honor, and for slaves, plantation discipline, replaced law as the mechanisms for resolving conflict and punishing wrongdoers.[6] Legal historians have paid attention to pressing constitutional questions, to dramatic criminal cases, or to broad questions of the relations between legal and economic development in the South, far from the circuit trials that mattered so much in local culture.[7] This chapter will travel from the county courthouse to the slave market, drawing the connections between the two.

So much of the daily business of Southern courts involved the commercial law of slavery—about half of the trials in the Adams County Circuit Court—that we cannot understand the place of law in Southern culture without visiting the courthouse during a trial for breach of warranty of a slave. Civil trials involving slaves were the routine events bringing townsfolk and planters together to fight over their human property and, in the process, to hash out their understandings of racial character.[8] Through rituals invested with all the trappings of state authority, both white and black Southerners again and again made the journey from slave market to courthouse.

At local trials, whites worked out their relationships with slaves, and with one another *through* slaves. While white men rarely faced criminal prosecution for striking out at slaves, they quite often found themselves in court for civil suits regarding property damage to the slave of another. At trials, nonslaveholding whites had the chance to exercise power as jurors and as witnesses, telling stories about the character and mastery of defendants who were far more likely to be wealthy planters. Slaves, too, with no officially sanctioned opportunity to exercise agency, both consciously and unconsciously influenced the outcomes both in the slave market and in the courthouse, despite the dangers inherent in outright efforts at manipulation. Lawyers, who played the role of transmitters of culture as they traveled from town to town, made their careers in the legal practice of the slave market and invested the fruits of their careers in the slave market. In these ways, the institutions of slavery, law, and the market grew intertwined.

The county to which our traveler made his journey, Adams County, Mississippi, was in some ways unique and in some ways representative of the Deep South. Adams County held within its boundaries a large population of slaves, some of the richest planters in the South (the "nabobs") living in suburban estates, a free black community numbering about two hundred, and a town of white working people living on the bluff overlooking the Mississippi River. Below the bluff, "Under-the-Hill" was a raucous port known for gambling, drinking, and brawling with the famous "Bowie" knives first used in its barrooms. Natchez and its environs contained most of the wealth and population of rural Mississippi, and in the early years of statehood, in the 1820s, Natchez was a political center as well. Although the presence of a very wealthy planter class made Adams County unusual, over one-third of the county's white households contained no slaves at all.[9] In fact, the very wide range of wealth and slaveholding among the whites of Adams County, together with its large slave population, active slave market, and excellent surviving records, combine to make it a revealing point of entry into the courtrooms of the plantation South.

· · · · ·

From the old settlements of South Carolina and Louisiana to the frontier of the Old South-West in Alabama and Mississippi, the organizing units of Deep Southern society were the plantation and the county. With an overwhelmingly rural population and few manufacturing or commercial centers, towns formed around that central political, cultural, and economic institution, the county courthouse.[10] Circuit courts, held for one or two weeks twice every year in most Southern counties, drew men, women, and children from all over the county.[11] Beginning in 1832, circuit courts were held at the Adams County Courthouse every May and November.[12]

Court Week was a social event in Natchez, as in small towns across the South.[13] Although many people attended the county courts held monthly by justices of the peace to adjudicate disputes over small amounts of money and prosecute petty crimes, circuit courts were major events. One Georgia lawyer recalled that "[f]amilies would come in wagons and carts, and bivouacing round the villages at night, their camp-fires gave them a cheerful aspect during court-week."[14] Men attended court because they were litigants, jurors, or witnesses, or because their interests might be affected by a case in other ways, as guarantor of a note, creditor, or debtor. In Mississippi, whether or not they had business there, "a large number" of women as well as men "went for the recreation and excitement attendant upon such occasions; many more went to get 'something to drink,' as it was always very plentiful on those occasions."[15] On the courthouse steps, citizens gambled, drank, brawled, listened to oratorical flights of rhetoric, and debated politics.[16]

In attendance at courts were men, women, and children from all walks of life. By 1817, when Mississippi achieved statehood, the Natchez district was the biggest population center in Mississippi.[17] The traveler arriving at the courthouse on a spring day in 1830, for example, might first have met some of the wealthy planters arriving by liveried carriage from the suburban estates that skirted the town.[18] One frequent visitor to the court—as both a plaintiff and a witness in slave-related trials—was planter-judge John Perkins, who owned eighteen thousand acres of cotton plantations in Mississippi and northeastern Louisiana, with homes at Somerset, Louisiana, Columbus, Mississippi, and The Briers at Natchez. Arriving at the courthouse, Perkins would have greeted other gentlemen planters and their wives, as well as friends and acquaintances from town, affluent merchants like Jacob Soria, the auctioneer, and Andrew Brown, the lumber company president and sawmill owner.[19]

The courthouse was often the scene of political orations, and at times heated disagreements arose. Residents of the Natchez environs were more likely than other Deep Southern planters to be Whigs and Unionists, especially the wealthy planters and businessmen.[20] Natchez did, however, produce some well-known Democratic politicians, including the fervent states'-rights advocate and Calhoun compatriot John A. Quitman, who won the gubernatorial election in 1838 with the support of Natchez townspeople but not Adams County planters.[21] Approaching the courthouse to hear Quitman speak about the nullification crisis, the traveler would have found gathered there a raucous collection of workingmen, many foreign-born, especially British and Irish, with a smattering of Germans and French, and others who haled originally from Virginia and Maryland. Most of these town-dwellers were middle-class and owned few slaves or none at all.[22]

The traveler arriving at the courthouse would not have seen only white faces. Slaves made up 73 percent of the population of Adams County in 1830; most of the slaves of Mississippi lived in Adams County and the neighboring counties. The enslaved population, however, was largely dispersed in the rural plantations, with only 15 percent of slaves living in Natchez, whereas whites, and the small population of free blacks, were concentrated in town.[23] Thus the view from the courthouse square would have been different from the view along the route. The slaves who came to town for Court Week were probably body servants, carriage drivers, market people, and slaves directly involved in litigation; field hands stayed behind. In the 1850s, three out of four Adams County slaves lived on cotton plantations of fifty or more slaves.[24] The few town slaves likely to have crowded the courthouse square were probably employed primarily as domestic servants and in retail establishments; others were dockhands, draymen, brickmakers, and lumber hands.[25] They would have been joined by the members of a small free black "aristocracy" of Natchez, which included six families owning five to twenty slaves and some real estate.[26] Other, much poorer free blacks, might also have joined the crowd milling about in the square—peddlers, prostitutes, and day laborers.[27]

William Johnson was a leader of the free black community, a barber and independent businessman, protected by wealthy white patrons, who also kept a diary for which he has become justly famous. Johnson's journal entries illustrate the place Court Week commanded in the local culture. Almost every time circuit court was in session, Johnson noted that business was doing better because of it—because more people were in town to attend—or noted his surprise that business had not improved *despite* the court's being in session. For example, in May 1850, he wrote "Buisness not very Brish for Court times," and "Buisness rarther dull for Court to be in Cession yet," while in November Term of that year, business was much better during Court Week: "Greate many Persons in town." During one court session in 1844, Johnson noted that a bipartisan dinner for the governor was not well attended, because the circuit judge refused to adjourn court.[28]

Johnson's diary entries also suggest that civil disputes involving slaves commanded local attention just as criminal cases did. Many times he mentions legal proceedings involving slave stealing, slave beating, or other issues involving slaves. For example, on January 6, 1844, Johnson wrote, "A trial came of[f] before Esqr Woods to day and it was Parkhurst was tryed for stealing a Darkey belonging to Fields . . ." On May 10, 1850, Johnson mentioned a warranty suit over slaves between Rhasa Parker and William Pullam. On December 13, 1839, Johnson learned from Mr. Wales of Washington that Philo Andrews was "[s]till aliving and was seen some where in Mobile or in Mexico and told me He Left her in consequence of his Stealing a Negro and that he Proberly was now a Live and the property that had was Now, He thought, owend [*sic*] by Mr Brooks."[29]

Circuit courts were an arena not only for local culture, a meeting-place and focal point for the neighborhood, but also for a broader legal culture. That is, the lawyers and judges who rode circuit from county to county developed their own cohesive camaraderie, a romance and lore of the circuit, which instructed their membership in a distinctive sense of their profession, of what it meant to be a man of law. Many were convinced that it was the experience of circuit riding which forged the legal fraternity and was the single source of legal culture in the Old South. According to Charles Warren, "many older lawyers have been of the opinion that the largest and best part of the legal education of the past was this mingling of the whole Bar together in traveling from county to county, and from court to court, the enforced personal relations which were brought about, and the presence of the younger members of the Bar during the trials of cases by their seniors."[30] Circuit riding also gave lawyers an important role in cultural transmission, transporting ideas from town to town, and linking far-flung rural areas.[31] Whereas a relatively large, wealthy town like Natchez supported its own bar, many areas relied on the lawyers who rode into town with the judge for the circuit court.

Circuit riding could be hard work. Charles Jones Colcock, a judge on the South Carolina Court of Appeals, wrote to his wife in 1827 to complain about the difficulties of circuit life: "[W]e are in a dreadful situation as to business . . . there have been several extra courts . . . more business than we could dispatch in Two months." Dissatisfied, he concluded that he "wish[ed] most sincerely that I was on the other Bench or had a small living in any other way—for I am most heartsick of the duty—But it is in vain to complain. I am chained to the oar . . ."[32] Just as judges felt overworked, lawyers who did their work while on the circuit rather than waiting until they reached their offices, where they had clerks to help them, might stay up all night writing out the texts of their motions and appeals.[33]

Others drew a more vivid picture of circuit riding. Lawyers and judges on the circuit drank liberally and attended dancing balls and parties. Henry S. Foote, a prominent lawyer and governor of Mississippi, claimed that he was "painting no fancy sketch" when he said that he had "often seen judges remarkable for ability and learning, and who before their elevation to the bench had ranked high as lawyers both of learning and eloquence, so much overcome with strong drink while presiding in court, even when important trials were in progress, as almost to be unable to sit erect or get through the customary formalities of judicial proceeding without some grotesque and unseemly exhibition . . ."[34]

As a group, lawyers and judges were the wealthiest participants in civil trials involving slaves, and most closely identified with the planter class. Young men came to Natchez to practice law but nearly always turned into planters over the course of their careers.[35] The high level of slaveholding among lawyers, their close connections to the nabobs, and the fact that their practices depended heavily on the slave economy suggest the degree to which slavery helped to shape both legal culture and legal practice in the Deep South.

In many parts of the South, lawyers aimed to be statesmen. Lawyers who had built up lucrative practices had the choice to rise to the bench, to try their hand at politics, or to become planters. Charles Jones Colcock, who went on to become a justice on the South Carolina Court of Appeals, the state's highest court, wrote to his grandmother at the tender age of eighteen, explaining his decision to become a lawyer: "[A] lawyer may get into as much business as may be necessary for his support, as soon as he has finished his studies and been admitted to the Bar; besides the Bar is the true road to honor and preferment in this country, and I hope my brow may one day be a Laurelled one."[36] In Adams County, however, the well-trodden path from lawyer to statesman and politician was largely closed off in the years following the Panic of 1837, when Adams County's wealthy Whigs lost political power to the Democrats of the piney-woods counties of eastern and northern Mississippi. Natchez lawyers also disappeared from the state supreme court after 1832, when its judgeships became elective offices.[37]

Nevertheless, Natchez was known as "a mecca for lawyers." As Joseph Baldwin explained in a sketch of lawyers during the "flush times of Alabama and Mississippi," lawyers moved to the South-West because "it was extolled as a legal Utopia, peopled by a race of eager litigants, only waiting for the lawyers to come on and divide out to them the shells of a bountiful system of squabbling."[38] Particularly in the years following the Panic of 1837, "the dockets of the Courts were crowded with suits great and small, involving titles to lands and negroes, and all the intricacies of the law. The Circuit Court Clerks . . . and their deputies, and the Marshals and Sheriffs and their deputies, were busy night and day, issuing and serving process."[39] When John A. Quitman, who went on to be a general in the Mexican-American War and governor of Mississippi, first arrived in Natchez to practice law, he wrote to his father, "No part of the United States holds out better prospects for a young lawyer." The reasons Quitman gave had less to do with lawyering than with cotton planting. "[The planters] live profusely, drink costly Port, Madeira, and sherry, after the English fashion, and are exceedingly hospitable. Cotton planting is the most lucrative business that can be followed. Some of the planters net $50,000 from a single crop." Quitman left no doubt that his goal as a lawyer would be to achieve planter status.[40]

Indeed, many lawyers discovered that once they arrived at Natchez, their ambitions shifted. Joseph Ingraham, the "Yankee" who traveled the old South-West, found a connection between the vibrancy of the slave market and the relative paucity of politically active and well-known lawyers making their home in Natchez, observing, "A plantation well stocked with hands, is the *ne plus ultra* of every man's ambition who resides at the south. Young men who come to this country 'to make money,' soon catch the mania, and nothing less than a broad plantation, waving with the snow white cotton bolls, can fill their mental vision."[41]

This transition from lawyer to planter, and sometimes to planter-judge, was an important one among the lawyers who made their business representing parties to civil disputes involving slaves. One major dynasty of lawyer-planters began with Judge Edward Turner. Turner was born in Virginia, studied law in Kentucky, and came to Natchez in 1802, at the age of twenty-four. By 1815, he had built up a small legal practice and owned three slaves and twelve acres of land. In the 1820s he began to climb the ranks of the judiciary, first as a judge of the Adams County criminal court, then as a supreme court judge, and finally as chief justice of the High Court of Errors and Appeals. He also became a major planter and married into a nabob family, beginning a tradition followed by many young lawyers who came to Natchez from parts north. Both John A. Quitman and William B. Griffith, his law partner, married into Turner's family; Griffith married Turner's daughter, and Quitman his niece.[42]

The tradition continued with John T. McMurran, whose career highlights the influence of slavery in tracing this path from lawyer to planter. A native of Pennsylvania, McMurran read law in Ohio with an uncle and received no formal schooling. He came to Natchez with a letter of introduction to Quitman and then succeeded Griffith as Quitman's law partner in 1828. By 1835, McMurran was responsible for the largest practice in southwest Mississippi, as Quitman left the regular practice of law when he became a state senator. McMurran married another of Edward Turner's daughters, Mary Louise.[43] McMurran handled about a quarter of the court's business during the 1840s. Most of his legal practice, like that of most antebellum lawyers, involved debt collection, particularly on behalf of the Commercial Bank of Natchez. McMurran was the lawyer for the plaintiff in fourteen civil trials involving slaves during the 1830s, and defendant's counsel in three. This made him one of the most frequent repeat players in slave-related trials.[44]

McMurran put the money from his law practice into speculation on land and slaves. As Joyce Broussard-Hogan notes, "It is almost as if he abandoned litigation before the court [in the 1850s] in favor of land and slaves, although we know that he remained active as a prominent lawyer throughout the 1850s." By the 1850s, McMurran had investments in the Bank of New York, the largest bank contributor to the Union cause, often in the tens and even hundreds of thousands, and was handling investments for other major Natchez planters as well, including Stephen Duncan and A. P. Merrill.[45] He owned four plantations at various times in Mississippi, Louisiana, and Arkansas, and together with his law partner James Carson owned hundreds of slaves and thousands of acres in Adams County alone; his Natchez estate, Melrose, sat on 132 acres just outside of town, bounded by Quitman's Monmouth, Turner's Woodlands, and another brother-in-law's Linden. From his humble beginnings as a migrant with only his legal apprenticeship to recommend him, McMurran had became a wealthy planter and major slaveholder.[46]

Judges reflected the social background and politics of the bar as a whole. Before the new state constitution of 1832 introduced judiciary elections, judges were appointed by the governor. After 1832, although judges were elected, nearly all of the candidates were lawyers, and campaigns were more dignified than those for other positions.[47] In the first decades of the nineteenth century, a number of states had their supreme court judges ride circuit as well, which meant that they sometimes reviewed their own decisions on appeal, but by the 1830s, most states had established separate systems.[48] Even in the earliest times, when judges were less likely to have formal legal training, those who did not come from "gentlemanly" backgrounds met a backlash against their authority. Seth Lewis, the first chief justice of the Territorial Court in 1802, suffered such great scorn at Natchez as "an ignorant shoemaker" that he quit his position and went into private practice.[49]

Lawyers in Natchez, many of whom had been born or had studied in the North, aspired to join the ranks of planters and to take part in planter society. The bulk of their business was commercial litigation, which in Natchez meant slave-related trials. The great majority of these lawyers made no distinction between traders and others as clients, and there was no plaintiffs' bar or defense bar. While lawyers who did banking litigation might have particular banks as steady clients and might process land claims primarily, they represented buyers, sellers, hirers, and owners in disputes involving slaves. The typical lawyer turned his legal fees into slaves as soon as he possibly could. Often, these same lawyer-planters became the local judges. Simply put, their practices rested on slavery. In this way, slavery shaped legal practice, and lawyers and judges became invested in the institution of slavery.[50]

·   ·   ·   ·   ·

The slave markets that provided so many lawyers with their livelihoods—both as litigators and as slaveholding planters—did a vigorous business in the antebellum Deep South. Although foreign importation of slaves ended in 1808, owing to constitutional prohibition, the Deep Southern states continued to import slaves from the Upper South in ever greater numbers during the antebellum period.[51] Slave traders brought slaves from Virginia, Kentucky, and Tennessee to sell at the markets in Charleston, Natchez, and New Orleans. Overall, more than a quarter of a million slaves came into the Deep South from the Upper South each decade from the 1830s on. Local sales also accounted for a substantial part of the trade, probably more than half.[52] Individual slaveholders sold slaves to one another directly or used local traders as intermediaries. And slaves were sold by the sheriff at public auction when a slaveholder or his estate became insolvent. In South Carolina, the one state for which we have solid numbers, these sales amounted to one-third of all slave sales.[53]

The slave trade in Natchez spilled beyond the boundaries of Forks-of-the-Road. Before 1833, slaves were sold everywhere—off boats that docked at the landing Under-the-Hill; at shops on Main Street in upper Natchez; on the steps of the county courthouse in court-ordered sales; as well as at Forks-of-the-Road. To prevent what many viewed as an unseemly display, the town in 1833 passed an ordinance to prevent public sales by slave traders, which was stiffened in 1835 by a second ordinance prohibiting the exhibition by anyone of slaves as merchandise on street corners and in front of stores within the city limits.[54] By the 1830s, two-thirds of the slaves in the state had originally come from Virginia, with the remainder coming from Kentucky and other states.[55] Most slaves sent to the Southwest arrived at New Orleans by ship and continued up the river to Natchez between October and May; the firm of Franklin & Armfield sent an additional overland coffle each summer to Natchez. Altogether, in addition to many local sales, about thirteen hundred slaves a year came into the Natchez market from the upper South by the 1830s; this number may have doubled by 1860.[56] In 1902, General William T. Martin, who had been a lawyer in many slave cases, remembered that "[i]n some years there were three or four thousand slaves here [at Natchez]. I think that I have seen as many as 600 or 800 in the market at one time."[57]

Several Southern states periodically banned domestic importation, as did Mississippi from 1837 to 1846. These bans, however, were always overturned and do not appear to have made a dent in the trade.[58] Mississippi innovated another form of regulation in 1831, in reaction to the Nat Turner rebellion in Virginia, requiring imported slaves to register a "certificate of character" from the exporting state, guaranteeing that the slave was not a runaway or thief. This requirement was also quite simple to circumvent, as one trader explained: all one had to do was "to get two freeholders to go along and look at your negroes. You then tell them the name of each negro—the freeholders then say that they know the negroes and give the certificates accordingly."[59] Bans on the trade appear to have resulted from both economic and security considerations: sectional tensions between older, established areas that had no need of more slaves and newer areas; temporary economic panics; and reactions to well-known slave insurrections such as Nat Turner's.[60]

Prices continued to rise for slaves throughout the antebellum period, with the exception of the Panic years of the late 1830s and early 1840s. "Prime male field hands" in the New Orleans market sold for about $700 in 1846; their price had more than doubled by 1860 to upwards of $1,700.[61] To own slaves was to own appreciating assets, as important for their rising value as capital as they were for the value of their labor. This meant that, as Gavin Wright has explained, slaveholders were a class whose "economic interest centered in slave property." Slaveholders were "laborlords" rather than "landlords"; they moved around frequently and made little investment in towns or infrastructure.[62] Even the high level of land speculation in Mississippi and Alabama suggests that slaveholders were not particularly attached to their land. Slaves were their most important form of capital.

Slaves were also the cornerstone of the Southern credit economy. An exhaustive study of credit relations in one Louisiana parish outside New Orleans has shown that slaves, because they were readily convertible into cash, were "especially desirable for collateralizing debt arrangements." Credit sales of slaves ranged from a high of 37 percent of all slave sales (1856) to a low of 14 percent (1859), averaged 20 percent, and rarely had terms longer than twelve months, whereas land mortgages lasted two to five years.[63] Thus slaves were the ideal collateral for debts. The complex web of notes traded on slaves could, and often did, fall through in years of financial panic and high land speculation.

Other segments of the economy depended on slaves as well. Hiring, or leasing, provided an important way for both individuals and corporate entities, especially towns and cities, to obtain labor without making the major capital investment in slaves. Slave hiring may have involved as much as 15 percent of the total slave population.[64] In New Orleans, surveyor Joseph Pilie reported to the mayor on work done by hired slaves and convicts, including "29 negros by the month, 63 negros in chains, 28 negresses & 30 condemned men." They worked cleaning, paving, building, and repairing the streets, markets, and levees.[65] When a slave in the municipal works fell ill, the owner typically sought redress directly from the city before going to court. In 1815, an owner named M. Chardon petitioned the town council of New Orleans concerning a sick slave named Phoebe, whom he had placed in the jail for "correction." Because she was "strong and robust," she was put to work in the public works by Mayor N. Girod, who assured M. Chardon that she would be well taken care of, and that he would be recompensed for her labor.

No record remains of whether M. Chardon received payment for Phoebe's convalescence or for her wages. If not, M. Chardon likely would have brought suit in parish court for his $102.25, as happened so often in parish and circuit courts across the Deep South (Louisiana was divided into parishes rather than counties).[66] In some similar cases, owners sued hirers for mistreating a slave. More often, these cases resembled warranty suits in that hirers sued owners when the leased slave turned out to be "unsound," died, or ran away. In either situation, the trial revolved around the question of who should assume responsibility for the condition and character of the slave.

Hiring relationships also occurred among private parties. In January 1848, Francis Cooley of Woodville, Mississippi, hired the slave George to Benjamin Joor on behalf of Rebecca Wetherington. Joor paid Cooley with a note for $135 for the year, agreeing to pay physicians' bills and taxes on George. When Joor defaulted, Cooley sued in Adams Circuit Court. Joor answered with the defense that he did not "have the work labour care or diligence" of the slave George, who had run away several times during the year. Joor submitted three receipts paid to the sheriffs of Adams and Wilkinson Counties to retrieve George from jail. Rebecca Wetherington wrote to Joor in November: "George appears to have run away from you and has been caught by the Negro Dogs and badly bitten and committed to the Jail of Woodville and now requires strict attention to make him able to attend business. And now I request that you hire him to Mr. James Rawlins for the balance of this year and so by doing you will oblige." The suit settled for $118. The fact that slaves were fragmented property, with so many interest-holders in any particular slave, meant that there was no such thing as a simple, unitary master-slave relationship for most slaves and most masters.

Market transactions, credit relations, and hires all led to disputes that had the potential to land the parties in court. Most sales anticipated litigation at least indirectly by including an express warranty by the seller that a slave was "sound in body and mind and slave for life." Form bills of sale used by slave traders generally included spaces for the sex, name, and age of the slave, and for the warranty, which might be couched in varied terms. Some bills of sale explicitly excluded certain aspects of that particular slave's condition or character from warranty. For example, Emile Guerin sold to Augustus Koenig a slave named Nanette, "fully guaranteed against the redhibitory vices and maladies prescribed by law, with the exception of a disease, which she had about two years ago, which manifested itself in fits having the character of madness, and of which he is unable to say that she is cured, although she has not been afflicted by it for the said space of two years."[67]

When slave buyers were dissatisfied with their purchases, they tried to recover for the problems directly. Usually this meant confronting the seller and demanding that he accept the return of the slave and give his money back. Slave traders were more likely to settle such cases out of court than were private individuals. In their personal writings, planters wrote of their frustration with the legal system. Benjamin L. C. Wailes, a prominent doctor and planter of Natchez, became embroiled in litigation when the life estate-holder of his plantation Fonsylvania sold and mortgaged a number of slaves without permission. After an unsuccessful suit for eight slaves sold through Miles and Adams, New Orleans commission merchants, he wrote in his diary: "Note. Never engage in a law suit if to be avoided or have anything to do with lawyers without a written agreement as to terms and compensation."[68]

If they did not succeed in settling a dispute out of court, many dissatisfied buyers turned to the law. They had to be able to afford court costs and attorney's fees that ranged from about thirty dollars to several hundred.[69] Nevertheless, the people who brought their suits to county court were not the biggest planters in the Cotton Kingdom; they reflected the local population in miniature. In Adams County, about one-third owned between one and five slaves. For these plaintiffs, the illness, injury, or loss of just one slave could be devastating. Fewer than one-third were planters owning twenty slaves or more, and an even smaller number were extremely wealthy planters with hundreds of slaves and large plantations. The median plaintiff owned ten slaves and 280 acres and probably made his living through farming.[70] By contrast, defendants were the wealthiest parties appearing in circuit court. A full 22 percent were the greatest planters in Adams County, owning over fifty slaves within the county itself, not counting nonlocal holdings (such planters made up just 12 percent of the total population). Sellers were the greatest slaveholders, with the median owning sixteen slaves; the median buyer-defendant (sued for nonpayment of a note) owned only six slaves.[71] Relatively few sellers, whether appearing as plaintiff or defendant in Adams Circuit Court, were professional traders; only 24 out of 177 cases involved traders, and the majority of them were local traders who lived and worked in Natchez.

Buyers, sellers, owners, and hirers of slaves most often brought their disputes to the circuit courts of their county.[72] They went to court primarily to win monetary damages.[73] Their suits dominated the dockets of circuit courts and other courts of first resort at the county level.[74] In Adams County, about half of the trials in circuit court involved slaves, and most of those were civil disputes among white men regarding the disposition of their human property.[75] Of these civil disputes, a majority were suits for breach of warranty—66 percent of the appealed cases in the Deep South, and 52 percent of the trials in Adams County.[76] Suits based on express warranties could be pled as "breach of covenant" or as "assumpsit," both actions based in contract. In Louisiana, suits of this type were especially common, because the civil law codified consumer protections under the category of "redhibitory actions." One could obtain legal relief for the purchase of a slave who was proven to have one of a series of enumerated "redhibitory" vices or diseases, including addiction to running away and theft.[77] Although professional traders preferred cash sales or very "short" credit (notes payable in six months or one year), a significant number of buyers in local sales paid at least part of the slave's price with notes, some of them with much longer terms. In those cases, breach of warranty might be a defense to a creditor's lawsuit to collect the unpaid debt. Over the course of the antebellum period, litigation rose in the circuit courts, because of the growing population and economy, but slave-related litigation increased even more quickly, indicating the rising economic centrality of slaves.[78]

. . . . .

Had our traveler arrived at the courthouse on a typical day during Court Week, he might have attended the trial of a civil dispute involving a slave, such as the 1856 trial of *Andrew Brown v. Samuel Cox*, in which Brown sought damages for the shooting death of his slave Jake.[79] As he entered the courtroom, the traveler's eye would have been drawn to the judge's bench. The antebellum courtroom was arranged simply. Only the judge and the witness being examined sat elevated above all others. The judge sat on a chair or bench on a raised platform of wood or wrought iron. To one side sat the jurors, in twelve wooden chairs. To the other, plaintiff, defendant, and their attorneys sat at one table. The witness sat on a movable platform somewhere near the judge. There may have been rows of chairs for the onlookers, or the audience might have been relegated to standing on a lower level, on brick pavement, looking upward at the proceedings. Portraits of prominent judges adorned the walls of some courtrooms, and gaslit chandeliers descended from the ceiling.[80]

Trials could be raucous affairs. As Garnett Andrews, a Georgia lawyer, described it, "When I came to the bar, and for years after, we had no digest of the laws, nor Supreme Court . . . and not even rules of practice." This meant that trials were rather free-flowing affairs: without "precedents of adjudicated cases . . . to be relied on as guides, . . . hardly half the litigated cases were tried on their merits."[81] Whether or not it was actually true in practice, story had it that verbal and even physical violence erupted at trial in the Old South. The *New Orleans Bee* repeated a story about two lawyers "at a late term of the Court of Common Pleas in this county" who after "some altercation commenced bandying epithets, by no means complimentary to each other (as these good men do occasionally) when his honor, the Presiding Judge, remarked that 'it was presumed the members of the bar were gentlemen, and that they should treat each other as such.' 'Yes, your honor,' said one of them, 'I so understand it, but it is one of the legal fictions *not always borne out in practice.*' "[82]

Although the trial of *Brown v. Cox* lasted two weeks, there is no record of such theatrics at this trial. Still, it must have occasioned plenty of local interest. Andrew Brown was the largest industrial presence in Natchez. He ran the lumber mill, and he owned thirty-three slaves in 1850, making him the largest slaveholder within the town in that year; he also employed many whites as well as free blacks. Brown was popular among men of lesser means: he was one of only four wealthy men to serve in the local government of Natchez during the entire antebellum period, as town selectman in 1837–38. Samuel Cox, on the other hand, was an out-of-towner, staying at the home of Benjamin P. Swan, an engineer who lived in the downtown area.

The trial probably began with both parties' attorneys' delivering opening statements, which were argumentative rather than merely a recitation of the facts or the pleadings.[83] After opening statements, the testimony began. Andrew Brown presented his case first, and Swan was Brown's star witness. Swan testified that he had retired to bed on the night of October 20, 1856, when he heard a noise at the back door, which turned out to be the slave Jake. When Swan asked Jake what he was doing there, Jake "enquired did Mr. Stanton live there and . . . produced a paper which he said was a letter from his young mistress to Mr. Stanton which she did not want every body to see." When Swan looked at the paper, however, he found that it was not a love letter but merely "an old pass, dated Vidalia[, Louisiana, across the river from Natchez]." Swan seized Jake, believing he was there to rob his house, and called to Samuel Cox, a houseguest staying with his family for two weeks from out of town; the two of them took Jake, tied by a rope, into downtown Natchez, to the city guardhouse. Jake broke and ran on Franklin Street, heading toward the bluff. Cox called, "Stop or I will shoot," and "ran some thirty five feet before firing the first time, after a very slight intermission he fired the second time . . . the boy fell immediately." Although it was manslaughter in Mississippi to shoot anyone in the back, unless a "fleeing felon," there is no record of any effort to convict Samuel Cox criminally. Andrew Brown decided to sue for civil damages instead. At least four of the witnesses testified on Brown's behalf; record remains of only one defense witness.

Brown v. Cox was typical of civil trials in its volume of testimony; judging exclusively from the subpoenas that remain in the records, the average civil case involving slaves in Adams Circuit Court called at least five or six witnesses.[84] Many cases whose records survive intact involved twenty or more witnesses, a few as many as fifty. Witnesses were paid one dollar for each day they appeared in court, and four cents per mile traveled, until the pay increased by half in the 1830s.[85] Witnesses' costs could make a trial quite expensive. Most witnesses appeared in court on the day of the trial. Out of 434 Adams County witnesses, 112 were identified as nonlocal and had their depositions read into testimony.[86] Of these, 42 were from Kentucky, 32 from Louisiana, and 23 from Tennessee. The large numbers from Kentucky and Tennessee reflect the slave trade through these border states to Mississippi; Louisiana witnesses were most often from directly across the river, where many Natchezians owned plantations and may also have conducted sales during the years of restricted trade in Mississippi.[87] Even if a witness lived in Natchez, she might not appear in court. Women, in particular, often gave depositions in private to both attorneys in order to avoid a court appearance.

Nearly all witnesses in court were white. By law, dating back to 1807, no person of color, free or slave, could appear as a witness in any case "except for and against each other"; nevertheless, the Adams County Circuit Court accepted the deposition of a free man of color in at least one case, despite the objections of the other party.[88] (In New Orleans, with a much larger and more established community of free people of color, "colored" litigants and witnesses were considerably more common, some of them slaveholders themselves.) In Adams County, two-thirds of witnesses owned five slaves or fewer; however, some of the remaining third owned substantial numbers.[89] Defense witnesses were much more likely than plaintiff's witnesses to be slaveholders or even planters.[90] These statistics suggest two points. First, wealthier planters defending lawsuits called their wealthier friends and neighbors to testify for them. Conversely, however, those same wealthy planters could well have their names dragged through the mud by witnesses much lower in social rank than themselves.

Like most civil cases in Adams Circuit Court, *Brown v. Cox* was decided by a jury.[91] The jurors were chosen randomly from among the white men who were "freeholders or householders" in the county.[92] Freeholders were defined in 1811 as those "persons who have made the first payment or purchase of lands from the United States."[93] However, the tax rolls included not only property owners but all of those who paid a poll tax of fifty cents, and some of the jurors appear to have been such taxpayers. Furthermore, in Mississippi as in other Deep Southern states, it was permissible to convene bystander juries composed of qualified men who happened to be at court that day, if there were not enough jurors from the regular *venire*.[94] Bystander juries were the most likely to be people of the lower and middling classes. In order to qualify, jurors had to be male; between the ages of twenty-one and sixty; citizens; and they could not be convicts for "felony, perjury, forgery, or other offence punishable with stripes, pillory, or burning in the hand." Both parties had four peremptory challenges for jurors in civil cases. Similar rules governed jury selection in the other states of the Deep South.[95] Overall, the composition of the petit jury stands in contrast to the grand jury, whose members, in the last decades of the antebellum period, were not chosen at random and thus were substantially more likely to be planters.[96]

Brown's lawyers asked the judge to instruct the jury that killing a slave who was not committing a felony but only "fleeing to escape arrest" created liability to the slave owner for damages; that suspicion of a felony did not authorize killing the suspect; and that "the measure of damages is the proven value of the slave." The judge, probably Stanhope Posey, a young judge who lived in the neighboring county, gave all of these instructions. Cox's lawyers asked the judge to instruct the jury that it was lawful and justifiable for Cox to help Swan arrest Jake and take him to the guardhouse, if they believed that the slave was trying to break in; the judge gave those instructions. However, he refused to instruct the jury that "[i]f the jury believe that the Defendant did not shoot to kill the negro but simply to frighten him to make him slow, and further that he shot under the reasonable belief that the Boy had been guilty of felony from which shot said Boy was killed accidentally, they are to find for the Defendant."

Because the parties' attorneys suggested the jury instructions, the judge's role was rather limited. He gave or refused the instructions but added none of his own. The law on judicial instructions had changed over the course of the antebellum period. By the Limiting Act of 1822, judges were enjoined not to charge the jury as to fact but only to state the law. However, this statute was repealed in 1833 and replaced with one which far expanded the power of the jury by providing that the parties propose instructions, and the judge merely give or refuse them.[97] This was a great limitation on the judge's power. It left room for the jury to decide many questions of law on which the parties did not propose precise instructions, or on which both sides proposed instructions, and the judge gave both. Jurors during the antebellum period "were frequently told they had the right and power to reject the judge's view of the law." At the same time, judges could set aside jury verdicts.[98] Most commonly, in Adams County, as in other trial courts in this period, judges exercised their power by ordering a new trial, thereby sending the case to a second jury, and sometimes even a third. When a motion for a new trial was refused, the only option for a dissatisfied litigant was to appeal to the High Court of Errors and Appeals in Jackson.[99]

The jurors, of course, could have nullified; that is, they could have ignored the judge's instructions and found that Cox was justified in shooting Jake, simply out of the belief that a runaway slave is inherently threatening and dangerous. Yet the jury found for Brown and awarded high damages, the full fifteen-hundred-dollar price asked for Jake. Fifteen hundred dollars was an unusually large recovery in the 1830s. It seems likely that the jury found for Brown in part because he was prominent and popular in Natchez whereas Cox was unknown, rather than because of any community standard against killing slaves. In Natchez, white men routinely committed violence against slaves with impunity.[100] Most Deep Southern juries found it acceptable for a white man to shoot a slave in the back, on the theory that a runaway slave was per se dangerous.[101]

Without further knowledge about Andrew Brown, it would have been difficult to predict his victory in court. Overall, plaintiffs and defendants did equally well in Adams Circuit Court: 44 percent of cases ended in a victory for the plaintiff; 45 percent were dismissed or ended in a victory for the defendant; 8 percent were settled; and the remainder were non-suited or abated.[102] None of the known characteristics of slaves at issue could predict outcome (age, sex, color, or skill), and neither could the wealth of the defendant or of jurors. In warranty suits, buyers and sellers did equally well before juries—winning equally often in Adams County. The aggregate data suggest that despite variations in appellate doctrine from strong consumer protection to *caveat emptor* ("let the buyer beware"), juries largely decided cases on the basis of the stories, or "facts," presented to them in testimony, without great regional variation or bias toward one side or the other.

The best quantifiable predictors for a plaintiff to win a civil dispute involving slaves were the amount in controversy and the wealth of the plaintiff: plaintiffs were significantly more likely to win when smaller amounts of money were at stake, and when they were less wealthy overall. Juries were probably more reluctant to cause money to change hands when the sums were greater, and juries exercised class sympathy, finding more easily for farmers with a few slaves than for planters.[103]

Neither of those factors came into play in this case. In Andrew Brown's suit, his chief witness and many of the jurors probably had economic and social ties to him. Swan, despite his friendship with Cox, testified on Brown's behalf. In 1857, Swan was a forty-year-old engineer from Maine, a small slaveholder who had owned three slaves in 1850. Engineers in towns like Natchez made their livelihood on public works projects such as dams and bridges, in which Brown was almost certainly involved. Of the nine jurors for whom I obtained information, several had likely ties to Brown. J. W. Eggleston was a carpenter, who must have relied on Brown for timber. In the year of the trial, Eggleston was in his late fifties and owned no slaves of his own. James Orr was an immigrant from England in his late forties, a wagon maker, who likewise must have had a supplier relationship with Brown. Orr owned three town lots but no slaves. A. C. Britton was a cotton broker and banker (the Britton and Koontz bank remains in Natchez to this day) with whom Brown not only banked but stored cotton from his plantation. Britton, like Brown, was, for a town-dweller, a large slaveholder; he owned thirty-seven slaves in Natchez in 1860. The jury also included two nonslaveholders with no property, Thomas Bowen and B. B. Coyle; three small slaveholders, A. W. Marriner (three slaves), E. Craig (four slaves, one town lot), Samuel Burns (two slaves, one town lot); and one broker who owned ten slaves, William Gay.[104]

The jurors who decided *Brown v. Cox* were not unusual. Overall, a majority of jurors appear to have been town-dwellers, and a disproportionate number were tradesmen. Out of the Adams County sample, 42 percent of the jurors owned between one and five slaves, and another 21 percent owned no slaves, reflecting the population of the town of Natchez but not of the county as a whole, where large slaveholding was more widespread. Of course, these nonslaveholders could well have felt themselves personally invested in slavery as an institution. Some of them may have hired slaves as workers in their trades; others may have enjoyed their membership in the slave patrol or otherwise appreciated the status of a free, white man in a racially hierarchical society. However, only one out of twelve qualified as a "planter," owning more than twenty slaves, and about three-quarters owned no land measured in acres. A planter bringing or defending a suit involving slaves in Adams Circuit Court could be confident of finding only one of his ilk on his jury.

Nineteenth-century juries were expected to draw on their own local knowledge to some extent. As the South Carolina court held in 1834, the jury may act "in some degree from their own knowledge; that is why they are chosen from the vicinage [vicinity in which the cause arose]." Juries were an important check on the power of the judiciary because they could apply knowledge that might not be available to the judge. According to some historians, in an era in which judges were "making law" as never before, the role of jury was that of "an anchor in a shifting sea of legal doctrine." Other historians have emphasized the importance of the jury in guaranteeing the rights of nonslaveholders in the South, so that Southern law reflected community norms rather than slaveholding interests.[105]

Planters certainly complained about juries. One planter expressed his frustration to his lawyer, "If possible, get a jury of planters. Keep out the lofers [*sic*] that are generally about Natchez."[106] A Northern traveler, on visiting a Southern courtroom, expressed the sentiments of many planters when he wrote that "the juries look as if made up of scant materials where all the stock on hand was worked in. A more motley group I have never seen than today in the jury room."[107] This observer complained that "there is not a more ignorant & debased white population in the United States than the lower class of whites in Georgia. And it is from the fact of the numbers of these men on juries, that all legal questions which go to juries are deemed [by the planters with whom he conversed] not more certain than the throw of the dice."[108]

Despite some litigants' dissatisfaction with juries, the judges who sat on state supreme courts did not share their concern. The Deep South's highest courts affirmed lower court judgments 62 percent of the time in civil cases involving slaves. They were somewhat more likely to overturn a jury verdict in cases where the buyer had won at trial, or where the owner had *lost* at trial to another supervisor of a slave, or to an accused assailant of the slave. In Adams County, the only factor uniting the small number of cases appealed to the Mississippi High Court of Errors and Appeals seems to have been that slave traders were somewhat more likely to appeal judgments against them; John D. James in particular brought five or six suits to the high court. It may have been that local traders imagined they might attract more sympathy from the high court than from a jury. However, they did no better or worse on appeal than other plaintiffs. But while appellate courts seemed to be relatively more sympathetic to sellers, as well as to slave owners seeking recovery in tort, no clear pattern emerges. It seems likely that appellate courts also relied more on ideological constructs of "character" than on strict rules in favor of one party or the other.[109]

·   ·   ·   ·   ·

The one person about whom we know almost nothing in *Brown v. Cox* was the slave Jake. The most silent participants in circuit court trials were the subjects of the disputes: the slaves themselves. There is little evidence in trial records or other historical documents about slaves' presence in the courtroom. The central subject of a dispute, graphically brought to life in testimony, embodied in words, may not have actually appeared in person very often in the courtroom. I found only one example of a court order to bring a woman slave before the jury to display her physical "defectiveness." In another case, a slave seller complained on appeal in a warranty suit that the trial judge had used his own powers of observation to conclude that the woman slave was devoid of sense. In many cases, of course, the slave was escaped or dead, and no legal power could bring the slave to the courtroom. In other cases, slaves were unavailable because they had been resold, or simply because trials that went on for many days would take a slave away from work.

Those slaves who were living and had not successfully escaped may not have been present in the courtroom, but they were probably aware of the legal proceedings. It would not have been surprising if some of them tried to influence the legal process. Here again, the silences of the historical evidence frustrate contemporary readers. Such attempts would simply have been an extension of slaves' efforts to manipulate their own sales in various ways—to be bought by an owner who seemed promising; to remain with a family member or loved one; to avoid sale out of the neighborhood. Although conscious manipulation in all likelihood played a far smaller role in the courtroom than did litigants' *fear* of slaves' agency, it is likely that some slaves, for example, recognized the possibility of being returned to a former owner soon after sale if they demonstrated some "defect."

While legal records are silent on slaves' legal consciousness, other sources suggest that slaves were keenly aware of the law's influence on their lives. African Americans who fled slavery and went on to write or narrate their stories of bondage and escape often commented on the injustice of the white man's law—"*their* judges, *their* courts of law, *their* representatives and legislators."[110] Many, if not most, fugitive slave narratives listed the variety of ways that law made blacks into property and deprived them of rights, sometimes quoting statute books by section number and page.[111] As Frederick Douglass explained, "By the laws of the country from whence I came, I was deprived of myself—of my own body, soul, and spirit . . ."[112] Most prominent in this "litany of rights denied" for most ex-slaves was the ban on slave testimony in the courtroom.[113] Because of this ban, "[t]he temple of justice is barred against [the colored race]."[114] Jon-Christian Suggs, in a marvelous study of law and African American narrative, found that "African-American attitudes toward the law emerge as a complex welter of hope, cynicism, trust, and clear-eyed, even ironic, understanding."[115] He quotes Rev. G. W. Offley's argument "to his fellow men and women of color that the law is arbitrary and a man-made instrument that they should ignore when determining their own worth in the world."[116] Suggs points out that Harriet Jacobs' *Incidents in the Life of a Slave Girl* is "a template for the centrality of law in the slave narrative," and argues persuasively that writing by ex-slaves is obsessed with the law and with legal status.[117] Often they wrote with a great deal of bitterness, with the understanding that courts were for the white man: "[D]e only law mongst us niggers wuz de word uv ole Massa."[118] Harriet Jacobs noted that the slave girl or woman has "no shadow of law to protect her from insult, from violence, or even from death."[119]

Slaves were also acutely aware of themselves as objects of property relations and commercial transactions. As James Lucas, an ex-slave from Adams County who once belonged to Jefferson Davis, explained to a WPA interviewer, "When Marse Davis got nominated fur something, he either had to sell or mortgage us. Anyhow us went back down de country . . . I bleeves a bank sold us next to Marse L. G. Chambers."[120] Richard Mack noted that when he was ten years old, he was "not really sold, but sold on a paper that said if he didn't take care of me, I would come back—a paper on me—a kind of mortgage."[121] Slaves were cognizant of their status as divisible property: they could be mortgaged, put up as collateral in credit transactions, split between life estates and remaindermen (those who claimed a property interest in a slave after the death of a life-estate holder), or just plain sold down the river. Yet slaves could also be completely unaware of who had control of the interests in them at any given time; William and Ellen Craft discovered that they had been mortgaged only when their owner sold them to pay a debt.[122]

Solomon Northup told a tale of how his divisible status saved his life. When his cruel master, Tibeats, was about to hang him in a rage, Northup was saved by the overseer, Chapin. Chapin gave two explanations for his action on Northup's behalf: first and foremost, he explained that his "duty is to protect [William Ford's] interests . . . Ford holds a mortgage on Platt [Northup] of four hundred dollars. If you hang him he loses his debt. Until that is canceled you have no right to take his life." Only as an afterthought did Chapin add that "[y]ou have no right to take it anyway. There is a law for the slave as well as for the white man." Solomon Northup owed his life to the overseer's protecting the mortgage interest against the owner of the slave.[123] This anecdote, too, brought home the pressing significance of the slave testimony ban: Chapin allowed Northup to sleep in the "great house"—"the first and the last time such a sumptuous resting place was granted me during my twelve years of bondage"— because he feared that Tibeats would return to kill Northup, and he wanted white witnesses. "Had he stabbled [sic] me to the heart in the presence of a hundred slaves, not one of them, by the laws of Louisiana, could have given evidence against him."[124]

More commonly, slaves who were hired out called on their owners to protect them against ill treatment by hirers. Mary Carpenter remembered that her mother "wuzn't gona low no white man who didn' own er to tech er," so she sent a little boy slave to fetch her master, who not only saved her from a whipping by her "leesor" but "kep all de lease money he'd clected in advance for her suvvices, too!"[125] Georgia Smith's sister, Anna, simply ran away from the farm where she was hired out, and Georgia "found her hid out in our 'tater 'ouse." Georgia finally told their owner where Anna was because she had grown so ill and malnourished. After she had recovered, the owner tried to return her to the hirer, but Anna "cried and tuk on so" that he "told her she could stay home."[126]

Many ex-slaves wrote of their attempts to influence market transactions—along with their fear that such efforts were utterly futile. Charles Ball, for example, recounted his mother's attempts to keep from being sold separately from her child, but also about the danger of a slave's "speak[ing] the truth and divulg[ing] all he feels." When Ball himself was questioned by a prospective purchaser of whom he had "formed [an] abhorrent . . . opinion," he answered as neutrally as possible, that "if he was a good master, as every gentleman ought to be, I should be willing to live with him."[127] Ball hoped on the one hand to dissuade this "wretch" from buying him, and on the other hand to save himself from "the violence of his temper" should he "fall into [the buyer's] hands." Another former slave recounted the danger of being tricked by an owner: "The mistress asked her which she loved the best her mammy or her daddy and she thought it would please her daddy to say that she loved him the best so she said 'my daddy' but she regretted it very much when she found that this caused her to be sold [along with her father] the next day."[128] Yet there are many recorded instances of slaves' running away to former owners to keep their families together, or engineering sales to be closer to a spouse or relative.[129]

Given these efforts to influence market transactions, and slaves' awareness of the importance of law in their lives, it would not be surprising if some slaves realized in some instances that running away or illness could lead to a legal suit that might result in rescission of their sale. Yet it is likely that conscious manipulation was not the norm. Just as slaves realized the dangers inherent in influencing their sales, they recognized the dominance of white men in the legal arena. What the cases reveal instead is the *indirect* influence of slaves on legal proceedings: both as a result of the white participants' fears of slaves' manipulation, and as a by-product of slaves' efforts to resist their masters in other domains.

The slaves over whom white men took one another to court were most often young men, their average age twenty-three. Yet the aggregate statistics on age and gender cannot tell the full story. Buyers were as likely to bring suit for breach of warranty regarding an enslaved woman as regarding a man, and disputes over title involved women as often as men. Tort suits, efforts by owners to recover from other white men for damage to their slave property, account for the greater number of men who appeared as the subject of civil suit in Adams County courts. This may have been because men were more likely to be hired out, as well as more likely to rebel or run away when hired out or left with some other supervisor. Nearly every runaway slave in the sample was male.[130]

The slaves at issue in civil disputes were skilled craftspeople and domestic workers as well as field hands. In litigation, female skilled slaves were usually house servants, especially washers and cooks; male slaves were most likely to be carpenters or blacksmiths. Field hands' work was not considered skilled work. In sales documents, as cataloged in Gwendolyn Midlo Hall and Patrick Manning's *Slaves in Louisiana, 1735–1820*, the most common skills noted were agricultural skills—woodcutting, gardening, plowing, and field labor—because the Hall and Manning database counted fieldwork as a "skill." In Hall's and Manning's rural sample of sales and miscellaneous transactions, 38 percent of slaves sold as skilled fell into this category. Only 20 percent were domestic workers and 13 percent craftspeople (including carpenters and blacksmiths). New Orleans probate inventories included more mulattoes, more house servants, and more craftspeople. Overall, 35 percent of skilled slaves noted in estate lists were agricultural workers, 30 percent were domestic workers, 9 percent were craftspeople, and 14 percent worked in transportation or industry.[131] It does not appear from this comparison that skilled slaves were disproportionately represented in litigation, but it may be that highly skilled craftspeople were disproportionately represented *among* skilled slaves in litigation.

How did the outcome of these trials affect enslaved African Americans? The most serious effect on a slave still living would be a transfer from one owner's possession to another. In a suit for possession of a slave (an action for detinue or replevin), the remedy was usually to return the slave. However, the remedy for suits for damage to a slave, in an action for "trover" or "trespass," as well as many warranty suits, was monetary damages, which might mean that money would change hands between white people, with no change to the slave's situation mandated. Yet even in cases where damages were sought for a slave's defect under warranty, for example, the slave might be returned to her former owner because the buyer no longer wanted her. In South Carolina, it was customary practice to resell the slave complained of at auction (vendue), and to sue for damages amounting to the difference between the original sale price and the resale price; there were also resales in Alabama.[132] Under the Louisiana Civil Code, the remedy for a defective slave was rescission of the sale. In Mississippi, neither resale nor rescission seems to have been practiced.

Yet even in a situation where the slave remained with the same owner, one should not suppose that the slave's life was not altered by the lawsuit. An owner angered by a loss in court, especially a loss in face that he might trace to a slave's misbehavior, might take out his frustration on the body of the slave. Thus efforts to be returned to a former owner or otherwise to influence one's own disposition would have been as fraught with danger as attempts to manipulate one's original sale. Always, the slave would have to walk the line between working toward the desired outcome and planning for the opposite contingency. It is likely, then, that the influence of slaves in the courtroom was felt, and feared, more by masters, indirectly, than it was planned directly by slaves themselves.

. . . . .

The road from the slave market in Southern towns inexorably led to the courthouse. Along the road traveled dissatisfied buyers and sellers, owners and hirers; their neighbors coming to bear witness, weigh their case as jurors, or simply to observe; lawyers who made their living in the slave economy; as well as the slaves whose lives hung in the balance. On Court Day, these players participated in one of Natchez's major social rituals, invested with all of the manifestations of state authority. When they entered the courtroom, these men and women did not leave the marketplace behind. They argued for financial advantage in cases with high stakes. But they did so in the context of a culture in which not only profit but honor mattered, in the market and in the courtroom. Trials taught important lessons to both participants and spectators about white honor and black dishonor, and about the character of masters and slaves, and these lessons resonated in their daily lives.

TWO

HONOR AND DISHONOR

Like other slaveholding societies, the Deep South of the United States
was a society in which concepts of honor held an important cultural
place. Although in the popular mind, the Southern ethic of honor
is most associated with the chivalric code, the duel, and other gentlemanly
rituals, the earliest students of honor in the South recognized that this
gentlemen's code was intimately connected to, and dependent on, both
the institution of slavery and the honor available to all free white men
by virtue of their race.[1] The ethic or code of honor encompassed far more
than certain ritual performances; it governed the day-to-day relations
within households and communities, and between masters and slaves. The
white Southerner traveling to the marketplace, and then to the courthouse,
did not leave this world of honor behind. This chapter will begin with a
general discussion of Southern honor and then explore the ways honor
and dishonor played out both in the marketplace and in the courtroom.

. . . . .

"Honor" can mean many things in different societies. Southern honor
has been associated with militarism, regional nationalism, exaggerated
masculinity, and a heightened sense of pride or touchiness.[2] Vital to the
meaning of honor, however, is the sense of outer-directedness that stands
in sharp contrast to the inward-looking piety of the Puritan tradition.
Unlike conscience and guilt, inner-directed qualities that sharpened one's
private sense of good and evil, strictly between a man and his God, honor
depended upon reputation. Whereas the New Englander felt deeply the
strictures of conscience and guilt, the Southerner's behavior was guided
by a sense of honor and its inverse, shame. Upholding honor required
public display. The Southerner's great fear was to be publicly shamed or
dishonored. It mattered not so much whether he actually lied as whether
he was publicly accused of lying, or "given the lie." As a prominent
scholar of Southern honor has written, "[a]t the heart of honor . . . lies
the evaluation of the public."[3] Although honor began with an "inner conviction of self-worth," it also required putting that self-assessment before
the public and having the public confirm it.[4] Of course, conceptions of
honor were not unique to slaveholding societies, and it would be false to
say that "honor" had no meaning in the "free labor" North. But it is

surely the case that slavery sustained the environment which allowed an ethic of honor to flourish in the South long after it had ceased to hold sway in the North.

Unlike in the North, the concepts of *honor* and *character* were closely linked in antebellum Southern culture. The term *character*, in the antebellum period, was sometimes used to mean *reputation*, as in "he gave his good *character*," or "he had the *character* in the neighborhood as a thief." In court, witnesses could give "character evidence" by reporting on "the estimate attached to the individual by the community." One nineteenth-century treatise writer explained that in jurisprudence, "character is . . . convertible with 'reputation,' " provided that the witness could report on local, recent reputation.[5] This usage does not necessarily mean, however, that *character* referred to something less important because exterior. Whereas New Englanders recognized a strong division between external appearances and one's inner, "true" self, so that reputation could serve only as *evidence* of character, to nineteenth-century Southerners, appearances *were* what mattered.[6] Historians identify this distinction as a crucial difference between an honor-based and a guilt-based society.[7] *Character* in the North had come to mean something very internal, a matter of inner morality, which one had to struggle to express in one's manners. In the South, however, *character* meant at once one's true, essential nature and one's apparent, reputed nature, for they were one and the same. When I use *honor* to refer to a Southerner's personal attributes, the word is very close in meaning to *character*: to display or exercise *honor* is to have an honorable *character*. However, I also use *honor* to refer to the Southern cultural system—a code or ethic that provided a language and structure for disputation, governing what kinds of assaults on one's character would be a threat to one's honor, and what kinds of defenses would preserve one's honor in the face of a challenge.

This emphasis on external confirmation, and even definition, of one's character, had far-reaching consequences for Southerners' behavior and even modes of thinking. For example, Southern orality and physicality have been ascribed to the honor code: "The stress upon external, public factors in establishing personal worth conferred particular prominence on the spoken word and physical gesture as opposed to interior thinking or words and ideas conveyed through the medium of the page."[8] Certainly, the Southern penchant for violence was commented on by observers from without and within. Historians have chronicled the importance to white Southerners not only of dueling but of nose-pulling and other physical means of asserting one's honor in an altercation.[9] Likewise, politics took on particular importance in Southern culture, as "public life offered the opportunity to garner honor from the broadest of all audiences."[10] In a variety of ways, honor governed how white men in particular lived their lives in the antebellum South.

Honor was indisputably a gendered system. Although women, like children and slaves, could not participate in the masculine rituals of honor, white women were often spoken of as having honor; indeed, the defense of white women's honor was an important aspect of being an honorable white man. However, white women's "honor" was approximately synonymous with sexual virtue and purity. And white women were not expected to defend insults on their own behalf. The culture of insult, violence, and response was a male one. White identity and manhood were both defined and affirmed through the rituals of honor.[11]

Central to Southern white male honor culture, like its antecedents in traditional English honor culture, were "[t]he concept and practice of truth." As in early modern England, a time and place romanticized by white Southerners, a gentleman was known by his *word*, and "the social practices mobilized around the recognition of truthfulness, the injunction to truth-telling, and the interpretation of why gentlemen were, and ought to be, truthful were central to the very notion" of honor. It was not enough, however, to be honest. In order to have one's word believed, one had to demonstrate the attributes of credibility: detachment, independence, self-control. Thus the most serious insult in honor culture was to "give the lie" to one's adversary.[12]

Unlike in early modern England, however, the Southern code of honor was not the exclusive possession of gentlemen. Men of the lower class took part in their own rituals of honor, from nose-pulling to family rivalries. Most basically, Southern "common folk, though not given to gentlemanly manners, duels and other signs of a superior elan, also believed in honor because they had access to the means for its assertion themselves—the possession of slaves—and because all whites, nonslaveholders as well, held sway over all blacks." Historians have referred to this unifying principle as "*herrenvolk* democracy" or "white men's timocracy."[13] The coincidence of an ideal of honor with white *herrenvolk* democracy appears paradoxical at first glance. On the one hand, Southern gentlemen were expected to adhere to a "Code of Conduct" that prescribed very different ways of interacting with social inferiors, peers, and superiors. On the other hand, Southern politics depended on a belief that all white men were equals, that only blacks constituted the "mudsill" class. This resulted in a democratization of honor, a recognition that there were elements of honor in which all white men could partake, especially through acts of citizenship.[14]

The inverse of the proposition that honor was available to all whites on the basis of their race, of course, was the inevitability that all honor be denied blacks on the basis of race. Indeed, white honor and black dishonor were deeply linked; slavery supported white men's honor. Orlando Patterson, whose comparative study of slavery and "social death" remains a classic, quoted the Confederate soldier who "described his flag as symbol of 'an adored trinity—cotton, niggers and chivalry.' "[15] The soldier recognized an important symbiosis among slavery, the cotton economy, and the ethic of honor. Patterson elaborates on the links between slavery and honor: "[F]irst, in all slave societies the slave was considered a degraded person; second, the honor of the master was enhanced by the subjection of his slave; and third, wherever slavery became structurally very important, the whole tone of the slaveholders' culture tended to be highly honorific."[16] While there were honor-based societies without slavery, Patterson discovered no slave societies without an ethic of honor.[17]

Of course, it is important to distinguish between the dishonor of the slave and the dishonor of a white man. Because honor was available to all white men, they were also vulnerable to shaming—having honor taken away in a dramatic public display—as South Carolinian Preston Brooks tried to do to Massachusetts Republican Charles Sumner by caning him on the floor of Congress; or by calling a man a liar. If white Southerners did not believe that black people could have honor, how could slaves be *dis*honored? Although one could say that slaves were simply outsiders to the system of honor, incapable of having honor and therefore incapable of being dishonored, that would ignore the extent to which dishonor had to be continually reiterated and reinforced. Dishonor was an active process by which white men proved to themselves and to one another their superiority to enslaved blacks. James Oakes, in a chapter entitled "Outsiders," details the ways whites constantly reminded slaves of their place by dishonoring them: "As there is no greater dishonor than to be denied all standing in society, so there is no condition more completely dishonored by society than the social death of slavery." Although honor was most prized when it came from equals, honor thrived best in societies with a dishonored class, through whom and on whose bodies men could exercise honor. Oakes recognized that the "commonplace symbols of honor and dishonor" in Southern society were those "embedded in the normal workings of the master-slave relationship."[18]

The rituals of slavery bolstered white men's honor while dishonoring the slave. Historians have chronicled the many ways in which punishments went beyond what was "necessary" to enforce obedience, in order to humiliate and dishonor the slave. Slave codes emphasized crimes against deference so that slaves would be required to bestow honor on whites with the appearance of willingness.[19] Among these rituals of dishonor in the master-slave relationship were the ceremonies of whipping, which masters used not only for punishment but for humiliation. The symbolism of white children beating enslaved adults brought this aspect into relief, as did the spectacle of a slave woman being brutalized by a white man while her husband stood alongside helpless.

Furthermore, slaves appear to have *themselves* understood these interactions with whites in terms of honor and dishonor. The narratives of ex-slaves frequently mention the humiliation of moments of dishonor—the first moment the child realized his difference from white children when he saw a white child beat his mother; the moment when he realized that he did not know his father, or that he was to be separated from his brothers.[20] One historian has suggested that enslaved men exercised a range of responses to the humiliations of slavery, from "shameless" playing the fool, or "Samboism," in which the slaves acted outside the strictures of honor and shame, to covert efforts to "stain[] the vaunted honor of the master," to defenses of honor within the slave quarters.[21] Whether or not slaves in fact retained the codes of honor of the Fulani and other African tribes into the nineteenth century, the writings of ex-slaves suggest that they experienced whippings and other humiliating events in terms of masculine honor and dishonor. Frederick Douglass, for example, traced the moment he became "A MAN" to the day he defended the honor of an enslaved woman against an overseer and then resisted being beaten himself.[22] Douglass also commented ironically on white honor, which dictated that it was "cowardly" to knock down a slave woman in order to tie her up for a beating, but that it was honorable to bind her and give her "a 'genteel flogging,' without any very great outlay of strength or skill."[23] With this condemnation, he implied that *true* honor would demand the protection of black womanhood. As Kathleen Brown has shown in her study of colonial Virginia, slaves were early denied honor through being "ungendered": black women were not allowed respect for the integrity of their sexuality or their families, and many of the badges of masculinity in Southern culture—especially guns and alcohol—were withheld from many black men.[24] This "ungendering" seems to have been felt especially strongly by both enslaved women and men.

· · · · ·

Most prominent among slaves' remembered moments of dishonor were memories of slave sales, and especially the auction block. The slave market, more than anything, felt to slaves like the ultimate dishonor, capturing the essence of both unfreedom and debasement. Ex-slaves repeatedly referred to being sold "like cattle," one noting ironically that there was "a curtain, sometimes just a sheet in front of them, so the bidders can't see the stock too soon."[25] They often mentioned the humiliation of being undressed in the marketplace, poked and prodded like chattel, all humanity denied. Worst of all was the exposure of the black woman's body to white men, and the humiliation of the enslaved men forced to look on without being able to help her. Slaves recognized these rituals as part of being put in their place, being taught their status as property incapable of having honor.

White Southerners too "recoiled from the spectacle of the slave auction," suggesting that there was something dishonorable about participation in the market. Yet, as James Oakes points out, this very "disdain was itself part of the symbolism of slave sales—it demonstrated the master's sense of honor even as he sent the slave off to be sold."[26] Honorable white men participated in the market at the same time as they held themselves personally aloof from it, sometimes by sending agents to do their buying and selling, sometimes by exchanging slaves in private sales rather than with professional traders—and other times, simply by declaring their disdain even as they managed to overcome it.

Some historians have portrayed a market economy as incompatible with honor, assuming that participation in a market must automatically make men and women bourgeois and individualistic.[27] Yet at least in the antebellum South, the ethic of honor survived and coexisted with the values of the businessman. Even in the North, where bourgeois individualism is sometimes said to have triumphed during this period, there were strong voices of moral reform exhorting businessmen to maintain the "principles of mercantile honor" in debtor-creditor relationships. One moralist writing on bankruptcy urged that a creditor should deem "his honor of more value than even the preference of a large percentage of pecuniary gain."[28] In the North, bankruptcy legislation replaced moral exhortation, as businessmen ignored these pleas. In the South, however, while insolvency was "no longer a personal mortification," nevertheless "the old ways predominated: Southern legislatures did not enact bankruptcy laws, preferring instead debtor-relief devices."[29] The idea of honor in the marketplace still held meaning for Southerners who bought and sold slaves—which does not necessarily mean that they behaved any more honestly or with less concern for profit; it means, rather, that they cared not only about profit but about how they appeared in the eyes of others during these transactions and afterward.

Most fundamentally, the marketplace implicated the practice of truth in an immediate way. Back in eighteenth-century England, Daniel Defoe had commented on "the practical problems of constituting and maintaining credit and credibility," so vital to honor culture, "in trade and civil society generally."[30] Southerners were deeply involved with these problems, concerned with maintaining honor in the context of market participation.

As the previous chapter outlined, marketplace conflicts often landed the disputants in the courtroom. Some scholars have suggested that because of its honor culture, the South was relatively unbound by law, that "honor and legalism . . . are incompatible."[31] Their arguments surely have merit with regard to the criminal law: Southerners frequently commented on the necessity to avenge insults and assaults directly, rather than through legal prosecution. Yet even studies of the Southern criminal justice system note the extent of litigiousness in Southern civil courts. These commercial/legal battles became the occasion for slights to a man's honor, slights that required defense, and legal disputation created an important arena for the display of honor. Among white men, mechanisms of honor and of law lived side by side.

Many of the extralegal honor rituals historians have seen as evidence of the diminished importance of law took place literally in the shadow of the courthouse, and they spilled in and out of the courtroom. On the courthouse steps, or in the courthouse square, it was not unusual to see men coming to blows in affairs of honor. While duels generally took place in the early morning hours in secluded spots, other violent confrontations involving the defense of honor often occurred in public, and often among men of the law. Within one month in Natchez, the diarist free black William Johnson chronicled a "scuffle" between lawyer J.A.T. Midderhoff and "N. E. Turner," followed by Midderhoff's "Card" in the newspaper "denounc[ing] N E. Turner a base paltroon and an arrant Coward," and "a Terrible Flogging with a Large Lether Strap" which lawyer Ralph North gave to Judge Rawlings.[32] In 1844, Johnson recorded a fight at the Courthouse that grew out of legal proceedings in the courtroom. While the instigator of the fight, McClure, was fined two hundred dollars and sentenced to jail for four days, Johnson noted that a "Good many Persons was Surprised to find McClure So much of a Man."[33]

Bringing a man to law was one device in an arsenal of tactics among honorable men: posting a man a liar in a "Card" in the newspaper, suing him, and challenging him to a duel (or threatening him with a beating if he were considered a social inferior) were all escalating steps on the ladder of honorable gambits. Taking someone to court may have been seen by some as an admission of vulnerability that "place[d their honor] in jeopardy," but it happened so frequently that many who would not have called the courtroom an appropriate arena in which to defend assaults on their honor nevertheless ended up doing so there.[34]

The litigants were not the only ones who played their roles on a field of honor. To the "plain folk" who sat on juries, jury duty signified an important emblem of civic participation. To sit on a jury and to vote were the cardinal prerogatives of white men, jealously guarded against incursions by inferiors such as women or free men of color. While a free person of color might occasionally testify in court, one never took a seat on a jury. Jury duty in many jurisdictions, both North and South, was still restricted to property holders during the antebellum period, but increasingly Southern petit juries became a place for the exercise of "*herrenvolk* democracy," an institution in which ordinary white men could sit in judgment on gentlemen. Of course, to the planter class, the more democratic version of honor afforded to all white men through jury service threatened their own standards of gentlemanly honor. Thus the courtroom became the arena for conflict between two Southern codes of honor, with juries representing that of men of lesser means. As one historian has noted, just as men lower in the social hierarchy could exercise "social control" over the rich by abusing their slaves, jury service afforded those poorer men a "ballot" to vote against wealthy planters when these crimes reached a court.[35]

Lawsuits over slaves also provided an opportunity for white men to assert their honor in relation to their slaves. The rituals of trial—from the exposure of slaves' bodies to the erasure of their words—announced slaves to be people with no honor and reflected back to white men their power to deny honor to slaves. It is no coincidence that poor whites chose as a method to strike out at rich whites assaults against their slaves: in doing so, they not only hit their social superiors where it hurt, but they asserted their own social superiority defined as whiteness; they deployed the law's official nonrecognition of slaves' testimony to their own advantage; and they asserted white honor by dishonoring blacks.[36] Yet, in a variety of ways, at trial, slaves demonstrated their ability to influence white men's honor; their bodies, and at times their words, could make white men liars.

In civil disputes involving slaves, the values of the businessman and the gentleman were both drawn into the fray. In a culture in which being called a liar was the ultimate challenge to a man's honor, a breach of warranty suit itself was an insult. Slaveholders defended suits not only with claims about the soundness of the slave but with protestations about the strength of their own character.

One perceptive cultural historian has characterized the antebellum South as a culture of masks, whose members were especially preoccupied with appearances.[37] A warranty suit was about unmasking in a culture of masks. What lay beneath the mask the slave seller had donned for the buyer? Were appearances true? While warranty suits would challenge the honesty and character of sellers wherever they took place, North or South, courtroom proceedings to determine the truth behind appearances were particularly unsettling in a region where appearances meant so much. And although it was the dishonored slave who stood unmasked, in the marketplace and in the courtroom, the unmasked slave might have the power to unmask the master. The slave proven unsound could indirectly "give the lie" to the slaveholder.

At trial, when witnesses and litigants recounted stories of slave sales, they focused their tales on whether the seller had told a lie or behaved dishonorably. Ephraim Lynch, who was present when Henry Mays sold a slave named Simon to James Stroud, said that Mays "wouldn't have sold him if he were unsound, wouldn't put the cheat on him."[38] Witnesses sometimes used the phrase "a cheat" to describe a low price. In one Alabama case, a witness testified that the slave at issue "from his appearance at [the time of sale] was unsound and a cheat . . ."[39] Thus a warranty was not only a legal guaranty of money damages for an unsatisfactory purchase; it was a word of honor.

When sellers sold slaves without an express warranty, buyers wondered why. In some cases, sellers specified a defect or disease to explain why they were not giving a general warranty. But in others, they suggested that their word of honor should substitute for a legal warranty. If the sales contract did not contain an express warranty, the buyer trying to recover in court had to base his claim on the seller's oral promises about the slave and had to plead his suit as fraud or deceit. In one South Carolina case, the seller, Carter, got on the auction table himself with the auctioneer and "declared that the negroes were sold as they were. That there was no guaranty but that of title." According to a witness deposed in the ensuing litigation, "some person present asked, what is the matter with the negroes? . . . Carter replied he did not know; there they were, ask them any questions that they thought proper."[40] Some sellers went even further, claiming that it was beneath their honor to warrant slaves expressly. Their word, combined with a "sound price," guaranteed the soundness of the slave.[41]

Sellers also gave reasons as to why they were selling their slaves, both to allay fears that the slaves were defective physically or morally, and to deflect suspicion that the sellers themselves were professional traders or hard-hearted speculators. To have it reported in court that "the only reason the Defendant gave for selling her was that he had to [sic] many in his yard" gave the impression that one was a speculator.[42] Honor required the white Southerner to profess a certain distance from the marketplace, just as masters professed a distance from slave discipline, despite their active participation in both activities. Sarah Pearce called Andrew Chambless a liar by testifying that he bought a slave named Mary for five hundred dollars, and when asked "what he wanted with such a negro as that, for he could not trade her, and tell the Truth, he then said that he would not have her to keep, but he would not mind telling a lie to make a good trade."[43] Litigants took these assaults on their honor personally. Manes, who had traded Mary away, told William Hall that "he was sorry that the man he bought negro Mary of had traded his note, so that he could not defend, that he had been swindled in the purchase of said negro and would like to get at the man that did it in order to redress."[44]

Men wanted to avoid being called liars, but also to avoid being called professional slave traders, which was nearly the same thing, in popular lore. In one Adams County case, the witness first established that his own "business and pursuit [was] farming," but that he knew "of no reason why said negro was sold by Morgan, except for speculation. He was in the habit of buying and selling for profit."[45] By contrast, a "character witness" might testify that "Mr Johnson is a farmer and occasionally Buys them for his own use. I have never heard of his selling more than one or two in the 15 or 20 years I have known him."[46] Another witness explained that "I am acquainted with all the men that I bought these negros from and know them to be honorable men and of fair standing in society and that they warranted those negros to me to be sound."[47] Typical lawyer's interrogatories intended to cast doubt on the credibility of a witness, along with "Are you interested in the outcome of the suit?" and "Are you related to either of the parties to this suit?" included "Are you interested in the purchase and sale of negroes? Do you trade in negroes?"[48] Even professional traders tried to avoid being portrayed in stereotypical ways in court. The slave trader Samuel Davis, plaintiff in a warranty suit, succeeded in having stricken from the record the following testimony: "Witness states that said Davis had at times singular manner such as to induce persons to believe either that he was a fool or crazy; but if a man were to go to buy a negro from him or had any other money transaction with him, they would find that he was neither a fool or crazy, where money was concerned. Said Davis was a shrewd sharp trader and was so considered."[49] Despite the prominence of many slave traders, the convention that trading was a dishonorable profession allowed slaveholders to distance themselves from the consequences of their own sales of slaves.

Although Southern planters expressed their distaste for professional traders and the interstate slave trade, individual traders were often integrated into Southern planter society, particularly those whose business concerns extended into other areas, or those who ran successful plantations themselves. As one historian has written, "[t]o have a scapegoat 'evil' trader was a great convenience. But it was equally necessary, for practical purposes, that there be 'respectable merchants' dealing in slaves." Isaac Franklin and a few other major traders abandoned the business for full-time planting in the 1850s and 1860s and were accepted into society. Rice Ballard, Franklin's Natchez partner, owned slaves jointly with "the esteemed and socially prominent Natchez jurist Samuel S. Boyd." John D. James, another prominent Natchez and New Orleans trader, corresponded in a friendly manner with planter William Terry. Although he wrote to Terry about the slaves he had for sale, he also wrote, "Your Daughter Eliza at our house all yesterday . . . I was glad to see her look so well; I was at Mr Scotts about a week ago they were all well, Mary requests me to present her love & respects to you." Traders won at trial as often as did other sellers of slaves, despite the occasional declaration by appellate judges about "this species of humanity."[50]

·   ·   ·   ·   ·

One case involving a great planter, several important lawyers, and a major slave trader illuminates the ways in which matters of law became affairs of honor. Not only did a vast sum of money—$200,000 was as much as $6 million in today's dollars—turn on this dispute's settlement, but it implicated the character of all the parties involved and nearly led to deadly violence. Yet the conflict ended through negotiation, before a trial, perhaps because a slave trader thought it best to avoid an affair of honor in the courtroom with a prominent local gentleman.

In the fall of 1836, just one year after Isaac Franklin built the "Forks-of-the-Road" slave depot, Ballard, Franklin & Co., the Natchez subsidiary of Armfield, Franklin & Co., the South's largest slave-trading firm, imported a large number of slaves to be sold by Rice Ballard at Forks-of-the-Road. On February 1, Ballard sold forty-three slaves to Henry Turner. Turner's agent for his Dulac plantation in Terrebonne Parish, Louisiana, paid for the slaves with a one-year note bearing interest at 10 percent, with a verbal understanding of renewal. For five years, Ballard renewed the note. But in 1841, Turner refused to renew. Ballard demanded payment, and his Natchez lawyers, Alexander Montgomery and Samuel S. Boyd, brought suit in U.S. Circuit Court for damages of $200,000 in March of that year.[51]

Rice Ballard was well represented by local Natchez lawyers. Montgomery & Boyd were considered to be "at the head of the Natchez bar." Alexander Montgomery was the son of an early Natchez settler and territorial governor, and sat briefly on the circuit and supreme courts until the 1832 shift to an elective judiciary removed him from the bench. Samuel S. Boyd was a native of Maine, who arrived in Natchez in 1830 and joined into partnership with Montgomery. He became one of the largest slaveholders within Adams County, owning between fifty and a hundred slaves in the county at the time of *Turner v. Ballard*. Henry Turner, nephew of Judge Edward Turner, and a major planter, responded to Ballard's suit by asking his brother-in-law, John Quitman, to represent him in the matter. Quitman at this time was experiencing hard times in his political career and had returned to legal practice with a vengeance, seeking to make money to repay debts.[52]

By the end of 1841, Quitman and his partner, John T. McMurran, had developed a four-point defense. First, they challenged Ballard's Virginia citizenship, contending that he was a Natchez citizen, so that he should not be able to file suit in federal court (federal jurisdiction was available only on the basis of the "diversity of citizenship" between plaintiff and defendant).[53] Second, they argued that the "Caillou negroes," who represented one note for $63,000, were an unsound lot. Third, the other two notes, they claimed, charged interest at a rate of "ten percent discount," in violation of usury laws. Fourth, the sale violated the state constitutional ban on importing slaves as merchandise; the transaction had been a sham Louisiana sale to get around the ban.[54]

The litigation dragged on for over a year, with depositions, document discovery, and investigations. Quitman and McMurran attempted to coach their witness, Turner's agent, through his deposition, which they felt he gave the first time with too little specificity. Much of the lawyers' work was quite tedious tracing of the paths of the various notes, for which they hired an investigation firm. Turner's lawyers also spent several months trying to obtain discovery of Ballard & Franklin's account books, which they eventually won, so as to have documentary proof of the sale and notes.[55]

By mid-1842, however, the case had taken a personal turn. Already, at the end of 1841, Turner had revealed to Quitman that he cared deeply about the outcome and relied on Quitman heavily: ". . . in all cases of difficulty I must look to you for help and to speak candidly you are the only real friend I have." Turner contrasted Quitman with his own brother, who, he complained to Quitman, "aint worth a pinch of snuff between you and I." In this context, Turner anxiously asked Quitman about whether "any negro cases had come up" and what his "prospects" were.

Several months later, Turner's honor was at stake as well as his emotional well-being. On June 7, 1842, he wrote to Quitman, "I have a great deal to tell you about Ballard when we meet, that will make your blood boil, and I fear may end in a serious way." Unfortunately, the two did not meet for some time, so Turner decided to put the matter in writing, after all: he wrote to Quitman that he had spoken to Ballard's partner Armfield while they were traveling together by steamboat. Armfield had told Turner that "Ballard had used his influence every where to make people believe I had acted in a dishonest way about these claims and had succeeded in injuring my character with some about Natchez." Even worse, Armfield claimed that Ballard "had formed a determination to assassinate

[Turner] the first time we met." At this point, the innocent reader might infer that Turner meant "assassinate" metaphorically—that Ballard would assassinate his *character*. But this was the Deep South. Turner reminded Quitman of a night when the two of them had gone "under the hill and then over the river," probably for a night of drinking, and on the way back, Ballard had joined them for the walk up the hill. "Well that was the occasion on which he was to have shot me as he was then armed up to the teeth and publicly proclaimed his intention to that effect to many gentlemen in the City Hotel." When Ballard came back from their walk together to the City Hotel and was asked why he had not shot Turner, "he told the same gentleman that you had pledged yourself that his claims should be satisfied as soon as you had negotiated for Fielding's interest in this estate—thus casting an imputation on you as well as myself—intimating that we were afraid of him." Armfield had also told Turner that "if Ballard denied what he told me . . . he would publish him as a liar." Turner trusted Armfield's report, despite his partnership with Ballard, because, he said, Armfield was "in no way interested." Turner explained Ballard's behavior as a reaction to frustration that "Ballard had not the least hope of recovering at law." Turner himself was so incensed at the news that Ballard had threatened him that he had nearly returned the next morning to confront Ballard but was dissuaded by his agent from doing so. However, Turner concluded, "the rascal ought to be severely punished."[56]

We may glean from this correspondence several things. Henry Turner and John Quitman, Natchez nabobs, had been out carousing (going "under the hill" to the saloons at the riverside and "across the river" to Vidalia, Louisiana) with a notorious slave trader, Rice Ballard. If that was the first time they had met, then, until that point, all their transactions had been conducted through third parties: the slave sales involving large amounts of money, the notes, and the renewals of the notes, as well as all negotiations over unsound slaves, exchanges, and returns. Ballard appears to have felt his debtor's legal arguments and defenses to be enough of an insult to his honor that he proclaimed to other guests and barroom visitors at the City Hotel that he would resort to violence to settle the dispute. Turner, for his part, accepted completely the word of Armfield, a slave-trading associate of Ballard, so long as Armfield was "in no way interested" in the outcome of the suit. Despite his clear intimation of Ballard's lower social status, indicated by his determination that the "rascal should be *punished*," rather than engaged in a duel as an honorable social peer, Turner still felt that Ballard had the power to injure his reputation. Ballard had the "influence" to convince people of Turner's dishonesty, and to "injure [Turner's] character."

Turner took this threat to his character very seriously. He did not believe that using legal loopholes to avoid paying a debt to a slave trader constituted dishonesty; he believed that Ballard's threats sprang from frustration at his inability to recover at law, as advised by his lawyer, Samuel Boyd. Furthermore, he sought to involve his brother-in-law, Quitman, in the matter, by suggesting that Ballard impugned his character as well by tying Quitman personally to the satisfaction of his claims. As it happens, on March 2, 1842, Henry Turner and Quitman had bought out Turner's brother George's interest in the Palmyra plantation, including 5,710 acres of land, 230 slaves, and sixty head of cattle. In doing so, Quitman had assumed some of Henry Turner's debts—including the obligation to Rice Ballard. Thus Quitman was in fact personally liable for Ballard's claims.[57]

Quitman responded, however, not by getting personally involved, but by attempting to negotiate a speedy settlement to the suit through Ballard's lawyers, Montgomery and Boyd.[58] There is a gap in the documentary record here. We will never know whether Quitman tried to calm Turner down, whether there was any physical altercation, or what transpired in the gossip of the community that was not recorded on paper. We do not know what would have happened if, in August, Montgomery and Boyd had not written to Quitman and McMurran, making the first overture toward settlement. According to one historian, John McMurran was the calm partner: "While Quitman fought and fumed, McMurren [sic] took matters differently. A stout, highly logical fellow, he never turned dogmatic. Chuckling his way through a case, he won it and then walked out with his hand about the shoulder of his defeated rival."[59] Thus perhaps John McMurran was responsible for the decision to negotiate. The settlement discussions took ten weeks, and although at several points the negotiations nearly fell apart, the parties reached an agreement on November 1, 1842.[60]

Turner v. Ballard did not go to trial. Neither Henry Turner nor Rice Ballard suffered the ordeal of neighbor witnesses' going before neighbor jurors to testify to their characters as slave masters, as businessmen, or as plantation managers. This was not unusual; few great traders appeared as slave sellers in Adams Circuit Court.[61] The traders who allowed disputes to get to court were locals like John D. James and his family members, whereas large traders were more likely to avoid the courtroom, and to see negotiation over unsound slaves as a cost of business. As one slave trader explained, giving compensation for a slave who died was "bad but better than a lawsuit." Isaac Franklin, the largest slave trader in the South, made it a practice to return and exchange slaves complained of as "defective" rather than face litigation. Staying out of court was not only good business for big traders like Franklin and Ballard but also a badge of honor, an effort to escape the dishonorable taint of the trade. To Rice Ballard, the prospect of being portrayed to a jury as a disreputable trader who had dealt deceptively in the marketplace threatened to thwart his efforts to pass in polite society. Because he was a professional, it was unlikely that he could defend his honor at trial the way other slave sellers did; thus he opted to settle.

The legal issues in the case were not deeply felt by either side. There is every indication that Henry Turner did not pay his note because he could not or would not, rather than because a few of the slaves among a hundred were "unsound." Neither does he appear to have been an unwilling or unwitting participant in the ruse of a Louisiana sale to avoid the constitutional ban on sales in Mississippi. The constitutional ban was a favorite defense to notes given for the purchase of slaves, but it could backfire, because it was also considered by Mississippi courts to void all warranties given in slave sales, which benefited slave sellers and traders.

Yet despite the routine nature of the parties' legal and business dealings, *Turner v. Ballard* became an affair of honor as well as of money. Southern gentlemen were exquisitely sensitive to charges of false dealing. They took slights seriously as impugning their honor. They jumped quickly from words to blows or threats of violence. And despite superior social station, they feared opponents' ability to injure their "character" through gossip. Thus Henry Turner saw the resolution of this legal dispute as affecting far more than his pocketbook: his character, and his brother-in-law John Quitman's character, depended on his proving his case.

Furthermore, slave traders, no less than planters, had the best local legal talent at their disposal. The "leaders of the Natchez bar" represented Rice Ballard. Yet legal relationships were often wrapped up with personal, familial, and business relationships. John Quitman was Henry Turner's brother-in-law and close friend; John McMurran, who did most of the work on the case, was also related by marriage. Ethical concerns about conflict of interest do not seem to have entered into their minds when Turner and Quitman melded legal, financial, and personal relationships. Because of these close relationships, it was possible for Rice Ballard's challenge to Turner's honor to be a challenge to Quitman's as well.

· · · · ·

Just as the courtroom became the forum for white men's affairs of honor, this venue also provided an opportunity for whites to exercise honor through the dishonor of slaves. Slaves were dishonored in the courtroom both by the baring of their bodies and by the law's disrespect for their words. When ex-slaves discussed in their narratives the way the law touched their lives, inevitably they returned to the ban on slave testimony as the crowning injustice, as did Solomon Northup in his story about the evil master, Tibeats, whose crimes went unpunished because the witnesses could not speak in court. It was the silence that law imposed upon slaves which they felt most guaranteed their disempowerment. Treating the slave's word as a lie, and shutting it out of the courtroom, was the best way for white men to deny slaves access to honor as well as justice before the law. This distrust of the word of "servants," racialized in the American South, had its origins in the general English "association between mendacity and servility," and in the "wide agreement that the servant's word was *not* his bond."[62] A culture that made a man's word his badge of honor stripped people of honor by denying them words.

A notorious murder case from Natchez brings home the power of the slave testimony ban. Baylor Winn was reputed in Natchez to be a man of color, a member of the same free black community as the diarist William Johnson. He and Johnson had exchanged friendly visits, rode and hunted together, until Winn began cutting timber on land Johnson claimed, and Johnson declared Winn to be "not an Honerable Man." In 1851, in the midst of the dispute, Winn ambushed and shot Johnson, in the presence of one enslaved and two free African Americans. Before he died, Johnson named Winn as his murderer. Winn was jailed, and the coroner's jury "returned a verdict that Johnson came to his death by a wound or wounds inflicted by Baylor Wynn [*sic*]." The prominent lawyer, and later Civil War general, William T. Martin acted as the special prosecutor to bring Winn to justice for Johnson's murder. Martin was hamstrung, however, by the slave testimony ban. His only hope to prove Winn the murderer was to demonstrate to the court Winn's "negro blood"; only if Winn were of color could the eyewitness testimony of blacks be admitted against him. Two juries deadlocked over this question, and the state gave up its efforts to convict Winn when a jury voted that he had not been proven to be a "negro." Johnson's murder went unpunished. It is not surprising that blacks, free and enslaved, saw the testimony ban as a license for whites to kill blacks with impunity.[63]

Sometimes this silencing literally erased slaves' stories from the historical record. Less dramatic than a murder trial, *Forniquet v. Lynch* was a little replevin case that appears from the trial record to have been a boring ownership dispute, with little testimony, small amounts of money in controversy, and no interesting legal issues.[64] On the face of it, Charles Lynch, the governor of Mississippi from 1836 to 1838, sued Edward P. Forniquet in 1834 over possession of the slave Ellen. Only one deposition remains in the record, that of planter Richard Terrell. The case was dismissed. However, the correspondence between Governor Lynch and his lawyer, George Winchester, reveals a vivid human story behind the scenes; it demonstrates the myriad ways in which the law dishonored, and erased the agency of, both slaves and free blacks.

The story begins in 1803. In that year, Charles Lynch bought a slave, Bob Leiper, in Kentucky, and moved with him to Natchez. Lynch must have been at least Bob's third owner, as he had taken the last name "Leiper" from one owner, and a second, Meriwether, sold him to Lynch. Lynch explained that he then "permitted Bob and his family to reside in Natchez, and under the control of Micajah Terrell, Judge [Edward] Turner, and others, to hire himself out." To the community, Robert Leiper, Sr., was known as a free black. He lived with his wife, Rhoda, and started a large family, many of whom lived as free or hired themselves out. In 1826, Lynch officially freed Bob Leiper, his wife, and daughter Charlotte, and recorded the deed with the judge of Concordia Parish. Apparently there were conflicts between Lynch and Leiper over the emancipation, because Lynch later claimed to his lawyer George Winchester that the emancipation never formally took place. In his claim in the replevin case, Lynch stated, "About 1826 or 7 [he] agreed to emancipate Bob and some of his children upon certain terms, with which Bob and his family have not complied. None of them have ever been legally emancipated, but several of them are permitted to have their freedom and are considered as free by the Governor." The record does show, however, that subsequent to the disputed emancipation, Lynch sold to Bob Leiper his son Robert, Jr., and a Natchez lot; Bob bought his granddaughter Matilda from someone else and then freed his son, granddaughter, and another daughter. In 1838, Robert Leiper, Sr., his daughter-in-law, and two grandchildren sailed for Liberia; local historians suggest that "former Governor Lynch must have been still selling Leiper children to the free Leipers remaining in Natchez [in 1841]."[65]

At all events, it is undisputed that before 1826 Bob Leiper was not free but quasi-free. He lived apart from his master, raised his family, and hired out his own time. In May 1822, Leiper purchased a slave for his own use, Ellen, at a sheriff's sale. According to Lynch, Leiper paid for Ellen himself, but the bill of sale was given to Christopher Kyle, a white Natchez merchant, who assigned her to Bob in May 1825 "to keep as his own until called for by him."[66] Ellen lived most of the time with the Leipers at Natchez, but Lynch "had the girl in his possession at Monticello in 1827 or 8," at which point Lynch explained to Winchester that he "let her go back to Natchez with old Rhoda and to remain with her, as she was old and in bad health, the girl might render her some service."[67]

When Ellen turned sixteen, in 1829, a slave belonging to Edward P. Forniquet applied to Bob Leiper to marry Ellen. Leiper made it a condition of his consent to the marriage that Forniquet should buy Ellen "until she was of age when she would become free." Forniquet's slave, Ellen's husband, paid Leiper's note himself, perhaps from wages earned working overtime, and only "under these representations" was Forniquet "induced to purchase." As Governor Lynch's lawyer, George Winchester, observed, Ellen's husband "is much attached to the girl."[68]

At this point, however, Lynch decided to exercise his rights of ownership, informing Leiper in essence that any slave who belonged to his slave was his slave too. Now, of course, in 1830, Bob Leiper no longer belonged to Lynch. But whatever had passed between Lynch and Leiper over the controversy about his emancipation had obviously stayed with Lynch. He sent an emissary to Forniquet to demand Ellen, "but Forniquet refused to give her up." Lynch also bought the execution of Micajah Terrell against Christopher Kyle's estate, "to avoid any difficulty from Kyle's title." Some time passed before Lynch took legal action. He wrote to his lawyer, George Winchester, in February 1837, that he would pay Forniquet about $100 (the $200 Forniquet paid Bob Leiper for Ellen, minus $100 for her hire) in order to have Ellen back. Forniquet replied that he was willing to rescind the sale if Lynch would submit the matter to arbitration under John T. McMurran.[69]

Despite Edward Forniquet's willingness to settle, the matter dragged out for several more years. One letter from Lynch to Winchester concerned legal action against the estate of Meriwether, the Kentuckian from whom Lynch originally acquired Bob Leiper.[70] The letter mentioned at least four depositions already taken in that suit; it also referred to a deposition of Anselm Lynch, to prove Ellen's residence with Governor Lynch during the year 1826, before he let her return to Leiper's wife Rhoda. There is no other record of this case, nor of its outcome.

On March 21, 1839, Charles Lynch filed a complaint against Forniquet in Adams Circuit Court. Lynch's complaint alleged that Ellen and her two children were worth $2,500, and demanded the money or the slaves, plus payment for hire. Forniquet retained Montgomery and Boyd, the same lawyers who argued Rice Ballard's case, to represent him in the matter. The trial record contains only one set of interrogatories, served on a neighbor planter by Winchester's associate, asking him whether he was acquainted with Lynch's father and with Robert Leiper, and whether he had ever heard either Lynch or his father speak about the freedom or ownership of Leiper. The case was dismissed two terms later, November 1840, but it appears to have been dismissed by the judge, and Charles Lynch paid the costs, so there may have been some kind of settlement.

Forniquet v. Lynch reveals that a case which appears from the legal record to have been a dispute between two white men was in fact about a black man's dishonor. This case was only incidentally between Governor Lynch and Edward P. Forniquet. It was really about Lynch's putting Robert Leiper in his place: a subordinate place. Lynch gave Leiper quasi-free-

dom—but he was "free" only so long as he observed unspoken boundaries. When he reached for the prerogatives of the master class—the
prerogatives of *whiteness*—he had to be disciplined. First, he bought a
slave; at this juncture, Lynch simply reminded him of who owned whom
by beckoning Ellen to live with him for part of a year, before sending her
back to old Rhoda. But when Leiper tried to *sell* a slave for profit, Lynch
took legal action.

The case illuminates power relations among whites, free blacks, and
enslaved blacks. First, there is the fact of freed slaves' owning their own
slaves. Some free blacks bought family members in order to give them
freedom. In one sad South Carolina case, a free man of color, Liles, bought
his sick wife from a former master, Bass, just months before she died.
Feeling no pity, the master gouged his former slave for $600, despite the
fact that he would have gotten almost nothing for a sick woman on the
open market. When Liles sued Bass for breach of warranty after her death,
the trial judge opined that "we cannot deprive [Bass] of his good bargain."[71] However, in Natchez as elsewhere, many slaveholding blacks
were masters like others; William Johnson fills his pages with his troubles
over his unruly slave Stephen and the necessity for frequent whippings.
Here, Robert Leiper bought a girl slave for his own use as a domestic
servant until she turned twenty-one, when he agreed to set her free. Perhaps he saw this as a type of apprenticeship for her; perhaps he hoped
that a young woman house servant would allow his wife to enjoy certain
luxuries or freedoms; or perhaps he hoped for some kind of intimacy
with this young woman. Unfortunately, the records remain silent on the
relationship between Robert Leiper and Ellen.

The case highlights the precarious position of free blacks—above slaves
but below whites in the Southern hierarchy. In the 1830s, the South was
moving swiftly to assert the color line rather than the slave/free line as the
boundary that mattered. *Forniquet v. Lynch* illuminates the role of law
in ordering relations among the three groups and maintaining the hierarchy. In the correspondence, there is evidence of slaves as moral agents,
trying to live honorably within the constraints of slave society. A nameless
male slave tried to marry Ellen, approaching Leiper first. He then worked
to raise the money to buy Ellen from Leiper, although in practice this
meant that his owner had to buy her. All of these transactions involved
people of color centrally: the main players were Leiper, Ellen, and Ellen's
husband. But "the law" here is nearly synonymous with "the white man."
The law not only helped the whites to assert their ownership in Ellen's
body, but it silenced Ellen, her husband, and even the free Robert Leiper,
removing them from the dispute as parties and even as witnesses.

In *Turner v. Ballard*, Henry Turner's honor and character as a white
gentleman were put on the line by the legal conflict arising from his com-

mercial dealings with a trader of slaves, and by his refusal to pay for slaves whom he deemed defective. In *Forniquet v. Lynch*, the law literally erased the black principals in the dispute, and all evidence of black moral agency, remaking a legal conflict as between two white men. Charles Lynch dishonored Bob Leiper, and the legal process confirmed his dishonor.

. . . . .

Yet despite the law's power to erase slaves' agency, to silence their words, and to dishonor them, courtroom disputes also gave slaves power to throw their masters' honor into question, sometimes through the courtroom repetition of slaves' own words. White Southerners were obsessed with the fear that slaves were deceiving them, and continually frustrated that slaves were so inscrutable and difficult to read. As Steven Shapin has pointed out, the problem of "read[ing] the[] characters" of servants was a perennial one in traditional honor culture, and it was only greater in the slave South.[72] A master who could not read slaves well ran the risk of being duped by them, and nothing was less honorable than being fooled by a slave. Slaveholders were constantly on the lookout for trickery by slaves, and their fear lent greater urgency to the project of proper slave "management." In the courtroom, these fears constantly emerged, opening the possibility that slaves' resistant acts could become the basis for a litigant's challenge to his opponent's honor.

As will be discussed at length in chapter 5, the most common mention in court of a slave's deceit was to characterize a slave as feigning physical illness. Hardy Stevenson complained that he had bought the slave Esther only because her seller "represented said slave to be sound and to be deceitful in pretending to be sick frequently and . . . said all that she needed was a master who would drive her . . ."[73] Instead, he charged, Esther was truly ill. In *Laurence v. McFarlane*, Fanny's former owner testified that although Fanny complained of rheumatism, "it was more from an unwillingness to work than from want of ability."[74] A good master, these litigants and witnesses suggested, was one who could see through this deceit and make a slave work. A slave buyer, however, might argue that the slave's deceit was an example of a general dishonesty and "bad character" that justified a recovery of damages, as did the buyer in *Cozzins v. Whitacker*, whose witness testified that the slave Anthony was "lazy and . . . affected to be sick" when in fact "there was nothing the matter with him."[75]

Slaves could also feign mental illness or incapacity by putting on fake fits or acting as though they did not understand what was said to them. Questions of insanity will be addressed more fully in chapter 5, but the stories about deceitful pretense of insanity mirror the same fears as those of feigning physical illness. Even when the parties generally agreed that a slave was insane, they felt it necessary to point out that her symptoms were "utterly irreconcilable with the idea of deception."[76] In a breach of warranty case for an allegedly insane slave, the seller often suggested that the insanity was feigned, as did this seller's lawyer in a cross-interrogatory to the buyer's overseer:

3. What were the symptoms of insanity, if any, which you discovered about the negro Lawson? Were they constantly on him, or did they return only occasionally? Was not the said Lawson an artful designing fellow and do you not believe he *affected* to be deranged? Do you not remember that he pretended to be in love, and did he not state *that* as the cause of his derangement, and did not the plaintiff order him to be whipped saying he pretended only to be deranged, and that he would whip him out of his love fit, or words to that effect?

Here, again, the master was expected to discern a slave's trickery and take action; to suggest that he did not or could not would be an insult to the master's honor.

But the most disturbing deceit by a slave was not to simulate illness or even insanity, but to pretend to be a white man. The issue of "passing for white" arose in lawsuits by owners against railroads or ferryboats for transporting a runaway slave. The common carrier's defense was often that a reasonable person would have taken the slave for a white man. In one Georgia case, the owner introduced a witness who had seen Sam in Chicago, "passing as a white-man . . . Saw him take drinks at the bar with white men." Although "to a casual observer," this witness said, Sam "did not show any negro blood, he shewed the negro from the nose down." The railroad put on witnesses who "swore that they had *seen* Sam about pl[ainti]ffs store for a year or more and considered him a *white man*—that they had dealt with him in the store as a clerk of the pl[ainti]ffs bought goods of him and paid him money—that his complexion was light his hair straight and his general appearance to ordinary observation that of a white man one offered had been in the habit of calling him Mr Wallace and regarded him as a member of the firm."[77] That a slave could "pass" as white meant that whites could imbue "property" with honor and character, albeit by mistake.

Thus witnesses presented evidence of slaves' attempts to resist their masters by avoiding work, escaping, or "passing" as white. This resistance may even have been imagined by slaveholders anxious about their own ability to control their bondspeople. But the fact that the possibility of deception lurked behind every case of a "defective" slave thwarted whites' efforts to turn these cases into exercises of mastery and control.

Even the ban on slave testimony, the most effective legal mechanism to dishonor slaves and render them invisible before the law, did not survive courtroom battles intact. Despite the rule in every state that slaves could under no circumstances testify against whites, a rule which applied to out-of-court nonhearsay as well as live testimony, slaves' words were frequently repeated at trial. The rationale for the rule was simple: slaves were mendacious and unworthy of taking the oath to testify; their words could not be the basis of liability or culpability of a white person. Yet, time and again, in warranty cases, slave statements regarding their own condition were allowed, almost always against a white man, the slave seller. Thomas Cobb notes in his treatise that this was the main exception to the rule, owing to "the necessity of the case."[78] As one witness in a warranty case commented, "persons about to purchase negroes invariably interrogate them as to their health." Slave buyers relied on slaves' words in the marketplace, and they could not do without them in the courtroom.

Most of the time, witnesses reported slaves' words at trial without drawing judicial comment. It was common for witnesses to refer to slaves' statements in their testimony without either party's objecting. If no party objected, evidence of the use of slave testimony did not appear in the appellate opinion. For example, in *George v. Bean*, several witnesses testified that "the girl complained of a pain in her head and side" and "complained . . . of debility . . . of being overcome by hurt." The Mississippi High Court granted the plaintiff-seller a new trial on other grounds, never mentioning the admission of slave statements in its opinion.[79] In one South Carolina case, a witness testified that "the Negro said he had eaten dirt," and another that Romeo "after a drinking frolic would complain of a stoppage in his water," to which no one objected.[80] In a case that involved competing medical testimony, one doctor testified that a slave "said she was unable to attend to her duties about the house" because of an "enlargement of the tendons of her ankle." The other doctor, who argued that the swelling was only mild rheumatism, testified that "she said she had runaway, and took a cold, and that the swelling arose from that."[81]

The reported statements sometimes went beyond mere medical symptoms. One Natchez witness reported that an enslaved woman "had a short time before [she was sold] taken *some medicine to clear herself* (meaning thereby to produce abortion as this affiant understood)."[82] Another testified to a slave's statements about his ownership: "[T]he overseer went with him to the negroe's cabbin, where he was sick, saw and spoke to [the slave], asked him who he belonged to, and answered, to Mr Sauve and that said Barnaby sold him to him . . ."[83] At other times, a witness referred to the negotiations that had taken place between the buyer and the slave at the time of the sale, as when Thomas Gadsden remembered that "Philander stated to [the buyer] that he was unsound; had a shortness of breath, occasioned by a fall from a house." When asked, on cross-examination, how this information had been elicited, Gadsden replied that the buyer had "interrogated the negroes," as buyers always did.[84] The need to consult slaves in daily life, and especially in the marketplace, made it difficult to exclude their words in the courtroom.

Often, the opposing party objected to the admission of slaves' words at trial, but the judge overruled the objection. In the Pickens County, Alabama, Circuit Court, William Murrah's attorney asked Dr. Jesse Peebles about Phoebe's illness, including the following interrogatories:

> 11. State what account the negro woman Phoebe gave to you of the causes and length of her diseased state? How long she had been laboring under a cough and difficulty of respiration? Whether she had been cupped blistered or scarrified and what for? Who had been the physician . . . Whether she had ever afterwards felt well? State what she described her feelings to be and to have been since said former sickness? . . .
> 12. State how the symptoms [she] described accorded with your own opinion . . .

Despite the fact that the defendant excepted to the eleventh and twelfth interrogatories "because predicated on the sayings of a slave," Dr. Peebles answered the questions.[85] In one Adams County, Mississippi, case, the defendant based his motion for a new trial on the judge's ruling allowing "so much of the deposition of said Collins as relates to and is founded upon hearsay and the statements of the negro Caroline." The judge allowed the jury to hear the deposition that "the girl Caroline stated that she was sickly and had been in bad health for several years, and had been sold several times and taken back," and the jury found for Caroline's buyer. The defendant lost his case and his motion for a new trial.[86]

When these cases reached a higher court, judges invented creative excuses for what seemed like a long step out of bounds: first, they took care of any hearsay objections on the grounds that the statements fell into the hearsay exceptions of *res gestae*, or verbal acts; second, they ruled that since doctors routinely used a slave's statements about her own condition as one criterion on which to base their medical opinions, such statements could be admitted in the context of the doctor's opinion. Yet, eventually, even sick slaves' declarations to laymen were allowed. It was impossible to hear suits about the condition of human beings without hearing from the human beings themselves.[87]

The Mississippi High Court of Errors and Appeals, in *Fondren v. Durfee*, decreed that a sick slave's declarations to his master about his present illness were admissible as "verbal acts, indicating the nature and character of the disease under which the slave is laboring," and then arrived at the dubious conclusion that "being made to the master, who is interested in the welfare of the slave, [the slave's declarations] are presumed to be honest." This holding was a far cry from the expectation that a slave will dissemble illness to get out of work. The court also rationalized the presumption of slave honesty by the fact that slaves' declarations were "constantly acted upon by medical men as true statements."[88] In an early Alabama case, the Alabama Supreme Court took this logic so far as to admit a slave's declarations to prove *scienter*, or bad faith on the part of the seller, putting great power in the hands of the slave.[89]

The Alabama court reconsidered this question in *Bates v. Eckles & Brown*. At trial, Dr. Peterson testified, "In conversation with the negro, I learned from him, although he made the statement with extreme reluctance, that he had been subject to similar attacks before . . ." Mary Treadwell also explained that Toney "made frequent suggestions as to the treatment to be used, which led to inquiries on my part, as to whether he had been before afflicted in the same way. He replied that he had been subject to similar attacks and had generally been relieved by drinking soap suds . . . [and] by being put in a barrel of warm water." Sarah Stephens added that she heard Toney "suggest the use of red pepper, which he generally carried in his pocket . . . he often asked for syrup and said meat would hurt him . . ."[90]

Although the defendant-seller objected to this testimony, the Alabama court ruled that slaves' declarations "are admissible evidence upon the principle of *res gestae* as well as from the necessity of the case."[91] However, this court decreed that slave statements regarding previous illness would be admissible only if made to a physician. The court cautioned that if it went too far in allowing statements as reported to other witnesses, such as "the female witnesses who disposed in this case," then "it would be an easy matter to prove slaves unsound by their declarations of their unsoundness, oftentimes feigned as an excuse to avoid labor, or to procure a change of masters."[92] The judge recognized that the possibility of a false "warranty" coming directly from a slave increased the risk of a master's investment and increased the risk of the master's losing his own honor and character as a master if he honored the deceit of the slave.

. . . . .

In the marketplace and in the courtroom, white Southern men sought to safeguard honor as well as profit. Disputes involving slaves held the potential to threaten a man's honor. On one level, they did so as any market dispute might, by raising the possibility that a man was a liar. Yet it was important that white men worked out their relationships *through* transactions involving slaves. This meant that whites' relations to blacks ordered relations among whites as well. Because white honor depended on the dishonoring of slaves, conflicts in the marketplace and courtroom took on dimensions of honor—not only because they called into question white men's honesty but because they called into question their mastery.

Most dangerous of all was the possibility that a master had been deceived by the slave himself. The ban on slave testimony was an essential element of the dishonoring of slaves, and the introduction of slave testimony threatened both the cultural system of honor and a legal system predicated on the denial of the slave's moral agency. When slaves' words were repeated at trial, they introduced the specter of the deceitful slave manipulating whites right into the courtroom. The possibility that a slave might deceive one into believing in his illness, idiocy, or whiteness impugned a white man's honor in the deepest way. Legal actors expended a great deal of effort to handle these threats to honor and law: the stories they generated about the characters of masters and slaves were a part of that endeavor.

THREE

SLAVES' CHARACTER

IN 1821, South Carolina judge Abraham Nott addressed the difficult question of whether, in ordinary slave sales, a buyer could expect that the slave he or she bought would have a good character.[1] While sellers rarely warranted a slave's "moral qualities" in writing, there was some precedent in South Carolina for the rule that "a sound price warrants a sound commodity." The state Supreme Court had applied the "sound price rule" to slaves in 1793, explaining that "all imaginable fairness ought to be observed, especially in the sale of negroes, which are a valuable species of property in this country."[2] This "sound price rule" operated to imply a warranty of soundness even into a contract for slave sale that did not contain any express language about the slave's health or fitness for labor.[3]

Why should the rule not extend to a slave's "moral qualities" as well? After all, a slave who ran away was as unproductive as a slave who fell ill. Judge Nott gave the answer: to allow the litigation of a slave's moral qualities would be "worse than opening Pandora's box upon the community."[4] Nott gave several reasons for thinking this litigation dangerous and open-ended: First, he argued that slaves' character was so dependent upon their masters and on their particular situation that no general rule could be formulated. Second, he argued that moral standards varied so greatly that it would become necessary to extend the warranty to "the smallest deviation from the strictest line of moral rectitude." Third, he expressed discomfort about the prospect of slave character's being an object of extended discussion in the courtroom. His opinion betrays the practical concerns judges had about the problems of litigating slave character; it also reveals a deeper uneasiness about the wisdom of opening up slave character as a subject of inquiry at the very moment slaves were to be treated as objects of ownership and transfer.

Despite the efforts of appellate courts in South Carolina and other states to keep slave character out of the courtroom, cases involving warranties of moral qualities reached the courts frequently in actions for fraud or deceit, when buyers charged that sellers had orally vouched for the slave's moral qualities or character.[5] Slave character also went on trial whenever a slave's runaway habit or other "vice" became an excuse for a white person to shoot or beat the slave; further, owners or hirers might give a slave's character as an excuse for her illness or death. "Moral qualities" included not only the general character of the slave but his or her "habits" of drinking, stealing, and running away. In Louisiana, the action of redhibition extended specifically to the "habit of running away," "addiction to theft," and other "vices of character . . . in proportion to the degree in which they disable[d]" the slave.[6]

When litigants and witnesses discussed slaves' character, distinct images of the good and bad slave emerged in civil trials. The commodification of slaves' character and labor shaped the way witnesses spoke about them. Furthermore, gender narratives had a profound impact on racial imagery, not only because white Southern stereotypes of black women and men were reproduced in the courtroom, but because slaves' perceived shortcomings as laborers were interpreted in ways that would not challenge those stereotypes. And when witnesses, lawyers, and judges told stories about why slaves had the character they had, and behaved the way they did, they developed certain stock stories about the origins and development of slaves' "runaway" character, which determined the outcome of many warranty and hire cases. The "medicalization" of slave "vice" colored accounts of slave character in many cases, but particularly in those involving women. In a variety of ways, these cases forced lawyers and judges to confront slaves' moral agency, as they did when witnesses noted a slave's own reasons for behaving a certain way, when a slave's action resulted in a tort, or when a slave deceived a white man—and the stories lawyers and judges told tended to minimize or deny slaves' agency.

Moral agency meant more than simply that slaves had human qualities. What was threatening to the legal system's effort to treat slaves as chattel was evidence that slaves behaved as morally reasoning, self-governing agents. Yet the logic of the legal system itself guaranteed that litigants in civil disputes would open the door to such evidence, and that it would take *work* to rationalize this evidence away—to explain it in other terms. Both law and the honor culture found the moral agency of slaves threatening, but it was in the legal arena that white men were forced to confront the contradictions such agency raised. In everyday life, whites often recognized that slaves made moral choices and tried to govern their own lives, without that recognition challenging their commitment to seeing slaves as racially inferior beings who benefited from bondage. From the perspective of honor culture, slaves' agency was threatening in its capacity to throw masters' honor into question. Slaves acting as moral agents in disputes between white men were slaves acting *out of their place*. When they did so, they raised the stakes in courtroom conflicts over commerce, and legal actors worked hard to put them back in their place.

· · · · ·

Parties in the antebellum courtroom painted a picture of good and bad slaves that sometimes contradicted the stereotypes popularized by polemicists on both sides of the slavery debate. The stereotypical slaves historians have named in Southern culture—the childlike, lazy, and dishonest "Sambo," the rebellious "Nat," the average "Jack," the sexual "Jezebel," and the motherly "Mammy"—provided white Southerners with important ways to understand their relationships with enslaved African Americans, but not all of these characterizations emerged in the courtroom.[7] Black women were rarely portrayed as harshly as black men who were identified as "Nats," nor were they portrayed in sexual terms as "Jezebels." Furthermore, witnesses' characterizations of good slaves as honest, intelligent, and industrious calls into question the depth of their belief in "Sambo" and highlights the fact that the qualities slaveholders prized were those most useful in a market economy. Most descriptions of slaves included an estimate of dollar value, and most disputes hinged in one way or another on the slave's skills as a worker. Suits involving the skills of a slave, in particular, brought the intersection of black identity as capital and as labor into relief.

Southerners needed a spectrum of images to deal with individual slaves in their daily lives.[8] Witnesses at trial often described slaves in terms that did not fit into the simple stereotypes propagated by appellate judges and the authors of legal treatises, particularly in recognizing the personalities, human motivations, and skills of individual slaves.[9] Slave sellers generally advertised their slaves to be "a No. 1 boy," "honest, industrious and free from vice," or "honest, sober, humble and not given to be a runaway."[10] In one Louisiana case, the seller's witnesses proved William's honesty by testifying that he, "a boy of good character perfectly honest and sober[,] . . . used to be sent to the house of the most respectable men in [town] to shave them when they did not like to come to the shop." William "was well informed and well acquainted with amounts and generally managed [his owner's] affairs."[11] Likewise, an overseer testified that Aglae was "very industrious very clean,"[12] and Lucinda's owner advertised her as "an honest trusty servant" who "always brought her wages in."[13] Honesty and industry were qualities that both male and female slaves might exhibit.

Occasionally, witnesses referred to slaves' intelligence or morality.[14] In *Pilie v. Lalande*, one witness reported that a female slave was "quick and intelligent," another that she was "of good disposition intelligent and a good servant."[15] On the other hand, black intelligence could be a negative attribute from a white point of view, particularly in a woman. In one case, Farmer tried to return Kitty to her seller because "she knew too much . . . the essence of Farmer's objection was that the slave was too smart."[16] The slave known as either Harry or Charles was described as "a very pert, smart boy" and "a shrewd cunning boy" by witnesses for both the buyer and seller in a warranty dispute; but the seller's witness also declared that he was "too cunning for his good," and a previous owner of the slave remembered warning the plaintiff, who "had a mind to educate him & get his assistance in the store," that "the Boy was rascal enough already without an education."[17] Intelligence could lead to rebellion.

A bad slave's characteristics included faithlessness, dishonesty, indolence, and insubordination. The same slaves whom sellers portrayed as honest and trustworthy, slave buyers suing for character defects accused of being "vicious and worthless, habitual and dangerous runaway," "ill disposed, faithless, inconstant, unsteady, disobedient, and bad in all respects," or "dishonest, lazy and vicious."[18] A particularly bad slave, Lawson, "was violent and headstrong and abused the smaller negroes."[19] Another witness in Adams County Court described his former slave Jesse as "a notorious scoundrel,"[20] bought in chains and sold in the stocks. Such vehement denunciations of the slave's whole character as degraded and vicious almost always attached to male slaves. Witnesses might characterize enslaved women as lazy but did not employ the same stereotype of savagery to describe rebellious women.[21] For example, in one case over a runaway woman slave, the buyer's most detailed complaint about her character was that she was "as smart a negro as any, if she would stay."[22] In other cases, the buyer merely argued that the female runaway was crazy or idiotic.[23]

Vice in enslaved men was frequently connected with dishonesty and faithlessness in ways suggesting that masters could normally expect honesty and loyalty from slaves. If all slaves were mendacious "Sambos," this expectation would make no sense. Sometimes one party, usually the seller, would invoke the "Sambo" stereotype, arguing that one cannot expect too much even from good slaves: "[I]t [is] very common amongst Negroes to steal a little and run away."[24] This bore out the stereotype of slaves as mendacious and mischievous, though generally harmless. Yet there was a strong counterstory which insisted that, in fact, well-treated, good slaves were both honest and trustworthy. Indeed, in the same case, the witness being deposed made plain that he did not "believe most negroes would [steal and run away.]"[25] Thus while Southerners in court spoke of bad slaves as dishonest and vicious, they usually meant to distinguish these individuals from the general character of all black slaves.

The emphasis on honesty and industry also suggests that these were characteristics whites highly prized in slaves. Given the market context of these legal disputes over slave character, such valued characteristics had a precise market price. Because slaves were such an important form of capital in the antebellum South, positive descriptions of their character were often accompanied by an estimate of value, such as "being a fine fellow honest industrious free from vice and such an one as would command a good price" or "a Negro woman slave whose character was exceptionable and was considered not so valuable on account of her bad qualities but was worth as he considered $400."[26] Conversely, a slave's bad character also had a price; one Georgia overseer sued by the plantation owner for beating his slave to death won a judgment that "[i]t is very obvious that a negro's bad character detracts from his value, and ought to lessen the damages for killing him."[27] One slave trader defended a warranty suit by explaining that the slave January was worth $800 but for the vice of running away and had been sold at a "reduced price" of $300; January's character discount was $500.[28] Constantly putting a numerical value on a slave's character guaranteed that whenever slaves were viewed as people, their property aspect also intruded. Commodification meant always thinking about slave character in dollar terms.[29]

Witnesses and sellers also described good or bad slaves in terms of their work skills or the jobs they performed. In the valuation of slaves, skills could weigh in the balance against qualities considered to be defects in slaves, such as old age or high temper. Philander, for example, "was an old man about 50 years old; he was represented as a very good carpenter; though he was old, yet he might be more valuable on account of being a mechanic."[30] In another warranty case, Sally "was a pretty good looking old woman—was a House servant, and capable, but very high tempered— she was an *excellent Cook*." Sally was put into the workhouse "for her impudence"; one witness reported her buyer's having said that he could not manage her; and a former owner testified "that Sally was a very capable servant and objectionable only as respected her temper—which was intolerable."[31] In these cases, skills, age, and "temper" each factored into the calculus of these slaves' prices.

When a buyer sought to recover the price of a slave, it was usually legally insufficient to prove that a slave lacked the skills the seller represented him or her to have.[32] However, a skills claim could supplement another claim of unsoundness to the benefit of the buyer. It could be that evidence of a seller's having lied about a slave's skills tended to prove to the trier of fact that the seller had also lied about other things. Or it may have been that the skills claim itself carried *some* weight as a redressable injury but not enough weight standing alone. For example, in *Brocklebank v. Johnson*,[33] the buyer's primary claim was that Romeo was a drunkard and suffered illness from his drinking. In addition, though, he wanted to prove that Johnson had misrepresented Romeo to be a good bricklayer. The trial judge instructed the jury to consider both claims, but that for the skills claim, "the Plaintiff could only recover the difference in value between a Bricklayer and a common negro." Brocklebank won both a jury verdict and an appellate judgment that he could recover for deceit even if Johnson had given no written warranty of Romeo's character or his skills as a bricklayer.[34]

The Louisiana Supreme Court heard several of these mixed-claim cases involving women sold to do housework. Women were disproportionately represented in both warranty and hire disputes over skilled slaves. Indeed, if a buyer sued a seller for a breach of warranty in the sale of a woman slave, and the case did not involve physical illness or death, the complaint was most likely that she did not perform sufficiently well as a house servant. The facts of the cases, as set out in the trial testimony, highlight the different characterizations of women and men who refused to work. For example, Grenier Petit sued Jean Laville because the slave Aglae "was neither a washer nor a good subject."[35] The plaintiff called witnesses who testified that they had tried Aglae as a washer and "she did not appear to understand any thing about washing." One, Mme. Felix, "gave her two shirts to wash and after keeping them during four hours she returned them without having finished them." She testified on cross-examination that "she can say in an hour if a person is a washer or not." A woman who worked for Mme. Felix testified that she had been obliged to rewash the two shirts Aglae washed, and that although she "is not a washer by trade," she "is a good judge of washing."

It is impossible for us to determine whether Aglae did not know how to wash shirts or simply decided not to wash them as a form of resistance, but it is significant that all the witnesses agreed that Aglae's defect was her lack of washing skills rather than her rebelliousness or even laziness—in stark contrast to cases in which male slaves failed to complete work and were branded rebels of bad character and habits. Why white Southerners found it easier to imagine black women as incompetent than as vicious is open to conjecture. Perhaps it was too far a stretch to think of a female house slave, a "Mammy," as a rebel; perhaps gendered notions of competency made it easy to attribute incompetence to black women. Certainly, the absence of white fear of "Nat" when the slave at issue was a woman made masters slower to conjure up a vicious rebel at the first failure to obey orders. In any event, it appears that behavior on the part of a woman which might have been interpreted as deficiency in character in a man was more often portrayed as deficiency in skill.[36]

The debates over a slave's skills often revealed that judicial standards for the level of skill or for the amount of work reasonably expected of a slave were remarkably low. In *Chretien v. Theard*, William Rogers, a carpenter, testified that the male slave Lafortune was "expert in neither trade of Carpenter or Joiner, that . . . Lafortune is not more expert in them than an intelligent man who has never learnt said trade." Although several other witnesses corroborated this account, the judge gave great weight to the testimony of two witnesses who had known Lafortune many years earlier and said "that he was capable of executing work when market [*sic*] out to him." The judge wrote that "[t]his I think is as much as could be expected of an unlettered slave. It could not be supposed that he could calculate the dimensions and proportions of a building. It was not to be expected that a slave should be a master workman."[37]

It was clear that William Rogers believed that Lafortune, sold as a "carpenter and joiner," should have the skills of a carpenter and be able to perform his work better than even an "intelligent man" without training. By contrast, the judge implied that a slave carpenter could meet a lower standard than a "carpenter"; the judge did not consider an "intelligent man" to be the appropriate reference point for "an unlettered slave." While ordinary Southern whites expected slaves to meet a level of skill as well as industry, judges justified their decisions in these cases in a way that avoided inscribing in the law too high a standard for slaves, one that might undermine the "Sambo" stereotype. Thus the paternalism expressed at the appellate level conflicted with the demands of the market economy for skilled labor.

Finally, slaves' status as capital and as labor intersected. Litigants argued vehemently over a slave's skills in determining the slave's dollar value. For example, in *Stone & Best v. Watson*, the buyer succeeded in proving a slave unsound because of illness but also wanted to show that her "value if sound" should take into account that she was reputed to be "a No. 1 seamstress" and in fact was not.[38] In *Campbell ads. Atchison*, one witness testified that "he would not have given a Dollar for" Sally, for whom the buyer had paid $350, "but that she ought to have brought $250." His reason for considering her worthless was her temper, but he recognized that her skills would bring money on the market. Another witness testified that Salley "would *at the present time be worth $350,* but for her temper [which lowers her price to] 0 . . ."[39] In *Porcher ads. Caldwell*, a witness testified "that a first rate cook would be worth $500," but that because of the slave's poor cooking skills, he "dont think the negro worth $350 if she had been sound."[40]

The cases involving slaves' skills show several sometimes contradictory impulses by all parties involved: witnesses' attribution of intelligence, ability, and efficiency to enslaved people; judges' unwillingness to set high standards for slaves' labor; the constant juxtaposition of paternalist rhetoric with discussions of slaves in terms of dollar value; a focus on women's inability rather than their insubordination. Yet, for the most part, disputes over skilled slaves avoided the starkest contrasts between the good slave and the bad slave, for the very reason that the suits presupposed a competency on the slave's part that defied stereotypes.

. . . . .

Disputes involving runaway slaves, unlike those regarding slaves' skills, highlight the schizophrenic racial iconography of white Southerners: The hope that slaves were happy "Sambos" and "Mammies" was always balanced by the fear that if the bonds of slavery were loosened, the childlike slave would revert to a savage beast. What the trials help to illuminate about this child/savage duality, however, is the multiplicity of stories about what made a slave into a child or a savage, and about which slaves were one and which the other. Slave buyers and sellers, hirers and owners, told different stories about the dependence of slave character on masters' influence, and about the immutability of slave "vice."

As George Fredrickson has shown, Sambo and Nat were two sides of the same coin: according to Southern white racial theory, "the Negro was by nature a savage brute. Under slavery, however, he was 'domesticated' or, to a limited degree, 'civilized.' Hence docility was not so much his natural character as an artificial creation of slavery."[41] As Mississippi Valley physician and ideologue Samuel Cartwright put it, "the negro must, from necessity, be the slave of man or the slave of Satan."[42] White Southerners believed that black character was plastic. One Virginia planter wrote that "[t]he character of the negro . . . is like the plastic clay, which may be moulded into agreeable or disagreeable figures according to the skill of the moulder."[43] But they did not think it was infinitely plastic: "innate racial traits limited his potential development to a more or less tenuous state of 'semi-civilization.' "[44]

This picture of black character as malleable to a certain point should be contrasted with Southern ideas of white character development. To a great extent, Southern ideals of white character depended on slavery, and, implicitly, on a contrast between black and white. From Scottish moral philosophy, white Southerners inherited the idea that the "moral sense" was an innate faculty of all white men.[45] This moral sense could be developed through education, or it could be left in the rough, but all white men had it.

By the nineteenth century, most white Southerners believed that blacks were bereft of a moral sense that could be educated. While proslavery writers did not state their conviction of black moral inferiority in terms of "the moral sense," this equation can be inferred from their repeated assertions that blacks could not benefit from moral education because they lacked the necessary prerequisites.[46] Therefore, the plasticity of slave "character" did not necessarily equate with moral development as understood by educated whites. Rather, Southern ideologues emphasized the *imitative* abilities of the black slave. As Dr. Cartwright wrote, "When made contented and happy, as [slaves] always should be, they reflect their master in their thoughts, morals, and religion, or at least they are desirous of being like him. They imitate him in everything, as far as their imitative faculties, which are very strong, will carry them."[47] Thus slaves well governed might *mimic* moral development without actually having their own moral faculties to develop.

In warranty cases, the malleability of slave character was essentially a seller's story. Only a seller would suggest that the slave's character depended on good government by a master. By contrast, the buyer unhappy with a runaway or "vicious" slave preferred to portray the slave's character as immutable. This particular slave, according to the typical buyer, was an incorrigible savage under any circumstances. Buyers painted a world in which slaves were born with particular characteristics, just as whites were. Alternatively, while malleable character made slaves seem childlike but human, immutable viciousness could render an enslaved person subhuman.

The seller's story of malleability played into the paternalist defense of slavery by shifting the focus from the slave's character to the master's treatment of the slave. One case decided on appeal by Chief Justice John Belton O'Neall of the South Carolina Court of Appeal illustrates this shift. In *Johnson v. Wideman*, the buyer (Leonard Wideman) portrayed Charles as an insubordinate and vicious drunkard and runaway, while the seller (Jonathan Johnson) claimed that he behaved badly only under bad government.[48] Although the original trial records of this case are lost, the South Carolina Court of Appeal, in an unusual opinion, reprinted the report of the trial judge, including the testimony and briefs. More than forty witnesses, most of them small slaveholding farmers, appeared in the courtroom in the lower Piedmont county of Abbeville to discuss the character of the slave Charles.

Witnesses for Leonard Wideman, a planter with fifty-nine slaves and one of the largest extended families in the county, testified that Jonathan Johnson, a fifty-one-year-old planter and tradesman, had committed fraud in the sale of Charles. According to defense witnesses, Johnson had represented Charles to be sober, honest, and humble; they asserted that Johnson had said "he would trust him with money," and that "a boy of ten years old could control him." Instead, according to Alexander Cummins, a farmer with two slaves of his own, "Charles would get drunk; he would not work; he let his coal kiln burn up; was insolent; he was very often drunk; he saw him once lying behind the shop, and at another time in the woods. He (Charles) stayed with the defendant about two months and then ran away."[49]

According to the buyer-defendant, not only was Charles lazy and insolent, but he cursed his overseer and attacked or threatened other white men. "He was saucy: [I] saw him shove a white man, named Cramer, down. He did not bring much custom to the shop: he threatened to beat another white man named Wells," testified John Russell, who kept the grog shop at the crossroads known as Trick'em. Russell also reported that in threatening Wells, Charles told him, "[N]o one man ever had or ever should master him." Another witness recounted that Charles had struck a white man with whom he had been gambling. He also described an incident at the racetrack in which Charles had intervened in a quarrel between his former owner, Wiley Berry, and another white man: "Charles came up behind his master, shut up his fist and swore that he wished he was a white man." Twenty-eight witnesses testified to Charles' drinking, swearing, laziness, and general insolence. William Adams, a farmer with five slaves, even recounted a story in which Charles pulled a knife to prevent Adams and his brother from pulling Charles' two big dogs off his own little dog.[50]

The defense maintained that Charles had been a runaway and a drunk when Johnson, the seller, had owned him. John Wideman, the defendant's son, testified that his brother, a child at the time, was whipping Charles' wife, when she "broke and run, crying and calling for her husband." When Charles learned that the witness's brother was whipping her, "he swore he would mash him to the earth." At another time, John and his brother chased Charles from the kitchen; he turned and offered to fight them.[51]

Other witnesses who lived near Johnson told stories of Charles' swearing that he would not live with Johnson, hiding in a willow thicket when there was work to be done, and asking a storekeeper for a ticket (a pass). Major William Eddings, who owned six slaves, estimated Charles' value at $1,000 when Johnson bought him from Berry, "taking him *as he was*," because of his skill as a blacksmith. On the day of the sale, according to James Spikes, "Charles quarreled with Berry: charged him with keeping his wife, shut up his fist and was walking towards Berry, when Johnson prevented him." When the plaintiff-seller tried to argue that a firmer master could have reined in Charles' misbehavior, defense witness Sherwood Corley testified that "he had often helped to tie and whip [Charles]" when Berry owned him; "it had no effect on him; he would curse his master as soon as taken down."[52]

In short, according to the buyer-defendant in this case, Charles was the epitome of the dangerous and outlaw male slave: he threatened white men with violence; he refused to work unless he wished to; he did not respond to whipping; he ran away at will; he tried to defend his wife's honor against white men; he not only acted as though he were equal to a white man, he *said he wished he were a white man*. In all of these offenses, according to the buyer-defendant, Charles was impervious to varying treatment; he was immutably vicious.

The plaintiff-seller's witnesses, however, told a different story. According to them, Charles was a drunkard and an "insolent negro" only when he lived with Wiley Berry, "himself a drinking, horse-racing man" (from whom Johnson bought Charles). Wiley Berry was a planter in the neighboring county of Edgefield. As Lewis Busby, a toll-bridge keeper who owned thirteen slaves, explained, "He had heard of [Charles'] drinking. He had borne the character of an insolent negro: but not in the time he belonged to the Johnsons." Others testified that Charles was humble and worked well; that when Johnson owned him, "he was not so indolent as when he belonged to Berry." Berry had exposed him frequently to spirits and had whipped him often. Alexander Presley testified that Wideman knew Charles' reputation, and told Presley that Charles "was under a bad character . . . as he could out-general old Wiley Berry, he must be bad." Thus Johnson's case rested on the contention that Charles was a good slave when managed well, and the only evidence of his insolence came from his behavior under Berry and under Wideman himself. In the alternative, Johnson argued that Wideman knew Charles' bad character before he bought him.[53]

The chief justice of the South Carolina Court of Appeal, John Belton O'Neall, sat as circuit judge in this case. Instructing the jury, he asked, "[W]hat moral qualities would be so material, as that a misrepresentation of them would have the effect to rescind the contract?" and answered "that any quality represented to exist, which, if it did not, would have the effect of diminishing in a considerable degree, the usefulness and value of the slave, would have that effect."[54] He went on to enumerate those of Charles' vices that might qualify: "Habitual drunkenness was I told them, such a vicious habit as would justify them in rescinding the contract," but "occasional intoxication, not amounting to a habit," would not be enough. "An habitual runaway was, I thought, a material defect," but again, "*occasional flights of a slave from his master's service for special causes would not constitute any material moral defect.*" And honesty, O'Neall instructed the jury, "was a material moral quality in a slave: but nothing short of general dishonesty would show a defect in this behalf. For occasional thefts among the tolerably good slaves may be expected . . ."[55]

But O'Neall added a strong caveat. While all of these qualities in a slave might justify nonpayment of a note, he stated that "the policy of allowing such a defence might be very well questioned. For, most commonly such habits were easy of correction by prudent masters, and it was only with the imprudent that they were allowed to injure the slave. *Like master, like man* was, I told them, too often the case, in drunkenness, impudence, and idleness."[56] The jurors, apparently accepting this argument, found for the plaintiff-seller, Jonathan Johnson, and the higher court, in a short opinion by O'Neall himself, affirmed the verdict.

The stories of buyer and seller in *Johnson v. Wideman* highlight the way that mutability of a slave's character could dominate litigation over a slave's "vice." Charles, in the courtroom, appeared to be both child and savage, but Wideman claimed that he was a savage *no matter what*, whereas Johnson made the claim that Fredrickson documents: Charles was "a child *in his place*, and a savage *out of it*."[57]

O'Neall's instructions contained, in microcosm, several of the stories about slaves' character development. He drew a number of dichotomies: "occasional intoxication" vs. "habitual drunkenness"; "occasional flights . . . for special causes" vs. "habitual runaway"; "occasional thefts" vs. "general dishonesty." Like "Sambo," the typical slave could be expected to drink, run away, and steal a little—only when these acts came to define his character would he be considered defective. On the other hand, black character, even more than white character, was formed through habit, and masters were responsible for slaves' habits.[58] The trial judge, as well as the supreme court, largely accepted Johnson's argument that Charles' misbehavior could be attributed to the freedom Berry gave him and the bad example Berry set. This theory of slave "vice"—"like master, like man"—removed agency from the slave and portrayed the slave as an extension of his master.[59]

. . . . .

"Some months after the said Negroe man had run away he learned . . . that the same Negro was a runaway," explained one witness in a Louisiana case.[60] The distinction between the act of running away and the character of a runaway, drawn at length by the trial judge in *Johnson v. Wideman*, had several impulses. On the one hand, it was a simple recognition that masters lacked absolute control over their slaves; to define runaway character or dishonesty by a single act would open the floodgates to warranty suits, because resistant acts simply happened *too* often. But it was more than that: the exercise of proving a runaway character or habit defined the slave by his vice and made the vice into an immutable essence. An Alabama case may illustrate.

In 1849, Walker Reynolds sued William Ward for payment of an $800 note, given for the purchase of a slave named Bill.[61] In defense, Ward, a planter with considerable holdings in land and slaves, claimed that he should not have to pay Reynolds for Bill, because Bill was a runaway, and that Reynolds had deceitfully represented Bill as "a negro of excellent character and recommended him in every particular extolling him both as to character and value." Indeed, according to Ward, Reynolds had explained that the only reason he was selling Bill was "that there had been a disturbance between the negro and another about a negro woman the wife of the other."[62]

Reynolds, the seller, read into testimony the depositions of several witnesses to show that Bill had been a good slave when he owned him. William Wilson, an illiterate town-dweller, testified that "I never knew or heard of said negro Bill to resist or rebel against his owner or any other person who had authority to control him." In answer to cross-interrogatories by Ward's lawyer, Wilson made a good start, reiterating that Bill was "active, able, and willing," but then added that "with this exception that he would occasionally run away." Wilson probably lost his value as a plaintiff's witness when asked, "Had the said Bill the reputation of the Red fox and was not that reputation acquired by his running away and the difficulty in his being caught?" Wilson admitted, "He had the name of the Red fox and was hard to catch when out."[63]

On reexamination, the plaintiff-seller's attorney asked Wilson, "Do you not believe the habit of running away by which Bill acquired the reputation of Red fox arose from imprudence of the plaintiff by his making unnecessary threats . . . ?" Wilson explained that "if Bill had belonged to some persons he would not have run away, and it was well understood that if he expected to get a whipping beforehand he would leave." In this case, the plaintiff's counsel was in the odd position of arguing that his own client's slave management had been so deficient—in "making unnecessary threats"—that the slave had run away from his seller, but that this action did not prove he would run away from his buyer.

Several witnesses testified both that they knew Bill as "Red fox" because of his skill at evading the slave patrol *and* that he was an excellent worker. William Mecham, who described Bill as a "stout, active and good-looking negro," claimed that he knew Bill to have run away only once: "One time he came to me one morning and said his master had got mad with him, he wished me to go home with him which I did." Micajah Lisle, who thought Bill a "*pert* active negro" also knew of only one runaway episode, when "I came across the boy Bill once in the woods . . ." Cunningham Wilson stated that Bill was "in mind and body as far as I know as sound as any man—black or white." On cross-examination, Wilson admitted that "I did know him to run away, I cannot state how often, several times, one time he went out a horse hunting and staid some time, how long am unable to say." He also said that the name Red fox "was acquired from a race one night with dogs having run well but was caught."

However, Cunningham Wilson concluded that Bill's value was "set with full knowledge of his character he having worked for me at harvest . . . and a better hand I would never desire." The plaintiff-seller sought to prove that Bill's selling price had already been discounted for his runaway habit. Each witness was asked to estimate Bill's value, and to explain whether their estimate included a discount for the "Red fox" reputation. At trial, Ward was the first party to introduce these witnesses' depositions into testimony, but only the sections that referred to Bill's character as a "Red fox" and a runaway. Reynolds read the omitted portions about Bill's hard work and high value. Both the trial court and the appellate court found for the seller, decreeing that he should be able to recover Bill's market value, taking into account his "character and qualities." Despite Bill's runaway character, Bill was not valueless.

In this case, the seller argued that Bill ran away only when he was afraid of being whipped, or when his master acted unreasonably, but that Bill had a good character. The buyer argued that being a runaway *was* Bill's character; Bill was a Red fox. Many warranty and hire disputes over runaway slaves hinged on just this distinction between the act of running away and the *character* or *habit* of a runaway. To some extent, this distinction amounted to tacit recognition of the area of rights slaves had carved out for themselves, and of masters' lack of absolute control over slaves. Despite increasingly strict statutory restrictions on their movements, many slaves continued throughout the antebellum period to "go abroad" at night, to visit wives on other plantations, to hire themselves out, and even to live in town apart from their masters. This tacit recognition is particularly evident in Louisiana law, which codified strict definitions for a true runaway habit, as opposed to merely "going abroad."

Yet the run away/runaway distinction was more than just accommodation on the part of whites; it was an effort to define slave character in terms of habits. If a slave ran away once, it was acceptable to attribute that action to a rational motive, but if this dangerous habit became routine, then slaveholders treated that habit as a vicious character trait or a disease. Because, according to this view, a slave could have no reason to want his freedom, he must simply have a runaway vice or habit. As John Staples, a witness for the buyer in *Hagan v. Rist*, explained, "I do not know why [John] runaway [sic] he certainly had no reason I think it is a natural vice with him." Staples portrayed John as immutably vicious. The buyer's overseer corroborated this testimony by saying that John "ran away without any cause whatever," in contrast to a slave who was whipped or had other reasons.[64] Therefore John must *be* a runaway. Without this run away/runaway distinction, the comment that "[s]ome months after the said Negroe man had run away he learned . . . that the same Negro was a runaway" would make no sense.[65]

Slave buyers, hirers from whom slaves ran away, or persons accused of shooting runaway slaves emphasized slaves' immutable viciousness and their own proper exercise of control over the slaves. In *Moran v. Davis*, the slave Stephen ran away from Davis, who had hired him from Moran. Moran then sued Davis for the price of Stephen; in answer, Davis replied that Stephen "was of bad and insubordinate character and difficult to manage and keep in proper subjection . . . Defendant says he used only so much and such means as were necessary to keep said negro under control . . . [He] was unruly and insubordinate and would not submit to the control of the defendant." The jury agreed that Davis should not have to reimburse Moran for the loss.[66] Hirers, buyers, and people accused of damaging the slave of another always wanted to convince the jury that the slave at issue *was* a runaway, that his character as a runaway was immutable.

By contrast, witnesses at trial frequently mentioned that a slave had run away once but called her a good slave at the same time. Henry Doyle testified that Capt. Samuel Cotton had told him that Mary "was dissatisfied at living in the county and that she had run away from Mr. Rogillio [*sic*] . . . He also stated that she was among the best servants he had ever owned."[67] A witness for the plaintiff in a suit to retrieve damages for a runaway slave shot in flight testified that Spencer was "a likely boy worth twelve or fourteen hundred—never heard anything against his character except that he had run away."[68] These witnesses portrayed slaves who had once or even more than once run away, but who did not have the character of a "runaway"; their character was defined by something other than running away.

Again, issues of commodification always arose at moments of character determination. In one Natchez case, Jonathon Guice sued John Holmes for possession of a slave he claimed Holmes had illegally detained from him. Guice's lawyer questioned several witnesses about the slave John: "[W]hat is his character, was he in the habit of running away?" Holmes' lawyer then cross-interrogated: "What was the value of such boy when addicted to running away? What is the difference between the value of slaves who are confirmed runaways and those not having this vice, all other things being Equal?" The witnesses all agreed that John had a good character, was not a runaway, but that a runaway was worth less than half "as he otherwise would be if not a runaway."[69]

· · · · ·

Buyers realized that if a slave's vice was a "habit" akin to a disease, she was reduced to a status closer to animal than if her vice was a purposeful one; just as sellers knew that if she was merely the product of her owner's management, that brought her closer to a child. Both of these notions were implicitly contrasted with some conception of immanent human "character." Both complete malleability and immutable "addiction" to vice negated the idea that a slave behaved a certain way out of the conscious choice of a rational mind, or the yearnings of a human soul.[70]

The legal tendency to medicalize slave vice by portraying character defects as "habits" or "addictions" drew its inspiration from mid-nineteenth-century versions of biological racism. Perhaps the most active expositor of these pseudoscientific theories was Dr. Samuel Cartwright, who acted as a physician-witness in slave cases in Natchez, Mississippi, before moving to New Orleans to become the only "Professor of Diseases of the Negro," in the Medical Department of the University of Louisiana, in the 1840s.[71] Cartwright propagated the notion that "negroes" not only were inferior but in fact constituted a different, subhuman species; he propounded what historians have called "states'-rights medicine," giving "medical" justification for the Southern way of life.[72] In a series of articles in *DeBow's Review*, Cartwright articulated theories that intertwined polygenesis; the physiological bases of black inferiority; and "negro diseases," of which the causes were physiological, symptoms behavioral, and cures a combination of behavioral and physical measures.

Cartwright located the central distinction between blacks and whites in a complicated feedback linking the nervous system, blood, and lungs. "The great development of the nervous system . . . would make the Ethiopian race entirely unmanageable . . . defective hematosis . . . is the true cause of that debasement of mind which has rendered the people of Africa unable to take care of themselves." Black people, Cartwright contended, rebreathed their own air, unlike whites: "In bed, when disposing themselves for sleep, the young and old, male and female, instinctively cover their heads and faces, as if to insure the inhalation of warm, impure air . . . The natural effect of the practice is imperfect atmospherization of the blood—one of the heaviest chains that binds the negro to slavery." Blacks needed slavery, Cartwright explained, because they needed white men's authority to "vitalize and decarbonize their blood by the process of full and free respiration, that active exercise of some kind alone can effect."[73] Cartwright argued that medically, slaves were like children: in their susceptibility to scrofulous (lymphatic) diseases; in their anatomy (livers, veins, sensitive skin); in their fear of the rod; and in the fact that they were "easily governed by love combined with fear" and "required government in every thing."[74]

Two diseases were of special importance to Cartwright's medical handbook for slave owners: "drapetomania" (the disease of running away) and "Dysthesia Ethiopica, or Hebetude of Mind" ("what overseers call Rascality"). Cartwright explained that drapetomania was caused by masters who did not recognize that "negroes" are by nature "knee-benders" from whom "awe and reverence must be exacted . . . or they will despise their masters, become rude and ungovernable, and run away." To cure drapetomania required keeping slaves in "that submissive state which it was intended for them to occupy . . . and treat[ing them] like children, with care, kindness, attention, and humanity . . ."[75]

According to Cartwright, rascality could also be attributed to lax management or excess freedom: "Dysthesia Ethiopica . . . attacks only such slaves as live like free negroes in regard to diet, drinks, exercise, etc."[76] The proper treatment, in order to stimulate the liver, skin, and kidneys, was to wash and oil the slave, then to slap his skin with a broad leather strap and put him to hard work, which would increase his circulation. Keeping the slave hard at work posed no danger, because, conveniently, according to nature's laws, it was impossible to overwork a slave. Cartwright wrote, "A white man, like a blooded horse, can be worked to death. Not so the negro . . . The white men of America have performed many prodigies, but they have never yet been able to make a negro overwork himself."[77]

Samuel Cartwright has been viewed by some historians as a marginal Southern thinker, whose ideas were accepted only on the fringe of proslavery thought. William Stanton dismisses Cartwright as "that brutal Louisiana physician and publicist . . . with his banana-skin humor, who appeared only on the periphery of the controversy to comment, cheer, or make impolite noises of disapproval."[78] This viewpoint is valid only with respect to Cartwright's theories on polygenesis. Few Southerners accepted Cartwright's attempt to reconcile the separate origins of blacks with the Bible by showing that Eve was tempted in the Garden of Eden not by a serpent but by a "negro gardener," and few believed that blacks outside slavery were slaves to a serpent/Satan.[79] However, belief in the existence of "distinctive peculiarities and diseases of the Negro race" was far more widespread. Other authors published articles by that title not only in *De-Bow's Review* but in a number of other Southern periodicals.[80] The links between body and behavior were widely accepted by antebellum Southerners. While few Southerners may have used the technical terminology of "drapetomania," some did refer to "dysthesia ethiopica" and "cachexia africana" (dirt eating) in court and were accustomed to talking about running away and other slave behaviors in terms of "addiction" and "habit."[81]

The Louisiana Civil Code labeled theft as an "addiction" and running away as a "habit."[82] To prove a slave a runaway or a thief, it was thus necessary to demonstrate that this "condition" was of long standing and had manifested itself a certain number of times for a given duration.[83] Because Louisiana was the only state that codified slave vices of character, perhaps it is understandable that it was the only state where this impulse to reduce moral qualities to medical bases took legal form. Certainly, it had the effect of reducing the slave to something more animal than human. Yet the description of running away or other vice (such as theft or disobedience) as a "character," a "habit," or an "addiction" was widespread in other states.[84] Throughout the Deep South, medical metaphors contributed to legal efforts to define slaves' characters by their "vices." Chapter 5 will discuss further the role of medical discourse in the litigation of character in court.

.   .   .   .   .

All of the explanations of slave character and behavior outlined above—as functions of slave management, as immutable vice, as habit or disease—operated in some way to remove agency from enslaved people. Reports of slaves who took action such as running away on their own impetus and for their own rational reasons fit uneasily into these accounts. Yet because slaves did behave as moral agents, reports of their resistant acts persistently cropped up in court. At times, witnesses provided evidence of slaves acting as moral agents; on other occasions, the nature of the case required acknowledgment of slaves' moral agency. Occasionally the courts explicitly recognized slaves' human motivations as the cause of "vices." More often, these stories were recorded in the trial transcripts but disappeared from the appellate opinions. Just as judges were reluctant to recognize slaves' skills and abilities, they feared giving legal recognition to slaves as moral agents with volition, except when doing so suited very specific arguments or liability rules. Recognizing slave agency threatened the property regime both because it undermined an ideology based on white masters' control and because it violated the tenets of racial ideology that undergirded Southern plantation slavery in its last decades.

For example, in one Louisiana case, a witness for the plaintiff-seller, while testifying that the slave Caleb was "punctiliously honest and trustworthy," explained that he had never heard of "Caleb absenting himself from the plantation but once, there being no white persons on the plantation he and his wife had a quarrel and he (Caleb) was out, I believe all night . . ." Another witness testified to a conversation in which the slave seller explained that although the slave had run away four or five times, "it was generally for the fear of being whipped . . ."[85] The appellate court referred to the latter comment but not to the former. If a slave ran away for fear of being whipped, that suggested a mechanical reaction to stimuli within a master's control; fear of whipping could easily be integrated into a theory of vice as a function of slave management. However, running away because of a quarrel with one's spouse connoted a slave's control over his own family life and his own decision making, interpretations that fit poorly into accepted theories of slave behavior.

In *Reynolds v. White*, the buyer-plaintiff complained that Sam was a runaway and a thief. On one hand, we have George Malcolm's testimony that Sam "stay[ed] away sometimes one day, sometimes more" and that "plaintiff was obliged to tie up said boy and nail up his gates to keep him at home." On the other, we have White's witness, C. J. Cook, who knew Sam to have been "absent" only once when White owned him, "to wit; the boy's mother was sick and the physician left a prescription for her; the boy was sent out with other prescription[s] to the Druggists after candlelight that boy did not return for 24 or 48 hours . . . and Mr. White and family thought the boy was lost and witness was of the same opinion. The boy was in the constant habit of getting out to play whenever he could and would return." This "play" Cook did not consider to be running away.[86]

Similarly, in *Anderson v. Dacosta*, a witness for Mathilda's seller described her as one who "liked to play and amuse herself" but nevertheless "bore a good name and character and was of a mild disposition." Another witness who spoke well of Mathilda denied that she was a runaway, explaining that she was only "in the habit of going back to the places where she was hired before," and that "all she wanted was a master to look to her and not to allow her privileges to run about."[87] In both of these cases, several witnesses for the sellers, rather than arguing that new masters bore responsibility for slaves' character, suggested that they ran away for their own reasons—to return to former owners, possibly to see family members, or even out of playfulness. Of course, this evidence of slave agency could shade into an argument that stronger discipline could prevent its exercise.

At the level of witnesses' testimony, hire cases often brought forth evidence of enslaved people's acting of their own volition. For example, one Georgia owner sued a railroad for taking his hired slave to Brunswick, when he had been hired to work on the South Western Road or the Muscogee Road. The railroad's lawyer cross-examined one witness to suggest that the change in work assignment came out of the slave's own preferences, not the needs of the railroads: "Do you know defendant carried said negro to Brunswick? Did not the negro run away and go towards Brunswick? Did defendant ask leave to carry said negro to Brunswick, or did he not say to you that the negro wanted to go there. And did he not tell you that he ran away?" The witness replied, "I do not recollect that he said the negro wanted to go. After the negro[']s death Def[endan]t said something in regard to the negroes having become attached to some of the negro women that went to Brunswick and this being a reason why the negro went off with them. I do not think Def[endan]t said he ran away, but that he went along with the other hands and overseer . . ."[88]

Witnesses often presented evidence of slaves trying to go back to former masters or, when hired out, to their present owners.[89] Judge Hackleman sold a slave "because he said he wanted another master—said he thought he ought to be allowed to go to preaching when he wanted to. He ran away from witness once. [G]ot dogs and caught him. Told him I would whip him if he did not finish his task the day before—He did quite finish it and went off."[90] Another slave ran away because, one witness reported, "he did not wish to go to Texas."[91] Mary, a Natchez slave, ran away because she "was dissatisfied at living in the country," although she had been purchased "to satisfy a negro boy . . . named Henry who wanted her for a wife. Mary was the same slave who had reported to a witness that she had "taken *some medicine to clear herself*," which he took to mean "thereby to produce abortion."[92]

Abram Martin sued Charles Bosley when they could not agree on how to divide a lot of slaves they had bought together. According to a witness present at the "division," two slaves asserted their own, contradictory preferences for the transaction: "[T]he fellow said if he was parted from [a certain woman slave] he would destroy himself he further observed that if he did not get her for a wife he would destroy the girl or himself and the girl would not live with him or have him for a husband and they were then parted and had been parted for the voige [*sic*]."[93] Buyers and sellers who recognized slaves' family attachments might also try to take advantage of them; in *Winn v. Twogood*, the seller had reassured the buyer that the slave would not run away because he was attached to a woman slave included in the sale.[94]

In court, witnesses often referred to slaves' exercise of agency at the moment of sale. As Walter Johnson shows in his study of New Orleans market culture, buyers often asked slaves what they thought of a sale; likewise, with no prompting, slaves spoke up to influence their own disposition—to discourage unwelcome buyers or encourage promising ones.[95] In courtroom testimony, these statements provided evidence of buyers' expectations and sellers' representations, but particularly of the susceptibility of both to slaves' own influence. In one South Carolina case the buyer, Smith, "stepped up to Bob, and asked Bob how he would like him for a master. Bob said he would not suit. Smith replied to Bob, 'I have not come to consult you; I have bought you.' . . . 'it is of no use for you to run, for I have my dogs, and can catch you.' Bob replied, that he would run from no man." Faced with the prospect of an unwelcome sale and no chance of escape, Bob committed suicide. The issue in the case became whether Smith or Bob's seller should bear the cost of Bob's death before his "delivery" to Smith.[96] An Alabama buyer based his claims about the seller's fraud on testimony that the slave on the auction block, apparently trying to avoid being sold, had announced that she was diseased, whereupon the auctioneer said "audibly, in a jocular way, 'hush, you are not diseased, you have eaten too many peas or potatoes, and they have swelled your belly.' " [97] In *Dunbar v. Skillman*, the slave buyer had explained to several of his neighbors that he believed the slave to have been a runaway in the past only because he was "allowed . . . liberty in a store" by one owner and was "abused" by the next; at the sale, the buyer told the seller to unchain the slave and asserted that "if he bought him he did not wish him abused." He then "asked the boy if he would live with him—when the boy replied he was very willing to live with him." When the slave nevertheless ran away not long afterward, the buyer sued the seller for redhibition under Louisiana law.[98]

Slaves who influenced their own sale, hire, or other disposition compromised their own commodification. Any risky venture might introduce unreliability into a transaction. But slaves were different from other risky investments because slaves *themselves* could increase or decrease their own value.[99] Testimony about the role of slaves' volition in slave transactions extended their influence into the legal arena.

. . . . .

Louisiana courts were the only ones in the Deep South that occasionally accepted evidence openly of slaves' own motivations to explain their running away. This was probably because Louisiana had such strict codified parameters for the "habit of running away"—up to a certain point, a slave's behavior might be only "*petit marronage*" ("little running away"); after that point, the slave was a runaway. Because the definition of the runaway habit was strictly set out in the Civil Code, it may have been easier for judges to recognize a slave's personhood when his or her behavior fell outside the strict definition.[100] For example, the New Orleans parish court did not consider that a slave's running away to visit his wife made him "a runaway." Ludger Fortier sued for the rescission of a slave sale because the slave left three days after the sale for several hours. According to defense witnesses, the slave had a good character, had never been whipped by his former owner, and had run away only to visit a slave woman on a neighboring plantation. The court denied Fortier's claim, finding that "[n]egroes sometimes absent themselves from their masters in the night without being runaway."[101] Similarly, in *Bocod v. Jacobs*, the Supreme Court noted that a slave's running away "may be the consequence of the displeasure of being sold—of his dislike of the new owner."[102] In *Nott v. Botts*, the trial judge found "nothing extraordinary in the fact of a negro coming from Kentucky, where they are treated almost on an equality with their master, running away in Louisiana," implying a slave's desire for greater autonomy.[103] All of these characterizations of slave motivation aver reasons that are rational, not products of mismanagement, "disease," or immutable viciousness.

The fact that Louisiana's definition of a runaway led to greater recognition of slaves' human agency had ramifications for litigants in nearby states. One Mississippi case became a referendum on the applicability of Louisiana law to local conditions. In 1848, John D. James, a Natchez and New Orleans slave trader, sold nine slaves to Joseph J. B. Kirk, a Natchez horse trader, in Point Coupee Parish, Louisiana.[104] In 1849, Kirk filed suit against James in Adams Circuit Court for $750 on the basis of James' warranty, executed under Louisiana law, that "said Slaves were free from the redhibitory vices and diseases." Kirk complained that one of the slaves, Simon, had run away repeatedly and finally drowned during an escape attempt.[105]

Both James and Kirk asked for jury instructions based on Louisiana law. Judge Posey refused to give several of James' instructions but did explain the Louisiana Code on redhibition to the jury. James appealed the lower court decision on the ground that the jury had applied an "arbitrary rule of evidence of another state."[106] James argued that Louisiana was traveling down a slippery slope toward recognition of slaves' personhood, and protection of slave buyers, a course that Mississippi should not follow. "For illustration, suppose that by the laws of Louisiana negro slaves are competent witnesses to prove the vice in a companion . . . Again, let us suppose that one of the redhibitory vices warranted against was a habit of drinking." Admitting slave testimony, argued James, was as outrageous as warranting that a slave would not run away.[107]

James' argument about the dangers of accepting Louisiana's protections for slave buyers in Mississippi reveals general fears about litigating character in cases of implied warranty. While a buyer's rule that strictly codified vices as "habits" made it possible to treat slaves as subhuman, buyer-claimants also introduced arguments about slaves' human agency, which threatened a law of sales in which slaves were property only. Judges resisted extending protections to buyers because they did not want to open the Pandora's box of putting slave character on trial. Going to trial risked long, involved proceedings (and possible hung juries) on the question of masters' treatment of slaves. In *James v. Kirk*, the testimony dwelt on whether a master was "as good a disciplinarian . . . as any of his neighbours." But Pandora's box held more than simply the difficulty of administering cases about property with unusual (human) qualities. Because these market transactions were risky, and slaveholders became personally invested in the outcome, slaves had the most chance to influence them by their behavior.

Judges outside of Louisiana recognized slave agency most directly in tort cases, in which a slaveholder sued another for damage to a slave when under the other's control. Most commonly, the defendant in such a case was an industrial hirer, or a common carrier, usually a ferryboat. Common carriers were generally held responsible for damages to property on board, which they insured. In *Trapier v. Avant*,[108] the trial judge tackled the question of "whether negroes, being the property damaged, they should form an exception to the general rule of liability in the carrier." He determined that slaves should not be an exception. "Negroes have volition, and may do wrong; they also have reason and instinct to take care of themselves. As a general rule, human beings are the safest cargo, because they do take care of themselves." According to the judge, the humanity of the slaves did not present enough of a problem to alter the general property rule. "Did this quality, humanity, cause their death? certainly not—what was the cause? The upsetting of the boat. [W]ho is liable fore the upsetting of the boat? The ferriman; there is an end of the question."[109]

The dissenting judge, however, pointed out the problem created by slaves' human agency: if the slaves had run away or thrown themselves overboard before the ferryman had a chance to reach them, then holding Avant responsible would amount to converting his contract into a guarantee of the slaves' "good morals and good sense." To Judge Johnson, the dissenter, slaves' humanity—their desire to escape and even to commit suicide—prevented the application of the usual liability rule. He explained: "These people like ourselves possess volition and physical powers which nothing short of the [illegible] can contain. Fetters may restrain their physical powers and the [illegible] may suppress the visible emotions of the will. But these restraints once removed, nothing short of omnipotence can infallibly circumscribe or put bounds to their powers . . ."[110] Thus both the majority and the dissent based their opinions about the applicability of a general liability rule to slaves on considerations of slaves' moral agency. In the tort case, unlike a breach of warranty case, judges found it impossible to deny that slaves were intervening actors in the causal chain. However, unlike the criminal law, which explicitly treated slaves as people so that they could be punished for crimes against whites, tort law resisted altering its rules for slave property. Torts pushed the logic of the black slave's dependent character to its outer limit: the position that won out in this case accepted that logic—but the dissent suggests the strains it caused.[111]

Another boat case illustrates the *Avant* dissenter's position that whites could not be held responsible for actions taken by enslaved blacks of their own "free will." In *Gorman v. Campbell*, in which a slave drowned while working as a hired boat hand, the ferry owner claimed that it was the slave's own fault that he died. Gorman, the slave owner, claimed that the boat owner must be held liable because he was responsible for the slave and had improperly employed him in clearing the river of logs. Richard Bishop, testifying for Gorman, stated:

> [I]t is not the custom of the . . . rivers to employ negroes hired for Boat Hands in clearing obstructions from the river or opening new passages for the Boats (added later) unless it is unavoidable at the time or necessary . . . The boy Sam of his own accord, in presence of the captain went into the river and commenced cutting a log. That he was about half an hour cutting the log in two—and the captain present during the time—that the water was very swift at the place he was cutting, and when he had cut the log—to save himself from being carried down stream he jumped upon another log which projected into the water, but which gave way and was carried down stream by the current with the boy on it—that in floating down his hat fell off, and in endeavoring to recover it, he sank suddenly, and was soon found, a short distance below . . . [112]

The captain and engineer of the boat testified that "the boy . . . was not drowned from the improper management of the owners of the Boat—Express orders being given by the witnesses for the negroes to engage in the work of choosing [navigating] the river." The court charged the jury that if they believed the slave was engaged in the work of his own free will, the boat owner was not liable. The jury found for the boat owner. The plaintiff appealed on the ground that the court's instructions amounted to a statement "[t]hat it was not necessary to use coercion with this kind of property." The plaintiff clearly understood that recognizing a slave's agency threatened the bonds of slavery.[113]

In effect, not recognizing slaves as agents with free will meant holding all supervisors of slaves strictly liable for their character and behavior; recognizing slaves as agents, conversely, meant that supervisors were not required to "use coercion" to compel slaves' behavior. The first option created the equivalent of a warranty of moral qualities in the tort context, with all of its attendant difficulties—the second option threatened anarchy.

On the other hand, judges in hire disputes frequently used legal analogies to horses or real estate, which had the effect of minimizing the person/thing distinction and de-emphasizing slaves' moral agency.[114] This may be because suits over hire fell under the law of bailment, or rental property, which meant that they were classified more closely with real property, especially real estate. Ironically, chief justice of the South Carolina Supreme Court John Belton O'Neall wrote that it was slaves' very humanity that required the real estate analogy for slaves in hire cases: although slaves are chattels personal, he explained, "yet they are moral agents, subject to the same feelings; and have a right to protection from abuse as other human beings. All natural, civil, and acquired rights, which a slave might exercise as a free man are necessarily from his situation, transferred as an incident of slavery to his master." Therefore, the hirer, like the land tenant, should have only limited rights to alter the leased property.[115] Courts compared a slave's falling ill or running away during the hire term to "the loss of the house by fire"; they compared the injunction not to treat a hired slave cruelly to the requirement that "after [a hired horse] is exhausted, and has refused its feed, the hirer is bound not to use it."[116] In one Alabama case, the issue was whether a hirer was required to work a slave in order to keep the slave in good working condition, in the same way that he might be required to milk a cow or exercise a horse.[117] Through the abstraction of claims about slaves into general property claims, judges made it possible to think of slaves less as human agents and more as things.

.   .   .   .   .

Parties in court opened Judge Nott's Pandora's box when they based their claims on slaves' moral qualities or volition as moral agents; when their witnesses testified that slaves took action for their own reasons; or when those witnesses repeated slaves' own words. Judges, however, tried to shut the box by privileging accounts that emphasized slave behavior as a function of masters' character or management, or medicalized slave vice into insanity or idiocy. Lawyers and judges confronted slave resistance by promoting stories about the origins and development of slave character and behavior that removed rational agency from slaves. In this way, the law created an image of blackness as an absence of will, what Patricia Williams has called "antiwill."[118]

Yet reading trial records also reveals how incomplete a picture of "the law" appellate opinions provide. If what happened in courtrooms, in the common experience and consciousness of ordinary people, was "law," then it is impossible to identify one integrated version of "the good slave" under "the law." Buyers, sellers, hirers, owners, and overseers all told different stories about why slaves behaved as they did and had the "character" they had. They drew on images at large in Southern plantation culture, shaped by shared narratives of race, gender, and commodification of slaves' character and labor—but they also refashioned those images for the legal arena, and for their own advantage at trial. The portrayal of slave character as malleable, dependent on a master's management, benefited slave sellers and owners; "medicalizing" slave vices as "habits" or "addictions" benefited buyers, as well as nonowners who "damaged" slaves.

Because the conflict devolved so often into a debate over mutability or immutability of character, the focus inevitably shifted from slaves to masters. Mastery and the character of masters came into question directly under the dictum of "like master, like man," but indirectly as well in every decision about a slave's character that reflected in some way on her master's control, will, or honor. These cases mattered in Southern culture precisely because putting black character on trial put white character on trial.

FOUR

MASTERS' CHARACTER

HAD PUTTING black character on trial not implicated white character, Southern whites would not have experienced civil trials involving slaves as significant or important. These cases mattered to Southern whites, and challenged Southern judges and juries, precisely because they called into question the mastery and, implicitly, the statesmanship of the white men who litigated them.

Warranty and hire cases put mastery on trial when litigants portrayed slave character as a function of treatment or management by masters. Tort cases involving neglect or cruelty offered parties and judges an opportunity to articulate standards of management even more directly, as juries decided whether a slave had been properly treated. A trial could become the forum for a man's neighbors to discuss not only his local reputation for slave treatment but all aspects of his plantation management: selling and trading, the employment of overseers, growing crops, even breeding slaves.[1]

Historical appraisals of the antebellum Southern slaveholder have been dominated in the last decades by the question of "paternalism." In Eugene Genovese's view, both slaveholders and slaves were committed to a paternalistic system, defined as a set of "mutual obligations—duties, responsibilities, and ultimately even rights," which allowed slaveholders to govern as a prebourgeois ruling class.[2] In the opposing view, Southern slaveholders were profit-maximizing capitalists, whose words and actions can be analyzed as extensions of their economic interests.[3]

To some extent, it is useful to think about the image of the white master that emerges from "private law" trials in terms of paternalism; the phrase most often used as a standard for a good master was "like the prudent father of a family." Yet witnesses and judges at trial conjured up a good master more complicated than merely "the prudent father of a family"; he was a statesmanlike disciplinarian and a smart manager of a plantation—which meant being a shrewd businessman. This image of mastery suggests the importance of both honor and profit making to the white men of the plantation South, and the extent to which slavery and the law helped to construct "whiteness" in terms of honor as well as profit.[4] Furthermore, while paternalist rhetoric was useful to help build up a master's image, it entered the legal doctrine only at the point where masters' own behavior was not at issue—when a hirer, overseer, or agent had charge of the slave.

Putting to one side the question of how the law contributed to the development of a certain kind of economy, civil cases help to illuminate the ways in which the law worked to establish what it meant to be a master, and therefore what it meant to be a white man, in Southern plantation society.

Of course, no single ideal of mastery emerges from trials involving slaves as property. The legal "standard" of mastery set out by judges in these cases did not always coincide with the admiring or disparaging comments witnesses made about particular masters. Just as judges favored certain of witnesses' interpretations of slave character and behavior, judges emphasized particular strands of Southern ideology about slave management and mastery—different ones from those emphasized by people who came to testify in Southern courts. Buyers, sellers, hirers, owners, and overseers all told different stories about why slaves behaved as they did, all of which reflected on their masters' character. In the courtroom, the parties drew on stories about mastery that were at large in antebellum Southern culture, but "the law" also helped to shape those stories. Furthermore, enslaved people who were allowed no voice in the courtroom nevertheless helped to create the law because their resistant acts forced these conflicts to the surface.[5]

. . . . .

In warranty cases, the master's own treatment was put at issue because it could be an excuse for a slave's illness or vice. When lawyers for the master posed interrogatories, they typically tried to build a case for his good plantation management and solicitous treatment of slaves. Witnesses pointed to certain favorable aspects of the treatment of slaves, sometimes without even being asked or prodded to do so: a sick slave's being brought up to the plantation house; the employment of good physicians; good food and work hours for all the slaves. All of this testimony helped to build the image of the good master as a kind father to his black "family."

In a typical interrogatory, a defendant's attorney asked, "What kind of a Master the Plaintiff is, whether he treats his slaves well, what is his character as regards the master of slaves, *good* or *bad*."[6] Testimony to prove a master good included evidence about the food, clothing, medical attention, and shelter given to the slave: "That [Egerton] had the same allowance as the other slaves, three pounds and a half of meat a week with as much bread as they could eat—the rations of Egerton were doubled but he still complained . . . After he was taken down the second time he was taken into the house of Mrs. Herring, where he was attended to by her and family night and day, and had as much attention paid him, as if he were one of her own family."[7] In another Natchez case, Dr. Nathaniel

Vanandigham deposed that when he attended a slave, "the girl was in a comfortable cabin."[8] Similarly, in *Townsend v. Miller*, Eliza Roach deposed that "[t]hese negroes received immediately the attention of Dr. Hamilton who was living in the house of Benjamin Roach my husband after his leaving Dr. Cartwright was then called in to them."[9] In answer to the interrogatory "Was Armstead's food while sick, that of good wholesome food such as bread, meat, butter, coffee, tea, soup &c. . . . Did Armstead have sufficient warm cloathing, lodging and other necessaries suitable to his health, and his disorder while sick?" Elizabeth Dromgoole answered "[t]hat Armstead was comfortably lodged, cloathed, dieted and nursed, that a physician was immediately employed."[10] Comments to indicate good treatment included the assertion that "Silvia . . . was treated well—Kept in Mrs. Stroziers room all the time [that she was sick]."[11] Testimony that slaves were kept in the main house or in the mistress's room, and that they ate the varied diet of the white household, suggested that the good master treated the black and white members of his "family" with the same solicitousness.

Masters tried to prove that they treated their slaves well in order to show that slaves who ran away were not reacting to ill treatment. Thus it became a trope to intone that a slave ran away "without cause" or "without provocation":[12] "[O]n the 2d day of May 1858 the said slave without having been chastised or otherwise ill-treated, absconded and ran away," complained one slave buyer. The seller interrogated the buyer's witnesses about "how he was treated by Major Gatlin—how Major Gatlin is in the habit of treating his slaves . . ." J. B. Milner answered, "[S]aid boy Jim remained with said Gatlin about 2 month, when he Jim absconded without provocation . . . As to the treatment of Mr Gatlin toward his negroes I think he is a reasonable man and treats his negroes very humanely."[13] In another Louisiana case, an overseer claimed, "I am certain that the boy ran away from no bad treatment, he was kindly treated, but he appeared incompetent to appreciate it . . ."[14] In answer to the question, "Do you know how said Wyatt treated his slaves—is he a very humane and kind master or is he rather a hard master—state all you know . . . ?" one witness answered, "While Peter Wyatt owned Davy he lived at my house and I had the opportunity of knowing his course of treatment to David. He was humane and kind, nor do I think he ever gave him any cause to run away."[15] Or, as one attorney summed it up, "Did Toney run away from bad treatment or the badness of the negro himself?"[16]

While this evidence—that masters and their witnesses competed eagerly to demonstrate their kindliness to their slaves—could be read to uphold a "paternalist" ideal, it is worth noting that litigants used such expressions for highly instrumental ends. Evidence of paternalist concern for slaves could justify outcomes in favor of either buyers or sellers. If Toney, in the above example, was "bad himself," then a buyer who proved his kindness as a master should not be held responsible for Toney's running away; if Toney's new master treated him badly, he should be held responsible. The legal rule leading to the second outcome, *caveat emptor* ("let the buyer beware"), has been considered a hallmark of capitalism in early-nineteenth-century sales law.[17] Whereas the consumer-protective "sound price rule," which implied a warranty of soundness from a "sound price," was premised on the notion that commodities had intrinsic value that should determine their fair or "sound" price, the rule of *caveat emptor* assumed that the free market should set both prices and contract terms such as warranties. If private parties wanted a warranty, they should contract for it; fairness had nothing to do with it. Thus paternalist rhetoric engendered and supported a market-based legal rule—hardly evidence for a precapitalist socioeconomic system, as Eugene Genovese has characterized the antebellum South.[18]

Genovese's use of "paternalism" has generated controversy well beyond what I shall discuss in these pages. However, it is sufficient to note that recent work has contested his picture of a prebourgeois, precapitalist South by showing the coexistence of paternalism with capitalism in diverse societies, in part by defining "paternalism" more narrowly.[19] Genovese views paternalism as a form of social relations involving reciprocal duties and obligations, and a form that is necessarily tied to a prebourgeois socioeconomic system. Shearer Davis Bowman, who compares Southern planters to Prussian Junkers, believes that "the label paternalism should be limited to a type of upper-class ideology, one that persists into the late twentieth century and was widespread in the nineteenth-century Western world, urban as well as rural, free as well as slave."[20] The trials bear out this more limited definition: paternalist ideology was perfectly compatible with legal rules, like *caveat emptor*, that promoted capitalist relations.

This harmony between paternalist ideology and capitalist legal rules should not be surprising when we consider that planters' paternalism co-existed comfortably with a vigorous interest in buying and selling slaves. Any litigant in a warranty case, by definition, would seem to have shattered the paternalist ethos of keeping his black "family" together. Yet the myth of the reluctant master and the evil trader allowed white Southerners to maintain both a paternalist ideal and a vigorous, often ruthless slave market.[21] Witnesses in court betrayed no sense that it was dishonest for an ordinary planter to be a good businessman with respect to his plantation, *provided that he did not step over the line to become a professional trader.*[22] Witnesses often mentioned that a planter or farmer was a frequent buyer and seller of slaves: for example, "Morgan . . . was in the habit of buying and selling for profit";[23] "He bought him to sell again";[24]

"I have always been a farmer and am a farmer yet but have been trading on negroes some for the last ten or twelve years."[25] In none of these situations did the witness hint that there was a pejorative aspect to market participation. Being a wise planter also meant knowing the value of slaves and knowing how to get a good deal in a transaction. As one agent for a planter explained, "[W]itness has bought more than 500 negroes before this and has not been deceived in relation to the soundness of one of them."[26] Another planter wrote to his agent, "Everything . . . is left to your Judgment and discretion in both of which I have the fullest confidence. You know the value of negroes, you are a Judge of them."[27] Thomas Alexander deposed that Samuel Cartwright was "a man of good business habits and knows how to keep servants [handwriting unclear]."[28]

Paternalism was compatible with a profit-maximizing ideology because slaves were themselves capital in the antebellum South.[29] Thus as many planters explained, humanity coincided with economic self-interest. As one Mississippi planter wrote, it was better to "tak[e] care of our present capital . . . than [to] wear[] it out in quest of another, if even larger . . ."[30] If this policy were followed, he wrote, "humanity and self-interest need not be separated."[31] Another wrote that "throwing humanity aside," and because of the high price of slaves, "it behooves those who own them to make them last as long as possible."[32] Mississippian Andrew Flynn advised his overseer that "the children must be very particularly attended to, for rearing them is not only a duty, but also the most profitable part of plantation business."[33] Wise planters, according to these writers, harnessed humanity to serve the demands of capital.

In one situation that came frequently before the courts, however, the interest-humanity equation was broken. When a slave was hired out to another person, usually for a year term, that person had far less economic incentive to treat the slave kindly. What is noteworthy about paternalism in the private law of slavery is that judges introduced paternalist rhetoric in the case of hirers, not masters themselves. Appellate doctrine sought to put the hirer in the position of the master, by re-creating the incentives to conserve slave capital.

In hire cases, judges invoked the paternalist injunction to treat a slave as "the prudent father of a family" treats his kin. Paternalist rhetoric arose particularly in cases in which a slave fell ill or died during a hire term, and the owner and hirer disputed who should bear the cost of the lost labor and doctor's bills, or even whether the hirer should be held liable for the slave's full price. Hirers were to pay medical bills under normal circumstances.[34] In most jurisdictions, during a hire term, the hirer bore the risk of the slave's illness or running away, but not of death.[35] In an 1824 Alabama case, Judge Minor reviewed the law of bailments, "contracts for the rent of houses, &c., or for the hire of slaves." He noted that "loss of the house by fire, or of the labour of the slave by sickness, or his running away during the term" did not discharge the hirer from paying the price of hire, because the hirer is "considered as a purchaser for a limited time . . . subject . . . to the same risks as if he were a purchaser of the fee simple . . . As applicable to contracts for the hire of slaves, [these principles] appear to be supported by sound considerations of humanity and policy."[36] Judge Minor here set up the legal rule equating hirers with substitute masters for a term ("purchaser for a limited time") without resorting to the familial metaphor, although he did note that humanity supported the rule. Obviously, paternalist rhetoric was not necessary to justify rules against "waste" of slave property—yet it reappeared time and again.

In one Georgia case, as Judge Lumpkin explained the hirer's obligation "to use the thing, be it servant or horse, or anything else, with due care and moderation," he decreed that a hirer must treat a slave as a "good and prudent father of a family" would treat his children.[37] With respect to the standard of care for a hirer, Louisiana's differed little from those of other states. For example, in *Buhler v. McHatton*,[38] the owner's lawyer argued that "[e]very dictate of humanity demands, that a slave, afflicted with a serious disease, should, in the hour of her affliction, be treated with the greatest care . . . it must be such as a prudent father possesses for his own child." He went on to complain that even though Mr. Devall "claims to be a regular practitioner," "so far from regarding her as a patient, thrown upon his hands for treatment, he looked at her alone as a menial, and I think, but one single and isolated time, gave or attempted to give her, a dose of medicine . . ."

The typical interrogatory in a hire dispute raised the charge that a hirer did not treat his hired slaves the same way a master would: "Did or did not the defendant feed and clothe the said hired negroes well and treat them in every respect like his own, in sickness and in health, and did or did not the manager on the said defendant's plantation treat the said negroes with as much forbearance and kindness as any other negroes on the plantation?"[39] Inevitably, the witnesses for the hirer insisted that he did.

In one such case, the owner charged the hirer with "carelessness and negligence in treatment of a negro girl named Adeline the property of plaintiff whereby the said girl died," because he did not employ a physician for Adeline when she was sick.[40] According to Robert Mosely, Beverly Wilkinson had promised to treat Adeline "in a careful proper and moderate manner and in the event of her sickness she should receive from him proper and careful treatment and attention suitable and necessary for her situation and if necessary he would employ a Physician to attend her."

Wilkinson had subhired Adeline to A. B. Hughes, who "himself was confined to his room by Sickness" when Adeline fell ill. Adeline was treated by Hughes' overseer, "one Moore," who "gave medicines—that he bled her on Tuesday night and then applied mustard plasters to her wrists and stomach that the witness left her about twelve o'clock on Tuesday night apparently easy . . . Moore stated that he had overseed some thirteen years and during that time he had treated all cases of sickness with all negroes under his charge that he thought he could manage and not to call in a physician unless the case was thought dangerous and that he did not consider the negro girl to be dangerously sick." The jury found for Wilkinson. The Alabama Supreme Court, however, reversed and remanded the case twice, on the ground that the owner should recover the amount of hire—although not the full value of the slave. Despite Hughes' having shown that he treated Adeline as he treated his other slaves, the court reserved a higher standard of slave treatment, including the employment of a physician in the case of serious illness. The important thing, according to Judge Stone, was that a hirer use "that 'degree of care used by the generality of mankind in relation to their own slaves.' "[41]

Juries were more reluctant to hold a hirer to an affirmative standard of disease prevention. Samuel Davis sought $2,000 damages from Philander Wood for his refusal to deliver up a certain slave named Charles Clark after the contract of hire had expired, and further charged that Wood had breached his contract to "use the said slave in a moderate careful and proper manner" by exposing Charles Clark to a yellow fever epidemic. Davis requested that the judge instruct the jury that Wood became liable for the loss of Charles when he refused to deliver him up on July 30, 1853, and that Wood was liable whether or not Charles' death from yellow fever occurred "from the negligence of said Defendant or not." The judge gave both instructions. Wood asked the judge to instruct the jury that if he had held Charles as a security for the payment of horses, he was not bound to deliver up the slave until the debt was paid. Further, he asked for an instruction that he could not be liable for Charles' death if the slave died "under medical treatment and the defendant took good and prudent care." The judge gave these instructions as well. The jury found for Wood.[42]

It is somewhat surprising that official solicitude for the health and care of slaves emerges so strongly in disputes over hire. Analogies to real estate and other forms of bailment or tenancy should have been sufficient to create legal rules protecting owners from hirers' "wearing out" their human property. Yet paternalist ideology provided the framework for the law and provided the cues for litigants to argue their cases in terms of how well they conformed to a standard of good mastery.

. . . . .

Contesting mastery in the courtroom, witnesses invoked an ideal far more complicated than just that of a kind father. Witnesses valued a particular style of mastery that reinforced slaveholders' authority in Southern society: good masters were detached, maintained a superior mien, and punished their slaves in the right way. The Southern system of honor called for the proper level of condescension to inferiors.

A good master not only gave his slaves solicitous treatment, especially when they were ill, but disciplined them with a firm hand. He knew the right amount of discipline to apply with difficult slaves. Gardner Davis complained that the slave Stephen "was of bad and insubordinate character and difficult to manage and keep in proper subjection"; Davis averred that he "used only so much and such means as were necessary to keep said negro under control . . ."[43] In one form or another, a master always tried to present the picture "that he [was] as good a disciplinarian with his slaves as any of his neighbours."[44]

The goal of proper treatment was to get the maximum labor out of a slave. Both kind treatment and whipping were to be used only if they succeeded in getting work out of a slave. One overseer explained that Billy "was first put at the house and very mildly treated but nothing could be got out of him," after which Billy was "put in the field he would leave his work and runaway without any cause he was then whiped but still nothing could be got out of him."[45] Some slaves, it was recognized, would not respond to whipping; others would work well, according to their owners, but only if kept in line by corporal punishment. Those slaves who required greater discipline or supervision might not suit for fieldwork but could be turned into productive laborers in the house. The good master could discern the best way to manage the particular slave at issue.

A good master did not get overexcited. In *Borum v. Garland*, Garland had hired Henry from Borum. "Henry was whipped by the patrol at the house of his wife, on the next day the plaintiff [Borum] at the request of the boy Henry gave him a pass to return to his wife's house: on that day or night the boy ran away without having returned to Garland's possession." The next day Garland and Borum met, and Garland "remarked that he did not blame plaintiff he expected under the same circumstances he would have acted similar but would have held himself answerable for his act." Borum, "whose nervous system was very much deranged[,] remarked in a state of excitement that Garland should not have the boy again even if he came back."[46] The jury in this case found for Garland, and the higher court affirmed. By contrast, when Phillips' slave, hired to Maury, ran away back to Phillips, "Maury demanded the slave being free from excitement and telling Phillips that the slave should go into no one's

hands but his own and should not be treated harshly." Maury's explanation of this encounter in his appeal convinced the Alabama Supreme
Court to reverse the case in his favor.[47] The Southern "Code of Conduct"
required men of honor to treat equals as equals and inferiors as inferiors.
To allow the ultimate inferior, a slave, to ruffle one's calm would be dishonorable.

As Kenneth Greenberg has shown, this style of Southern mastery both
reflected and reinforced Southern statesmanship. "The statesman in the
legislative hall and the master on the plantation exercised the same style
of government."[48] The ideal master and statesman was dispassionate and
detached, eschewing overt shows of power; just as the statesman preferred
to be *pressed* into service, the master bore the *burden* of his servants.[49]
Further, "masters, like statesmen, also sought honor. They aimed to exercise authority through the public display of superior virtue and intelligence." The best master never inflicted punishment on slaves in anger,
used a low tone, and avoided administering whippings himself, leaving it
to an overseer or to another. For example, hirers often returned slaves to
their owners for whipping. As one hirer explained, "I did return him to
his owner—the reason was that I did not want the trouble to correct him.
I believe he was corrected by his master, who returned him to me . . ."[50]
Both owners and hirers sometimes sent slaves to the county jail, or to the
Charleston Work House, for example, to be whipped for a fee rather than
soiling themselves and their clothing with blood.

To allow himself to be inflamed by passion would bring the master
down to a lower level. This aloof style of punishment reinforced the master's authority in the same way as did a statesman's delivery of an oration.
"Just as the oration, regardless of its subject, established the superiority
of the orator, so the words of admonition to a slave established the superiority of the master."[51] This correspondence between mastery and statesmanship for whites is the flip side of the relationship between slavery and
dishonor for blacks uncovered by Orlando Patterson and others.[52]

．　．　．　．　．

A recurrent theme in planters' published writings was the need for *system*
in slave management. As one Georgia-Alabama planter wrote, "the peace
and harmony, if not the profits of the planter, might be greatly promoted
by more rule and system in the regulation of the labor of the farm."[53]
Southern agricultural periodicals constantly published various planters'
"rules" for plantation management, rules for food, work hours, and so
forth. These rules Southern writers analogized to "a code of laws," for
which "[a] tribunal exists" to pass judgment.[54] The master sat as judge

of that tribunal. As William W. Fisher III has written, "the pride many Southerners took in the ability of masters and overseers to deal with most instances of slave 'misconduct' on their plantations was based partly on . . . their conviction that honor entails, among other things, 'policing one's own ethical sphere.' "[55]

Judges, too, emphasized the importance of a good plantation manager's having his own code of laws. As the Alabama Supreme Court noted in a case of an overseer's whipping a slave for theft, it was "quite as well, perhaps better, that [the slave's] punishment should be admeasured by a domestic tribunal [rather than by the State]."[56] Thus the focus on "system" was not merely a reflection of Northern-style ideals of coolness, rationality, and modern managerial philosophy; rather, it reflected the belief in the honorable gentleman's ability to govern his own domain dispassionately. One case may illustrate.

A. W. Walker bought a plantation from J. S. Cucullu, along with a gang of fifty-eight slaves.[57] Walker sued because ten of the slaves "were afflicted with serious maladies, diseases, and defects of body." The trial turned on the testimony of the overseer, who had also been on the plantation for one month while Cucullu still owned it. Antoine Landier Sr., the overseer, described himself at the time of the trial as a planter, age sixty-one. He made the case that "this gang of negroes . . . appeared to him to be negroes enjoying all the benefit of health . . . a strong bodied set" when Cucullu owned them, but that when Walker took over, "it is his opinion that the said slaves have lost at least 25% of their value by the loss of their health and strength." Landier contrasted the management prescribed by Walker with proper slave management: "[I]n the summer season negroes of well regulated plantations are turned out at work at 4½ o'clock in the morning and returned to their quarter at 7 o'clock in the evening and in the summer are allowed of said time two hours or 2½ to take their meals in winter they have one and a half for the same object . . . whilst the plantation belonged to Mr. Cucullu, said Cucullu always allowed his negroes full time to take their meals . . ."

Unfortunately, Walker did not live up to Cucullu's standard:

[W]hilst he was overseer of Walker's plantation and in the winter season he used to call the gang to work at about three and a half hours after midnight and that the gang were released from work at night not before nine or ten o'clock and this was done by the witness by order of the said Walker, the negroes says witness always took their meals in the opened field and whether the weather was good or bad, they were never allowed to go to their cabins to take their meals and were allowed just the necessary time to take said meals and witness says that since he has left overseeing said Walker's plantation, the same plan is always carried on . . .

The contrast between Cucullu and Walker, according to the overseer, extended not only to food and working hours but to discipline as well. "Witness says that Joseph Cucullu treated well his slaves, and when the said Cucullu's slaves for want of discipline misbehaved themselves he the said Cucullu used to shut them up in his lockup and rarely said witness was [it that] the said Cucullu had to make use of corporal punishment as his said slaves were orderly and well disciplined and that very little whipping took place on said plantation." Walker, on the other hand, "treats badly his negroes and . . . the corporal punishment made use [of] by him in the chastisement of his slaves was by severe whipping and by locking them up in the cachot or dungeon and the said whipping consisted in making use of the strap or palette and very often inflicted as many as one hundred licks to one boy at a time . . ." Not only was Walker too harsh a disciplinarian, but he transgressed the customary boundaries of time off allowed for slaves: "Said slaves were allowed neither Sundays nor any other festival days, that they have not an hour to wash their clothes at any time that they are bound to wear their same clothes the whole time . . . [they] are in a state of stealthiness unconceivable and the stench that comes from their bodies from their want of clothes from wearing unfit and dirty clothes . . . [they are] overworked, overstrained, and badly fed . . ."

Walker's ill-treatment of the slaves had predictable effects, both physical and moral. Although "the slaves belonging to said Cucullu and sold to Walker had no bad character or never ran away" when Cucullu owned them, under Walker's management "five negroes of the said gang ran away and this marronage [running away] was caused by the great restraint and severity of uncommon treatment inflicted . . ." Several other witnesses gave similar testimony; one witness testified that "he has seen the said Walker whip in a cruel manner his slaves and particularly a young girl 11 years old, whom he whipped or caused to be whipped at three different times the same day, eighty lashes each time and furthermore the said Walker overworked his negroes." Thus, according to these witnesses, any illness or running away on the plantation since Walker bought it from Cucullu could be attributed to Walker's bad mastery.

However, also in evidence was the record of a criminal prosecution of Augustus W. Walker for "harsh, cruel & inhuman treatment towards his slaves," in which Walker had been found not guilty. The judge in the criminal case explained the flexible standard for punishment of slaves: "Here then is the measure of chastisement and the rule imposed to the master, the master can chastise; the slave is entirely subject to his will; the punishment must necessarily depend on the circumstances . . . if the case is a grave one, the chastisement will probably be severe, if the slave is of a robust constitution, the chastisement may be increased . . ." In this case, the Louisiana court found Walker to be a good master, above all because he did not "strike[] at random with passion or anger" but had a *system* for plantation management and discipline:

> The Court now comes to the facts and what does it see, the Defendant has a pretty large gang of negroes on his plantation, he feeds them well, he clothes them well, he does not want that his overseers strike his slaves without consulting him, he never chastises his slaves without cause, they rise at daybreak, they have half an hour for breakfast and for dinner one hour in winter and one hour and a half in summer, they leave the field labour at dusk and are employed in the evening in putting order about the yard or quarters and in cleaning the mules . . . who can find fault in this manner of acting . . . *It is childish to suppose that a master who is generally careful of his slaves . . . would have gone beyond the rules, which he has always imposed on him and so far would have exposed his own interests. This may be expected from a man who strikes at random with passion or anger and without cause, Mr Walker is quite another man* . . . (Emphasis added)

This case presented two stories about a good master, that of the witness and that of the judge in the prior criminal case. The witness, Landier, argued that a good master gave his slaves enough to eat, did not work them too hard, gave them free time in accordance with local custom, clothed them well, and used only mild discipline, relying on the general contentment of his labor force to keep problems to a minimum. Landier emphasized an important thread in the Southern ideology of mastery: the coincidence of humanity and "interest." In other words, humanity was good business. The judge, sanctioning a much harsher regime, echoed other themes of the statesmanlike master. While he found evening work hours acceptable, if not in the field, he believed it most important that a master should have a regular system of "rules" which he "imposes on him[self]." Such a man, who chastises only with cause, exercises supervisory authority over the whole plantation, and never strikes out in passion or anger, would never break his own code—it would be "childish" to imagine that he would. The judge's master here is the picture of the Southern statesman.[58]

. . . . .

Perhaps the best way to reexamine the hypothesis that slavery law upheld paternalist ideals of mastery is to examine contests involving bad masters—masters who abused or neglected their slaves. Paternalists called for "reasonable correction"; deterring bad behavior through *certainty* rather than severity of punishment; never whipping out of passion or anger; and matching the severity of punishment to the crime.[59] Yet trials revealed the malleability of these standards. While those who abused slaves in passion or anger, out of proportion to their alleged crimes, were most likely to suffer some kind of penalty in court, as a general rule the law on cruelty was quite lenient.

As one planter wrote, laxity by masters was of far greater concern than harshness: "Some few persons are too strict with servants; but for every one who errs in this way, one hundred may be found who go to the opposite extreme and let them idle away their time and do no more than half work."[60] Planters in their published writings expressed exasperation at the freedoms slaves had carved out for themselves: cultivating a garden patch; trading in an underground economy; drinking liquor; owning dogs or guns; visiting spouses "abroad" at night; visiting in town or on other plantations on Sunday; staying away from work during Christmas week. They insisted that well-run plantations did not allow such freedoms.

Both witnesses and judges clearly saw laxity or neglect as the greater lapse in mastery. It was bad mastery to allow a slave to jump ship, to play with fire, to "run about," to hire his or her own time, or to return to an owner on her own or with another slave in charge—in other words, to give a slave too much freedom.[61] Witnesses often made comments implicitly disparaging a master's management, such as "All she wanted was a master to look to her and not to allow her privileges to run about."[62]

In another Louisiana case, Sarah Hill placed Edmund in James White's hands to sell for a commission. Edmund ran away when White "carelessly and with the grossest negligence entrusted the said slave to the care of another slave and sent him thus accompanied to the wharf of steam boat landing of . . . New Orleans." The court found that "sending a slave nearly white down to the wharf under the charge of another slave is not the prudence which should characterize the action of an agent."[63] Similarly in *Barber v. Anderson*,[64] the judge ruled that a hirer giving a girl slave a pass to go back to her owner and letting her go did not meet the standard of prudence for a hirer.

Sellers in warranty cases often portrayed buyers as lax masters. One seller, Jean-Pierre Michel, answered a breach of warranty complaint, asserting "that if [the slave] is now a thief or a runaway . . . the same had originated with him since he belonged to the said [buyer] and has been caused by the neglect and bad management of his master the [buyer]."[65] In this case, the seller charged that the buyer, Robert Ogden, had allowed William to hire his own time "in New Orleans, Baton Rouge and elsewhere . . . [and] upon steamboats." Ogden's brother, on cross-examination by Michel's attorney, explained that he had "no knowledge of [Ogden's] permitting [William] to hire his own time other than giving him a writing to enable him to find a place." Later, however, he admitted that his brother had told him that William once did hire his own time "for a short time," and that "on two occasions only" his brother hired William on steamboats. Furthermore, when Ogden spent a winter in New Orleans, he left William in Baton Rouge "as I understood to take care of his house and lot at Baton Rouge and cultivate his garden . . ." This damaging testimony convinced the jury to find for William's seller, Michel, and the Louisiana Supreme Court affirmed their verdict.

Similarly, in a hire dispute, William Randolph sued Israel Barnett, the owner of a steamboat, for the value and hire wages of a slave, Dempsey, who had been hired to the steamboat. Randolph accused Barnett of negligently allowing Dempsey too much freedom on board his boat, so that he was able to escape. Barnett answered that "the said negro in a fit of intoxication leaped from on board of the Steam Boat . . . and was drowned or escaped from the possession of said Defendant without any negligence or misconduct of him the said Defendant." Unfortunately, only interrogatories with no answers remain in this record.[66]

A master's laxity could always become the issue in a case involving a slave alleged to have a bad character. In Natchez, John Perkins complained that John Hundley had sold him a vicious and lunatic slave, Lawson, who was "violent and headstrong and abused the smaller negroes." He also contended that Lawson was subject to fits of mental derangement, as the result of which Lawson had died in a fire in the cotton gin. Hundley, however, tried to build a case that Perkins had been a lax master, who had given Lawson too much freedom, and that this laxity had caused Lawson's bad character and even mental disease. Hundley's attorney cross-examined Hugh M. Coffee, Perkins' overseer: "Was the negro Lawson permitted to sleep in the gin and to have a candle or fire therein? And if so, why was this permitted if he was subject to derangement?" Coffee answered that "[t]he plaintiff's negroes were plentifully fed and clothed and regular Work was required of them . . . Plaintiff was a very particular man in regard to Fire and did never permit this fellow Lawson or any of his Negroes to leave their cabins with fire or lights in the night to go to the gin or anywhere else."[67] Furthermore, Coffee complained that Lawson was "ungovernable," that Coffee "could do nothing with him," and that his derangement was real rather than feigned. Nevertheless, the jury accepted the case that Perkins had not been a good enough master to govern Lawson firmly and to detect his "artful" deceit; they gave Hundley a verdict for Lawson's full price.

. . . . .

As we saw in *Walker v. Cucullu*, it was notoriously difficult to get a criminal conviction for cruelty to slaves, particularly of a master who beat his own slaves. William W. Fisher III suggests that courts often justified this refusal to criminalize cruelty by the argument that "physical abuse of slaves was dishonorable behavior that would be condemned by the community," and that social sanctions were preferable to legal ones.[68] Yet cruelty also came before courts in civil cases: in the case of a master, when witnesses accused masters of causing slaves' bad behavior or illness by cruelty; and in the case of those other than the owner, when the owner brought a suit for civil damages for the abuse of his slave. In both these situations, it was much more likely than in the criminal context that the jury would be willing to agree that cruelty had taken place, and witnesses were more willing to testify to cruelty.[69] Nevertheless, provided that the slave abuser showed the "badness" of the slave, he could justify the abuse. As one court held, "It is certainly for the interest of the master, that the slave should be taught habits of industry; and, as a moral, sentient being, should learn that his happiness depends upon the appreciation of virtue and a conformity to its precepts. If these sentiments cannot be inculcated by the force of moral suasion, it is certainly allowable, and it may be a duty to inflict corporal punishment."[70]

Of course, it is worth remembering that the low judicial standard for cruelty to slaves was set in a legal context that also allowed men to beat their wives, children, and free domestic servants. In divorce cases, the standard for cruelty in wife beating remained the "rule of thumb" throughout the nineteenth century: whipping a woman with anything wider than a man's thumb was considered cruel. Courts hesitated to get involved, particularly in claims of mental cruelty, because of the perceived dangers of intruding into the domestic sphere, the dominion of the master of the house. As for the child, a father had "power to chastise him moderately."[71] The child did have "rights which the law will protect against the brutality of a barbarous parent," but, again, courts were very reluctant to interfere. Indeed, Tapping Reeve argued that the proper standard for a reviewing court should be that "the parent . . . be considered as acting in a judicial capacity, when he corrects . . ."[72] Furthermore, the nineteenth-century master had the right "to give moderate corporal correction" to "apprentices and menial servants who are members of his family," but "only while the master stands *in loco parentis*."[73] Yet the level of violence considered acceptable in cases of slave beating or murder cannot be compared to this parental standard of correction.[74] The pages of trial transcripts involving the abuse of slaves were soaked in blood.

In warranty trials, accusations of cruelty were something witnesses used to disparage masters, and to suggest that they should be held responsible for slaves' illnesses or running away, but they rarely determined the outcome of the case. In one Georgia warranty case, Silas Gordon sued Malcolm Moseley for selling him a boy slave, Daniel, who died of "dropsy."[75] Moseley, however, contended that Daniel's disease was a result of cruel treatment by his new master. He introduced a doctor who testified that "exposure to bad weather—over labor—late hours at night—with bad treatment and indifferent doctoring are well calculated to produce such a disease as Daniel's."[76] Several witnesses testified to "the general character and reputation of Silas Gordon the plaintiff for his bad and cruel treatment of his slaves." In the trial transcript, the words "bad and cruel" were added in pencil. Then the following words were crossed out: "that he was in the . . . unusual habit of treating his slaves with great cruelty—that he fed them badly, clothed them badly, worked them hard and exposed them to labor at night, out in all kinds of weather . . ." Furthermore, the witnesses offered to prove that Gordon had been indicted for cruelty to his slaves.

Gordon, however, successfully objected to all this evidence. Thus Moseley's appeal argued that Judge Warner, of Troup Superior Court, had erred in excluding evidence of cruelty. Justice Starnes of the Georgia Supreme Court rejected Moseley's appeal, explaining that "testimony of a man's general character and reputation, in the treatment of his slaves, is nothing more than hearsay testimony, and is inadmissible." In Georgia, at least, courts were reluctant to allow allegations of cruelty to determine the outcome of a warranty case.[77]

Lawyers and litigants, however, still tried to use these allegations to their advantage. Sometimes, in a warranty case, the seller's attorney would introduce allegations of cruelty that were not directly on point but would impugn the credibility of the buyer. For example, when Smith sued slave traders Meek and Johnson for breach of warranty in a sale of thirteen slaves, most of the testimony revolved around the question of whether the slaves had contracted the measles while they were stationed at Forks-of-the-Road, Natchez.[78] The sellers posed this cross-interrogatory to Smith's witness, David H. Love: "Did you or not whip severely a slave by the name of Harry or Henry belonging to said Smith and cut his testicles and did he or not die from that cause?" This question was clearly thrown in to impugn the witness's credibility; all the other interrogatories and cross-interrogatories concerned the illness of two slaves, Wiley and Betsy, who had apparently come down with the measles.

The judicial approach to a master's cruelty was quite permissive in Louisiana as well.[79] An 1834 law created an exception to the rule that two runaway episodes proved a runaway habit, in the case of cruel and unusual punishment by a new master.[80] In *Hagan v. Rist*,[81] John had run away from his buyer twice within the two months after the sale, and had been more than eight months in the state before the sale, giving rise to a presumption of a runaway habit.[82] The seller-defendant charged that the buyer's cruelty had caused the runaway episodes. The trial judge, however, refused to accept this excuse. He noted that medical evidence did establish "that a very severe flogging lacerating the back in its whole extent had been inflicted upon this slave" by the buyer. However, because the whipping was administered after the slave had run away several times, it could not "in any sense be considered as the cause of his running away." Furthermore, such a flogging, regardless of its timing, probably did "not even enter into the strictest letter [of the proviso that cruel treatment overcomes the presumption of a runaway habit] . . . because a flogging on the back although severe, can scarcely be considered an *unusual* punishment on a plantation for a slave who was, as proved[,] a confirmed and obstinate runaway." Whipping, no matter how severe, did not amount to cruelty because it was the *usual* punishment for slaves.

.　.　.　.　.

Cruelty did become the central legal issue in a civil trial when someone other than the owner beat or shot a slave. The typical owner's trespass complaint took the form that the defendants

> with force and armes did seize and lay hold of a certain Negro boy slave . . . did pull and drag the said slave about and then and there with their fists & sticks & cowhides & whips gave and struck the said slave a great many violent blows—and then not only greatly bruised and wounded the said slave but the said slave was thereby disabled for a long space of time to wit for the space of six days . . . from doing and performing his ordinary labor and in consequence of the many bruises and scars . . . rendered less valuable . . .

In this case, the owner sued his overseer and his neighbor for beating Hamilton sixty-one stripes after the slave was caught stealing from the neighbor, while the owner was away in Kentucky. The jury assessed the overseer thirty-one dollars in damages and found the neighbor not liable.[83]

Overall, juries were quite skeptical of owners' complaints that supervisors had abused their slaves. In suits that were appealed to a higher court, owners won in twenty-four cases, and supervisors won in twenty-six at the trial level. However, appellate courts were more sympathetic to owners' claims and overturned substantially more jury verdicts for supervisors than for owners. After appeal, owners had won thirty-three cases, and supervisors only half that number.[84]

Many of the shooting cases involved slaves who fled and were chased by dogs, then shot in the back. The jury was asked to determine whether flight counted as the kind of resistance justifying death. It was difficult to argue that a fleeing man threatened one's own life, but of course, in their minds, he did threaten society at large. For example, John Morton, a slaveholder in Columbus, Mississippi, gave James Holbert authority to shoot buck- or large shot in hunting his slave Spencer with his "trained negro dogs" in Pickens County, Alabama. Holbert enlisted John Bradley to help him, and Bradley shot Spencer in the head. However, Dabney Duncan testified that "Defendant said he meant to shoot him in the legs but just as the gun went off the negro fell or slipt into a hole that brought his head into range." Morton tried to argue that the killing was not justified because Bradley was not in danger from Spencer; Bradley introduced evidence that a grand jury had refused to indict him for the crime, and that he had followed the instructions Morton gave Holbert. The jury found for Bradley.[85]

Merely pursuing runaways with dogs, however, never counted as cruelty. In a Georgia case, Gardner Davis hired Stephen from Augustus Moran and ran him with dogs "into the creek where he was drowned." The court charged that "[u]nder ordinary circumstances the owner the hirer or the overseer of a slave, has the right to pursue the slave if he runs away with such dogs as may track him to his place of concealment, to follow him up untill the slave may be captured, provided it be done with such dogs as can not lacerate or materially injure the slave." The jury found for Davis.[86]

A trial judge sympathetic to the owner (or to the slave) could bind the jury with instructions that were specific enough. In one Alabama case, many witnesses from Perry County offered testimony that something other than a beating caused death. Samuel Nelson, a forty-four-year-old Irishman, had hired the slave Sam from John Bondurant, a young farmer, in 1851.[87] One Saturday night, Sam disobeyed orders to stay home and instead went to visit his wife on another plantation. The following Monday morning, when he saw the overseer coming, Sam "picked up a club, put it under his arm," and went to the house of his owner, Bondurant, who tied him and whipped him "thirty licks." When he returned to Nelson's place, Nelson and his overseer tried to punish him, but Sam "resist[ed] to the last," even trying to cut Mrs. Nelson's face with a knife. Sam, whom one witness described as "the most furious and worst looking negro he had ever seen," could not be subdued even by "30 or 40 licks" administered by all the white men present. Finally, according to the witnesses, he was tied and whipped; six days later, Sam died." A doctor gave testimony that "the whipping alone did not cause the death"; death resulted in part from Sam's "head striking a root on a stump in the fall" and in part from Sam's "exhaustion . . . from his exertions running and resistance." However, the trial judge charged the jury that if they believed the whipping to be even a partial cause of the death, then they must find the defendants liable, even if they believed that Nelson "had a right to whip [Sam], and that he had a right to call assistance" in whipping him. The Supreme Court of Alabama reversed this verdict, remonstrating with the trial judge that this instruction was clearly in error; what mattered was not whether Sam had been tied, nor whether whipping had caused his death, but only whether the whipping was a "lawful act," which in this case it was.[88]

Regardless of the type of punishment involved, cruel treatment could always be justified by proof that a slave was sufficiently incorrigible. Even cruelty to a woman made sense if she transgressed the line of propriety. Dinah, a dressmaker, "had not sent a Dress home which she was to send that day . . . she sent word back she would not send it until she got it done." This act of "insolence," sending John Lovett "insulting language and also his sisters in law," justified the severe beating Dinah was given. One witness testified that Dinah, after the whipping, had "bloodblisters . . . on her rump was bleeding profusely from her womb . . . one of her teeth was knocked out." A doctor who examined her found her face bruised, her back whipped "but not as badly as lower down . . ." Another physician, Dr. Knott, submitted an affidavit to the effect that he "considered her at the time [of his examination] seriously injured." However, witnesses to the whipping itself did not deem it cruel. S. G. Mitchell testified that he had not seen Lovett whip Dinah himself, but that Lovett had directed two male slaves to take hold of her. Mitchell noted that "she appeared to be making more noise than was necessary. After witness went off he heard her halloo murder." Another witness did see the defendant whipping Dinah "pretty severely." But when Lovett "pulled up her clothes to show WB Phillips how he had whipped," it turned out that he "had given her a genteel whipping." It also seemed to count for something that Lovett "appeared to be trying to get her out of a public place to his house." At all events, Lovett won the suit.[89]

Indeed, the trial records make quite clear that women were given no preferential treatment by overseers and masters. In cases where cruel whipping was at issue, solicitousness for a slave's gender arose in only one circumstance: when she was pregnant. Two Mississippi hire disputes provide a contrast.

In 1851, Alexander McKowen, an Irish-born merchant with no slaves of his own who had hired the slave Mariah from E. L. McCoy, allowed his overseer to whip Mariah with a "moderate-sized whip" one hundred lashes. She died soon afterward. A young Irish-born farmhand who had witnessed the whipping said that he "did not think the whipping cruel or unusual," and "had seen negroes worse whipped," but being "annoyed or disgusted with the noise," he had "retired from where the whipping was done." McKowen pointed out that "no slaveholder can say that this punishment was too severe—or that it exceeded the custom of the country . . . Under the naval discipline code until recently modified, it was not at all unusual to impose upon the bare back of the *white* sailor at one time a hundred lashes with the cat o'nine tails—much severer than this negro whip." Such a comparison of a woman with a navy man makes clear that no shadow of chivalry influenced the case. McKowen also reminded the jury that one hundred lashes did not break community norms—the "custom of the country." Finally, McKowen's doctor testified that the beating might not have caused Mariah's death, but rather that "apoplexy intervened," and that Mariah "was of a habit predisposed to apoplexy," as shown by the fact that Mariah "resisted and fought" her overseer, even taking "*violent hold of the private parts of his body* [emphasis in original]." The jury found for McKowen, and the Mississippi High Court of Errors and Appeals overturned the verdict only on the ground that the hirer could not be held responsible for his overseer's acts.[90]

A similar Mississippi hire dispute led to a very different outcome in court because pregnancy was involved. In *Trotter v. McCall*, the thirty-year-old farmer Hugh McCall, who also owned no slaves of his own, whipped his hired slave Betsey one hundred lashes on her bare back—but Betsey was pregnant. She gave birth to a child who was "puny and sickly, and died in a few days."[91] McCall sued William Trotter, Betsey's owner, for detaining Betsey when she fled to him. Pregnancy brought forth the paternalist rhetoric that mere black womanhood could not, for slave children were capital. Doctors testified to the dangers of miscarriage, and Trotter, a lawyer-planter who acted as his own attorney, rhapsodized about the immorality of so mistreating a pregnant slave "for no other cause than making an attempt to runaway": "suppose under similar circumstances a man should hire out his Daughter . . . and the party to whom she was hired should give her one hundred lashes on the Bare Back . . . ought the father to pay Damages for refusing to surrender his daughter . . . I think not." Two juries in a row made up of mostly young farmers with no or few slaves awarded damages to McCall. Trotter enlisted one of the leading lawyers practicing in Jackson, George Potter, to argue his appeal to the High Court of Errors and Appeals, which reversed the jury verdict, noting McCall's justified fears about "injury to the slave, who was then in a delicate condition peculiar to females."[92] Trotter himself had written and published a *History and Defense of African Slavery*, in which he discussed the value of a pregnant woman: "On all large farms there are frequently a large portion of the slave women . . . in a state of pregnancy . . . and this class of slaves, if properly taken care of, are the most profitable to their owners of any others . . . It is remarkable the number of slaves which may be raised from one woman in the course of forty or fifty years with the proper kind of attention."[93]

It was possible for owners to win against hirers who made an insufficient effort to portray the abused slave as dangerous or vicious. In one Louisiana case, an owner recovered for cruel treatment when it led to the suicide of a slave hired to a steamboat as a fireman. His owner, also a fireman, accused the captain of the *Yalla Busha* of treating David so badly that he was driven to jump overboard.

> That on the trip of said boat from New Orleans to Shreveport, said negro was taken sick with the fever . . . the negro was then forcibly compelled to go to work which he did but shortly afterward being exhausted by the heat of the fire he went back to his bed, when the engineer following the order of the captain went for him and whipped him back to the furnace and on the way said negro attempted to jump overboard, then the engineer forced him to go to work again but said negro being exhausted and unable to bear this cruel treatment jumped overboard and was drowned . . .

The captain, in defending his actions, suggested merely that the suicide was an unexpected result of his treatment, but did not justify the treatment by reference to David's character. The trial judge juxtaposed a paternalistic horror at this maltreatment with a concern for the property loss: "Besides the immorality and impropriety of the odious act which caused a man's death, the perpetrators of that outrageous deed are liable unto the master for his pecuniary loss . . ."[94]

An owner recovered for cruelty to his slave by a mob of white men in Madison County, Alabama, in part because an unrelated white witness testified on his behalf, in part because the men had no contractual relation giving them power over the slave, and in part because of the nature of the cruelty.[95] The men accused of cruelty, Daniel Curry and the Townsends, contended that the slave Lewis had stolen and killed some hogs. According to Admiral Dale, who testified on behalf of the owner, "I saw them all—They came to the house . . . on horseback, some of them had large hickory sticks, and Daniel Curry had a heavy Bull whip, one of the largest I ever saw, they called me out and I went down to the gate where they were. I did see the said defendants commit a trespass on said negro slave named Lewis."[96] Dale was in his eighties at the time of this incident, living in a household with Captain Willis and Elizabeth Routt, wealthy farmers who owned sixty slaves, and young William Jeffries, a teenage student. The slave Lewis belonged to the estate of William Jeffries' father. Daniel Curry and the Townsends were neighbors, all farmers and younger men. Curry was illiterate and owned no slaves of his own; the Townsends, however, were a large family, who owned four households in the neighborhood, and among them hundreds of slaves.[97]

Dale went on to recount that Edmund Townsend had accused four of the estate's slaves of killing his hogs. Dale challenged Townsend to prove it, so Townsend summoned Harrison Curry, who claimed that he had found "some negroes" by the hogs' pen, who ran from him. Dale expressed his disbelief. "I asked him if the negroes were riding or walking; he said he could not tell. I replied the moon near her full, a bright moonlight night, and you could not tell whether they were riding or walking?" Dale at that point questioned the slaves—Lewis, Jacob, Solomon, and Henry—who had been accused of hog killing, suggesting that he would take their word over Edmund Townsend's. Townsend reacted violently. When one of the slaves contradicted Townsend, explaining that Lewis had been sick in his mother's cabin at the time the hogs were killed, "Edmund Townsend jumped up, and with a large hickory stick raised, told him to shut his damned big mouth or he would split his damned brains out, and told him to clear himself a damned son of a bitch, and drove him off. He said he would have them whipped—if he couldn't do it he would have them before a Justice of the Peace." Edmund Townsend, the patriarch of a large family and the biggest plantation in the neighborhood, was used to getting his way.

Dale begged Townsend to wait until the owner's return, but "Edmund Townsend swore he would whip them *then*." Townsend's brother, Parks, "said he thought they ought to have a light whipping." Meanwhile, Dale saw the two Currys "sitting on the fence plaiting a thong to the Bull whip." Then the Currys and Samuel Townsend Jr. went out to where the slaves were, "leaving me arguing with Edmund Townsend and trying to persuade him to drop the matter." When Edmund Townsend joined the rest, Dale "remained alone with my head hung down, not knowing what to do, and for the first time in a long life felt intimidated." When he heard cries and "the crack of the whip," he went out to find

> Parks Townsend with Jacob tied on the lane, and Sam Townsend Jr and Harrison Curry were in pursuit of Solomon and Henry who had ridden off on their horses . . . I found Daniel Curry whipping Lewis and Edmund Townsend standing behind him. Lewis' hands were tied together above his head, to the body of a small tree, with his face to the tree, his feet were also tied together, and a very large rail was placed between his legs and on the rope to confine his feet to the ground. His belly was against the tree and he was so tied that he could scarcely move. They had whipped him till the blood was streaming down his back.

Dale tried to stop Curry, who did not stop until Dale "put [his] hand into [his] pocket as if [he] were armed." After Dale made another slave untie Lewis, "Edmund Townsend continued in a great rage and said that if he caught any of the negroes of this place on his premises, damned if he didn't shoot them or have them shot." At this point, Lewis "had some eight to ten severe gashes on his back and hips in some of which I could bury my finger."

The cruelty of this near-lynching impressed both jury and judge in part because of the manner in which it was carried out. Edmund Townsend *would not wait*; he whipped in passion and anger; he did not enact even a semblance of a "domestic tribunal" to discover the perpetrator of the hog killing; he did not care about fitting the punishment to the crime or the criminal. This mob behavior must have offended the jury's sense of masterly conduct. The jury in the case consisted almost exclusively of slaveholding "farmers," with holdings ranging from 350 acres and a single female slave to 61,800 acres and 228 slaves. Two of the small slaveholding jurors were near neighbors of the litigants; the rest lived in the neighboring district. All of them had experience as masters of slaves.[98]

If Edmund Townsend had been a hirer or owner of Lewis, he and his henchmen might have gotten away with what counted as a "trespass" in this case. The standard for a hirer seems to have been at once higher for good treatment and more lenient for cruelty, mirroring the more obliquely articulated standard for mastery: masters should be good but, provided they ran their own show by their own code, could get away with amazing cruelty. Hirers, legally put in the position of masters, were allowed the same standard, but neighbors, common carriers, and other whites were not.[99] They were not expected to watch over slaves the same way, but they could not be allowed to beat them to death either. Of course, as in the *Nelson* case, if other white men would testify that death was accidental, juries would accept their word; but if the other white witness testified to the abuser's passionate irrationality and inhumanity, jurors deemed the treatment culpable.

·   ·   ·   ·   ·

Just as "private law" disputes over slaves helped to create the meaning of blackness through the stories parties told about black character, they also helped to establish the cultural meaning of whiteness. To be a white man in Southern culture involved a set of meanings about honor and mastery, which were contested by litigants and witnesses in trials over the warranty and hire of slaves. If these cases turned only on the question of whether a man was a good paternalist, only the most devout Christian would have cared. But because the statesmanlike master represented the proper way to live up to the honorable "Code of Conduct" of Southern gentlemen, disciplinary style and plantation management became arenas of conflict. The volume of literature on Southern planters' shelves devoted to plantation and slave management should give a clue to the importance of these conflicts to the culture as a whole.

The cases also show the symbiosis of definitions of black and of white character. Wherever the argument that black character depended on management by a white man appeared, that white man's *good* character depended on the demonstration that *bad* black character had other sources. Yet, just as with slave character, the definitions and the arguments were not monolithic. Witnesses and litigants used descriptions of good and bad masters to gain advantage in disputes between buyers and sellers, hirers and owners. Judges, however, reserved paternalist language for the project of making hirers into substitute masters for a term. Likewise, while parties in the courtroom painted a picture of the good master as reasonable, detached, and humanitarian to the extent that such a stance made good business sense, judges emphasized the aspect of Southern ideology that called for masters to govern their domains according to a system, preferably with a code of laws and a "domestic tribunal." Finally, despite paternalist rhetoric against cruelty, the only cruelty that led to liability, as a rule, was that committed by those other than masters or hirers, in a manner that violated ideals of statesmanlike mastery—or against a pregnant woman.

Northern abolitionists always said that the worst thing about slavery was how it depraved white men's character. Slaveholders defending slavery tried in various ways to disprove this accusation, and even to show that white men improved their character through governing. By the final decades before the Civil War, most Southern slaveholders were keenly aware of the relationship between their role as masters and their character. The courtroom was one arena in which slaveholders and other white Southerners worked out their hopes and fears for themselves and their future.

FIVE

BODY AND MIND

IN THE SUMMER of 1860, John Blair of DeSoto Parish, Louisiana, bought a young male slave from a Georgia trader doing business in New Orleans. The slave he purchased, Hillier, did not stay with Blair for long. According to Blair, "he ranaway again and again," and each time he "was captured by [Blair]." Blair tried to return Hillier to the trader but was asked to keep him "till the [yellow] fever abated in the City." Finally, Hillier escaped at the end of the summer and managed to evade capture until early November, "when he was found to be almost in a dying condition from exposure." According to Blair, Hillier died of peritonitis (inflammation of the abdominal lining) as a "direct consequence of the redhibitory vice of running away," and he sued the trader in New Orleans district court for Hillier's price and the costs of medical care during his illness.[1]

Ten witnesses testified at trial, including several doctors. The plaintiff's witnesses emphasized that Hillier was treated well and that he was chained only to prevent his escape. Blair's brother was "certain that the boy ran away from no bad treatment, he was kindly treated, but he appeared to be incompetent to appreciate it . . ." Furthermore, according to this witness, Blair fed Hillier an excellent diet: "three and one Half pounds Bacon or Pickled Pork one Peck meal and one pint Molasses per week." Two doctors testified about their postmortem examination of Hillier's body: "[H]is bowells were covered with small white specks resembling somewhat the specks of butter upon buttermilk . . ." The defendant, by contrast, attempted to make the case that Hillier was badly treated—overworked and excessively punished—and that running away was frequent on that plantation.

The outcome of the trial was typical of warranty (or in Louisiana, redhibition) disputes over a slave's disease and death: Blair recovered a jury verdict, and the appellate court affirmed it. On its face, the case exemplified the mundane nature of most civil cases where the state of a slave's body was the central issue in dispute. Such contests over whether a slave was "sound in body and mind" at the time of sale or hire were the most common cases involving slaves—not only in Louisiana but throughout the South, at the trial as well as the appellate level.[2] In Adams County, Mississippi, where breach of warranty of physical soundness cases constituted half of all slave-related trials, a plurality concerned slaves with consumption, scrofula (a lymphatic disease), or heart conditions.[3] Yet detailed descriptions of slaves' bodies, vehement disputes over the causes of death, and involved medical testimony on the progress of illness filled dozens of pages of trial transcripts in even a simple case of "negro consumption" (miliary tuberculosis). In these cases, one theme recurs: the relentless objectification of slaves counterposed by the repeated intrusion of slaves' moral agency.

Even in cases like John Blair's suit, in which the slave's physical condition was the legal issue, character came into question in a variety of ways. At the most general level, *all* cases involving slaves required the parties in the courtroom to read slaves' bodies, because bodies seemed to offer the most concrete signs of slaves' condition. Yet these readings rarely remained on the physical plane; slaves' bodies offered clues to their character, and whites felt their own character to be judged on the basis of their ability to read slaves' bodies. Further, there were a variety of specific ways in which cases that began with the physical implicated the moral: cases like Hillier's in which a slave's character contributed to a physical illness; as well as a range of cases in which moral, mental, and physical blurred—those involving insanity, "idiocy," and drinking.

Slave masters and litigants wished that slaves' bodies were easy to read, that all defects and characteristics could be plain and apparent on the surface. That slaves' bodies contained hidden mysteries, that slaves could conceal and dissemble, and that observers could see different things or reach different interpretations of slaves' bodies: these were sources of frustration both to slave masters in general and to courts in particular. Increasingly, the courts' answer to the problem of the unknowable slave body was to turn to medical expertise. To reach judgments about slaves' bodies, minds, and character, litigants called in third-party experts, doctors, who made it their business to fathom the mysteries of black bodies, which many declared to be "other," wholly different from white bodies. During the first half of the nineteenth century, when courts were just beginning to rely on scientific and medical experts for specialized knowledge, and when doctors were using the opportunity to testify as a way of shoring up their new professional identity in a public arena, Southern doctors established themselves as a profession by affirming their status as experts on slaves' bodies. In so doing, doctors made claims to honor as professional men, whose judgment could be trusted because of their honorable detachment and superior knowledge.

Yet even medical expertise did not solve the problem of reading slaves' bodies. For doctors had to rely on slaves' own words to diagnose their illness, so that medical testimony brought slave agency into the courtroom by forcing the tribunal to consider a slave's own construction of his or her condition. Warranty suits over sick slaves raised the specter of "feigned illness," which suggested that blacks could deceive whites as to the state of their bodies. Doctors tried to handle this problem by claiming to have medical methods to discern feigned illness, which became an emblem of the Southern medical profession. As doctors' professionalization in the antebellum South was bound up both with testifying in cases involving slaves and with developing a racialized, purely "Southern" medicine, courtroom conflicts over sick slaves became a nexus for white fears about black disease, dirt, and sexuality, about the unknowability of slave bodies and the impossibility of controlling slaves' moral agency. Once again, slaves' agency threw into question the honor of the white men who claimed to know and to control them.

Particularly in areas in which Southerners believed mind, body, and morals to overlap, doctors betrayed their frustration with slaves' efforts to control their own bodies at the same time that they "medicalized" slaves' unruly character traits as having biological, racial roots. By privileging the testimony of doctors, the courtroom heightened the tendency to "medicalize" the discourse about blacks in Southern society. The legal process shaped racial discourse in these cases as well: by making people take sides in an adversary process, it changed the way they looked at slaves and what they said about them; the legal process anointed experts, making medical doctors authoritative in court; and it colored all interactions with the anticipation of litigation.

.   .   .   .   .

Slave buyers in the marketplace read slaves' bodies, trying to judge for themselves whether slave traders and sellers were representing them fairly. When prospective purchasers undressed slaves, they thought they could read hidden information about slaves' age and condition. One ex-slave from South Carolina remembered that her grandmother had had to open her mouth to show her teeth, "de way dey do when dey sell hosses," in order to "know effen dey wuz sound."[4] As discussed in chapter 2, these rituals of the slave market reaffirmed to white buyers and sellers that slaves could not have honor, and slaves experienced them as acts of dishonor. But they also point to the *embodied* nature of slaves' dishonor. Kenneth Greenberg describes the undressing of slaves in the marketplace as an aspect of slaves' "unmasking"; to white Southerners, slaves were "people who lacked the power to keep themselves from being unmasked."[5] In a culture that prized surface appearances, lacking control over one's own outer layer was a rank humiliation.

Sellers, however, tried to do more than simply to lay bare slaves' bodies for buyers' examination and interpretation; they sought to give those bodies words. As Walter Johnson has shown in a study of the New Orleans slave market, slave sellers "wrapped the slaves in description," hoping to persuade buyers to make a purchase by matching their fantasies to a slave.[6] For example, a buyer who imagined himself as a great gentleman planter, presiding over a cotton plantation, sought field hands who could help him fulfill that self-image; a buyer who saw himself in an elegant household bought manservants or maids who would fit that picture. Sellers played on these imaginings through their descriptions, talking about color, height, and weight, as well as character, disposition, and intelligence, although slave traders tracked slave prices strictly by gender and age.[7]

Warranty suits turned the marketplace inside out. The complaining buyer, or the buyer explaining why he refused to pay his note, used the description of a slave to convince judge and jury that he had been duped by an unscrupulous seller, and possibly by the slave herself. The sick slave was one who did not match the buyer's hopes of cotton bales piling up on a smoothly running plantation; his disappointment could be bitter, because the slave represented his ticket to a different station in life or the maintenance of his current way of life. Slave sellers, on the other hand, repeated their marketplace descriptions of slaves, echoing the call of the auctioneer in their testimony. Sometimes the body of a slave was read for signs of character, as when attorneys asked witnesses about marks and suggested that marks of the whip revealed something essential about the slave's character—or about her master's. At other times, the slave's body was discussed simply as a piece of property, a commodity, each of whose parts could be priced. In all instances, describing slaves provided witnesses and litigants the opportunity to establish themselves as authorities on slaves' bodies, either as one who knew this particular slave best, or as one who could read slaves' bodies particularly well. And in each case, the ritual of unmasking reasserted the honor of the white man and the dishonor of the slave.

The first description of a slave's body in a lawsuit appeared in the complaint. Slaves were identified by name, age, gender, and sometimes color; this identification was followed by a brief description of the unsoundness of which the buyer complained. The form of the complaint allowed no room for even brief mention of more specific identifying features. At trial or in depositions, however, lawyers for both parties asked witnesses to describe slaves. They sought to elicit information that would identify the slave—proving that the witness knew her well—and that would indicate her state of health at a particular time. Jonathan Prude has suggested, in a study of runaway slave advertisements, the rarity of Southern whites' devoting enough attention to the "lower sort" to give detailed descriptions of their appearance.[8] Yet in trial depositions—read out loud at Court Day in the county court, as public as runaway ads and accessible to those who could not read newspapers—whites were often able to describe slaves with particularity.

Typical attorney's interrogatories asked whether a slave was "sound or unsound," and asked for a description of the slave's "appearance, gait, manner of carrying himself . . . other marks or signs of health."[9] Some interrogatories included identifying characteristics: "Did you ever know a slave of copper complexion called Ellick about 24 years old, 5 feet 8 or 9 inches high and weighing about 180 pounds?"[10] More often, however, the details of a slave's appearance were reported in the witness's answer. These varied from such vague terms as "large and fine-looking"[11] to very detailed portrayals: "the negro woman Becky was very black; of good skin, of a trim figure, of rather a graceful manner moving with ease, weighing he supposed between one hundred and twenty five and one hundred and thirty five pounds and about five feet two or three inches high with good teeth and rather thick lips."[12]

In warranty and hire trials, witnesses were vague about age. Southerners who displayed great pride in their ability to pinpoint slaves' dollar value showed no dismay at their inability to gauge the age of slaves whom they had known since birth or even claimed to have raised. Dr. Joseph Guy deposed that he could "only guess at [an enslaved woman's] age altho I have known her almost from her infancy . . ."[13] The brother of Bob's owner, who shared the same household, testified that he thought Bob "was about 28 years old, something older than represented in the bill of Sale," but on cross-examination admitted that he did "not pretend to state the exact age of said negro, it is hard to tell their age with accuracy."[14] Buyers recognized that they ran the risk of being misled. Elizabeth Dangerfield testified that "she bought Isabella for twenty five years of age but believes she may have been as old as thirty years."[15] This uncertainty about age persisted despite buyers' best efforts in the marketplace. Ex-slaves describing their sales often mentioned inspections designed to ascertain age: "One bidder takes a pair of white gloves they have and rubs his fingers over a man's teeth, and he says, 'You say this buck's 20 years old, but there's cups worn to his teeth. He's 40 years if he's a day." John Glover, a South Carolina slave, claimed that buyers "[c]ome en open you mouth en examine you teeth en dey wouldn' miss you a year." Yet few buyers seem to have felt so confident that they had not missed a year.[16]

By contrast, even vague physical descriptions could be accompanied by quite precise estimates of monetary value. Dr. Nelson testified that a slave was a "brown skin woman of medium size and he supposed her about 30 or 35 years old . . . if sound and healthy would have been worth $1300 . . ."[17] Witnesses were able to testify concerning the discount in value for slaves of varying ages or physical characteristics.[18] Just as specific skills added a precise increment to a slave's price, particular defects or deviations from the norm justified a discount, and experienced slave buyers and sellers knew the right amount.[19] These valuations were important in the determination of damages. Usually, a plaintiff sued for the price of a slave (or the difference between price paid and value when unsound), for the cost of labor lost, and for medical expenses incurred in having the slave treated.

One important aspect of slave descriptions, as both an identifier and an indicator of value, was color. Walter Johnson has noted that "[t]raders sold slaves according to lineage, but buyers bought them by color."[20] In other words, sellers promised that a slave had a certain proportion of black and white blood—a "mulatto," a "griffe," a "quadroon"—but buyers believed their eyes rather than sellers' words. In court, witnesses often reported on both color and "blood"; in doing so, they claimed a knowledge of the slave that could not be obtained at first sight. For example, it was common to note that a slave was "yellow" or light-skinned, but a "full-blooded negro" or "not known to be a mulatto."[21] Robert Abernathy testified about Wondy that "as complexion he was not a very black negro, but had none of the appearance of the mulatto in him."[22] Several witnesses reached the same conclusion about Burrell in another Adams County case. Robert McCary found him "of a dark color but not the Blackest Negro I ever saw there was apparently no white Blod in him," while Elizabeth Mayberry thought Burrell was "not a mulatto nor was he as black as some negroes."[23] There appears to have been no set rule about whether light or dark color added to a slave's value. As Frederick Law Olmsted noted in his travels, while one slaveholder "reckoned yellow fellows was the best a little; they worked smarter," another "didn't fancy yellow negroes 'round him; would rather have real black ones."[24] Ex-slave Henry Banner commented, "Yellow niggers didn't sell so well . . . Black niggers stood the climate better. At least everybody thought so."[25]

In order to prove their knowledge of the slaves, most witnesses were able to give detailed descriptions, including facial features, color, distinguishing marks, and numerical estimates of height, weight, and age.[26] In a typical case, one doctor deposed that "Gilbert was a stout made black man about 5 feet 8 inches high full face tolerable good looking and about from 21 to 23 years of age, Isaac was a slendermade man of yellow copper colour, about 5 feet 5 or 6 inches high, slow of speech, of mild humble address and about 25 or 28 years old. I do not recollect any particular marks on either of said Negroes . . ." Another witness said that "Gilbert . . . is a black negro about six feet high of sprightly appearance sold to me to be about nineteen or twenty years of age . . . Isaac was rather of a copper colour low heavy set about twenty one or twenty two years of age," and a third that "Gilbert was a large strong, active fellow weighing about 180 lbs about twenty one or two years of age, of very black colour,

Isaac was a strong built fellow a shade lighter in colour than Gilbert and weighing about 150 pounds, twenty four or six years of age."[27] Descriptions of facial features usually emphasized, whether consciously or unconsciously, those which were considered racially distinctive—flat noses and wide lips, for example.[28] Furthermore, there was no discernible difference in thoroughness between descriptions of men and those of women.[29]

The trial provided a unique setting for white Southerners to describe slaves. Testifying in a legal dispute required, first, identifying the subject matter of the dispute. One could not bear witness in a case involving a slave without first establishing through physical description that one knew the slave. The ritual of identification began each episode of questioning, whether in oral testimony or in written deposition. Through detail in descriptions of color, size, age, and especially value, witnesses could establish their credibility and even expertise. Of course, they often looked ahead to the main event, describing a slave as "likely" or "good-looking" in anticipation of an argument that she was sound. But many descriptions were relatively unself-conscious iterations of those aspects of black bodies which white witnesses could remember, those which mattered, and those which would signify to their listeners that they knew the slave.

Once witnesses established their ability to identify a slave, they offered descriptions to prove the slave's soundness or unsoundness. Parties in the courtroom read slaves' bodies for signs of character as well as disease. The way a slave walked or carried herself, the speed at which she worked, the size and appearance of her limbs, marks of punishment or of medical treatment all provided evidence of her condition.

Slaves complained of as unsound were described as "valueless and offensive," of "swarthy appearance," and as having "a sleepy dull look."[30] Sometimes the descriptions went into quite intimate details. The plaintiff's attorneys in *Hill v. Elam* questioned several witnesses about Burrell's anus: "Did you know that Berrell [*sic*] had then and for some time previously a 'pistula in ano'? Did you or either of you ever examine said Berrell about the 'anus', or any other private part for a 'pistula' [*sic*] or any other disease?" One answered that he "never knew the boy Burrell to have fistula in anno nor could he have had this disease while I knew him, without my knowing—I never made any examination but have seen him frequently riding bear back on horses—" In another Adams County case, the doctor testified that an enslaved woman's "most prominent symptom [of inflammation of the intestines] on my first visit was an intolerable itching about the anus, the parts adjacent being slightly excoriated by constant scratching."[31]

Somewhat surprisingly, few buyers went to court to complain that enslaved women were poor "breeders." I found only one case in which a plaintiff directly complained that dirt eating "rendered [the slaves] un-

profitable as breeding women."[32] Yet concern for pregnancy and repro-
ductive health ran very high. As discussed in chapter 4, even lax standards
for brutal masters could be stiffened in the case of a pregnant woman.
Buyers sued occasionally for diseases of an enslaved woman's reproduc-
tive system, but not disproportionately so in relation to medical historians' estimates of their incidence in comparison to other diseases. There
were suits in which buyers sought to return slaves who turned out not to
be pregnant, but they were usually seriously ill or dying as well.[33] Witnesses occasionally mentioned a slave's pregnancy, abortion, or "condition as to her monthly courses."[34] Most often, the concern was a "disease
of the womb," which in many cases turned out to be fatal.[35] Doctors also
often attributed ill health to amenorrhea or menopause.[36]

To prove soundness, witnesses described slaves as "sprightly" and
"healthy," never missing a day of work. Occasionally, male witnesses referred to enslaved women as "good-looking" or having a "good figure,"
but they did not go beyond that to discuss them in more overtly sexual
terms. The image of the black woman as "Jezebel" did not reveal itself in
descriptions of enslaved women at trial.[37] This may have had more to do
with taboos on official recognition of interracial sex than it did with actual practice, as the high prices certain "fancy" women commanded indicate that they were sold for sex.[38] However, buyers disappointed with
such purchases did not have recourse to the courts, unless they invented
another pretext for their complaint. To acknowledge sexual intimacy with
a slave would have violated the honor code, although such relationships
were tacitly approved.

Witnesses trying to prove soundness also tried to show that they themselves were in a good position to know the health of the slave. One way
to do this was to display knowledge of the slave's family: for example,
John B. Righter testified that "I was acquainted with his family they were
a healthy stock of Negroes and he whilst I owned him . . . Gilbert was a
sprightly stout and active boy and well disposed . . ."[39] The defendant's
attorney in another case asked two witnesses, "Did you know the slave
Bob? What were your means and facilities generally of being well acquainted with his bodily condition and health?" One answered, "I am
satisfied that the said slave Bob was a sound healthy negro in body and
mind," but unfortunately he "knew nothing about [Bob's] parents." On
the other hand, witnesses did not want it thought that their close knowledge of the slave might interfere with their objectivity: as William King
explained, "That Boy was the best boy witness ever knew. He was *raised*
with him. Tho he don't think his friendship and kind feelings affected his
valuation."[40]

William King's reassurance that friendship would not get in the way
of valuation reminds us of the main point of all descriptions of unsound

bodies: to win money damages in court. Thus witnesses were often called upon to testify to the discount in value they attributed to any particular disease or defect of a slave. So, for example, in *Watson v. Boatwright*, witnesses testified that a slave's price was discounted one hundred dollars for venereal disease. In an Alabama case, Charles Gingles warranted Joe, who was eight years old at the time of sale, to be "sound in mind and body with the exception of his legs," and promised to "make him good to [the buyer]" if his legs kept him from being "a serviceable boy." Testimony at trial showed that seven years later, Joe "could and did pick cotton," at the rate of "half to two thirds of a hand," despite the fact that his legs had deteriorated. A large number of witnesses were called for both sides to testify about Joe's market value, and it was left for the jury to sort the matter out. The trial judge instructed the jury to award damages amounting to the difference between Joe's value and that of a "serviceable boy," and they awarded the buyer six hundred dollars. Knowing a slave well and knowing the state of his health often meant putting a price on it.[41]

Perhaps the most important way to read a slave's body for signs of character was to read its marks. Marked bodies held great meaning for antebellum Southerners. Marks on a slave's body were often a code identifying a vicious slave.[42] The ex-slave Solomon Northup explained, "Scars upon a slave's back were considered evidence of a rebellious or unruly spirit, and hurt his sale."[43] Kenneth Greenberg has argued that slaveholders tended to believe that marks spoke for themselves as evidence of slave vice; that white Southerners "cared not a whit" for the story behind the scars.[44] However, in court, complaining buyers made that story important. Even in the marketplace, slave sellers had a difficult time explaining marks: their desire to portray themselves as good masters could come into conflict with their concern for a slave's price. If scars meant slave vice, that could hurt the sale; yet the alternative interpretation saw scars as evidence of ill-treatment. In court, attorneys often asked about marks as a way of finding out about the past: "Could you Judge from his appearance that he had been ill treated?" asked one Louisiana attorney, to which the reply was "[t]hat he saw no marks of it."[45]

In warranty trials, then, marks on the body were ambiguous signs. They could prove an earlier illness—showing that a slave had been bled or had had "scrofulous ulcers."[46] "Heroic" treatments for illness frequently resembled an assault on the slave's body, and many slaves saw regular medicine that way, distrusting the heavy use of blistering and "cupping." Marks on the body could also be signs of beatings, which might be used to show either a slave's vice *or* ill-treatment.[47] These descriptions could be quite terse, offered in the course of longer remarks—"his back pretty well marked with a whip"[48]—or more detailed. Owners who testified

about a slave's marked body may have been concerned to present themselves as masters who knew the character of their slaves, rather than as
fools surprised by their slaves' behavior.[49] Often, interrogatories asked
specifically about marks, trying to elicit information on a master's treatment. A typical exchange went like this:

> "Was or was not said negro mutilated at the time—did you or not examine
> said negro carefully[?]"
> "I do not know that he was mutilated, but I saw that the negro was bad off.
> I examined him pretty carefully."
> "Was it or not . . . at Montgomery very cold[?]"
> "It was very cold . . ."
> "Did you or did you not see any evidence of said negro having been bitten
> by Dogs[?]"
> "I did not."[50]

By contrast, the cross-examiners of this witness tried to suggest that the
marks were evidence of the slave's character, asking, "Was not said negro
a runaway—was he not in the habit of running away—had he not run
away before?"

Marked bodies held a double-sided significance for readers of character.
The character of the slave revealed itself through the mark of the whip,
to those who assumed all beatings to be justified. But the character of the
master suggested itself as well. The master might appear to be harsh or
cruel, for chasing a runaway with dogs, or he might appear savvy, for
knowing and correcting his slave's vice. Either way, the body itself spoke
in the same way as did the ambiguous act of running away. Because slaves'
character always potentially reflected masters' character, slaves' bodies
always potentially mirrored masters as well.

White Southerners' "regard" for black bodies in civil courtrooms takes
on meaning in an "Anglo-American culture . . . [that] was broadly per-
suaded that the knowable was the visible and was fascinated with the act
of perception."[51] As with runaway ads, the acute focus on the bodies of
enslaved men and women to some extent "resembled the careful iteration
of property in documents like wills and probate records," for slaves *were*
property.[52] But the body of a slave represented not only a piece of property
nor merely an instrument of labor but an investment in a way of life: a
slave could make a white man into a master; with enough slaves, he became a planter.[53] When white Southerners in court turned their gaze to
black bodies, they rationally tallied dollars and cents, but they also projected their own desires onto those bodies, seeing promises made and
promises betrayed. The slave in the market augured bales of cotton at
year's end; the slave in the courtroom had produced only heartache, complained the disillusioned buyer. In describing slaves' bodies, witnesses and

parties described what they valued in their slaves—a particular color, depending on whether they were field or house workers; strength; a docile character; and so on—and they put those values in monetary terms. But they also revealed white Southerners' ambivalent obsession with the black body: their fear of its power and their desire to master it.

·   ·   ·   ·   ·

The Southern doctor was the ultimate reader of slave bodies and therefore an important player in the slave market. Doctors oversaw slave sales, examined slaves in traders' pens, gave "certificates of soundness" for evidence in future litigation, and performed postmortems on slaves who died after sale. Just as the marketplace always stood in the shadow of the courthouse, doctors' exams, certificates, and postmortems foreshadowed their testimony in court on behalf of buyer or seller, hirer or owner. Southern doctors were the foremost experts in trials involving slaves, appearing in the courtroom as often as they did in the slave yards.[54] Medical writers validated their expertise with the claim that slaves required a specialized "negro medicine." As part of the practice of racial medicine, physicians' role as arbiters of slave "soundness" was vital to the effort of medical regulars to establish the Southern medical profession.

Yet at the same time physicians positioned themselves as trial experts, their credibility often depended on slaves' own reporting of their condition. Doctors feared slaves' deceit in reporting illness, but the source of their authority was the slave as an agent capable of speaking authoritatively about her own condition.

In one rare instance, the handwritten notes of the defendant's attorney, apparently scribbled during the trial, survived with the trial transcript of a Natchez, Mississippi, case. The notes suggest a lawyer's view of medical testimony and its uses. First, the lawyer summarized the medical testimony:

> J.N.H. Wood—proves that measles broke out on Smith's place in April and continued on the place until July—knows 15 or 20 had measles—25 or 30 died on the place three men own 140 negroes—place generally healthy . . .
> Mr. Johnson proves that measles usually lasted 3 or 4 weeks . . .
> Owen was present at the sale. Knew the measles were at the place—Smith inquired whether the measles were among the negroes—and was assured there were no opportunity to catch measles, saw Wiley 2 days after and he was sick saw him after with evidences of measles on him 9 or 10 negroes sick at one time =
> Dr Pollard—prove character of disease—
> Dr Davis in system 7 to 14 days before development . . .

Coleman went to Smiths at request of Love saw 17 sick—Love was sick—
negroes had no comforts . . .
Dr. Coleman was at Smith's April 21, 1836
   Wiley was in a situation which might have resulted from measles—Betsey
also inflammation of stomach & Bowels . . .

On the reverse of his memo paper, the lawyer scribbled arguments:

If A threw a log into the street, the stumbler may recover . . .
a mad dog bite—can't recover unless the owner knew he was mad
. . . If the negroes were unsound and died by mismanagement—seller is not
liable.

Then he gave his opinion of the medical testimony: "2 unprofessional
men call measles." On another scrap of paper, he had written:

Dr Hogg—a physician—the balance unprofessional—
= moved Heaven and earth to obtain medical assistance!
= He sais Dr Davis testimony conflicts with that of Dr Hogg—this is a mistake
= M. put away the sick negroes in a rest-house—no evidence of this . . .[55]

These cryptic notes indicate a number of things about the conduct of a
warranty trial. First, a seemingly routine case involving two slaves who
contracted the measles drew on the testimony of not one, not two, but
six doctors. Second, an important way to discredit witnesses was to suggest that they were "unprofessional." Conversely, to testify authoritatively in court was an important way for a medical man to establish himself as "professional." Finally, medical testimony provided crucial links
between masters' responsibility and slaves' condition. A medical opinion
that disease depended on "mismanagement" benefited the seller when a
slave fell ill under the buyer's care; an opinion that a disease could lie
dormant in the body for a period of time, such as from before the sale
until a month afterward, benefited the buyer. Doctors testified not only
to slaves' symptoms but to masters' care—"negroes had no comforts"—
and speculated about the course of diseases they little understood—"in
system 7 to 14 days before development." Lawyers, in turn, depended on
and distrusted doctors. When faced with conflicting medical testimony, a
lawyer first tried to suggest that the doctor for his side was "a physician,"
and that the other doctors, "the balance," were "unprofessional"; and
then to show that the testimony did not in fact conflict. In either case, the
matter turned on the testimony of doctors.
   The second quarter of the nineteenth century saw a new use of medical
experts in the courtroom. In both England and early America, medical
witnesses rarely appeared in court during the eighteenth century; when
they did so, they were called by the court rather than by the litigants, or

they testified as other lay witnesses, rather than as experts.[56] The concept of medical jurisprudence was a nineteenth-century phenomenon. In this period, James Stringham gave the first formal lectures on medical jurisprudence at Columbia, and T. R. Beck wrote *Elements of Medical Jurisprudence*.[57] The first edition of Isaac Ray's *Treatise on the Medical Jurisprudence of Insanity* and other treatises on identifying insanity in court also appeared in the 1830s. The development of medical jurisprudence both as a practice and as a formal category was part of a process of medical professionalization, establishing as experts regular physicians, as opposed to irregulars such as homeopaths, osteopaths, midwives, and practitioners of folk medicine, all of whom flourished in the antebellum South. Yet contemporary writers on medical jurisprudence (as well as modern-day historians) overlooked probably the most common medicolegal practice of doctors in the antebellum South: examining slaves and testifying in court as to their physical and mental condition.[58]

One doctor in the 1850s commented on this gap in the medical jurisprudence literature. A series of articles appearing in the *Savannah Journal of Medicine* in 1858 and 1859 presented guidelines doctors might use in certifying slaves' soundness or unsoundness. Dr. Juriah Harriss, a professor of physiology at Savannah Medical College, introduced his subject with the lament that this "question of great import to the Southern physician and slave owner" had not received systematic analysis despite its being such a large part of the business of Southern medicine. "Physicians in the South are daily called upon to give medical evidence in court . . . to pronounce upon the soundness of a negro slave . . ."; however, the medical opinions given were too "haphazard," biased, and arbitrary.[59] To introduce more regularity into the system, Harriss suggested a definition of unsoundness: "a chronic or constitutional [disease, which] incapacitates the negro for the performances of the usual duties of his calling, viz: hard labor, or tending to shorten life; or an acute disease of such a character as will probably leave as a sequence, a chronic affection, which will more or less incapacitate the negro for manual labor; or again an acute disease, which will render the negro liable to subsequent attacks of the same affection."[60] He then went on to discuss injuries to the head, injuries to the spine, tumors, scrofula, syphilis, and other diseases.

Not only did testifying in slave cases make up the bulk of the typical doctor's work as a courtroom expert, but it contributed to the development of the Southern medical profession in general. Southern medical writers like Dr. Samuel Cartwright argued for a distinct Southern medicine based on the unique "diseases and peculiarities" of an enslaved black population. In one of his advice articles to slave owners, Cartwright enumerated the "negro diseases," including "negro consumption" (what is now known as "miliary tuberculosis," a deadly form of the disease believed by some Southerners to attack blacks more frequently than whites), and drew the connection between physicians' diagnostic role with respect to "negro diseases" and their role in litigation:

> It is of importance to know the pathognomonic signs in its early stages, not only in regard to its treatment, but to detect impositions, as negroes afflicted with the complaint are often for sale; the acceleration of the pulse on exercise incapacitates them for labor, as they quickly give out and have to leave their work . . . the seat of negro consumption is . . . in the mind, and its cause is generally mismanagement or bad government . . .[61]

Although ordinary physicians may not have had many opportunities in daily practice to act on the racial theories of polemicists like Cartwright, trials involving slaves gave doctors the occasion to testify about "cakesciaaffrina or negro consumption," "negro syphilis," and other "negro diseases." The belief in "racial medicine," or the medical otherness of blacks, was partly based in real differences in immunities to certain diseases and partly the product of ideological commitment to theories of racial hierarchy. Todd Savitt has written that many "southern physicians . . . wrote about racial medicine [and i]n a sense, all those who wrote on the subject were providing a defense for slavery."[62] Of course, most of the physicians who appeared in court were *not* proslavery writers; as Steven Stowe has shown, they approached slaves' bodies in diagnosis and treatment with a pragmatic attitude, often noting no racial distinction in their medical notebooks.[63] But in vital ways, the fact that diagnosis and treatment took place in the shadow of the marketplace and the courthouse altered the way doctors approached slaves.

Even before a dispute led to trial, doctors gave certificates of soundness or unsoundness for use in litigation. For example, in one South Carolina case, Dr. Lee's certificate read, "I certify that Joe has a curvature of the spine and small limbs . . . I do not consider him capable of enduring continued hard work."[64] Dr. North certified that Maria was "valueless and offensive."[65] In another case, a doctor testified that "plaintiff wished him to give a certificate of boy's unsoundness . . . but witness refused."[66] On many occasions when doctors were called to examine slaves, whether before sale or afterward, the possibility of litigation, symbolized by the certificate of soundness or unsoundness, colored the interaction.

In suits involving diseased or injured slaves, doctors frequently testified on both sides of a case, and conflicting medical testimony was the rule rather than the exception. This "bickering and squabbling of medical witnesses" mirrored the state of medical jurisprudence in general, which medicolegal writers warned made it difficult for doctors to be taken seriously as professional experts. The very activity of giving expert testimony that gave doctors authority also threatened to diminish it. As one judge in Dallas County, Alabama, charged the jury, "the testimony of physicians was a matter of opinion merely."[67] For example, in one Natchez case, four doctors performed a postmortem on Ellick, a mulatto slave who had "complained of pains in the chest and at times his bowels out of order" before his death. Two of the doctors testified in court for Ellick's owner "that the adhesions of the heart were of old standing," based on the postmortem. This went to prove that Ellick's seller, the trading firm Griffin Pullam & Co., should be held financially responsible for his death. However, Dr. Edward Blackburn testified for the slave traders that he "for eight years had been connected with hospitals . . . had made very many dissections, was in the habit of making post mortem examinations of the bodies of those who died in said hospitals." Based on this experience, he could conclude from the other doctors' testimony that "no physician could form a well grounded opinion as to the age of the disease discovered . . . [except that it was] of at least 3 or 4 months standing." As Ellick had been sick in his buyer's care from July to November, according to Dr. Blackburn, the illness might have developed in the time after the sale.[68]

Doctors disagreed not only on the duration of a particular condition or disease but on whether the slave's condition was curable at all. In one South Carolina case, Dr. Horlbeck testified that a slave was "as much cured as she could be; she might have temporary relief." The doctor himself "would not have purchased her as a sound negro" because "she was deformed." He thought this "clearly visible to anyone who would examine." Dr. A. G. Ward, on the other hand, had examined the slave at the same time as Dr. Horlbeck "and thought it a case of rheumatism . . . regarded the case as curable." He "differed with [Dr. Horlbeck]." Furthermore, Dr. Ward "said if he wanted a negro for a plantation, he would not have made $50 difference in her value for this defect."[69] Sometimes disagreement went so far as disparagement of the other doctor's care. In a case about a slave carpenter who died after sale, the attending doctor, Dr. Bailey, "thought it a decided case of dropsy,[70] thought his case a hopeless one" and the disease "of long standing." The seller called to the stand Dr. Ogier, who thought Philander's disease was "aggravated by the cold" and that he "would not think himself justified in quitting a patient under such circumstances"; had he been in attendance, "he would have bled or cupped Philander."[71]

In many trials, even when there was no profound disagreement among doctors, an astonishing number of doctors testified to a slave's condition. For example, in a suit for the $640 price of the slave Caroline, Dr. James M. Whitfield, Dr. Daniel B. Cliffe, Dr. Chevalier, Dr. Hugh Lyle, Dr. C. H. Stone, and Dr. Branham all testified about Caroline's "monthly courses" or menstrual cycle.[72] These were not "experts for hire"; all of these witnesses were established local physicians with plantation practices among both whites and slaves. The money expended on examinations by so many doctors heightened the urgency of these warranty suits. To bolster the claims of buyers trying to recover from sellers, doctors often testified to the expensive medical bills the buyers had incurred. Whereas Todd Savitt estimates that the typical planter spent two or three dollars a year per slave on doctors, in warranty suits plaintiffs routinely claimed to have spent fifty to several hundred dollars on medical expenses. In one Natchez case, for example, a doctor claimed that his bills "exceed Three Hundred Dollars for attendance upon Gilbert and Isaac."[73]

Doctors attempted to establish their expertise by demonstrating their knowledge of slaves' most important characteristic in warranty suits: price. Doctors put a dollar value on the discount for a particular disease or defect and claimed to bring special expertise to difficult situations, such as that of a hereditary disease. For example, Dr. Drake testified that "consumption . . . is hereditary and of course [Sofa's] children cannot be as valuable as if they were born of a healthy mother . . ." While Dr. Drake knew "of no general rule to determine the discrimination of the price of children born of such parents as were diseased with consumption," he took it "as a plain common sense one with myself in purchasing, that half the price paid for those that have not such hereditary complaint, would be a fair price." Dr. Kendall, on the other hand, thought that "75 percent would be a very fair price for the children of Sofa."[74]

As one aspect of setting themselves apart as a profession, doctors in court emphasized the inadequacy of medical diagnosis and treatment by nonphysicians and irregulars. Testifying in court gave regular physicians the opportunity to assert a standard of care for slaves that required examination by a regular physician. In one complicated dispute, Mosely hired a woman slave to Wilkinson, who subhired her to Hughes. When she became ill, Hughes' overseer administered medicines, bled her, and applied mustard plasters to her wrists and stomach. In court, "Moore stated that he had overseed some thirteen years and during that time he had treated all cases of sickness with all negroes under his charge that he thought he could manage and not to call in a physician unless the case was thought dangerous and that he did not consider the negro girl to be dangerously sick." Dr. Ames, however, testified on behalf of Mosely, that

within the last few years the treatment of diseases had undergone a change and that the treatment of congestive fever particularly had undergone a change in the country . . . all he could say from Moore's description was that the disease was probably congestive fever or partaking of that character, that if the disease was congestive fever Moore's treatment was injudicious that the bleeding was mischievous and that the application of the mustard was in his opinion rendered necessary in consequence of the bleeding that the effect of the bleeding if the disease was congestive fever was to produce a depression of the powers of life.

On the other hand, "if the disease was intermittent fever, then the treatment of the case by Moore was correct." Wilkinson then asked Dr. Ames "if there was not many respectable physicians in the neighborhood of Montgomery who would probably have treated the girl in the same manner that Moore treated her if the disease was congestive fever," to which Dr. Ames, over the objection of Mosely's attorney, answered that there were "respectable physicians" who would have done the same thing.[75]

While doctors often appeared to offer testimony for hire to the highest bidder, they took care in court to present themselves as truthful, authoritative observers. Dr. Luke Blackburn, a prominent Natchez physician who went on to become governor of Kentucky, admitted in court that he sometimes examined slaves for the slave trader Samuel Davis. However, he expressed anger at "having been called in as he was passing, by Davis," to examine a woman slave whom he recognized "as one that had been returned by some one to Davis who had sold her, was subject to epileptic convulsions or fits, that he Davis knew it." Although Blackburn did "not know of his own knowledge that the negro was unsound, as it is impossible to tell unless you see them with the fit upon them," he "knew the negro woman had been returned to Davis as a fitified negro. This was the second time that Davis had called on witness to pass an unsound negro. The other was a negro woman sold by Davis to Dean Snyder, diseased with pox, when Davis warranted to get sound or well in a certain time, and who was afterwards returned." Davis successfully objected to all of this testimony of Dr. Blackburn, and it was crossed out but legible in the trial transcript.[76]

Frequently, doctors gave evidence based on postmortem examinations made solely for the purpose of furthering litigation. The incidence of postmortems is noteworthy, because they were performed not in criminal cases but in civil disputes, to determine the monetary value of the slave's body at issue. Sharla Fett has singled out postmortem examinations as one of the practices that "heightened African American distrust" of physicians because it " violated slave community norms of proper behavior in healing and burial."[77] Southern doctors routinely dissected slave bodies in hospitals and medical colleges to learn about anatomy; to slaves, these operations not only "devalued and objectified African American bodies . . . [but] also violated the correct relationship with the dead established through African American rituals of burial and mourning."[78] This violation must have seemed as deep, if not deeper, when postmortems were performed not to gain medical knowledge for its own sake but to determine the outcome of a lawsuit to allocate property rights in slaves. Dissection after death was the final dishonor to a slave's body.[79]

Not only were civil trials concerning slaves one of the best opportunities Southern doctors had to dissect bodies after death, much more common than criminal autopsies, but the postmortem was in fact a prerequisite to any plaintiff's claim over a dead slave. Indeed, the Louisiana Supreme Court held that failure to perform a postmortem barred a buyer's effort to recover damages for a recently purchased slave who had died.[80] Under the Louisiana Civil Code, as well as under the common law, a buyer had to prove that a disease existed before the sale in order to recover damages, and many used postmortems to make the case for a long-standing ailment.[81] Parties and doctors also used the evidence from postmortems to show that they had given the slave good care. One owner offered testimony to show that he "gave all proper care and attention to said slave," including having "had [the slave] attended by a physician during life and [having] caused a post mortem exam to be made after death."[82]

The most chilling recitals of postmortems came in cases involving the cause of a slave's death in tort suits by owners against those who had beaten or shot their slaves. One hirer, sued for damages for beating a slave to death, brought in a doctor to perform a postmortem to prove that "whipping alone did not cause the death" of the slave Sam. Instead, the doctor explained that Sam's "head striking a root or stump in the fall . . . might possibly have produced death"; moreover, "that the boy was exhausted to a considerable extent from his exertions running and resistance." He concluded that "all contributed their proportion, and that the whipping . . . did not of itself cause the death." The judge charged the jury that "unless they believed that only the whipping caused the death . . . the plaintiff [could not] recover," and the jury found for the defendant.[83]

Beyond the stated reasons for reporting on postmortems, descriptions of dissections put slaves' bodies on display in the courtroom with vivid immediacy. While living slaves may sometimes have been exhibited in court for examination by the jury, in cases involving slaves who had died, accounts of postmortem examinations came as close as possible to such a public demonstration.[84] On one occasion, the bloody clothes of a woman slave were passed around as an exhibit.[85] Southern doctors often used slaves as medical specimens for public exhibition; postmortems allowed them to extend this display into the courtroom.[86] They did so in gory detail, as when several doctors testified about the "adhesions of [one slave's] bowels," noting that "in cutting through the adhesions of the bowels the knife grated."[87] This display after death again reaffirmed slaves' dishonor.

. . . . .

Recitations of postmortem examinations gave doctors primary control over the representation of slaves' bodies. Neither lay witnesses nor slaves themselves could make sense of the internal architecture of the dead body as doctors could. By contrast, slaves still living spoke about their own pain and illness, and both owners and doctors made decisions—whether to put a slave to work, how to treat her—based on slaves' own words. This need to rely on slaves' accounts of their own bodies made doctors in particular uncomfortably dependent on slaves.

Apprehensions that slaves were "feigning illness" imbued the writings of Southern doctors even more than those of planters. As historians of Southern medicine have shown, "suspicions of pretended illness shaped southern physicians' ideas of examination, diagnosis, and treatment of slave patients."[88] Such suspicions also shaped doctors' courtroom testimony and the legal arguments that relied on it. An important part of doctors' reading of slaves' bodies was reading for deception. Just as parties in court claimed that slaves were not really diseased but only pretending (see chapter 3), doctors gave evidence that they had "diagnosed" slaves as deceitful. One Georgia doctor testified that he had told the slave's master that she was "practicing a deception on the family . . . and treated her accordingly."[89] Indeed, antebellum Southern doctors "looked upon feigned illness among slaves as a medical problem" to be treated in that light. Because discerning deception was part of diagnosis and treatment, it "became for southern physicians another proving ground of their professional authority."[90] As one medical student observed, "slaves' complaints of sickness 'demand at the hands of the Physician a more careful investigation than those of whites,' not for reasons of pathology or physiology but because slaves' complaints almost always involved some degree of deception." Therefore, Southern-trained doctors were needed who knew how to diagnose deceit.[91] Doctors capitalized on this authority in their own transactions: one doctor, who himself sold an old woman slave as sound, told the buyer that "she complained of being sick but that she was able to do the house work."[92]

Medical "battles of the experts" in court, which presented one of the greatest challenges to doctors' professional authority, often revolved around questions of feigned illness. In the Georgia case of disputed epilepsy mentioned earlier, in which Dr. Joseph Reese "thought that [the slave] was practicing a deception . . . and treated her accordingly," another doctor contradicted him vigorously. Dr. E. C. Hood testified that he had seen the woman "lying in a stupid comatose condition with laborious respiration pupils of the eye dilated . . . [he had] little doubt but that said negro had had a fit . . ."[93]

The ex-slave Henry Bibb explained the dangers to the slave of slave-holders' fears of slaves' feigning illness: "At the time of sickness among slaves they had but very little attention. The master was to be the judge of their sickness, but never had studied the medical profession. He always pronounced a slave who said he was sick, a liar and a hypocrite; said there was nothing the matter, and he only wanted to keep from work." Because Bibb's master always suspected deceit, he treated slaves with red pepper tea, so that the slave "would rather work as long as he could stand up, than to take this dreadful medicine." Only "if it should be a very valuable slave" was a physician sent for—and physicians posed dangers of their own.[94]

Southern doctors always balanced their relationship to their "client," the master, with their relationship to the patient, the slave. But in the courtroom forum, this balancing act was doubly difficult, for several reasons. From the doctor's point of view, two new relationships were added to the doctor-patient and the doctor-client relations; first, he was now working for one side in an adversary process, and second, he was involved in a public display of expertise.

Furthermore, from the perspective of the legal system, the slave's authority as a patient was doubly threatening in a court of law. For, in court, reports of slaves' own account of their symptoms threatened a legal system based on slaves' "incompetence" as witnesses. Yet, as Walter Johnson points out, it was "a difficult project" to get "information about slaves' bodies and pasts without asking them—describing slaves' inward experience while maintaining their outward legal silence."[95] Judges accommodated this difficult project by inventing the creative excuses chronicled in chapter 2 to eliminate objections to hearsay slave testimony. Recall the legal fictions used to justify slave testimony: statements made to a doctor were *res gestae*, which doctors routinely used as a basis for their medical opinions; therefore they were presumed to be true. Thus doctors' professional authority, which depended on slaves' own statements about their well-being, rescued those statements from the usual presumption of unreliability and deception on the part of slaves. Furthermore, doctors' suspicions of slaves' deception became submerged by doctors' eagerness to be considered experts in court; doctors credentialed themselves with assurances of their professional ability to detect fakery.

At the intersection of medicine and law, slaves had an opportunity to influence the commercial transactions involving their bodies because of doctors' dependence on their own accounts of their medical conditions. In order to rid the courtroom of even the specter of slaves' agency, doctors asserted their professional authority as the highest experts on slaves' bodies. They also "portray[ed] the tendency for deception among slaves as a racial characteristic of African Americans," which helped to deny slaves' own moral reponsibility and ability to manipulate whites.[96] Always, slave buyers and sellers, as well as their witnesses in the courtroom, tried to read slaves' bodies *against* their words, branding slaves' bodies with their masters' words. In doing so, Southern whites dishonored slaves and made their bodies objects of white people's contests of honor and professional authority. For a slave's body might literally *give a white man the lie*— it might make a liar of him. This gave slaves potential power, especially power through their words, against which both buyers and sellers struggled.

Just as doctors had to rely on slaves to report their own medical conditions, they had to rely on slaves to follow their medical instructions. As Dr. Samuel Cartwright wrote in frustration, slaves could not "be depended upon to report or let their indisposition be known, until they are nearly half dead and can no longer conceal it."[97] Thus one frequent legal argument in a warranty suit was that the slave herself had brought on illness or had allowed the illness to worsen by disobeying doctor's orders. In these cases, moral concerns blurred with medical ones as witnesses expressed frustration with slaves' unruliness and unreliability. Physical illness once again came down to questions of character.

Doctors blamed slaves for eating dirt, having sex, eating fruit when ill, or for just not taking care of themselves. One Georgia doctor complained that he had considered the slave in question, who had been ill with "Typhoid Fever, complicated with dysentery," to be "one of his best *cures*" until the slave disobeyed instructions. Five days after the doctor completed treatment, "I saw him near my office eating peaches and watermelons and I rebuked him severely. It was the next day after this that I was called in again . . . The Boy had relapsed and as witness believed it was caused solely by his imprudence in eating the peaches and watermelons."[98] Another doctor complained that Simon could have been cured if "the directions of witness were strictly carried out," but instead, "the boy Simon did not take such care of himself as he should have done . . ."[99] In several cases, one party alleged that dirt eating caused the slave's disease.[100] In *Ramsey v. Blalock*, one of the seller's doctors "thought it probable [Martha] might have been affected by eating dirt . . . as she showed some signs of Dropsy which may be produced by eating dirt," but a doctor for the buyer "saw no signs of any disease caused by eating dirt."[101] One woman slave was blamed for living with her husband "as man and wife," because "[i]f she was afflicted with cancer of the womb in copious menstruation a married life (or sexual intercourse) [was] not beneficial but injurious to her."[102] As Sharla Fett has pointed out, "antebellum physicians tended to racialize the 'unruliness' of black patients" who did not follow instructions.[103] Thus arguments about the causes of a physical illness could implicate questions of slaves' immutable vice. Sellers tended to argue that slave owners were responsible to doctors for following medical instructions; buyers claimed that slaves themselves autonomously caused their illness. Yet this argument, because it depended on slave agency, could benefit the seller. Therefore, buyers had to try to suggest that the illness had a life of its own and could not be affected by either slave or master.

. . . . .

Moral and medical arguments merged in a variety of cases in which a character issue led to medical problems or was understood in medical terms—these cases represent the inverse of those discussed in the first section of this chapter, in which suits about physical problems implicated character in some way. Disputes over slaves' falling ill from running away or drinking, or about slaves' insanity, raised the problem of physical diseases with moral causes, or ailments in which the physical and moral were inseparably intertwined. In cases of drinking and insanity, medical arguments that minimized the element of moral agency tended to predominate.

Many suits arose from slaves' falling ill after running away, like John Blair's effort to win damages for the death of Hillier from "exposure."[104] In one case, the slave "was frostbit while runaway," and another "died . . . which I attributed to his having been exposed while runaway."[105] As one witness explained, "[I] should think that a negro having run away from his master and gone into the back of the woods, living in dampness, would be very likely to contract such disease as well as many others."[106] The diseases of runaway slaves could be blamed directly on their vices. In Louisiana in particular, where running away was a "redhibitory vice," tracing a causal line from running away to disease or death provided a loophole from time limits on warranties of physical soundness.

Another habit that could lead to illness, and therefore reduce a slave's value, was drinking. If the slave was a skilled worker, drinking might interfere with his or her ability to perform a skilled job, such as bricklaying, baking, or laundry.[107] At other times, "drunkenness was the cause of the disease" of which a slave died, usually a disease of the liver, or of accidents such as drowning.[108] To elicit testimony about drinking, attorneys asked witnesses how often a slave drank, whether he or she lost any time at work from drinking, and, more generally, whether a slave was "greatly addicted to intemperance and the use of spirituous liquors." For example, in one Natchez case, the buyer's lawyer submitted these interrogatories to an out-of-state witness:

> Was or was not said negro woman greatly addicted to intemperance and the use of spirituous liquors?
> Had or had not said negro woman become almost useless by the too great indulgence in drink?

Do you or do you not know that said Franklin was apprized of and knew at the time he sold said negro woman to the defendant, that she was a great drunkard?

Were you or were you not present at the sale of said woman to said deft. If yea state whether the said plaintiff did not use every art and care to conceal from the deft the fact that said woman was a drunkard?

Was or was not said negro woman greatly injured by the use of spirituous liquors?

Was it or was it not almost impossible to suppress the inclination, which said woman had for drink?

How much was said negro woman diminished in value by her indulgence to strong drink?

Was or was not the character of the said negro woman as given to the deft by the plff at the time of sale correspondent with the truth and the fact?[109]

Drinking occupied an intermediate position between physical illnesses and vices of character, such as dishonesty and running away, which were clearly moral failings on the part of slaves (and potentially masters). Among medical doctors, there was already some understanding of alcoholism as a physiological disease or mental disorder. Dr. Benjamin Rush, a prominent proponent of environmental theories of behavior and a founder of both American psychiatry and the early temperance movement, as well as Dr. Thomas Trotter, a British physician, were two of the earliest advocates of the theory that alcoholism was a disease. Rush described a process of addiction and claimed that once an "appetite" or "craving" for alcohol had become fixed in an individual, the victim was helpless to resist. Rush and other temperance advocates saw alcohol as an "enslaver," drawing rhetorical links between temperance and abolitionism.[110] Trotter took this theory even further, claiming that "in medical language, I consider drunkenness strictly speaking to be a disease; produced by a remote cause, and giving birth to actions and movements in the living body that disorder the functions of health."[111] Dr. Isaac Ray, author of the first treatise on the medical jurisprudence of insanity in the United States, encouraged the view of drunkenness as a mental illness. He argued that drunkenness was proximately caused by a pathology of the brain, which, in turn, became an "efficient cause . . . and act[ed] powerfully in maintaining this habit." The phenomena of addiction, Ray argued, "strongly remind us of some of the manifestations of moral mania," and he quoted the French writer Esquirol approvingly in suggesting that drunkenness was a first stage of madness.[112]

Despite the beginnings of a medical theory of alcoholism as a disease, most Southern doctors were so far from decrying alcoholism as to use drink in their medical practices as a restorative and a palliative. Dr. Samuel Cartwright complained that when he settled in Natchez in the 1820s, there were only a few "temperance physicians" in the vicinity. "All the rest believed in the hygienic virtues of alcoholic drinks, and taught that doctrine by precept and example." Cartwright went on to exclaim that all of the temperance doctors were living, or died of old age, whereas "every physician of Natchez and its vicinity, thirty years ago, whether practising or retired, who was in the habit of *tippling* . . . has long since been numbered with the dead!"[113] Of course, Cartwright and other temperance physicians were fighting an uphill battle in a culture in which drinking (within limits) was a way of life and even a badge of honor for Southern white men.

It should not be surprising that slaveholders were most likely to disparage the effects of drink when they were talking about slaves. Southern whites emphasized alcohol as "a powerful agent of disinhibition capable of unleashing [slaves'] violent and irrational behavior"; they portrayed an "image of drunken blacks as a rebellious, intractable population."[114] Indeed, relationship to drink was a defining feature separating whites from blacks: white men had access to drink and the drinking rituals of white honor culture; black men did not. Kenneth Greenberg has pointed out how much of the apparatus of Southern criminal law was aimed at keeping slaves and free blacks from gaming, and keeping whites from gaming with them;[115] laws against selling spirituous liquors to slaves or free blacks accomplished the same goal of dishonoring blacks by denying them access to these cultural rituals. In Adams County, a majority of criminal cases involved either gaming or selling liquor to slaves. Although such prosecutions certainly aimed to quell the sources of slave rebellion, they also disciplined slaves who tried to claim access to white honor culture, and whites who crossed the color line to help them do so.

Moral views of drinking remained strong during this period; even most educated advocates of temperance considered alcoholism to be a moral failure. Between 1830 and 1840, national temperance societies began to stress that the drunk was a moral sinner who could stop drinking if he so desired. Influenced by this emphasis, abolitionists, including ex-slaves such as Frederick Douglass, portrayed alcohol as another aspect of enslavement itself. Douglass wrote that drink was a key weapon of the enslaver: "When a slave was drunk, the slaveholder had no fear that he would plan an insurrection; no fear that he would escape to the north. It was the sober, thinking slave who was dangerous, and needed the vigilance of his master to keep him a slave."[116] Douglass painted the effects of alcohol as almost the inverse of what some slaveholders claimed.

In court, when describing slaves' drinking, witnesses tended to the more "modern" explanation of alcoholism as an addiction for which it was "impossible to suppress the inclination." This medicalization of alcoholism was in line with white Southerners' general reluctance to attribute moral qualities—even moral failings—to slaves. Indeed, in a case like *Johnson v. Wideman*, in which the judge decreed that the rule for slave character was "like master, like man," the slave Charles' drinking was blamed on the drinking of his former master, who had set a bad example and "exposed him to spirits." In other cases, masters were not expected to bear responsibility for their slaves' drinking precisely because drinking was classed as an immutable vice, habit, or disease. Drinking was also an instance of slaves' exercising agency, often breaking the law, to take part in a ritual of white male honor culture, so slaveholders may have put extra emphasis on alcoholism's medical aspects as a way to remove agency—and honor—from slaves.

· · · · ·

The merging of moral and medical took clearest shape when white Southerners claimed that black slaves were insane. The association of blackness with madness had a long past in Western culture, but proslavery ideologues gave it an ironic twist in the antebellum South. On the basis of the error-ridden census of 1840, which cataloged fewer black "lunatics" in the slave South than in the state of Maine, they argued that insanity was incompatible with slavery; the enslaved black was contented and mentally healthy, but freedom would literally drive her mad. The number of suits brought by slave buyers alleging slaves' insanity is particularly interesting, given the "consensus among those who owned and observed slaves . . . that they were much less susceptible to mental derangement than free blacks or whites," and that "the reason for this low rate of insanity among slaves . . . was their simple lifestyle."[117] Indeed, after the Civil War, it became a commonplace that "insanity among slaves was scarcely known," whereas freedmen were in a state of "mental decay."[118] Thus the claim of insanity nearly always attached to slaves who tried to attain freedom: runaway slaves.

The idea that slaves were blissfully free of mental perturbation bolstered not only the proslavery position but also the medical view that "the boundary between mental and physical illness [was] permeable and indistinct"—that madness had physical and moral roots.[119] One South Carolina judge explained the popular theory:

> We do know, from actual observation, that a defect of understanding may result from physical causes . . . Mr *Craddock* speaks of lunacy as a *disease* . . . Dr. Zimmerman, who says he visited all the hospitals in France, thought that the maniacs might be distributed into 3 classes,—the men who became so through pride, the girls through love, and the women through jealousy.

Now, admitting this conjecture to be correct, it does not prove that these diseases did not result from a defect of physical organization . . . Both the mind and body must ultimately be diseased. For a disease of the mind soon produces one of the body.[120]

The emerging discipline of psychiatry emphasized both physical and moral causes of insanity, including blows on the head and "excessive study, disappointment, grief, trouble, &c."[121] Physical causes, however, like blows to the head, were hard to avoid; moral causes could be alleviated through "moral treatment"—the creation of a proper environment, either in one of the newly established asylums or at home.[122] Thus the keepers of the new asylums focused on mental disease as "a violation of natural, that is conventional, behavior . . . related in part to immorality, vice, and filth."

The new medical jurisprudence of insanity divided insanity into the categories of idiocy and imbecility, both of which arose from "defective development of the faculties," and mania and dementia, attributable to "lesion of the faculties subsequent to their development."[123] Mania could be intellectual or affective, a disease of the will or of the morals. The idea of "moral mania," promoted by Isaac Ray and others in the medical community, was widely resisted by the courts in criminal cases, in which they preferred to attribute criminal responsibility to anyone who was capable of knowing the wrongness of his or her actions. Yet, during the antebellum period, the idea of "moral insanity" gained a considerable hold within the new psychiatric profession, and among the proponents of medical jurisprudence. The legal writer Francis Wharton, known for his treatises on evidence and criminal law, published a treatise on "mental unsoundness" in 1855, approvingly citing Ray and the French psychiatrist Pinel on "moral mania."[124]

Given these associations between mental illness and morals, it makes sense that moral failings and mental incapacity or illness should have been conflated in suits over "defective" slaves. Yet what is striking about warranty suits is the gender differential in cases about insanity. While both men and women were the subject of warranty suits by reason of insanity, most cases involving men had to do with epileptic fits, whereas a broader range of behavior caused owners to invoke the term "insane" for an enslaved woman.[125] As chapter 3 has shown, the legal tendency to portray slaves' character defects as "habits" or "addictions" had the effect of "medicalizing" slave vice, reducing moral qualities to medical ones. This tendency to treat moral questions as medical ones seems to have been strongest when the slave at issue was a woman. There was no female "Nat Turner" in the Southern lexicon. When a woman resisted or refused to work, her behavior did not conjure up the same fears in the white mind as did a rebellious black man. In court, buyers or hirers of runaway women were more likely to question their sanity or mental capacity than their character.

Historians have long noted the nineteenth-century tendency to associate women with madness, but this has been considered a largely middle-class Victorian phenomenon—neurasthenic ladies at New England spas.[126] Yet, in the slave trials, the same assumptions about mental instability suggest that gender narratives of insanity may have been even more widespread than previously realized, although their implications for black women were very different. The fact that most runaway women who became the object of warranty suits were house servants is also noteworthy. One explanation for this may be that white Southerners were trying to maintain their image of "Mammy," and rebellious behavior lay too far outside of that image. Ultimately, though, placing black women's behavior in a medical framework reinforced their *dis*honor in white Southern ideology.

On January 3, 1834, Rose Icar, a New Orleans free woman of color, bought from Anthony Abraham Suares a twenty-year-old slave, Kate.[127] Icar paid five hundred dollars in cash for her slave and, by all accounts, bought Kate for her labor, not to gain her freedom. Not one month later, Icar was in district court, suing Suares for selling her a runaway. Rose Icar's petition to the court complained that "three or four days after the said slave had been taken possession of . . . it was discovered that said Slave was crazy, and she also ran away from her new mistress . . ."

The witnesses for the plaintiff all described Kate's "craziness" in terms that raise the possibility that she was as sane as a slave could be, rationally resisting her position. Jean Dinot testified that "said Slave is not worth much. When she is asked to fetch one thing she fetches another . . . She is capable of setting fire to [a house], as she does not know what she is about . . . Witness has seen said Slave when sent by her mistress go away in quite a different direction talking to herself and gesticulating. Witness on one occasion met her going toward the Lake and asked her where she was going when she answered she did not know." On cross-examination, Dinot admitted that he had seen Kate only three times before seeing her in court, and revealed one other important fact: Kate spoke only English. Dinot did not know whether Rose Icar understood or spoke English.

Kate ran away, but she did not get far. She was caught and brought to the Police Jail of Jefferson, a neighboring parish. She managed to frustrate her jailor as well; she told him that she belonged to a Dr. Sealden. He asked where this doctor lived, and she told him, "Down there, down that Street." He was unable to extract any other information from her and came to the conclusion that "said slave is not of sound mind." The sheriff testified that he had seen Kate "act as a crazy person—she holloed danced

all night and could hardly answer when spoken to"; although he threatened her often to be quiet, "the threats availed nothing," which led him
to "the opinion that said Kate was crazy."

Two other witnesses reached the same conclusion. One based his diagnosis on the fact that "[s]he is of no use in a house—when her mistress
told her to do one thing she did another . . . ," although he also noted
that Rose Icar spoke only a few words of English. On cross-examination,
the witness explained that "when the Plaintiff told the slave Kate to do
any work she spoke to her in English in the best manner she could." He
never saw Kate do any work; in fact, "Witness was present when Plaintiff
told said slave to go and wash her clothes. She took her clothes and went
out of the House and ran away."

By contrast, the only defense witness told the court that when Rose Icar
had "informed [him] that Kate had absconded . . . [he] observed to her
that inasmuch as the Slave was a stranger and unacquainted with the city,
it was probable that she had lost her way, and that no doubt she had been
taken up and put in jail." When he suggested that Kate might be found
at the Jefferson Parish jail, Icar told him that it was up to Mr. Suares to
hunt for her, but "in none of the conversations which Witness had with
the Plaintiff in relation to this Slave, did she allege the slave to be crazy;
that during the whole time the Slave was under the superintendence of
the Witness, he observed nothing in her behaviour to induce him to believe that she laboured under any . . . derangement."

The trial court judge granted Icar a rescission of the sale on the ground
that Kate was a habitual runaway. The judge applied the January 20,
1834, act of the legislature which created the presumption that a newly
imported slave who ran away within two months after sale had had the
redhibitory vice of running away at the time of the sale. Furthermore, the
judge ruled that "the evidence of a personal inspection of the Slave satis-
f[ies] the Court that the Slave is . . . destitute of mental capacity . . ."
Suares appealed on the ground that neither Kate's running away nor her
craziness was sufficiently established; "the utmost that can be inferred
from the testimony is that she was rather stupid: this is an apparent defect,
if a redhibitory defect at all . . ." Suares also complained that the judge
erred in basing his judgment on his own impression of the slave. However,
the Supreme Court was "satisfied from the evidence in the record, independently of the impression made on the mind of the judge, by personal
inspection, that the slave in question was wholly, and perhaps worse than
useless."[128]

Kate acted as though she did not understand the English of her French
colored mistress, disobeyed her orders, avoided work, tried to escape, and
lied to her jailers. This behavior convinced her mistress and the witnesses
for the plaintiff, as well as the judge, that Kate was crazy. If we compare

her behavior to that of the runaway male slaves who came before trial courts in these cases, it is hard to distinguish what made her crazy and them vicious. It could well be that Kate would be judged mentally ill by the standards of modern psychiatry, yet if Kate had been a man, her refusal to take orders and her efforts to escape might have been seen as rebelliousness or viciousness; her owners would have feared violence or insurrection. Her drinking might have been emphasized more as evidence of intractable vice. But, as she was a woman, "moral qualities" vices were not seen as applicable to her; her actions did not instill a fear of violent rebellion. Insubordination must be lunacy.

Other cases involving "craziness" or "idiocy" of female slaves bear many similarities to cases in which male slaves were accused of vice. For example, witnesses for the buyer of the slave Melly testified that she whistled after answering any question put to her by a white person; that she was "much whipmarked and . . . did not seem to enjoy senses enough for common purposes"; and that she seemed to be an "imbecile." However, defense witnesses found Melly to have "common sense enough for a field hand"; "she did like any other person she did her work well and obeyed well orders"; and they commented that, although Melly talked to herself, "white persons are more apt to speak to themselves than negroes," so that could hardly be a sign of idiocy![129] The Louisiana court, in ruling that idiocy was an "apparent" defect, one that should be readily visible to the buyer at the time of sale, vented their frustration with deciding questions of slaves' minds and morals: "It is very difficult, if not nearly impossible, to fix a standard of intellect by which slaves are to be judged."[130]

In another Louisiana case, *Buhler v. McHatton*, the buyer, Buhler, tried to have the sale set aside on two counts: first, "because said Jane has proved entirely useless as a cook"; and second, "because she is *addicted to madness* . . . [emphasis added]." Buhler tried to show Jane's insanity with evidence of her burning up her clothes, an "act[] utterly irreconcilable with the idea of deception"; refusing to eat meat on Friday or Saturday; and "frequent paroxysms of weeping, superstition, and violence." Witnesses ascribed Jane's odd behavior to "religious enthusiasm and grief at being separated from her children." Buhler characterized her "weeping and lamenting a separation of children" as "superstitious monomania." The jury, unimpressed, found for the seller, McHatton. Justice Campbell, in affirming the lower court judgment, noted that Jane's behavior "did not attract particular attention, and was not noticed for a month or more," and attributed it to her "religious scruples."[131]

One attorney's brief gave a particularly revealing soliloquy on the impossibility of imagining an enslaved woman's taking moral action or having moral dilemmas. In *Walker v. Hays*, the woman sued upon had drowned herself and her child soon after being sold. The seller's witness, J. D. Hair, called Agnes "a girl of unusual good sense," and the jury gave a judgment for the seller. On appeal, the buyer's attorney argued that, by itself, the fact that Agnes committed suicide proved that she was "addicted to madness." He went on to consider all the rational reasons a person might have for committing suicide, and concluded that none of them could apply to an enslaved woman:

> When it is done to avoid disgrace by the man sensitive about his honor, or in accordance with the prevailing custom of a people, whose minds are darkened by superstition or when it is done from motives of patriotism to retrieve a nation's honor, or rescue it from ruin, or in despair of the liberties of one's country, or to avoid a more cruel fate, in a death of torture, as illustrated by the heroes of antiquity, rendered immortal by their wisdom and their valor; it is not for a moment contended that it proceeds from insanity.
>
> But how different all these classes of suicide from the one for our consideration: here is a poor slave with no patriotic designs or interests to subserve, no national custom to conform to, no disgrace to avoid, no terrible punishment to escape, buries herself and helpless child in a common grave . . . [132]

In other words, an enslaved woman could have no *honor*: no nation, no tradition, no courage. The only possible reason she could have for taking her life was insanity.

The medicalization of women slaves' rebellious character as insanity helped white Southerners to accommodate violations of their image of the female house servant as a docile nurse to white children. Yet it is well to remember that medical treatment for insane slaves did not necessarily mean kind treatment. Because of the omnipresent fear of slaves' feigning insanity, most owners resorted to whipping as a first therapy.[133] Dr. Cartwright's treatments for the mental diseases of running away and rascality included whipping and hard labor. Moreover, antebellum physicians, conceiving of insanity as *at once* a physical illness and an affliction having moral roots, it required both heroic physical treatments—bleeding, cupping, venesection—and moral treatment, which for slaves probably meant discipline. An 1847 article recommending the medical (as opposed to moral) treatment of insanity nevertheless noted disapprovingly that bleeding and "depletion" of the stomach with emetics were still common treatments for insanity, and instead suggested opium, morphine, laudanum, Dover's Powder, and a combination of conium and iron.[134]

Whereas for whites moral treatment in early-nineteenth-century asylums generally meant removal from the community, silence, and the absence of stimulating agents, and has understandably been seen by historians of psychiatry as an improvement in the treatment of madness, moral treatment for slaves might include "whipping, jail, or the trading block."[135] The English traveler Fanny Kemble told the tale of Sarah, a slave on Pierce Butler's Georgia plantation believed to be insane, who was recaptured after running away, "tied up by the arms, and heavy logs fastened to her feet, and was severely flogged."[136] The planter S. A. Townes wrote in 1835 that he had sold a slave who was "nearly an idiot" for six hundred dollars, "an excellent price for her."[137] Perhaps, then, it is not surprising that the best documentation we have of insanity in slaves is in breach of warranty trial records.

·   ·   ·   ·   ·

The conflation of physical, mental, and moral disorders in slaves meant that even ordinary warranty suits over slaves' physical illness brought black character into question. On the one hand, a slave's moral qualities and behavior could contribute to a physical illness, so that arguments about the slave's agency became entangled with arguments about new and old owners' responsibility for the slave's condition. On the other hand, an enslaved woman's rebellious behavior was often attributed to mental illness, which white Southerners believed to have both physical causes and moral roots. All of these crossovers between the physical and moral worlds imbued the reading of slaves' bodies with meaning.

The difficulty of "reading a slave's body against her/his word" brought into question the character of the white parties in the courtroom whose authority depended on their ability to interpret slaves' bodies.[138] Doctors, in particular, sought to become trial experts during this period. Yet at the same time that this new medical jurisprudence lent authority to physicians, the interpenetration of law and medicine increased the opportunity for slaves to influence the law by feigning illness or by getting their own words into testimony. Experts all tried to read slaves' bodies in court precisely because it was dangerous for slaves to speak for themselves.

EPILOGUE

THE first Union warships traveled up the Mississippi River to Natchez in mid-May 1862. On May 13, the mayor of Natchez let the commander of the USS *Iroquois* know that Union forces would face no resistance from local residents. Shots were fired on just one day in September, killing two civilians and one Union soldier. But Natchez was not occupied by the U.S. Army until after the fall of Vicksburg, in the summer of 1863. As soon as the Union forces arrived in town, they were "overwhelmed by a stampede of black refugees from the countryside," many of whom "had been on the run since the summer of 1862."[1] Some of these newly free people, known as "contraband," joined the armed forces in Vicksburg and were organized into "colored regiments"; others remained on plantations held by their former owners or abandoned and leased to Northerners, and worked for low wages. Those who stayed on plantations shocked their former owners with their new attitudes: William Mercer made a list in June of 1865 of "adult Negroes who have remained on the plantations," dividing them into columns of "perfectly faithful," "comparatively faithful," and "behaved badly, outrageously." About half fell into the last category. William Minor, a Union loyalist, despaired that his ex-slaves "are practically free, going and coming and working when they please and as they please. They destroy everything on the plantation—In one night lost 30 hogs. They ride the mules off at all times."[2] The world was changing, and relations among whites and blacks would never be the same.

Institutions changed as well, and courts were no exception. But change came slowly. The Adams Circuit Court closed its doors in 1863 and re-opened only in 1866, by which time the slaves of Adams County had gained their freedom. In the years after the Civil War, Deep Southern courts once again convened to hear the lawsuits that had been held over from before the war, as well as new lawsuits. Some state supreme courts were still dealing with the questions of breach of warranty for slave property well into the 1870s. Certain of these cases involved decade-old disputes sitting in limbo on court dockets while the courts were closed. In other instances, slave sellers and owners sued on notes given for the purchase or hire of a slave, and the debtor defended the suit on the grounds of breach of warranty of title, claiming that he had been sold a slave warranted to be "a slave for life," and that this had clearly not turned out to be the case.

In May 1865, Eliza Huntington sued James Brown in New Orleans to recover the price of an unsound slave, arguing that "the right of action arose prior to the adoption of the present Constitution [in which contracts for the sale of persons were illegal]," and its object was "not to assert the right of property in man, but to recover a sum of money . . ."[3] Mrs. Huntington won her suit, and similar cases were heard and won in the courts of the Southern states through the mid-1870s. Indeed, many breach of warranty and hire disputes were decided with no mention of the fact that slavery had ended in the interim between transaction and legal recovery.[4] In other cases, the transactions had taken place between January 1, 1863, the day of the Emancipation Proclamation, and the end of the war; the debtor sought to be relieved from his debt by arguing a "failure of consideration" because the slaves were already free in 1863 and 1864. Southern courts unanimously rejected that argument, declaring that the Emancipation Proclamation did not free the slaves.[5]

However, in some cases the litigants directly raised, not the timing, but the *fact* of freedom, seeking to evade financial responsibility for their last transactions in the twilight of slavery. There were two approaches to these cases, as Andrew Kull has shown.[6] Reconstruction constitutional conventions in several Southern states, including Louisiana and South Carolina, added constitutional provisions regarding the unenforceability of contracts for "slave consideration." These Republican conventions included many black delegates, some of them former slaves themselves. They saw the enforcement of notes given for "slave consideration" as an affirmation of the legality of slavery. As Robert DeLarge, a black delegate to the South Carolina convention, declared during debate, "I am not willing to admit that either myself or my fellow being ever was property . . . Let us, by our votes, deny that any human being was ever a chattel or a slave."[7] Others recoiled at the thought of courts in a free nation still handling matters involving human property. William J. Whipper asserted that he was "not willing that the machinery of our Courts should be used for the purpose of wringing the bone from the two dogs."[8] In nullifying contracts for the sale of slaves, these delegates sought both to keep courts from ever again handling legal matters involving human property and to affirm that humans, under natural law, could never have *been* property.

These constitutional provisions did not hold up in court. All of the state courts save Louisiana that ruled on this question, as well as the United States Supreme Court, held that the provisions contravened the Contracts Clause, "impairing the obligation of contract."[9] They dismissed the contract law arguments about breach of warranty of title, noting that such clauses had never been meant to be a guarantee of a slave's future status.[10] And they concluded that there was no justice in nullifying the debts of certain slaveholders, indeed, as one black delegate to the South Carolina constitutional convention had put it, to "benefit a class, the buyers," in "the last dying throes of the slaveholder." Another South Carolina delegate explained, "[T]hose who are indebted for slaves were stronger props in the rebellion than those who felt slavery insecure, and sold out." To nullify their debts was only to aid the last white Southerners to give up on slavery.[11]

Yet the impassioned arguments in Reconstruction conventions about natural law and the best way to free the legal system from the taint of slavery did not ultimately carry the day in the highest courts. What ultimately decided the courts was "a determination that the public interest in predictable rules governing commercial transactions outweighed the distaste many citizens might feel to see the disputes of former slaveowners adjudicated in the courts of a free nation."[12] The desire to keep contract and property rules free of human considerations remained powerful. And so these cases continued to be heard, and decided, for a full decade after the end of legal slavery.

.   .   .   .   .

While courts continued to decide disputes involving people as objects of commerce, other legal institutions had developed in the years after the Civil War. Most unsettling to life as it had been led, there was now a federal presence in the South, in the form of the Freedmen's Bureau and a variety of other federal agencies. Through these agencies, Adams County ex-slaves had their first opportunity to make claims on the government and to make their voices heard in legal proceedings. What they said did not please their former masters. In proceedings before the United States Claims Commission and the Court of Claims, both ex-slaves and free blacks proclaimed their own wartime loyalty to the cause of freedom and cast aspersions on the claims of their former owners to have supported the Union. Of course, in order to succeed in a claim before the commission, one had to prove one's loyalty, so the declarations of ex-slaves on one another's behalf should be recognized as instrumental arguments for the financial advantage of one of their own, as any legal argument would be. Yet the language these former slaves used to explain that all people of color supported the Union and desired their freedom made abundantly clear that they did not fit into the hopeful picture their masters had painted of a people content in bondage.

How did it come to be that ex-slaves were in a position to own property that could be confiscated by the Union Army? Some of them had hired their own time during slavery, working for wages or running a small business, and paying their masters a portion of their earnings.[13] Others had gained their freedom at some point in 1863 and had been able, through cleverness and hard work, to acquire property quickly. Henry Anderson, for example, had belonged to Dr. Luke Blackburn but had kept a wood yard and "paid his master so much for his time." During the war, Anderson continued cutting wood and also picked up cotton and wood floating in the river and sold it. Unfortunately, all of his wood and two bales of cotton were confiscated by the Union Army, and Anderson sought to be reimbursed for this property.[14]

Claims commissioners interviewed a number of witnesses to prove Anderson's loyalty. The ex-slave Gallian Wickliff, testifying on Anderson's behalf, explained that Anderson was "in favor of the people that gave him his freedom as a matter of course. He would have been a mighty curious man if he hadn't have been."[15] Similarly, William Chase, a witness for the ex-slave John Holdman, who had had two mules seized by the Union Army, declared, "I do not know as I can call to mind a black man that was disloyal."[16] William Lynch, who went on to become a member of the state legislature during Reconstruction, explained that free blacks supported the cause of the slaves as well: "The truth is that I know of no colored man in this town whether he was free or not whose sympathies was not with the United States . . . [the free black] was in full sympathy with the cause of his race . . ."[17] In Claims Commission testimony, ex-slaves also avoided the kind of ritual declarations of gratitude to kind masters that routinely show up in the interviews done by WPA workers decades later. As William Hardin, a slave who became a Union soldier, replied when asked by the commissioners whether he was in debt to his former master, "No Sir it ought to be the other way."[18]

In their testimony, former slaves made clear why white Southerners might have been misled as to where their loyalties lay. Several made reference to the necessity for blacks, slave or free, to hide their pro-Union sentiments for fear of lynching. Littleton Barber, who had managed to save enough cash while a slave of Waller Irwin to purchase a mule, escaped to Union territory in July 1863; the army confiscated his mule. Barber explained that although he supported the Union cause, he "took good care that no white persons heard me say anything, Col. Farrar hung too many men who just said that they were for the union." When alone, he and other blacks discussed freedom and concluded that the only thing they could do was "watch & pray."[19] Vinson Brady, an ex-slave who went into the Union Army also mentioned that the "Rebels" hanged "colored men" who expressed Union sentiments.[20]

When asked to testify on behalf of their former masters regarding loyalty to the Union cause, many ex-slaves subtly undermined their former masters' claims. Katherine S. Minor of the Oakland plantation, a member of the far-flung, wealthy Minor-Surget clan, sought to recover for large amounts of personal property confiscated by the Union Army when they occupied her plantation.[21] Although numerous white witnesses, many of them prominent members of the Natchez aristocracy, testified on her behalf, her former slaves contradicted them. Most of them did not directly declare that Mrs. Minor was disloyal to the Union, but simply reported facts that left no other inference possible. Polly Bell, a "colored woman," testified that Mrs. Minor had "shirts, caps and socks made for the Confederate Army," and Dennis Bell, who had been Mrs. Minor's slave coachman, "swears that she sent socks and cotton bats to the Confederate hospital." Bell, whom Minor's lawyer tried to dismiss as "an exceedingly bad negro," also remembered Minor's saying "that she hoped the Confederacy would succeed and said the Colored People would never be free." Although a few former slaves still living on the plantation testified on Minor's behalf, most of the former slaves questioned gave such damning testimony that Minor's lawyer felt compelled to point out, "[T]his testimony comes almost altogether from persons who by their station in society would not be likely to know much about Mrs Minors political opinions . . ." Edward Fletcher, the dining-room servant of Henry Chotard, another prominent nabob, claimed that Katherine Minor used to rejoice over Confederate victories.[22]

Lee Scott, one of Minor's former slaves, gave responses to questioning that were typical of this undermining strategy. When the commissioner asked him, "Which side was Mrs Minor on?" he answered, "That is hard for me to tell," but went on to recount that when the Union forces arrived, "She said they were coming to take and work us to death and put us to work harder than they did: and take us to Liberia or some other country, and work us to death." The commissioner asked, "What did she say about the Yankees: that they were cruel or kind people?" Scott answered, "She said they were cruel and would take all us colored under strap and carry us off to Liberia, that they were tight, but we would find the Yankees a little tighter." That was saying quite a bit apparently, because according to Scott, "Mrs Minor was pretty tight; she was a very close mistress: there were better mistresses than her." The commissioner asked Scott to be more specific: "Didn't she give you privileges of a church: didn't she have a church on her place?" Scott answered, "No sir, and whenever she catched us a singing of a hymn—" at which point, the commissioner decided it would be best to go on to another subject.[23]

Even Andrew Brown, the sawmill owner, so popular with Adams Country jurymen many years before, did not fare so well with his ex-slaves. After his death, his heirs attempted to recover the value of confiscated property from the Claims Commission. They appealed the denial of his claim to the U.S. Court of Claims, where extensive hearings were held. A number of proven Union supporters, white men all, were asked to testify about Brown's loyalties. All of them stated that Brown had been a Union man before secession, but avoided, or claimed to have no opinion on, the question of whether he took up the Confederate cause after secession. Brown's heirs' claim was denied, largely on the basis of ex-slaves' testimony. The claims commissioner interviewed thirteen men and women of color with regard to Andrew Brown's loyalty to the Union, and their testimony was unequivocal. Richard Sullivan, a cabinetmaker who had bought lumber from Brown's mill, averred that "after the War began Brown was a Rebel . . . at the time the federal troops surrounded Vicksburg he damned the Federal government in my presence." Burr Louis, who had been Brown's slave and a sawyer in his mill, joined the Union Army as soon as federal troops took Natchez. Louis told the commission that Brown had sent lumber to the Confederate Army to build barracks and that he had "frequently heard Andrew Brown curse the Damn Yankees and talk in favor of the Rebels." Another ex-slave, Anderson Thomas, had heard Brown say that "the North could not whip the South and that he was with the South." Charles Henderson, who had been owned by Brown, remembered that Brown had sent clothing and provisions to "the Rebels" and had sailed a boat in a pro-Confederate procession. Numerous other ex-slaves remembered the same procession and the Confederate flag above Brown's mill, both of which several white witnesses had trouble recalling. With no mention of the race of the witnesses, the commissioner reported to the Court of Claims that he was satisfied by this testimony "on the question of loyalty"; and saw no reason to take additional testimony of witnesses suggested by Brown's heirs. All such interviews could prove was that Brown "would say one thing to some people and one thing to others."[24]

The jurists who devised the bans on courtroom testimony of people of color would have felt entirely justified in their silencing efforts had they survived to see what formerly enslaved people said when finally given the opportunity to have their voices heard in a legal proceeding. As soon as they had the chance, the ex-slaves of Adams County seized the opportunity to make claims on the federal government, to let it be known which side they were on, and to subvert the claims of their former owners.

. . . . .

After the war, neither African American nor white Southerners ever had the same relationship to the market, nor indeed to the culture of honor, as they had had in slavery years. But the law retained its double character as an instrument of commerce that erased the humanity of its subjects, and as an arena for contest and resistance by those who insisted on their subjectivity. Race did not lose its salience to American society, and "doubleness" remained an important strategy for blacks trying to cope with that society into the twentieth century. As we reckon with the legacy of legal slavery, of persons as property, we should remember that law can both reflect us back to ourselves and help to shape our future. Because the law has many makers, it will only be as good as we are.

APPENDIX

NOTE ON SOURCES AND METHODS

THIS study is based on three databases of information from trial court records and other local records. The first database consists of 177 trials in Adams Superior Court (before 1832) and Adams Circuit Court (after 1832) involving slaves, drawn from a sample of 10,317 out of approximately 30,000 causes of action filed between 1798 and 1860. Typically, case files included a complaint, subpoenas for witnesses, and a warrant for the defendant. Only about 4 percent of these causes of action ended in a trial; most were undefended debt actions. If the case went to trial, the file also included transcripts of testimony, depositions, attorneys' motions, jury instructions, and, at times, even notes made by the judge or by an attorney. The cases were also cross-referenced with the Minute Books of the Circuit Court, in which jury lists were kept. The handwritten documents were tied and stored in metal drawers, in approximate chronological order. Within drawers, the files were not arranged in any particular order. I sampled every third drawer for the years 1798 to 1850, and every drawer for the years 1851 to 1860. After I had completed my research, graduate students under the supervision of Ronald L. F. Davis began cataloging the trial records; some of them are now stored in cardboard boxes according to a different numbering system. After comparing our tallies in January 1995, I believe there is reason to take their case counts with caution, because of the inadequacy of the categories they employed to classify cases.

I included the following information in the database for each case: case number, case name, date, type of case (e.g., warranty-illness, or assault-shooting), outcome of case, plaintiff's role (owner, buyer, seller, hirer), whether a trader was involved, the amount in controversy, and the name, gender, age, and skill or defect of the slave involved, if noted in the document. The sources for the Adams County "cases" database are the Adams Circuit Court Records at the Historic Natchez Foundation, Natchez, Mississippi.

The second database consists of 1,098 participants in the Adams County trials, including plaintiffs, defendants, witnesses, lawyers, and jurors. Jurors' names derive from jury lists in the Minute Books of the Adams Circuit Court, at the Historic Natchez Foundation, Natchez, Mississippi. All other names were found in the trial records themselves. For 364 of these people, I was able to locate wealth and occupational information. The sources for this data are the personal and land tax rolls for

Adams County, 1802–61, and the manuscript census records for 1830, 1840, 1850, and 1860. The database includes the following information: the year in which the property was assessed or the census taken; the participant's role in the case in which he or she appeared, or multiple roles in more than one case; the number of slaves owned; acres owned in Adams County; town lots owned in Natchez; total value of Adams County landholding; and occupation, if available.

A number of people in the database have several entries because I obtained information from more than one census or tax year; the full database includes 749 entries for 364 individuals. In order to obtain correlations between information contained in the cases table and information contained in the people table, I combined them using "linking tables" for plaintiffs, defendants, witnesses, jurors, and lawyers that linked case numbers to the ID numbers for the participants in each case. The linking tables included all 1,098 participants in the cases. Before linking the tables, I created a second "people" table, which contained only one entry per person, by extrapolating the value for each person closest to the year or years he participated in a trial. For example, Frederick A. W. Davis has four entries in the "people" table, for 1850, 1852, 1857, and 1858. He was a defendant in one 1853 trial. Davis had 8 slaves in 1852 and 9 in 1858; in 1853, therefore, he probably had 8. In 1850, his town lot was worth $4,000, and in 1857, it was worth $7,000; by extrapolation, it was worth about $5,300 in 1853. Then I merged this new single-value table with the linking tables and the case tables. With statistician Shulamith Gross, I ran a variety of two-by-two regressions in order to isolate those factors which correlated strongly with outcomes for plaintiff or defendant.

The final database consists of information from 503 cases involving slaves in state supreme courts. The sources for the database are the published appellate reports of state supreme courts, as well as the trial records of the state supreme courts, at the Departments of Archives and History for Alabama, Georgia, Mississippi, and South Carolina, as well as the Special Collections Archives of the University of New Orleans. This database includes information on the type of case, the plaintiff's role, the outcome at trial, the outcome on appeal, the amount in controversy, and the name, gender, age, and skill or defect of the slave involved.

The five states vary in the quality of their record keeping. In Louisiana, nearly all of the trial records of the state supreme court remain in the magnificent collection at the University of New Orleans. Only those cases tried at Opelousas have been lost. Louisiana records contain a report of oral testimony, recorded by the trial judge, as well as all motions and briefs on appeal. South Carolina, at the opposite extreme, retains only scattered supreme court records, with none before 1824 or after 1857. The remaining records include a report of oral testimony by the judge and summaries of the briefs on appeal. Quite often the published appellate opinion included much of this report as a "statement of the facts." Thus it is possible to learn a fair amount about South Carolina trials from the published reports. Similarly, in Georgia, where a good number of the trial records survive, appellate opinions reprint much of the trial report. In Georgia, Mississippi, and Alabama, about half of the trial records survived. In Alabama, these were copied into large Minute Books of the Supreme Court, which are uncataloged and shelved at random in the archives. In all, I obtained 111 trial records from Alabama, Georgia, Mississippi, and South Carolina, and 74 from Louisiana. In Louisiana, because of the great volume of cases, I reviewed only the trials that directly involved slave character, and relied on Judith Kelleher Schafer's exhaustive study for the remainder. See Schafer, *Slavery, Civil Law, and the Supreme Court of Louisiana.*

Because of the size of these databases, they are not reproduced here. However, the "Adams County cases" table, the "Adams County people" table, and the "five-state cases" table are all available on my website: www.usc.edu/dept/law-lib/agross/.

The following tables are derived from the information in the three databases discussed above.

TABLE 1
Types of Cases

	% of 5-State Sample (N =503)	% Verdict for P	% of Adams County Sample (N = 177)	% Verdict for P
Warranty	66	62	53	51
Hire	16	58	10	69
Replevin	4	71	32	43
Tort	12	55	4	50
Total	98	61	99	50

TABLE 2
Types of Warranty Cases

	% of 5-State Sample (N = 330)	% Verdict for Buyer (at Trial)	% of Adams County Sample (N = 92)	% Verdict for Buyer
Illness	44	60	68	51
Death	25	63	20	78
Runaway	18	54	5	50
Insanity	3	60	1	0
Other bad character	3	44	0	0
Idiocy	3	64	0	0
Skills	3	63	0	0
Drinking	1	100	0	0
Total	100	60	94	56

Note: This table underestimates the incidence of vices of character, drinking, insanity, and runaway slaves, because if the slave had one of these "defects," and also died or fell ill, the case was classified as "death" or "illness."

TABLE 3
Slave Characteristics

	5-State Sample (N = 394)	Adams County Sample (N = 151)
Total male slaves	58%	55%
Total female slaves	42%	45%
Skilled male slaves (as % of all male slaves)	17%	2%
Skilled female slaves (as % of all female slaves)	17%	6%
Average age—male slaves	25	24
Average age—female slaves	23	21

Note: In the Adams County sample, there were 68 cases (38%) in which no slave characteristics were noted save gender.

TABLE 4
Slaveholding of Parties in Court

	Number of Slaves Held %					
	0	1–5	6–10	11–20	21–50	50+
Plaintiffs (N = 61)	0	34	18	18	16	13
Def'ts (N = 60)	10	27	18	18	5	22
Jurors (N = 124)	23	48	10	10	6	2
Witnesses (N = 107)	25	43	12	7	9	4
Adams County (1860 Census, N = 1,083 families)	36	28	11 (6–9 slaves)	8 (10–19)	8 (20–49)	8 (50+)

TABLE 5
Outcome of Warranty Cases at Trial and on Appeal, by State

	% Verdict for Buyer at Trial	% Verdict for Buyer on Appeal
Alabama (N = 36)	55	45
Georgia (N = 31)	57	54
Louisiana (N = 195)	62	52
Mississippi (N = 22)	65	65
South Carolina (N = 46)	60	40
Total (N = 324)	60	51

TABLE 6
Reversals by High Court—5-State Sample (%)

	Affirmed	Reversed	Total
Warranty (N = 324)			
Buyer wins at trial	38	22	60
Seller wins at trial	27	12	39
Total	66	34	100
Hire (N = 61)			
Owner wins at trial	28	26	54
Hirer wins at trial	20	26	46
Total	48	52	100
Tort (N = 50)			
Owner wins at trial	34	18	52
Def't wins at trial	20	28	48
Total	54	46	100
All cases (N = 469)	62	38	100

TABLE 7
Outcomes at Trial in Adams County **Warranty Cases**

	# of Warranty Suits	% Verdict for Buyer
1800s	4	100 (N = 1)
1810s	6	50 (N = 4)
1820s	15	58 (N = 12)
1830s	36	45 (N = 33)
1840s	6	66 (N = 6)
1850s	21	77 (N = 17)
1860s	2	0 (N = 1)
Total	92	54 (N = 74)

Note: Settlements counted as plaintiffs' verdicts; abatements, nonsuits, and dismissals as defendants' verdicts. In some cases, incomplete records made the verdict impossible to determine; therefore, percentages in the right-hand column are sometimes based on a smaller number of cases, indicated in parentheses, than the total number of warranty suits listed in the left-hand column.

TABLE 8
Outcomes at Trial in All Adams County Cases

	# of Cases	% Verdict for Plaintiff
1800s	18	100 (N = 7)
1810s	12	60 (N = 10)
1820s	27	48 (N = 25)
1830s	54	37 (N = 46)
1840s	22	43 (N = 21)
1850s	77	59 (N = 37)
1860s	4	66 (N = 3)
Total	177	50 (N = 149)

Note: See note to table 7.

TABLE 9
Verdict by Plaintiff's Slaveholding (% of All Cases)

	Number of Slaves Held by Plaintiff (N = 50 Plaintiffs)				
	1–5	6–10	11–50	51+	Total
For P	20	12	14	0	46
Against P	16	6	20	12	54
Total	36	18	34	12	100

Note: The Fisher's Exact (2-Tail) Test for independence gave a result of 0.052, which shows an inverse correlation between verdict for plaintiff and plaintiff's slaveholding.

A logistic regression analysis of verdict for plaintiff by plaintiff's slaveholding used the category "RICH" = 51+ slaves, or landholding >400 acres or >4 town lots. The regression found RICH P to be highly associated with verdict. The odds for the plaintiff to win were 2.5 times better if the plaintiff was not in the category "RICH" than if he was. P-value = 0.1261 because of the small sample size of plaintiffs with wealth information available.

TABLE 10

Verdict by Amount in Controversy (% of All Cases)

	Amount in Controversy (N = 111 cases)				
	< $200	$200–$600	$600–$1,000	$1,000–$1,400	Total
For P	17	19	10	9	55
Against P	6	14	9	15	44
Total	23	33	19	24	99

Note: Fisher's Exact (2-Tail) Test for independence gave a result of 0.072, showing a strong association between verdict and amount in controversy.

A logistic regression analysis of VERDICT— P with AMTGRP (amount in controversy grouped into the above categories) showed verdict to be highly associated with the amount in controversy. The odds for P decreased by 1.001 per $400 increase in the amount (p-value = 0.01).

Other variables (DECADE, SLAVE GENDER, SLAVE AGE, JURORS' SLAVEHOLDING, WITNESSES' SLAVEHOLDING, and DEFENDANT'S SLAVEHOLDING) were not found to be significant factors in explaining odds for success of plaintiff vs. defendant. The only significant factors affecting the odds of a verdict for the plaintiff were plaintiff's slaveholding/wealth and amount in controversy, which were both inversely related.

TABLE 11

Amount in Controversy by Plaintiff's Slaveholding (% of All Cases; N = 55)

	Number of Slaves Held by Plaintiff				
	1–5	6–10	11–50	51+	Total
< $200	15	2	11	0	27
$200–$600	11	5	7	2	25
$600–$1,000	5	7	5	4	22
$1,000–$1,400	5	4	11	5	25
Total	36	18	34	11	99

Note: Because the sample size of cases in which both the amount in controversy and the plaintiff's slaveholding was small, we were unable to achieve significant results using a chi-square or Fisher exact test. However, a Spearman's correlation gave an ordered correlation of 28.3%, showing that plaintiff's slaveholding and amount in controversy are positively correlated. It is possible to say with 95% confidence that the correlation is between 3.5% and 53%.

NOTES

ADAH   Alabama Department of Archives and History, Montgomery, Alabama

CAH-UTA   Natchez Trace Collection in the George W. Littlefield Southern History Collections, Center for American History, University of Texas at Austin

GDAH   Georgia Department of Archives and History, Atlanta, Georgia

HCEA   High Court of Errors and Appeals Records, Record Group 32

HNF   Historic Natchez Foundation, Natchez, Mississippi

LSU   Hill Memorial Library, Louisiana State University, Baton Rouge, Louisiana

MDAH   Mississippi Department of Archives and History, Jackson, Mississippi

SCA-UNO   Supreme Court Archives, Earl K. Long Library, University of New Orleans, Louisiana

SCDAH   South Carolina Department of Archives and History, Columbia, South Carolina

INTRODUCTION

1. Thomas R. R. Cobb, *An Inquiry into the Law of Negro Slavery in the United States of America* (1858; reprint, New York: Negro Universities Press, 1968), 83. Cobb's treatise on slavery was a polemic defense of the institution. For more on Cobb, see William B. McCash, *Thomas R. R. Cobb (1823–1862): The Making of a Southern Nationalist* (Macon, Ga.: Mercer University Press, 1983).

2. Thomas D. Morris, *Southern Slavery and the Law, 1619–1860* (Chapel Hill: University of North Carolina Press, 1996). See also J. Thomas Wren, "A Two-Fold Character: The Slave as Person and Property," *Southern Studies* 24 (Winter 1985): 417–31.

3. A. Leon Higginbotham Jr. and Barbara K. Kopytoff, "Property First, Humanity Second: The Recognition of the Slave's Human Nature in Virginia Civil Law," *Ohio State Law Journal* 50 (1989): 511–40; Andrew Fede, *People without Rights: An Interpretation of the Fundamentals of the Law of Slavery in the U.S. South* (New York: Garland Publishing, 1992); Jenny Bourne Wahl, *The Bondsman's Burden: An Economic Analysis of the Common Law of Southern Slavery* (New York: Cambridge University Press, 1998). These scholars write against a tradition of studies of criminal law that sometimes seemed to justify the Southern legal system by showing the ways in which slaves as criminal defendants were given procedural rights, as well as those writers who have seen Southern judges as ambivalent about slavery or even antislavery. See especially A. E. Keir Nash, "A More Equitable Past? Southern Supreme Courts and the Protection of the Antebellum Negro," *North Carolina Law Review* 48 (1970): 197–241; Nash, "Fairness and Formalism in the Trials of Blacks in the State Supreme Courts of the Old

South," *Virginia Law Review* 56 (1970): 64–100; Arthur F. Howington, " 'Not in the Condition of a Horse or an Ox,' " *Tennessee Historical Quarterly* 34 (Fall 1975): 249–63. Higginbotham and Kopytoff, instead, seek to show that the law had no difficulty treating slaves as things. I have no quarrel with their critique of the earlier literature, but I think that judges who felt no moral angst about treating slaves as things might nevertheless have faced certain dilemmas in doing so.

4. Andrew Fede, "Legal Protection for Slave Buyers in the U.S. South: A Caveat Concerning *Caveat Emptor*," *American Journal of Legal History* 31 (1987): 323.

5. For an economic analysis of the law of slavery, reducing all contradictions to interests and efficiency, see Wahl, *The Bondsman's Burden*. William W. Fisher, III, in a historiographic overview of the appellate doctrine of slavery, notes that there are also historians who "acknowledge that the law of slavery, was riddled with genuine inconsistencies but contend that they were all the fruits of a single, fundamental contradiction—the incompatibility of slave socioeconomic relations . . . and bourgeois socioeconomic relations," while still others explain the inconsistencies as a relic of the genealogical origins of slavery law in Roman law, English common law, villeinage, and the slave code of Barbados. I agree with Fisher that "we can understand better the law of slavery by examining its relationships to Southern ideology." William W. Fisher III, "Ideology and Imagery in the Law of Slavery," *Chicago-Kent Law Review* 68 (1993): 1056–57. For the incompatibility of slave relations with bourgeois capitalism, see Eugene D. Genovese, *Roll, Jordan, Roll: The World the Slaveholders Made* (New York: Vintage Books, 1976); Mark Tushnet, *The American Law of Slavery, 1810–1860: Considerations of Humanity and Interest* (Princeton: Princeton University Press, 1981); for slavery law as a relic of past legal systems, see Alan Watson, *Slave Law in the Americas* (Athens: University of Georgia Press, 1989).

6. Quoted in Amy Dru Stanley, *From Bondage to Contract: Wage Labor, Marriage, and the Market in the Age of Slave Emancipation* (Cambridge: Cambridge University Press, 1998), xiii.

7. Judith Kelleher Schafer's work is the exception to the rule of doctrinal studies of private law. She has researched all of the trial records of cases involving slaves appealed to the Louisiana Supreme Court. Judith K. Schafer, *Slavery, Civil Law, and the Supreme Court of Louisiana* (Baton Rouge: Louisiana State University Press, 1994). Despite its comprehensive scope, Morris, *Southern Slavery and the Law,* relies almost exclusively on appellate reports. See also Tushnet, *American Law of Slavery*; Fede, *People without Rights*; David J. Bodenhamer and James W. Ely Jr., eds., *Ambivalent Legacy: A Legal History of the South* (Jackson: University Press of Mississippi, 1984). For an excellent study of *criminal* law, local culture, and slavery, see Christopher Waldrep, *Roots of Disorder: Race and Criminal Justice in the American South, 1817–80* (Urbana: University of Illinois Press, 1998).

8. In the most cited example, the majority of Southern courts refused to apply to slaves the rule that an injured worker could not recover from his employer from an accident caused by a coworker ("fellow servant"), a rule that was arguably crucial to industrialization in the North. The fellow-servant rule "subsidized" infant industries by displacing the costs of industrial accidents onto workers. See Lawrence M. Friedman and Jack Ladinsky, "Social Change and the Law of Industrial Accidents," *Columbia Law Review* 67 (1967): 50–82. Some courts

excluded slaves from the fellow-servant rule on the ground that slaves, unlike other workers, were not free to warn employers of dangers, nor could slaves be said to have assumed the risk of dangerous employment through higher wages (although their masters may have). See, e.g., Tushnet, *American Law of Slavery,* 45–49; Paul Finkelman, "Slaves as Fellow Servants: Ideology, Law and Industrialization," *American Journal of Legal History* 31 (October 1987): 269–305; Frederick Wertheim, "Note. Slavery and the Fellow-Servant Rule: An Antebellum Dilemma," *New York University Law Review* 61 (1986): 1112–48.

The only studies of breach of warranty suits have followed this approach as well, pointing out that while South Carolina allowed implied warranties for slaves ("a sound price implies a sound commodity"), other states followed the newer rule of *caveat emptor* ("let the buyer beware"), which some historians have seen as a hallmark of capitalist development. Fede, "Legal Protection for Slave Buyers," 322–58, 329–50; Morris, *Southern Slavery and the Law,* 104–13; Wahl, *The Bondsman's Burden,* 27–48. For a discussion of *caveat emptor,* see Morton J. Horwitz, *The Transformation of American Law, 1780–1860* (Cambridge: Harvard University Press, 1977), 58–62, 173–88. Horwitz portrays the decline of implied warranty as part of a more general transformation from face-to-face exchanges that emphasized "just price" and "fair value" to impersonal market relationships in which only the will of the parties, and not any inherent fairness of the contract, carried weight.

This emphasis on law and economy derives in part from an unfortunate dichotomy that has until recently held sway over Southern historiography, a dichotomy between portrayals of the antebellum South as capitalist and those seeing its essence as "paternalist" and precapitalist. If slavery caused modification of Northern legal doctrines, this model can provide evidence for the incompatibility of slavery with capitalism; on the other hand, if slavery fit neatly into commercial law, this alternative model suggests the capitalism of the South. Such extrapolations from legal doctrine to characterization of the South as a whole depend on a belief in the instrumentalism of Southern judges. A good critique of this debate appears in Morris, *Southern Slavery and the Law,* 10–14, 428–34. See also Walter K. Johnson's excellent review of Morris, "Inconsistency, Contradiction, and Complete Confusion: The Everyday Life of the Law of Slavery," *Law and Social Inquiry* 22 (Spring 1997): 405–33. For an attempt to explain Southern judges' ideology in terms other than instrumentalism or guilt, see William E. Wiethoff, *A Peculiar Humanism: The Judicial Advocacy of Slavery in High Courts of the Old South, 1820–1850* (Athens: University of Georgia Press, 1996).

9. See Ariela J. Gross, "Litigating Whiteness: Trials of Racial Determination in the Nineteenth Century South," *Yale Law Journal* 108 (1998): 181.

10. See, e.g., George M. Fredrickson, *The Arrogance of Race: Historical Perspectives on Slavery, Racism, and Social Inequality* (Middletown, Conn.: Wesleyan University Press, 1988), 211 (citing slave lists that included notations such as "African King").

11. See Fisher, "Ideology and Imagery in the Law of Slavery."

12. See Robert W. Gordon, "Critical Legal Histories," *Stanford Law Review* 36 (1984): 57–125.

13. See "Note on Sources and Methods" in the appendix for details on my research methodology.

14. Clifford Geertz, *Local Knowledge: Further Essays in Interpretive Anthropology* (New York: Basic Books, 1983), 211. In interpreting trials as performances with a constitutive role in culture, I have also been influenced by James Clifford, *The Predicament of Culture: Twentieth-Century Ethnography, Literature and Art* (Cambridge: Harvard University Press, 1988); Mindie Lazarus-Black and Susan F. Hirsch, eds., *Contested States: Law, Hegemony and Resistance* (New York: Routledge, 1994); Guyora Binder and Robert Weisberg, "Cultural Criticism of Law," *Stanford Law Review* 49 (1997): 1149–1220; Richard Wightman Fox, "Intimacy on Trial: Cultural Meanings of the Beecher-Tilton Affair," in *The Power of Culture: Critical Essays in American History*, ed. Richard Wightman Fox and T. J. Jackson Lears (Chicago: University of Chicago Press, 1993), 103–34; Stephen Greenblatt, "Towards a New Poetics of Culture," in *The New Historicism*, ed. H. Aram Veeser (New York: Routledge, 1989), 1–14; and the essays contained in *Performance and Cultural Politics*, ed. Elin Diamond (New York: Routledge, 1996).

15. In Louisiana, the action of redhibition allowed a buyer to have a sale rescinded if the slave exhibited certain "redhibitory vices" within one year of the sale. Absolute redhibitory vices included leprosy, madness, and epilepsy. Redhibitory vices of character included commission of a capital crime, addiction to theft, and the habit of running away. The habit of running away was defined as running away twice for several days, or once for longer than one month. Other vices such as drinking were redhibitory if so severe that the slave was "rendered worthless" by them. Furthermore, declarations of a slave's good qualities, such as a particular skill or good character, could give rise to a redhibitory action if the buyer could prove that was the main reason for the purchase. La. Civ. Code, bk. 3, tit. 7, chap. 6, sec. 3, "Of the Vices of Things Sold," arts. 2496–2505 (1824). This meant that Louisiana, in effect, recognized a broad action for fraud, encompassing many moral and mental qualities not usually considered warrantable. Most Louisiana litigation was instigated by buyers suing for redhibition; only 14 percent of redhibition cases involved sellers suing on notes.

Redhibition litigation was very common in Louisiana parish courts, judging from the cases that reached the state Supreme Court, probably because buyers did so well at the trial level. Buyers won 62 percent of their cases at the trial level, a testament to the consumer-protective cast of the Civil Code. They were less likely to win in that smaller number of cases in which they were sued on notes, perhaps because judges or juries believed that their claims about slave defects were afterthoughts, last-minute defenses. See appendix, table 5.

About one-quarter of all redhibition cases in Louisiana involved the habit of running away. Because of the explicit implied warranty for running away, more of these cases came up in Louisiana than in other states. However, the arguments raised look remarkably similar. For a discussion of Louisiana redhibition, see Judith K. Schafer, " 'Guaranteed against the Vices and Maladies Prescribed by Law': Consumer Protection, the Law of Slave Sales, and the Supreme Court in Antebellum Louisiana," *American Journal of Legal History* 31 (1987): 306–22.

16. Within Louisiana, a majority of the cases were brought to trial in New Orleans, although frequently they involved plantations outside the city limits, along the Mississippi River. Another distinctive feature of the Louisiana system was the preponderance of bench trials without a jury. This, together with the number of cases from New Orleans, does bring into question how much Louisiana cases could have had the same cultural resonance as did a trial in Adams County, Mississippi. Going before a judge in a big city is certainly not the same as being tried by one's peers in a small town.

17. For example, the average age of the slaves involved was 24 in the five-state sample and 23 in the Adams County sample; the male-female ratio in both was about 58–42. The only types of suit that appear frequently in the local sample but rarely in the appellate reports are *replevin* or *detinue* suits for "conversion" or possession of slave property. This is partly because these suits were less likely to be major disputes that would be appealed to a state supreme court, and partly because of the way I searched appellate reports. Therefore, warranty, hire, and tort disputes were overrepresented in the appealed cases. See appendix, tables 1–3.

The average amount in controversy was much higher in Adams County cases than in the five-state sample, because Adams County cases were more likely to involve more than one slave. This runs counter to the hypothesis that only expensive cases would be appealed to a higher court. In warranty suits, sellers who lost in court were more likely to appeal the jury's verdict, because the cases that went on to appeal were more often cases in which the buyer had won at trial. See appendix, table 6.

18. Fairfield District Court of Common Pleas Judgment Rolls, Boxes 13–14, 38–48 (1848–51, 1813–24), SCDAH. Laurens District Court of Common Pleas Judgment Rolls, Boxes 22–24 (1810–15). I sampled 339 causes of action from Fairfield District, S.C. (the years 1813–18 and 1848–51), and 171 causes of action from Laurens District, S.C., to find ten trials involving slaves: five conversion suits, two warranty disputes, two tort suits for assault on a slave, and one dispute over the hire of a slave. This 2 percent figure (10 out of 510) roughly matches that of Adams County (177 trials out of 10,317 causes of action), again because only about 5 percent of causes of action went to trial. Likewise, the subject matter of the cases appears to be roughly similar.

CHAPTER ONE
COURT AND MARKET

1. Michael Tadman, *Speculators and Slaves: Masters, Traders, and Slaves in the Old South* (Madison: University of Wisconsin Press, 1996), 96; D. Clayton James, *Antebellum Natchez* (Baton Rouge: Lousiana State University Press, 1968), 197.

2. Joseph Ingraham, *The South-West by a Yankee* (New York: Harper & Brothers, 1835), 2:192–93.

Slaves had been sold at the fork of St. Catherine's Road and Liberty Road for decades, but in 1835 Isaac Franklin, owner of the largest slave-trading firm in the antebellum South, built a permanent structure there. He did so despite the statewide ban on importation of slaves to the state in that year.

3. William W. Brown, *Narrative of William Wells Brown, a Fugitive Slave*, in *Puttin' On Ole Massa: The Slave Narratives of Henry Bibb, William Wells Brown, and Solomon Northrup*, ed. Gilbert Osofsky (New York: Harper & Row, 1969), 193–94. See also Henry Bibb, *Narrative of the Life and Adventures of Henry Bibb, an American Slave*, in Osofsky, 113–15.

4. Isaac Stier Autobiography, in *The American Slave: A Composite Autobiography*, ed. George P. Rawick (Westport., Conn.: Greenwood Press, 1977), Mississippi Narratives, pt. 5, vol. 10, supp. ser. 1, p. 2057.

5. The courthouse was built in 1819.

6. See, e.g., Edward L. Ayers, *Vengeance and Justice: Crime and Punishment in the Nineteenth-Century American South* (New York: Oxford University Press, 1984), 18, 32 (only a "circumscribed . . . segment of life . . . was controlled by law"; "honor and legalism . . . are incompatible"); Michael S. Hindus, *Prison and Plantation: Crime, Justice, and Authority in Massachusetts and South Carolina, 1767–1878* (Chapel Hill: University of North Carolina Press, 1980), 42–55 (dueling as a "negation of the law," 43; weak legal authority as a function of the Code of Honor in South Carolina); Christopher Waldrep, "Substituting Law for the Lash: Emancipation and Legal Formalism in a Mississippi County Court," *Journal of American History* 82 (March 1996): 1428 ("The state only reluctantly intervened in master-slave relations, regarding law as too burdened with procedure effectively to control human chattel. Owners realized law must be kept from their slaves"); Winthrop D. Jordan, *Tumult and Silence at Second Creek: An Inquiry into a Civil War Slave Conspiracy* (Baton Rouge: Louisiana State University Press, 1993) (important conflicts remain outside the formal legal system); Michael Wayne, *Reshaping Plantation Society: The Natchez District, 1860–1880* (Baton Rouge: Louisiana State University Press, 1983), 16 (plantation its own law); Michael Wayne, "An Old South Morality Play: Reconsidering the Social Underpinnings of the Proslavery Ideology," *Journal of American History* 77 (December 1990): 838–63 (important conflicts remain outside the formal legal system); Peter Kolchin, *American Slavery, 1619–1877* (New York: Hill and Wang, 1993), 127–32 (looking only at legislation, and noting that most slave discipline took place on the plantation). Bertram Wyatt-Brown, while recognizing that in Southern towns "[t]he courthouse, more than the church, was the center for local ethical considerations," has also focused exclusively on the criminal law, and on the extent to which the criminal justice system allowed extralegal sanctions to replace legal ones. Bertram Wyatt-Brown, *Southern Honor: Ethics and Behavior in the Old South* (New York: Oxford University Press, 1982), 366.

7. For studies of slavery and criminal law, see Waldrep, *Roots of Disorder*; Ayers, *Vengeance and Justice*; Philip J. Schwarz, *Twice Condemned: Slaves and the Criminal Laws of Virginia, 1705–1865* (Baton Rouge: Louisiana State University Press, 1988); Daniel J. Flanigan, "Criminal Procedure in Slave Trials in the Antebellum South," *Journal of Southern History* 40 (November 1974): 537–64; Hindus, *Prison and Plantation*. The obvious exception to this generalization about historians of slave culture is Eugene Genovese, whose theory of paternalism rests on an understanding of "the hegemonic function of the law." Genovese, *Roll, Jordan, Roll*, 25–49. My disagreements with Genovese's view are detailed in chap. 4. James Oakes' fascinating discussion of slavery and law centers on the *political* significance of law rather than the *cultural* connections and also focuses on statu-

tory law. James Oakes, *Slavery and Freedom: An Interpretation of the Old South* (New York: Alfred A. Knopf, 1990). For an early work pointing to law's importance in the South, see Charles Sydnor, "The Southerner and the Law," *Journal of Southern History* 6 (February 1940): 3–23.

For studies of constitutional questions, see, e.g., Robert M. Cover, *Justice Accused: Antislavery and the Judicial Process* (New Haven: Yale University Press, 1975); Paul Finkelman, *An Imperfect Union: Slavery, Federalism, and Comity* (Chapel Hill: University of North Carolina Press, 1981); James Oakes, " 'The Compromising Expedient': Justifying a Proslavery Constitution," *Cardozo Law Review* 17 (1996): 2023–56; William M. Wiecek, *The Sources of Antislavery Constitutionalism in America, 1760–1848* (Ithaca: Cornell University Press, 1977).

8. Civil suits were much more common in circuit courts than criminal cases; for example, during the years 1829–41, fewer than 600 criminal cases came before the Adams Circuit Court, whereas there were about 3,200 civil actions. The figure for criminal cases comes from Bertram Wyatt-Brown, "Community, Class, and Snopesian Crime," in *Class, Conflict, and Consensus: Antebellum Southern Community Studies*, ed. Orville V. Burton and Robert C. McMath (Westport, Conn.: Greenwood Press, 1982), 178; the number of civil actions is my own estimate. Edward Ayers estimated three or four civil cases for each criminal case in the typical Southern court. Ayers, *Vengeance and Justice*, 32.

9. In 1860, the census counted 1,083 free families in Adams County. Only 688 residents were heads of household who owned slaves within Adams County. Thus about 36 percent of free people (of whom only a handful were people of color) belonged to households with no slaves. Census of 1860, Adams County.

10. Orville Vernon Burton's excellent county study of Edgefield, South Carolina, discusses the county courthouse as the local seat of power and symbol of both political and cultural authority. Orville Vernon Burton, *In My Father's House Are Many Mansions: Family and Community in Edgefield, South Carolina* (Chapel Hill: University of North Carolina Press, 1985), 28–29. For colonial antecedents, see Darrett B. Rutman and Anita H. Rutman, *A Place in Time: Middlesex County, Virginia, 1650–1850* (New York: W. W. Norton, 1984), 125.

11. Some of the best work has been done on Virginia towns, especially in colonial times. A. G. Roeber has written persuasively about the centrality of Court Day as a social ritual in colonial Virginia towns. Roeber, "Authority, Law, and Custom: The Rituals of Court Day in Tidewater Virginia, 1720 to 1750," *William and Mary Quarterly* 37 (January 1980): 29–52. See also Rhys Isaac, *The Transformation of Virginia, 1740–1790* (Chapel Hill: University of North Carolina Press, 1982).

12. The statutory limit was eighteen days, but the average duration of a court term was much shorter than the statutory limit; usually the court concluded within one week in the early decades of the nineteenth century, and within two in the period 1830–60. If all the cases could not be determined within the period allotted, a special term of the circuit court was called, usually in January. T. J. Fox Alden and J. A. Van Hoesen, *A Digest of the Laws of Mississippi* (New York: Alexander S. Gould, 1839), sec. 3, p. 115.

In the territorial years, a court of common pleas was held four times a year, with full common law civil jurisdiction, as well as a supreme appellate court, once a year in each county, held by territorial judges with appellate jurisdiction. There were also superior or circuit courts presided over by one of the territorial judges, with general original civil and criminal jurisdiction, and appellate jurisdiction over county courts. For practical purposes, this meant that civil matters involving slaves came before superior courts, because the amount in controversy would almost always be too high for the court of common pleas. Likewise, after statehood, superior courts had jurisdiction over all matters involving fifty dollars or more, until, in 1832, the new state constitution established circuit courts separate from the High Court of Errors and Appeals. *Digest of the Laws of Mississippi* (1839), sec. 16, p. 119.

13. The correspondence of planters almost always included a mention of the circuit court when in session; as did the newspapers during May and November. Although criminal cases commanded the most attention, in Adams County, as in other jurisdictions historians have studied, the great majority of antebellum cases before the trial court were contracts disputes, and most of these were debt collection. This corroborates Thomas Russell's findings in South Carolina and Wayne McIntosh's study of St. Louis, Missouri. Thomas D. Russell, "South Carolina's Largest Slave Auctioneering Firm," *Chicago-Kent Law Review* 68 (1993): 1241–82; Wayne McIntosh, "One Hundred and Fifty Years of Litigation and Dispute Settlement: A Court Tale," *Law and Society Review* 15 (1980–81): 823–48.

Only titillating criminal cases such as murders by slaves received press coverage; civil cases were simply mentioned in one line. Likewise, newspapers occasionally published the list of grand jurors sitting at a circuit court, but never that of petit jurors. See, e.g., *Mississippi Free Trader*, November 8, 1854; *Natchez Daily Courier*, November 8, 1852; *Ariel*, July 20, 1825, 5; *Mississippi Messenger*, November 12, 1805; *Natchez Courier*, May 5, 1848. The *Mississippi Free Trader* commented on May 23, 1859, "[T]he Criminal Docket has drawn an unusually large crowd."

14. Garnett Andrews, *Reminiscences of an Old Georgia Lawyer* (1870; reprint, Atlanta, Ga.: Cherokee Pub. Co., 1984), 73.

15. A. J. Brown, *History of Newton County, Mississippi from 1834 to 1894* (Jackson, Miss.: Clarion-Ledger Co., 1894), 427.

16. "The circuit court week at Decatur, was often the occasion of much discord, large amount of drinking and fighting, and often the offending parties being brought before his honor to be reprimanded, jailed or fined. Large preparations were made by the hotel-keepers, the general merchandise dealers, and particularly the saloon-keepers to have plenty to drink . . . After court adjourned all restraints were thrown off, much disorder and many fights indulged in." Ibid., 428.

17. First visited by Europeans in 1682, it became a French trading post in 1714. The French abandoned the area after a bloody war with the Natchez Indians; after a brief period of English settlement in the last quarter of the eighteenth century, the Spanish built the first real town of Natchez, run by the Spanish government in Louisiana from 1783 to 1798. Half of Natchez's population arrived between 1802 and 1817, when Mississippi became a state.

18. Natchez grew during the 1820s and 1830s, its cotton planters amassing great wealth in land and slaves. Its landholding elites were rivaled only by those of coastal South Carolina and the "sugar bowl" of Louisiana. The Natchez "nabobs" included about forty planter families who lived mainly on the suburban estates skirting the town. Their land and slaveholding in Adams County did not

accurately reflect their wealth; in 1860, more than three-quarters of the largest slaveholders in Adams and the neighboring counties also had substantial holdings in Louisiana. Compared to the old elites of South Carolina, the Natchez nabobs were nouveau riche—most made their money in the nineteenth century.

William K. Scarborough, "Lords or Capitalists? The Natchez Nabobs in Comparative Perspective," *Journal of Mississippi History* 54, no. 3 (1992): 241–42. Three hundred and fifty "nabobs" owned 250+ slaves in the 1850 or 1860 census in all fifteen states, yet only seven owned 250+ in Adams County itself in 1850. Ibid., 240. See also Morton Rothstein, "The Natchez Nabobs: Kinship and Friendship in an Economic Elite," in *Toward a New View of America*, ed. Hans L. Trefousse (New York: B. Franklin & Co., 1977), 97–112. James, *Antebellum Natchez*, 139, 243, 136.

Many "nabobs" went North for their undergraduate education, and many maintained ties with the North. John P. Walworth, a prominent planter, and president of the Planter's Bank of Natchez, sent his son Douglas to study at Harvard and Princeton. Douglas wrote to his father that he thought "Yankees . . . lacked courage," and that he often found himself in arguments over slavery. Yet because of their Northern ties, and particularly their financial investments, most Natchez nabobs were Whig Unionists and much less politically active than their secessionist counterparts in South Carolina. Walworth Papers, MDAH; Scarborough, "Lords or Capitalists?" 259–62.

19. There were a number of merchants who crossed over into planting, and vice-versa; successful merchants like Frederick Stanton and Richard Abbey invested heavily in plantations and slaves, while planters became cotton brokers and funneled their profits into far-flung investments. John Hebron Moore, *The Emergence of the Cotton Kingdom in the Old Southwest: Mississippi, 1770–1860* (Baton Rouge: Louisiana State University Press, 1988), 239. Important social organizations such as militias and Masonic temples included members of both classes.

20. Most townspeople subscribed to the Democratic *Mississippi Free Trader*, while planters and wealthy businessmen subscribed to the *Natchez Courier*. James, *Antebellum Natchez*, 127–28. In 1850, one out of twelve Natchez whites owned slaves, and the average slaveholder owned four; the average Adams County slaveholder owned eighty-two. Ibid., 129.

21. New research into precinct voting shows that Natchezians voted Whig in state and national elections in the same majorities as did the rest of Adams County dwellers. Alan D. Constant, "The 1840 Presidential Election in the Natchez District, Mississippi" (M.A. thesis, University of Texas at Austin, 1993), tables 1 and 2 (Constant's work supersedes James' rough, and incorrect, estimates).

22. James, *Antebellum Natchez*, 94, 177, 230, 137. Nevertheless, there were small farmers in Adams County. There were 87 families owning fewer than 20 slaves, of which 24 owned no slaves, 11 owned 1–4, 16 owned 5–9, and 36 owned 10–19 in 1860. Moore, *Cotton Kingdom*, 142.

23. Even so, more than a third of the people of Natchez were black: in 1860, there were 2,131 slaves, 3,607 whites, and about 200 free blacks. Population Schedules of the Eighth Census of the United States, 1830, 1860. There were 135 free blacks in Adams County in 1830, and 225 in 1860. Census of 1830, 1860. By contrast, some of the piney-woods counties of Mississippi, Georgia, and Ala-

bama had total populations of a few thousand with only a few hundred slaves. Adams County had the eleventh highest slave population in the Deep South in 1830. Census of 1830.

24. In Concordia, Louisiana, where many Natchez nabobs owned plantations, 85 percent of slaves worked on large plantations. Ronald L. F. Davis, *The Black Experience in Natchez, 1720–1880* (Special Historical Study, Natchez National Historic Park, April 1993), 21.

By 1860, the white population of Adams County had grown, but the slave population had grown even faster: there were 5,648 whites and 14,292 enslaved blacks. Census of 1860.

25. Davis, *Black Experience*, 51; Census of 1860.

26. They were the Johnsons, the McCarys, the Barlands, the Fitzgeralds, the Fitzhughs, and the Woods. Davis, *Black Experience*, 59–60.

27. Life grew more difficult for free blacks of all classes beginning in the 1830s. That decade saw a tightening of the legal restrictions on free blacks and elimination of many of the legal rights that had separated them from slaves. In the summer of 1841, a campaign popularly known as the "Inquisition" was conducted against the free black community to discover violators of the strict laws of the 1830s and to deport them from the state. Moore, *Cotton Kingdom*, 264–66; James, *Antebellum Natchez*, 179.

28. *William Johnson's Natchez: The Antebellum Diary of an Antebellum Free Negro*, ed. William R. Hogan and Edwin A. Davis (Baton Rouge: Louisiana State University Press, 1973; Port Washington, N.Y.: Kennikat Press, 1968), 2:721–22, 757, 492 (May 13, 1850; May 16, 1850; November 11, 1850; May 29, 1844).

29. Ibid., 471, 720, 1:274. See *Parkhurst v. Field*, Drawer 317 Docket #142, November 1845, Adams Circuit Court Records, HNF; *Andrews v. Brooks*, Drawer 100 Folder 6, Docket #5, May 1820, Adams Circuit Court Records, HNF.

30. Charles Warren, *A History of the American Bar* (Boston: Little, Brown, 1911), 206.

31. Orville Vernon Burton, in his community study of Edgefield, South Carolina, found that "lawyers were . . . important in the spreading of ideas . . . [L]awyers linked Edgefield with the other South Carolina districts." Burton, *In My Father's House*, 21.

32. Letter from Charles J. Colcock to wife, January 24, 1827, Folder 3, Box 1, Colcock Family Papers, Collection 520, Howard-Tilton Memorial Library, Tulane University, New Orleans.

33. North Todd Gentry, *Bench and Bar of Boone County, Missouri* (self-published, 1916), 63–64.

34. Henry S. Foote, *Casket of Reminiscences* (Washington, D.C.: Chronicle Publishing Company, 1874), 265. (Foote also describes the bar of Natchez in Reminiscence no. 22, pp. 216–23.)

35. However, as they gained in economic power, they lost political strength in the state. In the early years of statehood, Natchez lawyers predominated in the ranks of the bar as well as in the political arena in Mississippi. The "Natchez Junto," which held sway in state politics during the early years, embraced most of the town's leading attorneys in the 1820s, including five of the state's attorneys general: Thomas B. Reed, Lyman Harding, Edward Turner, Aylette Buckner, and

Richard M. Gaines. Their political influence remained strong until the late 1830s; "lawyers from Natchez occupied the Mississippi governor's chair for fifteen of the first seventeen years of statehood." Natchez peaked in white population and influence just before the Constitution of 1832 created a large number of new counties in the northern and eastern parts of the state. James, *Antebellum Natchez*, 97, 113–14.

36. Colcock Family Papers, 1785–1917, Collection 520, Howard-Tilton Library, Tulane Uiversity, Folder 2, Letter dated August 13, 1819.

On the question of whether legal practice was a safe and financially rewarding path, Southern lawyers held mixed opinions. Henry St. George Tucker, a University of Virginia professor, told students that "the profession of the law is the most successful path, not only to affluence and comfort, but to all the distinguished and elevated stations in a free government." E. Lee Shepard, "Breaking into the Profession: Establishing a Law Practice in Antebellum Virginia," *Journal of Southern History* 48 (August 1982): 393. By contrast, in 1835, Virginia lawyer Thomas R. Joynes told his son that law was "not always and, in fact, not generally, the road to wealth. The practice of the Law is one of the most uncertain and precarious of all pursuits." Ibid. Shepard notes that "letters of advice . . . abound with effusive praise for the law and its practice juxtaposed with emotional warnings of the dismal prospects for success of even the most promising novice." Ibid.

37. James, *Antebellum Natchez*, 97, 113–14, 119; Moore, *Cotton Kingdom*, 243. Edward Turner and J.S.B. Thacher were the only Natchezians to serve on the High Court of Errors and Appeals between 1832 and 1861.

38. James, *Antebellum Natchez*, 97; Joseph Baldwin, *The Flush Times of Alabama and Mississippi* (reprint, New York: Sagamore Press, 1957), 34.

39. Horace S. Fulkerson, *Random Recollections of Early Days in Mississippi* (Vicksburg: Commercial Herald Pub., 1888).

40. Katharine M. Jones, *The Plantation South* (Indianapolis, Ind.: Bobbs-Merrill, 1957), 235–36.

41. Ingraham, *South-West*, 2:84–85.

42. Lawyers were leaders of many of the social organizations that cut across class lines in Adams County, such as militias and fraternal orders. A number of lawyers were officers or members of the most prestigious volunteer military company, the Natchez Fencibles, including Thomas Reed and John A. Quitman. Quitman and Reed were also Grand Masters of the Grand Lodge of the Odd Fellows, and a number of lawyers were prominent Masons. Quitman boasted to his brother in 1836, "I am President of a states rights association, of an anti-Abolition society, of an anti-Gambling society, of a Mississippi cotton company, of an anti-Dueling society, of a railroad company, director of the Planters bank, grand master Mason, Captain of the Natchez Fencibles, trustee of Jefferson college and Natchez academy, besides having charge of a cotton and sugar plantation and 150 negroes." Moore, *Cotton Kingdom*, 191; John A. Quitman Subject File, MDAH; Records of the "Natchez Fencibles," John A. Quitman and Family Papers, Box 1, Folder 2, LSU; Thomas Reed Papers, Box 1, Folder 1, LSU.

43. Mary Turner's sister, Fanny, married Lemuel Conner, whose notes of interrogations of slaves are now made famous by Jordan's *Tumult and Silence at Second Creek*.

44. Joyce Broussard-Hogan, "The Career of John T. McMurran: From Yankee Lawyer to Planter Elite in the Natchez District, 1823–1866" (unpublished manuscript, available at MDAH). McMurran's obituary rhapsodized about his mastery of "the questions of 'Quo Warrants,' the 'Forthcoming Bond Law,' the 'Valuation Law,' and the many varieties which the points arising on the protest of promissory notes assumed." *Natchez Courier*, in Box 1, Folder 3, Thomas Reed Papers, LSU.

McMurran's practice was not atypical. Aylett Buckner and his partners kept a docket of the issues they argued at Jefferson Circuit Court in the November Term, 1840; all were debts. Of these, one was "settled," one "supposed to be settled"; in two, the notes were "satisfied"; another had "been to the supreme court & back"; two would be fought ("Montgomery will contend in this case that he did not endorse the note" and "Defend this case"); and in one they lost a $995 judgment. A. P. Merrill–Aylett Buckner Papers, Box 1, Folder 10, LSU.

Lawyers' correspondence often included letters referring to unsound slaves as a defense to debts. There is no way of knowing how many debt actions involved sales of slaves unless the defense was actually argued in court and the testimony remains. However, the frequency of such mentions in letters suggests that this was very common. For example, B. Cozzens wrote to Joseph Allen on behalf of J. D. Tyler that a note Allen held "I presume to be a draft given to a Gent. in Tennessee for two negroes (Stephan & Hassett)," and that Stephan "proves unsound." Cozzens wanted to take the course that would "*avoid litigation*," so he was planning to advise Tyler "to loose [*sic*] $250 of the $300 paid and return the servants." Cozzens to Allen, March 12, 1847, Merrill-Buckner Papers, Box 2, Folder 13, LSU.

45. Broussard-Hogan, "McMurran," 11–12. It is no surprise that most nabobs were Unionists, considering that they diversified their investments into Northern real estate, securities, and railroad stock; even in their agricultural undertakings, they behaved like capitalists. Scarborough, "Lords or Capitalists?" 259–64.

46. Broussard-Hogan, "McMurran," 12. For another lawyer who became a planter through speculation on slaves using his first legal fees, see Biographical Sketch of Lyman Harding, April 22, 1859, in the J.F.H. Claiborne Papers, Book G, Roll 9, MDAH; Lyman Harding Subject File, MDAH. Edward Turner Subject File, MDAH. George Poindexter, an early lawyer who went on to become governor of Mississippi, doubled his slave- and landholding between 1807 and 1815, when he paid taxes on 58 slaves and 810 acres in Adams County alone. Adams County Personal Tax Rolls, Miss. Territ., Roll #299. William Vannerson, who moved to Natchez from Virginia in 1823 with a single slave, acquired 27 slaves during his active years in practice in Adams County in the 1830s before going on to become a Lawrence County probate judge. Adams County Personal Tax Rolls, Miss., Roll B-592.

Overall, the average lawyer in a slave-related case owned 13 or 14 slaves in Natchez; about 150 acres of land; one or two lots in town where he kept his law office, together worth nearly $9,000; a carriage; and a gold watch. However, this average reflects the period of time during which these lawyers were active in practice. Although there were certainly more "middle-class" lawyers who never succeeded on the scale of Turner or McMurran, only four lawyers of thirty-five paid no taxes on slaves during their active years of law practice.

The success of McMurran's generation meant an even more "aristocratic" life for the succeeding generation. McMurran's son, John, and Douglas Walworth got into "scrapes" stealing chickens, wrote letters to their female friends, hunted, and danced at fancy balls. Douglas Walworth, a young criminal defense lawyer, kept a diary of his daily activities. By his fifth year practicing law, he often went to the office only in the morning and rode horseback in the afternoon with his wife Rebecca (née Conner) or with friends. In 1859 he was elected city representative and stopped going to the office altogether. Letters, Folders 2, 5, 6, and Manuscript Volumes 2–7, Douglas Walworth Papers, LSU.

47. When Edward Turner of Natchez stood for office as justice of the Mississippi High Court of Errors and Appeals in 1840, his campaign circular—prepared not in his name, of course, but in that of his "friends"—proclaimed his "eminent legal ability"; his "strict adherence to those great moral principles, without which, all laws are vain, and civil liberty but a name"; his "thorough knowledge of the laws and policy of the State" as well as "an extensive acquaintance with the general principles of the Common Law and Equity Jurisprudence." F. Edward Turner Papers, Kuntz Collection, Collection 600, Howard-Tilton Memorial Library, Tulane University, New Orleans. "Yielding to the generally expressed wishes of the Bar and his numerous friends through the district, a reluctant assent, in accordance with the rule of his whole life, neither to seek nor decline office, he is placed before you as a candidate for your suffrages at the approaching election."

48. See n. 73 below for details on the court systems.

49. Seth Lewis Memoirs, 15–16, MDAH. Circuit judges during the antebellum period included Alexander Montgomery and Edward Turner, also major planters and important lawyers in private practice, as well as George Coalter and Stanhope Posey. Coalter and Posey were the most frequent judges' names to appear in trial records; but noting the judge's name was the exception rather than the rule. Posey lived in Wilkinson County, where he owned no slaves in 1830 but had become a small planter by 1860. Census of 1830, 1860. George Coalter moved to Mississippi from Virginia and joined the bar in 1810. He lived in Vicksburg, where he paid no taxes on land or slaves in 1831, 1842, or 1843. *Vicksburg Whig*, September 15, 1849. I am indebted to Christopher Waldrep for this information about George Coalter.

50. In their public pronouncements, lawyers and planters of Natchez were neither the greatest defenders nor detractors of slavery. In the early years, some of the great planters, such as Stephen Duncan, were colonizationists. There was a relatively high degree of manumission before 1830, and some ex-slaves were sent to Liberia. George Poindexter, a prominent Natchez lawyer, who served as congressman, senator, and governor of Mississippi, expressed the prevailing public position on slavery when he wrote in 1818 that slavery "is not a matter of choice whether we will have slaves among us or not; we found them here, and we are obliged to maintain and employ them." Mimi Miller, "A History of African-Americans in Natchez" (unpublished manuscript, available at HNF, January 1992). Both lawyers and planters, by the late antebellum period, had made the transition now well documented among white Southerners broadly: from "slavery as a necessary evil" to "slavery as a positive good." John A. Quitman, the rare Democratic planter-lawyer, declaimed in public and in private that slavery was as

right as it was good. His inaugural address as governor, on January 10, 1850, asserted, "We do not regard [slavery] as an evil, on the contrary, we think that our prosperity, our happiness, our very political existence, is inseparably connected with it . . . We *will* not yield it." John A. Quitman and Family Papers, LSU. Similarly, Douglas Walworth's private correspondence to his father discusses his defense of slavery "at the Miss Uphams" in the North. J. P. Walworth urged his son to "look with contempt and listen in silence to such petty politicians as run these little neighbourhood meetings . . . never allow yourself to get warm . . . I would not talk on it but refer such . . . to the Constitution of the United States"; it was unnecessary to argue the matter, he advised, as Southerners had already won so much from the Compromise of 1850 and "had all the great and good on our side." Letters between J. P. Walworth and Douglas Walworth, November 5 and 12, 1850, Walworth Papers, LSU.

51. Of the Deep Southern states, only South Carolina became a net exporting state during the 1820s. Louisiana, Mississippi, and Alabama remained net importing states through 1860, and Georgia, during the 1850s, was split between a net importing region in the west and a net exporting region in the east. Broadly speaking, eastern seaboard regions, settled early like the older regions of the Upper South, became exporters over the course of the antebellum period. Tadman, *Speculators and Slaves*, 6–7, 12. All five states imported an estimated 650,000 slaves between 1800 and 1859. Ibid., 12.

52. No reliable estimates exist of the actual percentage of slave sales that can be attributed to local noncourt sales. Michael Tadman suggests, based on newspaper advertisements, that they were outnumbered by local court sales; however, he also notes that bills of sale filed with the South Carolina secretary of state for 1847–62 show 75 percent local noncourt sales. While publicly filed bills of sale may be a skewed sample, newspaper advertisements may be as well, because many private sales involved face-to-face encounters among people who had no need to resort to advertising. In any case, his conclusion that the rate of local sales was "at least as high and probably higher than the per capita rate of interregional sales of Upper South slaves" is certainly right. Ibid., 112, 118–21.

53. Russell, "South Carolina's Largest Slave Auctioneering Firm," 1277–78.

54. James, *Antebellum Natchez*, 46. The 1833 ordinance declared it illegal for "any person to keep within the city of Natchez, negroes brought to this State as merchandise, for sale, nor shall any such negroes be offered for sale in said city, said commodity being considered, by this board, a nuisance, and dangerous to the health of the citizens." The ordinance applied only to "those persons commonly called negro traders" and exempted Natchez citizens. The ordinance was also not intended to prevent "any person from offering one or more negroes for sale at public auction, for any one day," but it did restrict people from offering any slave "for more than one day at any one time." *Code of the Ordinances of the City of Natchez, Now in Force* (Natchez, Miss.: Giles M. Hillyer, 1854), 151–52.

55. Traders advertising in Natchez newspapers almost always declared that their slaves came from Virginia; however, much of the litigation for breach of warranty concerned slaves who had come from Kentucky or Tennessee.

56. Davis, *Black Experience*, 15; see Thomas D. Russell, "A New Image of the Slave Auction: An Empirical Look at the Role of Law in Slave Sales and a Concep-

tual Reevaluation of Slave Property," *Cardozo Law Review* 17 (1996): 473–524, for an important discussion of court-ordered sales as a major component of the slave trade; Ingraham, *South-West*, 237–38; Wendell Stephenson, *Isaac Franklin, Slave Trader and Planter of the Old South* (1938; reprint, Baton Rouge: Louisiana State University Press,1968), 34–54. The 1832 Constitution restricted the slave trade; during the decade until repeal, Natchez traders frequently sold slaves across the river at Vidalia, Louisiana, to Mississippi buyers who specified Louisiana residence. Ibid., 63. According to D. Clayton James, slave traders with a permanent residence in Natchez, such as Rice Ballard, who sold on consignment for Franklin & Armfield, "did most of the local business and were exempt from the state tax of 1% on gross sales of slaves, which auctioneers and transient traders had to pay. The extent of the slave trade is suggested by the fact that for an unknown 'part of the year 1833' the Natchez sales of 32 non-resident slave merchants were $238,879." James, *Antebellum Natchez*, 198.

57. Quoted in Frederic Bancroft, *Slave Trading in the Old South* (Baltimore, Md.: J. H. Furst Co., 1931), 304–5.

58. The first ban on the domestic trade came out of South Carolina in 1787 and lasted until 1803. Tadman, *Speculators and Slaves*, 14. South Carolina banned the trade again between 1817 and 1818. *Statutes at Large of South Carolina*, vol. 7, ed. David J. McCord (Columbia: A. S. Johnston, 1840), Acts 2111, 2195. Despite initial caution among slave traders during restricted periods—Mississippi traders often executed sales documents across the Mississippi River in Louisiana—lax enforcement meant a gradual relaxing of their vigilance. Mississippi imported more slaves in the 1830s and 1840s than any other state, despite the ban. Ibid., 12.

59. Bacon Tait, quoted in Tadman, *Speculators and Slaves*, 88.

60. Ibid., 84–87.

61. Ibid., 116.

62. Gavin Wright, *Old South, New South: Revolutions in the Southern Economy since the Civil War* (New York: Basic Books, 1986), 18.

63. Richard H. Kilbourne, Jr., *Debt, Investment, Slaves: Credit Relations in East Feliciana Parish, Louisiana, 1825–1885* (Tuscaloosa: University of Alabama Press, 1995), 52. "In three of four years sampled in the decade of the 1850s (1850, 1853, 1856, and 1859), the slave market accounted for almost 80 percent of the total cash market for both land and slaves." Ibid., 50.

64. Morris, *Southern Slavery and the Law*, 132.

65. Report by Joseph Pilié, surveyor of the town to the mayor, August 2, 1831, Folder 8, MSS 44, Slavery in Louisiana Collection, Historic New Orleans Collection. "L'attelier de la ville se compose aujourd'hui de 29 nègres au mois, 63 nègres de chaines, 28 négresses & 30 condamnés; employés à nettoyer les rues, les marches, & la levee; rider les charpentiers, les forgerons & le pareur; creuser les foyes du faubourg Treme; placer des poteaux . . ."

66. Hire disputes constituted 16 percent of the five-state sample and 10 percent of the Adams County sample. See appendix, table 1.

67. Folder 44, MSS 44, Slavery in Louisiana Collection, Historic New Orleans Collection. See also bills of sale with warranty in Folders 18, 20, 22, 23, 26, 32, 33, 34, 35, 37. Warranties also included provisions for returns of unsound slaves.

See, e.g., Bill of Sale for Slaves, dated February 24, 1855, Box 2, Folder 16, A. P. Merrill-Aylett Buckner Papers, 1787–1870, LSU (". . . it is known and understood that the boy Dudley has a broken leg now not well but which I warrant to get well in due time to heal and if the leg does not get well I do hereby agree to take the said man Dudley back . . .").

68. Charles S. Sydnor, *A Gentleman of the Old Natchez Region: Benjamin L. C. Wailes* (Durham, N.C.: Duke University Press, 1938), 94.

69. Court costs included the clerk's fee, daily pay to witnesses and jurors, fees to justices of the peace for taking depositions, and the sheriff's fee for serving subpoenas and warrants. See "An Act to Establish the Fees of Justices of the Peace and Constables," Docket Book #2 of Magistrate Edward Turner, Natchez, Miss. Territ., F. Edward Turner Papers, Kuntz Collection 600, Howard-Tilton Memorial Library, Tulane University; *Digest of the Laws of Mississippi* (1839), Sec. 106 (witnesses' costs); *The Revised Code of the Statute Laws of the State of Mississippi* (Jackson, Miss.: E. Barksdale, 1857), sec. 17, art. 205, p. 513 (witnesses' costs). A long case involving many witnesses could cost hundreds of dollars. See, e.g., *Smith v. Meek*, Drawer 232, #76, April 1838, Adams Cir. Ct., HNF (court costs of $435.19; jury gave a verdict for $13,100.54, but this was vacated when the parties settled and the defendant paid costs).

70. These numbers derive from a sample of sixty-one plaintiffs in slave-related litigation. About one-third owned 5 to 20 slaves. The average wealth of a plaintiff was 44 slaves, 682 acres, and one town lot. The median buyer in a warranty suit owned 10 slaves, but the median plaintiff in a replevin or tort suit owned 14. There were five seller-plaintiffs, trying to recover on a debt for slaves; four of these were very small slaveholders or nonslaveholders, while one was a great planter, William B. Sessions, suing Dr. Samuel A. Cartwright! See appendix, table 4.

In Adams County as a whole, there were a significant number of nonslaveholders in the town of Natchez; in 1860, there were only 12 slaveholders in town with 20 or more slaves; 113 with 6–20, and 257 with 1–5, leaving a large majority with no slaves. In agricultural households outside Natchez, there were few without slaves (11 percent) in 1860, 28 percent with fewer than 20, 27 percent with 20–49, and 34 percent with more than 50. Overall in the county, 38 percent of slaveholding households held 1–4 slaves; 37 percent held 5–19; 12.5 percent held 20–49; and 12 percent held more than 50.

71. The median hirer owned 9, and the median defendant accused of a tort (such as beating a slave to death) owned 10. The averages were much higher, because of the unusual number of great planters included: the average defendant owned 62 slaves, 1,000 acres of land, one or two town lots, a watch, and a carriage; his land in the county alone was worth about $13,400.

72. There were lower-level courts in some counties, variously known as superior courts, inferior courts, or courts of common pleas, but these usually handled cases of less than fifty dollars, and the least expensive slave was worth several hundred dollars. There was also the possibility of bringing suit in a chancery court, or court of equity, which dispensed justice where a remedy was unavailable at law. Only a court of equity could grant "specific performance" of a contract, for example—an injunction requiring the parties to carry out the terms of the contract. Courts of law could only grant money damages for breach of contract.

During the antebellum period, courts of law and equity were merging in most of the South. For example, the Circuit Court in Adams County, Mississippi, had jurisdiction over both law and equity, although there was a separate Superior Court of Chancery during most of its life as well, with jurisdiction over equitable claims of five hundred dollars or less. Very few litigants brought their cases to the Superior Court of Chancery in Natchez, however; a sample of 179 cases included only three breach of warranty disputes involving slaves. In one case, the plaintiff brought his suit in chancery because he believed that he had no remedy at law if there was only "partial failure of consideration," that is, if the slave still retained some value. *Terrell & Stanton v. Ashley*, Docket #41, 1822, Series 203, Vol. 174, Box 5785, Sup. Ct. of Chancery—Western District, MDAH (slave woman Nancy "diseased with the Scrofula or King's Evil"). In another case, the present holder of a note sought relief from the equity court to avoid injury in "retribution" for harm caused by the slave's seller, the original holder of the note. *Smith v. Webb*, Docket #238, 1821, Series 203, Vol. 174, Box 5785, Sup. Ct. of Chancery—Western District, MDAH. In the third case, after losing two trials at law, slave seller Andrew Williams asked the chancery court for an injunction to stay the judgment of the circuit court in favor of the buyer, Joseph Brandt. Although no record remains of the disposition of the case, it is likely that this strategy failed, or more losers in circuit court would have availed themselves of it.

73. Just as plaintiffs rarely brought their slave-related claims to chancery courts, they rarely used equitable theories or sought equitable remedies in merged courts of law and equity. When they did so, they were liable to be informed that equity courts were not the place for contracts disputes; as the Mississippi High Court of Errors and Appeals explained, "your action is in covenant." *Davidson v. Moss*, Docket #7491, January 1841, HCEA, MDAH. Appeal reported in 30 Miss. 343 (1855). By this, the court meant that breach of contract claims belonged in courts of law, with the remedy of money damages.

There were unusual circumstances under which one might pursue an equitable claim. For example, if one sought rescission of the sale rather than money damages, in a common law state, equity was the only recourse. This rarely happened; in warranty cases, where the "merchandise" was "defective," most buyers wanted their money back and did not care about the disposition of the slaves, whereas most sellers wanted their notes paid rather than the slaves returned. In general, if a buyer won damages and the slaves were still living and not escaped, they were to be returned to the seller. See *Ingraham v. Russell*, 3 How. Miss. 304 (1839) (overturning jury verdict awarding $2,200 to buyer yet allowing him to keep slaves who were not totally valueless). But a buyer who paid with a note, became dissatisfied with a slave, and wanted to return the slave without waiting to be sued on the note could bring a bill of chancery to rescind the sale. See, e.g., *Hutchins v. Franklin*. Docket #102, October 1819, Superior Court of Chancery for the Western District [Natchez], Miss., MDAH.

74. Circuit courts were sometimes composed of the same judges who sat on the state supreme court in the first decades of the century; but by the mid-1830s, most states had separately constituted circuit courts. Mississippi had superior courts in each county with jurisdiction over all civil matters until 1822, along with a supreme appellate court. In 1822, separate superior courts of chancery

were established in four districts. Finally, under the 1832 state constitution, newly established circuit courts obtained concurrent jurisdiction over equity matters worth less than five hundred dollars, and all common law civil and criminal causes. Appeals from the circuit courts as well as the superior courts of chancery were heard by the High Court of Errors and Appeals. Similarly, Alabama, after statehood, established circuit courts through its 1819 Constitution and a Supreme Court composed of the same judges. Beginning in 1832, the Supreme Court was constituted separately and elected by the legislature; this gave way to general elections in 1850. In South Carolina, there were separate district (or county) circuit courts and chancery courts for the entire antebellum period; appeals went to a Court of Appeals in Law and Equity, composed of the circuit judges and chancellors respectively. Georgia had superior courts riding eleven circuits to every county, with jurisdiction over law and equity, with judges elected by the legislature; there was no Supreme Court until 1845. For details on Southern court systems, see Ralph A. Wooster, *The People in Power: Courthouse and Statehouse in the Lower South, 1850–1860* (Knoxville: University of Tennessee Press, 1969).

75. The vast majority of complaints filed in circuit court (96 percent) were simple debt actions that did not go to trial because the creditor won a judgment as an administrative matter, without the debtor's ever coming to court to defend the suit. It is likely that many of these suits which did not go to trial also involved debts for slaves, but it is impossible to know.

76. Of the five-state sample of warranty cases, 44 percent involved physical illness; 25 percent, death; 18 percent, runaways; 3 percent, other bad character traits; 1 percent, drinking; 3 percent, insanity; 3 percent, "idiocy"; and 3 percent, lack of skills. See appendix, table 2.

77. La. Civ. Code, bk. 3, tit. 7, chap. 6, sec. 3, "Of the Vices of Things Sold," arts. 2496–2505 (1824). See introduction, n. 16, for a discussion of redhibitory vices.

78. This was true both in Adams County and in the Deep South as a whole. In both the local and the five-state samples, litigation increased over time, but the increase was particularly steep among appeals, as the appellate courts grew busier over the antebellum period. In Adams County, litigation peaked in the late 1830s, following the Panic of 1837, but slave-related litigation as a percentage of all cases continued to rise over the entire period. Only 14 percent of the five-state sample of cases came to trial before 1830; a full 44 percent were heard after 1850. In Adams County, there were an average of 182 causes set per term in the 1820s; during the 1850s, there were an average of 710 causes on the docket per term, both civil and criminal. Issue Docket Books, Adams Circuit Court, HNF. Some of these were continued, some suffered judgment by default, and the rest were tried or dismissed.

79. *Brown v. Cox*, Drawer 354 #15, November 1856, Adams Cir. Ct., Miss., HNF. Actions of "trespass," for damage to the plaintiff's slave, whether by neglect, beating, shooting, or other means, constituted 12 percent of the five-state sample and 3 percent of the local sample. See appendix, table 1.

Besides torts suits like these, warranty cases, and hire disputes, the remaining category of civil litigation involving slaves comprised suits to claim possession of a slave, most often following a slaveholder's death, as his survivors fought over his estate. In other circumstances, possession or ownership of a slave was disputed because a runaway slave had been "taken up" by another; occasionally, a slave was actually stolen. In these suits, the plaintiff employed the legal fiction that he had "casually lost" the slave at issue, who had come into the defendant's possession "by finding"; the common law writs of action in these situations included "detinue," "replevin," or "trover." These suits made up 4 percent of the five-state sample and 32 percent of the local sample. See appendix, table 1.

80. Descriptions of courtrooms come from Gordon A. Cotton, *The Old Courthouse* (Raymond, Miss.: Keith Printing Co., 1982) (describing the Warren County Courthouse, built in Vicksburg in 1858) and Gentry, *Bench and Bar of Boone County*, 77.

81. Andrews, *Georgia Lawyer*, 19.

82. *New Orleans Bee*, Wednesday, July 16, 1845.

83. Although we have no record of openings by Adams County attorneys, records exist from South Carolina and Alabama trials involving slaves, and William L. Burke, Jr., has shown that opening statements were pervasive during the antebellum period. William Lewis Burke, Jr., "A History of the Opening Statement from Barristers to Corporate Lawyers: A Case Study of South Carolina," *American Journal of Legal History* 37 (1993): 25.

84. This number is necessarily inexact but is probably an underestimate. Sometimes only a subpoena list was available but no testimony. In these cases, it is possible to know only whether witnesses actually testified in court if receipts remain indicating how many days a witness served. On the other hand, where testimony survived but not subpoena lists, it is possible that more witnesses testified, or at least were subpoenaed, than those for whom testimony was recorded. Testimony is usually the most incomplete part of the record because it depended on the judge or clerk of the court to record, as opposed to complaints, answers, motions, and subpoenas, which were filed by the parties. For eighty cases in which I found subpoena lists, testimony, or receipts, there were 434 witnesses; however, it is likely that evidence of many others was lost.

85. *Digest of the Laws of Mississippi* (1839), chap. 37, sec. 106, p. 142; *Revised Code of Mississippi* (1857), sec. 17, art. 205, p. 513.

86. Unlike today, there was little pretrial discovery in antebellum cases. Although litigants had a right to obtain discovery of documents by petition, usually they built their cases on witnesses' testimony as to the contents of contracts and other documents. Lawyers frequently took depositions, but these were actually received as legal testimony by the court and read into the record before the jury, rather than merely being a pretrial information-gathering mechanism. In Mississippi, this practice dated back to the first Judiciary Act of 1807 in the Territorial period. Depositions were taken either by both lawyers, if local, or by a justice of the peace in a foreign locale using written interrogatories and cross-interrogatories sent by the lawyers. Witnesses answered orally, and their answers were copied down.

Such depositions were allowed for witnesses outside the territory, or with plans to leave the territory. After statehood, more detailed reasons for witnesses to forgo court appearance were enumerated in the statutes: age, illness, residence more than sixty miles from the place of trial, and gender exempted witnesses. Female witnesses did not have to appear in court, unless one of the parties filed an affidavit "that the personal attendance of such female in open court, is necessary for the ends of justice." In practice, some women did appear in court, but many took advantage of the deposition law. Depositions have survived in the legal record far more often than transcripts of testimony at trial, which were sometimes written up by the clerk of court, and sometimes by the judge himself after the fact. *Revised Code* of 1857, p. 514.

87. It is surprising that so few witnesses hailed from Virginia, given the level of slave importing from Virginia. However, these numbers are problematic because of the inadequacy of the record.

88. Act of February 10, 1807, sec. 9. People excluded from testifying "except for and against each other" included "[a]ll negroes, mulattoes, Indians, and all persons of mixed blood, descended from negro or Indian ancestors, to the third generation, inclusive, though one ancestor of each generation may have been a white person." *Digest of the Laws of Mississippi* (1839), sec. 110, pp. 143–44.

Beeler v. Leeper, Drawer 169 #26, May 1830, Adams Cir. Ct., Miss., and Book of Judgments NN, 382, HNF. Beeler's attorney, George Adams, objected to the testimony of Moses Wanzer, a thirty-four-year-old "Merchant Taylor" of color, living in New York, but the judge (probably Edward Turner) overruled the objection.

89. 43 percent of 107 witnesses for whom I obtained information owned between one and five slaves; and another 25 percent owned none. The average witness was a white man who owned seven slaves, about 180 acres of land, a town lot, and a carriage.

90. The average defense witness had sixteen slaves, 436 acres, and 1.5 town lots, whereas the average plaintiff's witness had nine slaves, 100 acres, and one town lot.

There were only sixty-three cases in which I could both identify which party called the witness and locate the witnesses in tax or census records. Therefore, we should take these results with caution.

91. Juries were listed only in the minute books of the court and not in the trial transcript. Thus I matched trials to juries only in those cases where the clerk noted in which minute book the trial was recorded. I was able to find jury lists for eighteen cases, one of which had two mistrials and three juries; I obtained information on an average of six jurors per jury.

92. The sheriff gave the clerk a list each year, and the clerk chose sixty of these for the *venire*. Before 1830, fifty-one were chosen every two years. *Digest of the Laws of Mississippi* (1839), sec. 122, p. 147. Jury selection was similar in other states. See *The Code of Alabama*, ed. John J. Ormond, Arthur P. Bagby, and George Goldthwaite (Montgomery: Brittan and DeWolf, 1852), pt. 4, tit. 2, chap. 6, art. I, sec. 3436, p. 613; *Statutes at Large of South Carolina*, 7:273; *A Digest of the Laws of the State of Georgia*, 2d ed., ed. Oliver H. Prince (Athens: published by the author, 1837), sec. 38, pp. 428–29.

93. Act of December 7, 1811, *Statutes of the Mississippi Territory* (Natchez: P. Isler, 1816), p. 27, sec. 8.

94. *Digest of the Laws of Mississippi* (1839), sec. 133, p. 150; *Code of Alabama*, pt. 4, tit. 2, chap. 6, art. I, sec. 3475, p. 618; *Digest of the Laws of Georgia* (1837), sec. 44, p. 430.

95. *Digest of the Laws of Mississippi* (1839), sec. 138, p. 150; sec. 142, p. 151; *Code of Alabama*, pt. 4, tit. 2, chap. 6, art. I, sec. 3439, p. 613; *Digest of the Laws of Georgia*, sec. 38, pp. 428–29.

96. A. Hutchinson, *Code of Mississippi, from 1798 to 1848* (Jackson: Price and Hall, 1848), sec. 136; Christopher Waldrep, "Black Access to Law in Reconstruction: The Case of Warren County, Mississippi," *Chicago-Kent Law Review* 70 (1994): 583–621. In Alabama, however, petit jurors were chosen not at random but from among those "esteemed in the community for their integrity, fair character, and sound judgment." *Code of Alabama* (1852), pt. 4, tit. 2, chap. 6, art. I, sec. 3438, p. 613. In South Carolina, the "best qualified" of those eligible were to be chosen. *Statutes at Large of South Carolina*, 273.

97. Hutchinson, *Code*, ch. 61, art. 9, sec. 14, from Circuit Court Act, March 2, 1833.

98. Alan Scheflin and Jon Van Dyke, "Jury Nullification: The Contours of a Controversy," *Law and Contemporary Problems* 43 (Autumn 1980): 54.

99. Renee B. Lettow, "New Trial for Verdict against Law: Judge-Jury Relations in Early Nineteenth-Century America," *Notre Dame Law Review* 71 (1996): 542–53. Whereas Lettow describes a general trend toward greater judicial control over jury behavior, in my view the Adams County trials suggest a great deal of jury power. Even granting a new trial, when it was used, only sent the case to another jury.

100. William Johnson reported a typical case in 1844: a slave was killed; an inquest was held; "They Looked at the head, found it very much Bruised. Did cut it Open Did not strip him nor Look at his back. No One, says One of them, is authorized to work without Pay and the Law Seys that a Dr shall have fifty Dollars for Oppening the head &c and no One would say do it So they closed the man up again and Said he Died with Congestion of the Brain, Thus it was and thus it is, &c." Hogan and Davis, *William Johnson's Natchez*, 500, August 19, 1844.

101. See chap. 4 below for a more detailed discussion of juries in tort cases.

102. This relationship changed over time: in the 1830s and 1840s, defendants did considerably better than plaintiffs, even when settlements are considered to be favorable results for plaintiffs (on the assumption that defendants would not settle unless there was some likelihood of a plaintiff victory). This result is not statistically significant, because of the small number of cases in the sample. In the 1830s and into the 1840s, during a period of financial panic, juries were more favorably inclined toward debtors. In warranty cases where a slave seller sued on a note, juries in the 1830s were more sympathetic to the debtor/buyer, who won in four out of five such cases, as contrasted with one out of two in other decades. In the more common cases where a buyer sued a seller for his money back, buyers and sellers each won about half the time, in the same ratio they did over the entire period. There was no significant change over time in the wealth of the parties, jurors, or witnesses.

103. The odds for the plaintiff were 2.5 times worse if he was a great planter than if he was not. The category "RICH" described plaintiffs with fifty-one or

more slaves (which also encompassed all large landholders) or owners of more than four town lots (which included wealthy town-dwellers who did not own land within the county). It is interesting that verdicts for the plaintiff correlated with plaintiff's wealth but not with defendant's wealth; because of the small number of cases in which all information was available for plaintiffs *and* defendants, it was impossible to compare the wealth of the two in a particular case. It is also very possible that a larger sample might have allowed greater correlation to be seen with defendant's wealth. See appendix, table 9.

104. Gay, an Irishman in his late thirties, appeared on five juries in civil slave cases in the late 1850s. Both Bosley and Mock lived on two-hundred-acre farms on Sandy Creek; Mock owned eight slaves and Bosley ten. The jury was heavy with planters; there were five major planters out of ten identified jurors. Of the nonplanters, John Helm was a middle-class merchant of Natchez, with five slaves, a carriage, a lot, and nearly $15,000 in sales; Louis Miller was a smaller merchant, with one slave and $4,500 in sales; and three jurors, including James H. McCoy (later a slave buyer), paid only a poll tax in 1830. In this case, the jury seemed willing to split the difference in a dispute between two small planters. *Mock v. Bosley*, Drawer 172 #52, November 1830, Adams Cir. Ct., Mississippi, HNF; Book of Judgments OO p. 88 (jury list); Personal Tax Rolls, Adams County, Miss., Rolls B-592, 595.

105. John Marshall Mitnick, "From Neighbor-Witness to Judge of Proofs: The Transformation of the English Civil Juror," *American Journal of Legal History* 32 (1988): 201 (by the nineteenth century, a juror was already expected to make judgment based on evidence and to be sworn if a witness); Stephen Landsman, "The Civil Jury in America: Scenes from an Unappreciated History," *Hastings Law Journal* 44 (1993): 605 (the jury as "anchor in a sea of shifting doctrinal law in the nineteenth century"); William Nelson, *The Americanization of the Common Law* (Cambridge: Harvard University Press, 1975), 13–23 (the jury a central instrument of governance with power over law and fact questions); Wyatt-Brown, "Snopesian Crime," 190 (the jury a "poor man's 'ballot' "); see generally Marjorie S. Schultz, ed., "Symposium: The American Jury," *Law and Contemporary Problems* 43 (Autumn 1980).

The problem of media's influencing the jury was apparently a concern even in the early nineteenth century: the grand jury foreman in one Adams County trial wrote an open letter to Judge Stanhope Posey, published in the newspaper, complaining of excessive media coverage of the trial for which he was a juror. *Mississippi Free Trader*, November 29, 1854, 3.

106. James Hill of Wilkinson County, letter to attorney Davis, in *Hill v. Elam*, Drawer 345 #83, May 1853, Adams Cir. Ct., Miss., HNF. The median juror owned just three slaves, one town lot, and no agricultural land at all.

107. *Bishop Whipple's Southern Diary*, ed. Lester B. Shippee (reprint, Minneapolis: University of Minnesota Press, 1937), 24. Bishop Whipple visited courts in Florida and Georgia.

108. Ibid., 44.

109. The five-state sample of breach-of-warranty suits appealed to higher courts comprised a group in which buyers had won 60 percent of the time at the

trial level. Sellers were rewarded in their appeals; appellate courts redressed the balance in favor of sellers, overturning a higher number of jury verdicts in sellers' favor so that buyers and sellers won equally often at the appellate level in the five-state sample as a whole. In Louisiana, buyers won at the trial level 62 percent of the time, but at the appellate level only 52 percent of the time. Thus despite Louisiana's vaunted consumer protections, the higher court overturned verdicts for buyers at a higher rate than they overturned verdicts for sellers. In South Carolina, buyers/sellers verdicts were 60 percent/40 percent at the trial level, and this ratio was inverted at the appellate level, with buyers winning 40 percent, sellers 60 percent. In Alabama, buyers'/sellers' verdicts were 55 percent/45 percent at the trial level, with this ratio inverted at the appellate level, again because the state's highest court overturned more verdicts for buyers than for sellers. In Georgia and Mississippi, however, the high courts left buyers' advantage intact: in Georgia, buyers succeeded 57 percent of the time at the trial level, 54 percent at the appellate level; in Mississippi, buyers won 65 percent at the trial level, and at the same frequency at the appellate level. Interestingly, only South Carolina and Alabama had a significant fraction of credit sales in their warranty litigation (sellers suing on notes). Thus high-court suspicion of breach of warranty as a defense may partly explain why sellers did so well in South Carolina and Alabama Supreme Courts. See appendix, tables 5 and 6.

110. Frederick Douglass, "An Account of American Slavery," in *The Frederick Douglass Papers*, ed. John W. Blassingame, ed. (New Haven: Yale University Press, 1979), 1:141. Italics added.

111. See, e.g., Bibb, *Narrative*, in Osofsky, *Puttin' On Ole Massa*, 76–77; William and Ellen Craft, *Running a Thousand Miles for Freedom* (reprint, New York: Arno Press, 1969), 13–15. Of course, the quotations from statute books may suggest coaching or editing by white abolitionists; however, the overall theme of the importance of law in maintaining slavery pervades all of the narratives.

112. Douglass, "My Experience and My Mission to Great Britain," in *Douglass Papers*, 1:37.

113. Oakes, *Slavery and Freedom*, 69.

114. Douglass, *Douglass Papers*, 1:37.

115. Jon-Christian Suggs, *Whispered Consolations: Law and Narrative in African American Life* (Ann Arbor: University of Michigan Press, 1999), 26.

116. Ibid., 27.

117. Ibid., 28 and chapter 1 passim.

118. Simon Walker Autobiography, in *The American Slave: A Composite Autobiography*, ed. George P. Rawick (Westport, Conn.: Greenwood Pub. Co., 1977), ser. 1, vol. 6: Alabama and Indiana Narratives, 404.

119. Harriet Jacobs, *Incidents in the Life of a Slave Girl* (reprint, New York: Oxford University Press, 1988), 45.

120. James Lucas Autobiography, in Rawick, *American Slave*, supp. ser. 1, vol. 8: Mississippi Narratives, pt. 3, p. 1339.

121. Richard Mack Autobiography, in Rawick, *American Slave*, vol. 2: South Carolina Narratives, pts. 1 and 2, p. 151. See also Jim Allen Autobiography, in Rawick, *American Slave*, supp. ser. 1, vol. 6: Mississippi Narratives, pt. 1, p. 54

("Mars John Bussey drunk my Mudder up. I means by dat, Lee King took her and my brudder George for a whiskey debt"); Sam McAllum Autobiography, in Rawick, *American Slave*, supp. ser. 1, vol. 9: Mississippi Narratives, pt. 4, p. 1352 ("Mr. Stephenson were a surveyor an' he fell out wid Mr. McAllum an' had a lawsuit an' had to pay it in darkies. An' Mr. McAllum had de privilege of takin' me an' my mother, or another woman an' her two; an' he took us"); Ephraim Robinson Autobiography, ibid., 1852 (". . . the Marster knew if he hurt you or killed you it was his loss. Once when a slave hand ran away and they were trying to catch him, another plantation owner shot his Marster's slave in the hip and magots got in the place. The slave died, and not only did the slave owner sue the other man but never spoke to him again"); Adline Thomas Autobiography, in Rawick, *American Slave*, supp. ser. 1, vol. 10: Mississippi Narratives, pt. 5, p. 2094 ("She, her mother, sister, and a brother were put on the block and sold to settle the debt at Ripley, Mississippi").

122. Craft and Craft, *A Thousand Miles for Freedom*, 11.

123. Northup Narrative, in Osofsky, *Puttin' On Ole Massa*, 285.

124. Ibid., 289.

125. Mary Carpenter Autobiography, in Rawick, *American Slave*, supp. ser. 1, vol. 3: Georgia Narratives, pt. 1, p. 143.

126. Georgia Smith Autobiography, in Rawick, *American Slave*, vol. 13: Georgia Narratives, pts. 3 and 4, pp. 58–59.

127. Charles Ball, *Fifty Years in Chains; or, The Life of an American Slave* (New York: H. Dayton, 1859; reprint, Detroit, Mich.: Negro Universities Press, 1969), 10–11, 69–71.

128. Rose Russell—Folklore, in Rawick, *American Slave*, supp. ser. 1, vol. 9: Mississippi Narratives, pt. 4, p. 1903. According to the interviewer, Rose "laugh[ed] as she t[old] how they fooled her away from the old plantation."

129. See, e.g., Adam Singleton Autobiography, in Rawick, *American Slave*, supp. ser. 1, vol. 10: Mississippi Narratives, pt. 5, p. 1946; Lewis Adams Autobiography, in Rawick, *American Slave*, supp. ser. 1, vol. 6: Mississippi Narratives, pt. 1, pp. 5–6. Walter Johnson, *Soul by Soul: Life inside the Antebellum Slave Market* (Cambridge: Harvard University Press, 1999), 176–88 (discussing slaves' "shaping sales").

130. One consequence of the fact that the sample contained many more male runaways was an age skew in the sample: Runaways tended to be older than other slaves in the civil courtroom, averaging thirty years of age, which pushed the mean age of male slaves higher than that of female slaves.

131. Of slaves listed with skills in probate inventories, two were male to every one female (as opposed to three to one in sales documents).

132. See, e.g., *Bennett ads. Carter*, Box 32, Collection 139—S.C. Court of Appeals at Law, available at SCDAH, appeal reported in Riley 287 (S.C. 1836); *Minter v. Dent*, 3 Rich. 205 (S.C. 1832); *Dinkins v. Parkerson*, Box 34, February 1839, S.C. Sup. Ct. Records, SCDAH, appeal reported in *Parkerson v. Dinkins*, Rice 185 (S.C. 1839); *Boinest v. Leignez*, 2 Rich. 464 (S.C. 1846); *Thorington v. Hogan*, Docket #2690, Book 60, 1839, Ala. Sup. Ct. Records, available at ADAH. Appeal reported in *Hogan v. Thorington*, 8 Porter 428 (Ala. 1839).

CHAPTER TWO
HONOR AND DISHONOR

1. John Hope Franklin, for example, writing over fifty years ago, showed "how the notion of honor diffused down to all free members of the society from its ruling-class origins . . . and . . . demonstrate[d] the direct causal link between the southern ruling class's excessively developed sense of honor and the institution of slavery." Orlando Patterson, *Slavery and Social Death: A Comparative Study* (Cambridge: Harvard University Press, 1982), 95, referring to John Hope Franklin, *The Militant South, 1800–1861* (Cambridge: Harvard University Press, 1956).

2. See, e.g., Wyatt-Brown, *Southern Honor*, 95, 34.

3. Ibid., 14. Wyatt-Brown suggests that the mid-nineteenth-century North was characterized by the "embourgeoisement" of honor, in contrast to the South's "traditional honor." Bertram Wyatt-Brown, *Yankee Saints and Southern Sinners* (Baton Rouge: Louisiana State University Press, 1985), 185.

4. Wyatt-Brown, *Southern Honor*, 14.

5. Francis Wharton, *A Commentary on the Law of Evidence in Civil Issues*, 3d ed. (Philadelphia: Kay & Bro., 1888), vol. 1, §564.

6. See Wyatt-Brown, *Yankee Saints and Southern Sinners*, 185–94; Kenneth S. Greenberg, "The Nose, the Lie, and the Duel in the Antebellum South," *American Historical Review* (1990) 95 (1): 63.

7. See, e.g., Bertram Wyatt-Brown, "The Mask of Obedience: Male Slave Psychology in the Old South," *American Historical Review* 93 (1988): 1233; Charles S. Sydnor, "The Southerner and the Laws," *Journal of Southern History* 6 (1940): 3. For an illuminating discussion of the legal and political ramifications of nineteenth-century Northerners' "look within," see Jacob Katz Cogan, "Note. The Look Within: Property, Capacity, and Suffrage in Nineteenth-Century America," *Yale Law Journal* 107 (1997): 473–98.

8. Wyatt-Brown, *Southern Honor*, 47.

9. Kenneth S. Greenberg, *Honor and Slavery: Lies, Duels, Noses, Masks, Dressing as a Woman, Gifts, Strangers, Death, Humanitarianism, Slave Rebellions, the Pro-Slavery Argument, Baseball, Hunting, and Gambling in The Old South* (Princeton: Princeton University Press, 1996); Ayers, *Vengeance and Justice*, 14–15; Wyatt-Brown, *Southern Honor*, 327–61.

10. Ayers, *Vengeance and Justice*, 16.

11. See Wyatt-Brown, *Southern Honor*, 50–55.

12. Steven Shapin, *A Social History of Truth: Civility and Science in Seventeenth-Century England* (Chicago: University of Chicago Press, 1994), 67, 107–9.

13. Wyatt-Brown, *Yankee Saints and Southern Sinners*, 187; George Fredrickson, *The Black Image in the White Mind: The Debate on Afro-American Character and Destiny, 1817–1914* (New York: Harper and Row, 1971), 61–71; J. William Harris, *Plain Folk and Gentry in a Slave Society: White Liberty and Black Slavery in Augusta's Hinterlands* (Middletown, Conn.: Wesleyan University Press, 1985), 5–6, 94–119; James Oakes, *The Ruling Race: A History of American Slaveholders* (New York: Alfred A. Knopf, 1982), 138–47; J. Mills Thornton III,

Politics and Power in a Slave Society: Alabama, 1800–1860 (Baton Rouge: Louisiana State University Press, 1978), 442–59; Ayers, *Vengeance and Justice*, 13–15.

14. See George M. Fredrickson, "Aristocracy and Democracy," in *The Arrogance of Race*, 134, 138–41. Fredrickson attributes this insight about the democratization of honor to Wilbur J. Cash. See Cash, *The Mind of the South* (New York: Doubleday, 1941). This paragraph draws from Gross, "Litigating Whiteness," 109, 157.

15. Patterson, *Slavery and Social Death*, 96.

16. Ibid., 79. See also Ayers, *Vengeance and Justice*, 26 ("There can be no doubt that cultures of honor existed for centuries before the South, or the New World, were known to Europeans; that cultures of honor flourished independently of slavery; and indeed that cultures of honor survive to the present. Nevertheless, it seems certain that honor would have died in the South without the hothouse atmosphere provided for that culture by slavery").

17. Of course, there were societies with slaves, such as ancient Israel, that did not have pronounced honor cultures. Patterson, like other historians of slavery, distinguishes "slave societies," in which slavery was "structurally very important," from "societies with slaves," where slaveholding did not become central to the culture. See also Ira Berlin, *Slaves without Masters: The Free Negro in the Antebellum South* (New York: Pantheon Books, 1974).

18. Oakes, *Slavery and Freedom*, 14–16.

19. Wyatt-Brown, *Southern Honor*, 363.

20. Oakes, *Slavery and Freedom*, 18–21 (citing ex-slave narratives).

21. Wyatt-Brown, "The Mask of Obedience," 1228–52.

22. Frederick Douglass, *My Bondage and My Freedom* (New York: Miller, Orton & Mulligan, 1855; reprint, New York: Dover Publications, 1969), 245–46.

23. Ibid., 94.

24. Kathleen M. Brown, *Good Wives, Nasty Wenches, and Anxious Patriarchs: Gender, Race, and Power in Colonial Virginia* (Chapel Hill: University of North Carolina Press, 1996), 179–86.

25. James Martin Autobiography, in Rawick, *American Slave*, vol. 4: Texas Narratives, pts. 1 and 2, p. 93. See also Laura Stewart Autobiography, in Rawick, *American Slave*, supp. ser. 1, vol. 4: Georgia Narratives, pt. 2, p. 594 ("Dey would line 'em up like horses or cows, and look in de mouf' at dey teef' and den march 'em down together to market in crowds on first Tuesday sale day"); Tom McGruder Autobiography, in Rawick, *American Slave*, vol. 13: Georgia Narratives, pts. 3 and 4, p. 76 ("We wuz put on the block just like cattle and sold to one man today and another tomorrow. I was sold three times after coming to this state"); George Womble Autobiography, ibid., 179 ("On the day that I was sold three doctors examined me and I heard one of them say: 'This is a thoroughbred boy . . .' "); John Glover Autobiography, in Rawick, *American Slave*, vol. 2: South Carolina Narratives, pts. 1 and 2, p. 140 ("I see em sell slaves heap of times . . . Bid em off just like horses en mules.")

26. Oakes, *Slavery and Freedom*, 20–22.

27. See ibid., 56–79 (discussing the connections between liberal capitalism and an ideology of individual rights); Oakes, *The Ruling Race*, 191, xi–xii, 69–73; see generally Robert W. Fogel and Stanley L. Engerman, *Time on the Cross: The Economics of American Negro Slavery*, 2 vols. (New York: W. W. Norton, 1989).

28. Edward J. Balleisen, "Reconstructing the Law of Failure: The 1841 Federal Bankrupty Act and the Culture of Debtor-Creditor Relations in America" (paper presented to the American Society for Legal History Annual Meeting, Seattle, Wash., October, 1998), 4, 6.

29. Wyatt-Brown, *Southern Honor*, 73.

30. Shapin, *A Social History of Truth*, 95.

31. Ayers, *Vengeance and Justice*, 18. See also sources cited in chap. 1, n. 6. But see Wyatt-Brown, *Southern Honor*, 401 ("Common law and lynch law were ethically compatible").

32. Hogan and Davis, *William Johnson's Natchez*, 1:336, 338. Pages of the newspaper often contained the "cards" of outraged and offended gentlemen challenging one another to duel. Duelists in 1827 to 1832 included lawyers Ralph North, William Shields, and Aylette Buckner. Edward Ayers has noted that "most duels were fought . . . between young men in the professions dependent upon the manipulation of language and image: law, journalism, and politics." Ibid., 25.

33. Hogan and Davis, *William Johnson's Natchez*, 2:492. Although an antidueling association arose in Natchez in 1828, and a committee of lawyers drew up a constitution providing for a "Court of Honor for the decision of all differences" to replace dueling, there is no evidence that the "Court" ever went into operation. Across the Deep South, lawyers walked the line between obeying the laws against duels and obeying the demands of honor, in a profession they deemed the path to honor.

34. Ayers, *Vengeance and Justice*, 18.

35. Wyatt-Brown, "Snopesian Crime," 174.

36. Thus Wyatt-Brown is wrong to conclude that the relationship of law and culture in the South "has more to do with relations among classes of whites than the familiar and overstudied repression of blacks"; whites asserted their honor not only in relation to one another but through the dishonor of blacks. Ibid.

37. Greenberg, "Masks and Slavery," in *Honor and Slavery*, 24–50.

38. *Stroud v. Mays*, Docket #483, September 2, 1849, Ga. Sup. Ct. Records, GDAH. Appeal reported in 7 Ga. 269 (1849).

39. *Moorhead v. Gayle*, Docket #1113, Book 32, pp. 289–93, June Term 1832, Ala. Sup. Ct. Records, ADAH.

40. *Bennett ads. Carter*, Collection 139, South Carolina Court of Appeals and Law, Box 32, Opinions 1837, SCDAH. Appeal reported in Riley 287 (S.C. 1837).

41. See, e.g., *Franklin v. Grissam*, Drawer 145 #74, May Term 1827, Adams County Cir. Ct. Records, HNF; *Alston v. Rose*, Drawer 112 #4, November Term 1822, Adams County Cir. Ct. Records, HNF; see also *Strozier v. Carroll*, Docket #3049, June 1860, Ga. Sup. Ct. Records, GDAH, appeal reported in 31 Ga. 557 (1860).

42. *Rodrigues ads. Habersham*, Collection 139, South Carolina Court of Appeals and Law, Box 37, SCDAH, July, 1842. Appeal reported in 1 Speers 314 (S.C. 1843).

43. *Manes v. Kenyon*, Docket #1552, April 4, 1855, Ga. Sup. Ct. Records, GDAH. Appeal reported in 18 Ga. 291 (1855). The slave Mary had been traded to Kenyon by Manes; Kenyon sued Manes for deceit on the basis of Mary's unsoundness. Sarah Pearce was a witness on Kenyon's behalf, testifying that Andrew Chambless, although interested in buying Mary from Kenyon, would have done so only as a swindle. Manes, meanwhile, felt that he had been cheated by whoever had sold Mary to *him*.

44. Ibid.

45. Deposition of J. M. Leatherman, *Hill v. Winston*, Drawer 336, #25, May, 1849, Adams County Cir. Ct. Records, HNF.

46. J. W. Kendall Deposition, ibid. Johnson sold the slave John to John Holmes in Tennessee. *Holmes v. Guice*, #57, Drawer 347, May 1854, Adams County Cir. Ct. Records, HNF.

47. Testimony of John B. Righter, *Abbey v. Osborne*, Drawer 275, #52, April 1839. See also *Randolph v. Barnett*, Drawer 188, Folder 2A, November 1832, #38, Adams County Cir. Ct. Records, HNF (Interrogatories to William Stroud and Julius Bettis of Louisiana: "Do you or either of you know the general character of said John Randolph for truth or honesty[?]"; to Moses Groves: "Do you know the general reputation of said John Randolph in your neighborhood for truth and veracity[?]"); Deposition of Moses Wanzer, *Beeler v. Leeper*, Drawer 169, #26, May, 1830, Adams County Cir. Ct. Records, HNF (Wanzer was "enough acquainted with Thomas Beeler to say that he *could not believe* him on oath, judging from his former character . . . he first knew him at Natchez Under the Hill as a speculator in upcountry produce, he next knew him in New Orleans prison, as being there on two years service for swindling a man out of a Boat load of Hogs . . ."); testimony of Cornelius Cooper, *Alston v. Rose*, Drawer 112, #4, November 1822, Adams County Cir. Ct. Records, HNF ("I tried to shame Allston for the trick he was trying to put upon Rose").

48. Cross-interrogatories to Major L. Smith and David James, *Powell v. Wells*, #33, Drawer 350, May 1856, Adams Circuit Court, HNF. See also Deposition of Richard J. Harris, *Guice v. Holmes*, #57, Drawer 347, May 1854, Adams Circuit Court, HNF ("I am not a negro dealer and never ha[ve] been . . .").

49. Deposition of Dr. Luke Blackburn, *Davis v. Wood*, #40, Drawer 348, May 1854, Adams Cir. Ct., HNF. Davis kept slaves with Thomas G. James and John D. James at Forks-of-the-Road.

50. Ingraham, *South-West*, 245. "Negro traders soon accumulate great wealth . . . Their admission into society, however, is not recognised. Planters associate with them freely enough, in the way of business, but notice them no farther"; Scarborough, "Lords or Capitalists?" 244; William Terry Papers, LSU; Tadman, *Speculators and Slaves*, 210. See also *Mississippi Free Trader*, November 15, 1854, 2 ("The reader is referred to the card of Mr. David Middleton, formerly of Natchez, who has opened a Slave Depot in New Orleans, No. 10 Moreau St. He is well known to this community, and will doubtless command a large share of their patronage . . ."); Richard Randall Tansey, "Bernard Kendig and the New

Orleans Slave Trade," *Louisiana History* 23 (1982): 159–78; Johnson, *Soul by Soul*, 54–55. Tadman, *Speculators and Slaves*, 192–209, shows the involvement of traders in the social, political, and economic life of the South. Out of 152 cases in my sample for which the outcome was known, the plaintiff won in 64 cases, the defendant won or the case was dismissed in 64, 11 settled, 5 ended in nonsuit, and 8 had other outcomes. Among trader-defendants, 9 won, 9 lost, and 3 settled their cases; among trader-plaintiffs, 2 won, 3 lost, and 1 settled.

51. Deposition of John R. Gwyn; Summons for Henry Turner, March 29, 1841; Letter from Henry Turner to John A. Quitman, April 9, 1841; Deposition of John M. Pelton, October 11, 1841; Quitman-Turner Correspondence, 1841–42, John Quitman Papers, N.S. 4062, ser. J, pt. 6, reel 6, Southern Historical Collection, University of North Carolina, Chapel Hill, N.C.

Civil suits involving slaves were extremely rare in the federal courts. Only five cases from the Deep South in the entire antebellum period contained any issues of warranty or replevin for slaves (I searched federal courts of appeal using Lexis for the key word "slave" for all years through 1861). It is uncertain why Ballard brought suit in federal court, unless he felt sure he would have no luck before a local jury in Adams County. Ballard declared himself a citizen of Virginia, although he was a transient trader, and Turner's lawyers considered challenging federal jurisdiction on failure of diversity grounds because Ballard was, in their view, a Natchez citizen himself.

52. Robert E. May, *John A. Quitman: Old South Crusader* (Baton Rouge: Louisiana State University Press, 1985), 108–9.

53. A federal court could exercise jurisdiction over the case only if there was a "diversity of citizenship" between the parties; if they were both citizens of Mississippi, the case would have to be tried in a circuit court in Mississippi.

54. Letter from Quitman to J. M. Pelton, October 2, 1841, Quitman-Turner Correspondence.

55. Discovery motion for Rice M. Ballard's account books, December 23, 1841; Letter from Quitman & McMurran to Pelton, December 28, 1841; Deposition of Glendy Burke, January 1842; Interrogatories to J. M. Pelton, January 1842; Quitman-Turner Correspondence.

56. Letters from Turner to Quitman, June 7, 1842, and June 26, 1842, Quitman-Turner Correspondence.

57. May, *Quitman*, 111. It took Quitman until 1857 to pay off Ballard's debt. Ibid.

58. Letters between Quitman & McMurran and Montgomery & Boyd, August 25, September 23, 24, and 25, 1842, Quitman-Turner Correspondence.

59. Harnett T. Kane, *Natchez on the Mississippi* (New York: William Morrow & Co., 1947), 278.

60. Terms of Settlement, November 1, 1842, Quitman-Turner Correspondence.

61. Yet it was great planters and their lawyers who kept their correspondence; thus historians may study their lawsuits. Few records remain of the smaller farmer who was the more typical plaintiff in a warranty suit.

62. Shapin, *A Social History of Truth*, 84, 92.

63. Hogan and Davis, introduction to *William Johnson's Natchez*, 55–62; *Natchez Courier*, June 20, 1851.

64. Drawer 245 #615, April 1839 (dismissed November 1840), Adams Cir. Ct., Miss., HNF. Replevin was an equitable remedy, in which the plaintiff asked the court to return property that had been wrongfully detained by another.

65. Statement of Lynch—Claim to Ellen, Folder 6, Box 2E906, Winchester Family Papers, CAH-UTA; Adams County Land Deed Records; Hogan and Davis, *William Johnson's Natchez*, 346 n. 21.

66. Apparently, Bob had Ellen "bid off" under two separate executions—an earlier one for $50 to some unknown white man, and then for $150 to Christopher Kyle. Kyle had recently completed the manumission of two female slaves and their children—Nancy and her two sons in 1819, and Caroline and her son in 1824; he eventually left most of his property to Nancy. Deed Book R29, Adams County Land Deed Records; Davis, *Black Experience*, 59.

67. Charles Lynch to George Winchester, April 4, 1838, Folder 2, Box 2E904, Winchester Family Papers, CAH-UTA.

68. George Winchester to Charles Lynch, March 21, 1837, Folder 1, Box 2E904, Winchester Family Papers, CAH-UTA.

69. Ibid.

70. Charles Lynch to George Winchester, April 4, 1838.

71. *Liles v. Bass*, Box 39, 1839, S.C. Sup. Ct. Records, SCDAH, appeal reported in Cheves 85 (S.C. 1840).

72. Shapin, *A Social History of Truth*, 92.

73. *Stevenson v. Reaves*, Docket #4043, Book 171, January 1854, Ala. Sup. Ct. Records, ADAH. Appeal reported in 24 Ala. 425 (1854).

74. *Laurence v. McFarlane*, Docket #1722, New Orleans, March 1829, SCA-UNO. Appeal reported in 7 Mart. N.S. 558 (1829). There were also several cases in which one party successfully objected to secondhand slave testimony, and the other party did not object to its exclusion. See, e.g., *George v. Greenwood*, Docket #3687, January 1856, N.O., *SCA-UNO*, appeal reported in 11 La. Ann. 299 ("Struck out: From the negro's statement he was carried to Texas—runaway and went back to Cherokee Nation").

75. *Cozzins v. Whitacker* [*sic*], Book 34, Docket #1261, January 1833, Ala. Sup. Ct. Records, ADAH. Appeal reported in *Cozzins v. Whitaker* 3 Stew. & P. 322 (1833).

76. *Buhler v. McHatton*, Docket #3448, March 1854, N.O., SCA-UNO. Appeal reported in 9 La. Ann. 192 (1854).

77. *Wallace & Wallace v. Spullock*, Docket #3608, December 1860, Ga. Sup. Ct. Records, GDAH. Appeal reported in 32 Ga. 488 (1861). See, e.g., *RR Co. v. Pickett*, 36 Ga. 85 (1867).

78. Cobb, *Law of Negro Slavery*, 231.

79. Docket #7418, December 1855, RG 32, Drawer 105, MDAH. Appeal reported in 30 Miss. 147 (1855).

80. *Brocklebank v. Johnson*, Box 28, April 1834, S.C. Sup. Ct. Records, SCDAH. Appeal reported in *Johnson v. Brocklebank*, 2 Hill 353 (S.C. 1834).

81. *Dinkins ads. Parkerson*, Box 34, 1839, S.C. Sup. Ct. Records, SCDAH. Appeal reported in *Parkerson v. Dinkins*, Rice 185 (S.C. 1839). See also *Gantt ads. Venning*, City Court of Charleston, S.C., January 1840, SCDAH, appeal reported in *Venning v. Gantt*, Cheves 87 (S.C. 1840); *Hillier v. Hume*, City Court

of Charleston, S.C., 1854, SCDAH, unreported; *Mangham v. Cox & Waring*, Docket #2952, Book 1856, 1st Div. No. 32, Ala. Sup. Ct. Records, ADAH, appeal reported in 29 Ala. 81 (1856); *Dean v. Traylor*, Docket #549, 1849, Ga. Sup. Ct. Records, GDAH, appeal reported in 8 Ga. 169; *Feagin v. Beasley*, Docket #2126, 1857, Ga. Sup. Ct. Records, GDAH, appeal reported in 23 Ga. 176; *Buckner v. Blackwell & Ballard*, Drawer 353 #23, May Term 1857, Adams Cir. Ct., Miss., HNF; *James v. McCoy*, Drawer 344 #69, May Term 1854, Adams Cir. Ct., Miss., HNF; *Herring v. James*, Drawer 329 #169, May 1847, Adams Cir. Ct., Miss., HNF; *Smith v. Meek*, Drawer 232 #76, April 1838, Adams Cir. Ct., Miss., HNF; *Rutherford v. Newson*, Docket #4018, December 1866, Ga. Sup. Ct. Records, GDAH, appeal reported in 36 Ga. 246 (1867); *Williams v. Vance*, Dudley 97 (S.C. 1837) ("Vance inquired of Robin's mother, whether Robin had ever had the measles, and she informed him that she had").

82. *Cotton v. Rogolio*, Drawer 202 #143, April 1837, Adams Cir. Ct., Miss., HNF.

83. *Barnaby v. Tomlinson*, Drawer 31, July 1799/1805, Adams Cty. Ct., Miss. Territ., HNF.

84. *Gantt ads. Venning*, City Court of Charleston, S.C., January 1840, SCDAH, appeal reported in *Venning v. Gantt*, Cheves 87 (S.C. 1840).

85. *Bush v. Jackson*, Docket #4012, Book 174 #14, January 1854, Ala. Sup. Ct. Records, ADAH. See also *Tilman v. Stringer*, Docket #2486, 1858, Ga. Sup. Ct. Records, GDAH ("counsel for defendant objected to the witness' stating any thing as to what the negro said in regard to her situation and that she complained—in the ground that it was hearsay—the Court overruled the objection and allowed the testimony . . . stated that the negro complained of head ache and said she had pains in her back and side and shoulders . . .").

86. *Hill v. Winston*, Drawer 336 #25, May 1849, Adams Cir. Ct., Miss., HNF.

87. See Thomas D. Morris, "Slaves and the Rules of Evidence in Criminal Trials," *Chicago-Kent Law Review* 68 (1993): 1209–40; Johnson, *Soul by Soul*, 172–76, 210–12.

88. *Fondren v. Durfee*, 39 Miss. 324 (1860).

89. *Stringfellow v. Mariott*, 11 Ala. 573 (1836).

90. *Bates v. Eckles & Brown*, Book 153, January 1855, Ala. Sup. Ct. Records, ADAH. Appeal reported in 26 Ala. 655 (1855).

91. 26 Ala. at 659.

92. Ibid., 660. The Alabama Supreme Court later limited the *Bates* holding, ruling in *Blackman v. Johnson* that a witness could not testify that a slave prayed or called on others to pray for him as evidence of sickness. *Blackman v. Johnson*, 35 Ala. 252 (1859); see also *Barker v. Coleman*, 35 Ala. 221 (1859).

CHAPTER THREE
SLAVES' CHARACTER

1. *Smith v. McCall*, 1 McCord 220, 224 (S.C. 1821).

2. *Timrod v. Shoolbred*, 1 Bay 325, 325 (S.C. 1793). The sound price rule was strengthened in the next two decades. See *Wells v. Spears*, 1 McCord 421 (S.C. 1821) (holding that an express warranty of title would not exclude an implied

warranty of soundness); *Stinson ads. Piper*, 3 McCord 251 (1825) (holding that the implied warranty extends to mind as well as body); *Smith v. Bank* of S.C., Riley Eq. 113 (S.C. 1837) (holding that only an explicit refusal to warrant soundness negated the implication of a warranty).

3. South Carolina was the only common-law state to adopt the "sound price" rule explicitly; Louisiana's redhibition law provided similar consumer protections. The Alabama and Georgia supreme courts both ruled that a purchaser could recover only for intentional fraud without an express warranty. *Cozzins v. Whitaker*, 3 Stew. & P. 322 (Ala. 1833); *Stroud v. Mays*, 7 Ga. 269 (1848). The Mississippi High Court of Errors and Appeals never ruled directly on this issue.

4. *Smith v. McCall*, at 224.

5. Louisiana's Civil Code included implied warranties for specific moral qualities of slaves, among them the habits of running away and of theft. La. Civ. Code, bk. 3, tit. 7, chap. 6, sec. 3, "Of the Vices of Things Sold," arts. 2496–2505 (1824). Alabama allowed buyers to recover for deceit involving oral representations of moral qualities. *Cozzins v. Whitaker*, 3 Stew. & P. 322, 322 (1833) (permitting the buyer to recover the price of a slave that was "so dishonest, lazy and vicious—of such a bad character and low repute, that he would not sell at a high price"). Georgia similarly rejected implied warranties but interpreted fraud broadly. See *Stroud v. Mays*, 7 Ga. 269 (1848); *Dye v. Wall*, 6 Ga. 584 (1849).

6. La. Civ. Code, "Of The Vices of Things Sold."

7. See John Blassingame, *The Slave Community: Plantation Life in the Old South* (New York: Oxford University Press, 1972), 133–34; Deborah Gray White, *Ar'n't I a Woman: Female Slaves in the Plantation South* (New York: W. W. Norton & Co., 1985), 27–61. The existence of "Sambo" as a personality type has been hotly debated; I am talking about "Sambo" only as a figment of white ideology.

8. See Fredrickson, *The Arrogance of Race*, 211.

9. Self-conscious legal writers of treatises, as well as appellate judges, drew heavily on such stereotypes of the black slave as a happy, docile "Sambo"; a rebellious "Nat"; or a sensuous "Jezebel." See Fisher, "Ideology and Imagery in the Law of Slavery," 1051.

10. *White v. Cumming*, Docket #357, Alexandria, 1826, available in SCA-UNO. Appeal reported in 5 Mart. N.S. 199 (La. 1826).

11. Testimony of William Rudder, *Castellano v. Peillon*, Docket #944, New Orleans, May 1824, SCA-UNO. Appeal reported in 2 Mart. N.S. 466 (La. 1824).

12. Testimony of Etienne Girard, *Petit v. Laville*, Docket #4660, New Orleans, June 1843, SCA-UNO. Appeal reported in 5 Rob. 117 (La. 1843).

13. *Pahnvitz v. Fassman*, Docket #512, New Orleans, June 1847, SCA-UNO. Appeal reported in 2 La. Ann. 625 (1847).

14. See, e.g., *Chretien v. Theard*, Docket #612, New Orleans, February 1822, SCA-UNO. Appeal reported in 11 Mart. O.S. 11 (La. 1822).

15. Docket #1724, New Orleans, March 1829, SCA-UNO. Appeal reported in 7 Mart. 558 (La. 1829). See also *Walker v. Hays*, Docket #6606, New Orleans, February 1860, SCA-UNO. Appeal reported in 15 La. An. 640 (1860) ("The plaintiff . . . established by Mr. Hair that [Agnes] was a very intelligent servant" [plaintiff's brief]).

16. *Farmer v. Fiske*, Docket #5248, New Orleans, December 1844, SCA-UNO. Appeal reported in 9 Rob. La. 351 (1844).

17. *Dunbar v. Skillman*, Docket #1575, New Orleans, March 1828, SCA-UNO. Appeal reported in 6 Mart. N.S. 539 (1828). Testimony of Robert Nelson, 6, George Long, 18.

18. Complaint, *Taylor v. Cochran*, Drawer 7 #1441, June Term 1802, Adams County Ct., Miss. Territ., HNF.

19. Memo, apparently by judge, *Perkins v. Hundley*, Drawer 91 #25, May Term 1819, Adams Cir. Ct., Miss., HNF.

20. Deposition of William Shaffer, *Tull v. Walker*, Drawer 70, May Term 1830, Adams Cir. Ct., Miss., HNF.

21. See, e.g., *Laurence v. McFarlane*, Docket #1722, New Orleans, March 1829, SCA-UNO ("sold [Fanny] because she was lazy"). Appeal reported in 7 Mart. N.S. 558 (La. 1829); *Gaulden v. Lawrence, Ga.* (slave lazy, although she was "warranted a #1 negro").

22. *Romer v. Woods*, f.w.c., Docket #1911, New Orleans, January 1851, SCA-UNO. Appeal reported in 6 La. An. 29 (1851).

23. See, e.g., *Icar v. Suares*, Docket #2649, New Orleans, February 1834, SCA-UNO. Appeal reported in 7 La. 517 (1835); *Briant v. Marsh*, 19 La. 391 (September 1841); and chap. 5 below.

24. *Cozzins v. Whitacker*, Docket #1261, Book 34, January Term 1833, Ala. Sup. Ct. Records, ADAH. Appeal reported in 3 Stew. & P. 322 (Ala. 1833).

25. Ibid.

26. Ibid.

27. *Williams v. Fambro*, 30 Ga. 232 (1860).

28. *Bonnet v. Ramsay*, Docket #1468, New Orleans, July 1825, SCA-UNO. Appeal reported in 6 Mart. N.S. 129 (1827).

29. See also Robert W. Fogel, *Without Consent or Contract: The Rise and Fall of American Slavery* (New York: W. W. Norton, 1989), 68 ("Masters even put a price on 'virtues' and 'vices.' Slaves labeled as runaways, lazy, thieves, drunks, suicidals, or having 'heredit vices' sold for average discounts of up to 65 percent as compared with slaves of the same age who were 'fully guaranteed' "); Frederick L. Olmsted, *Cotton Kingdom: A Traveler's Observations on Cotton and Slavery in the American Slave States* (New York: Mason Brothers, 1862), 2:81, 211 (discussing the valuation of slaves according to "blood," color, religion, and intelligence).

30. Testimony of Thomas N. Gadsden, *Gantt v. Venning*, City Ct. of Charleston, Box 34, January 1840, S.C. Sup. Ct. Records, SCDAH. Appeal reported in Cheves 87 (S.C. 1840).

31. *Campbell ads. Atchison*, Box 21, March 1827, S.C. Sup. Ct. Records, SCDAH. Appeal unreported. The word "old" in the first quotation was added to the transcript in a different ink.

32. Overall, it does not appear that either skilled slaves, house servants, or mulattoes were overrepresented in litigation. In litigation, female skilled slaves were usually house servants, especially washers and cooks; male slaves were most likely to be carpenters or blacksmiths. Field hands' work was not considered skilled work. In sales documents, as cataloged in Hall and Manning, *Slaves in*

Louisiana, 1735–1820, the most common skills noted were agricultural skills— woodcutting, gardening, plowing, and field labor—because the Hall database counted fieldwork as a "skill." In her rural sample of sales and miscellaneous transactions, 38 percent of slaves sold as skilled fell into this category. Only 20 percent were domestic workers and 13 percent craftspeople (including carpenters and blacksmiths). Of slaves listed with skills in probate inventories, two were male to every one female (as opposed to three to one in sales documents). New Orleans probate inventories included more mulattoes, more house servants, and more craftspeople. Overall, 35 percent of skilled slaves noted in estate lists were agricultural workers, 30 percent were domestic workers, 9 percent were craftspeople, and 14 percent worked in transportation or industry. It does not appear from this comparison that skilled slaves were disproportionately represented in litigation, but it may be that highly skilled craftspeople were disproportionately represented *among* skilled slaves in litigation.

33. Box 28, April 1834, S.C. Sup. Ct. Records, SCDAH. Appeal reported in *Johnson v. Brockelbank*, 2 Hill 353 (1834).

34. Ibid.; see also *Nowell v. Gadsden*, Charleston, Box 42, May 1848, S.C. Supreme Court Records, SCDAH, appeal unreported (breach of warranty for Lander because of illness and lack of skill as blacksmith); *Chretien v. Theard*, Docket #612, New Orleans, February 1822, SCA-UNO, appeal reported in 11 Mart. La. 11 (1822) (buyer "instantly discovered that [Lafortune] was neither a carpenter nor joiner . . . [he was] a drunkard and a thief and also an insubordinate slave"); *Athey v. Olive*, 34 Ala. 711, 712–13 (1859) (defendant refused to pay note because Matilda was crazy and because "Matilda . . . was represented by the plaintiff to be a good cook, washer and ironer, and seamstress, [but] that she came up to neither of these representations"). In Louisiana, it was legally sufficient to prove that the buyer had purchased the slave solely on the basis of the seller's declaration that she had skills she turned out not to have. La. Civ. Code, bk. 3, tit. 6, chap. 7, sec. 3, art. 2507.

35. *Petit v. Laville*, Docket #4660, June 1841, New Orleans, SCA-UNO. Appeal reported in 5 Rob. La. 117 (1841). See also *Buhler v. McHatton*, Docket #3448, New Orleans, February 1854, SCA-UNO, appeal reported in 9 La. An. 192 (1854) ("Jane has proved entirely useless as a cook, and 2d, because she is addicted to madness, insanity, or habitual craziness . . .").

36. Female slaves were overrepresented in litigation as compared to skilled slaves listed in sales documents, where skilled men outnumbered women two to one, and estate inventories, where the ratio was three to one. Hall and Manning, *Slaves in Louisiana, 1735–1820*.

While nearly half of all slaves listed in Louisiana probate inventories cataloged in *Slaves in Louisiana* had a skill noted, only 8.2 percent of Louisiana slaves were sold as skilled. In other words, sellers of slaves were reluctant to declare slave skills; they did not want to be sued for redhibition if a slave turned out not to have the skills she was declared to have. Bills of sale mention only a fraction of the skills noted in probate inventories. Of course, administrators of estates may have been motivated to note skills in more detail to raise the value of the estate.

37. *Chretien v. Theard*, Docket #612, New Orleans, February 1822, SCA-UNO, appeal reported in 11 Mart. La. 11 (1822). See also *Colcocke v. Goode*,

3 McCord 513 (S.C. 1826) (no implied warranty that one of a slave gang is a carpenter).

38. *Stone & Best v. Watson*, 37 Ala. 279 (1861).

39. *Campbell ads. Atchison*, Box 21, March 1827, S.C. Supreme Court Records, SCDAH (emphasis in original), appeal unreported.

40. *Porcher ads. Caldwell*, Box 37, March 1842, S.C. Supreme Court Records, SCDAH. Appeal reported in 2 McMullan 329 (S.C. 1842).

41. Fredrickson, *Black Image*, 53–54.

42. Dr. Samuel Cartwright, "Negro Freedom an Impossibility under Nature's Laws," *DeBow's Review* 30 (1860): 651.

43. H., "Remarks on Overseers, and the Proper Treatment of Slaves," *Farmers' Register* 5 (1837): 302.

44. Fredrickson, *Black Image*, 52.

45. See E. Brooks Holifield, "Scottish Philosophy and Southern Theology," chap. 5 of *The Gentleman Theologians: American Theology in Southern Culture, 1795–1860* (Durham, N.C.: Duke University Press, 1978). Many Southern theologians adopted the "faculty psychology" of the Scottish philosophers, which posited an innate " 'moral sense' antecedent to self-regarding motives and independent of revelation." Ibid., 130, 138.

46. See, e.g., J.D.B. DeBow, ed., *The Industrial Resources, Statistics, etc., of the United States, and More Particularly of the Southern and Western States*, vol. 2 (New York: D. Appleton & Co., 1854). More specifically, see John Campbell, "Negro-Mania: being an examination of the falsely-assumed equality of the various races of men," ibid., 196 ("Lawrence remarks, that the difference of color 'between the white and the black races is not more striking than the preeminence of the former in moral feelings and in mental endowments.' "); Chancellor Harper, "Negro Slavery, Address at the Society for the Advancement of Learning, of South Carolina," ibid., 205 ("Objection answered—'The slave is cut off from the means of intellectual, moral, and religious improvement, and in consequence his moral character becomes depraved, and he addicted to degrading vices'"; arguing that the slave cannot improve himself because he has no capacity for moral character development). See also Cobb, *Law of Negro Slavery*, 37–38 (considering "[t]he development of his moral character, when in contact with civilization," and finding that blacks "exhibit the same characteristics" of moral degradation, whatever the circumstances).

47. Samuel Cartwright, "Dr. Cartwright on the Caucasians and the Africans," *DeBow's Review* 25 (1858): 53–54. See also Cobb, *Law of Negro Slavery*, 35 ("[T]he negro . . . is imitative, sometimes eminently so, but his mind is never inventive or suggestive. Improvement never enters into his imagination").

48. Rice 325 (S.C. 1839). In this case, the seller sued the buyer because he did not pay his note.

49. Ibid., 326–28; Leonard Wideman, 39, Jonathan Johnson, 9, Alexander Cumming, 49, Manuscript Population Schedules of the Sixth Census of the United States, Roll 501, Abbeville, South Carolina, 1840 Census.

50. Rice at 330–35; Abbeville 1840 Census.

51. Rice at 332–33.

52. Ibid., 334–40 (emphasis in original); Abbeville 1840 Census.

53. Rice at 337–39; Abbeville 1840 Census; Manuscript Population Schedules of the Fifth Census of the United States, Roll 172, Edgefield, South Carolina, 1830 Census.

54. He began by instructing the jury that the defendant could not recover tort damages for the plaintiff's deceit; the only question would be whether the defendant was obligated to pay the one-hundred-dollar note. Ibid., 342. This was a legal issue that cropped up frequently: the distinction between breach of warranty, a contract action, which could result only in a return of the slave and/or refund of the price; and deceit, a tort action, for which the injured party could recover punitive damages. However, the judge, having settled the legal issue, made it clear that the moral issues would decide the case. He also instructed the jury that they must find evidence of fraud in order for the buyer-defendant to win.

55. Ibid., 342. Emphasis added.

56. Ibid., 342–43. The jury found for the seller-plaintiff, Johnson; Wideman appealed on the grounds that the judge's instructions had biased the jury for the plaintiff by ruling out damages for the defendant. In a per curiam opinion, which at that time referred to an unsigned unanimous opinion, the high court affirmed Justice John B. O'Neall's lower court judgment. In 1839, S.C. Supreme Court justices sat on the circuit courts as well, and it was not unusual for them to later renew their own opinion. Ibid., 344–45.

57. Fredrickson, *The Arrogance of Race*, 215.

58. See also *Cozzins v. Whitacker*, Book 34, Docket #1261, January 1833, Ala. Sup. Ct. Records, ADAH, appeal reported in 3 Stew. & P. 322 (1833) (stating that "[plaintiff's w]itness Mr. Henry Fort proved . . . that he Anthony would steal chickens &c and run away and that, that was his character," but defendant's witness, Mr. Madden, testified "that it was very common amongst Negroes to steal a little and run away, it was greatly owing to the kind of master or owner they had"); *Perkins v. Hundley*, Drawer 91#25, May, 1819, Adams Cir. Ct., Miss., HNF (noting that Lawton was good slave under his master, but "after his master died [Lawton] became a little unruly which was the reason of his being sold").

59. The South Carolina high court accepted this line of reasoning in other cases as well. See *Lowry v. M'Burney*, 1 Mill 237 (S.C. 1817) (the seller argued that "no man could warrant the *future conduct* of a negro after a sale . . . That a negro with proper treatment and good management, might behave very well to one man, while on the contrary he might behave very much amiss to another master. A difference of treatment, bad company, and the temptations of a village where drunkenness and intoxication prevail, and vicious habits are predominant, might seduce even the best of slaves to go astray"; the trial judge "left case to jury," and the higher court affirmed the jury verdict for the seller). See also *Hiligsberg v. New Orleans Canal Co.*, Docket #2555, April 1832, N.O., SCA-UNO, appeal reported in 6 La. 288 (1832) ("A change of the mode of labor, uneasiness at a change of habits may induce a negro to run away who had not previously had the habit of doing so").

60. *Castillanos v. Peillon*, Docket #944, New Orleans, SCA-UNO, May 1824. Appeal reported in 2 Mart. N.S. 466 (1824).

61. *Ward v. Reynolds*, Docket #4181, Book 221, Perry Cty. Cir. Ct., January 1858, Ala. Sup. Ct. Records, ADAH. Appeal reported in 32 Ala. 384 (1858).

62. Ibid.; Manuscript Population Schedules of the Seventh Census of the United States, Perry County, Alabama, 1850, M432, Roll 23.

63. *Ward v. Reynolds*; Perry County, Alabama 1850 Census.

64. Docket #4503, New Orleans, June 1844, SCA-UNO. Appeal reported in 8 Rob. 106 (La. 1844). Likewise, Abram Taylor complained, Pompey was "ill disposed, faithless, inconstant, unsteady, disobedient, and bad on all respects," and "John Cochran and Peter Watts well knew him to embrace the earliest opportunity to return to his old masters . . . Pompey never would remain or live with any other person or master than [Cochran or Watts]." *Taylor v. Cochran*, Drawer 7 #1441, Adams County Ct., Miss. Terr., June 1802, HNF.

65. *Castillanos v. Peillon*, Docket #944, New Orleans, SCA-UNO, May 1824. Appeal reported in 2 Mart. N.S. 466 (1824).

66. Docket #1561, April 1855, available in Georgia Supreme Court Case Files, GDAH. Appeal reported in 18 Ga. 722 (1855). In *Thornton v. Towns*, Jesse Thornton charged that Andrew Towns had violated a hire contract by his cruel treatment of several slaves; Towns argued that Golding's bad character fully justified his harsh treatment. Docket #3869, January 1865, Ga. Sup. Ct. Case Files, GDAH. Appeal reported in 34 Ga. 1225 (1865).

67. *Cotton v. Rogolio*, Drawer 202 #143, April 1837, Adams Cir. Ct., Miss., HNF.

68. *Morton v. Bradley*, Docket #4175, Book 215, June 1857, Ala. Sup. Ct. Records, ADAH. Appeal reported in 30 Ala. 683 (1857).

69. *Guice v. Holmes*, Drawer 347, 1854, Adams Cir. Ct., Miss., HNF.

70. White supremacists often gave immutable viciousness, or at least underlying savagery, as proof of the subhumanity of the entire Negro race. See Fredrickson, *Black Image*.

71. Samuel A. Cartwright Papers, Folders 1, 3, 5, LSU. Anonymous biographical sketch included in Folder 1. In Natchez, Cartwright traveled in nabob circles and was a large planter himself. Though a Whig, Cartwright was close friends with John A. Quitman and Jefferson Davis. In 1844, Quitman requested Cartwright to withhold his "great influence" from the Whig tariff; however, later that year, Cartwright gave an address at Natchez in favor of the tariff, and Henry Clay wrote to thank him for it. The citizens of Pine Ridge, a plantation district outside Natchez, presented Cartwright with a "splendid vase with suitable inscription" for his services in the 1833 cholera epidemic. Ibid. Cartwright's racial theories were apparently well known to the black community of Natchez. When one of Cartwright's women slaves committed suicide by jumping off a ferryboat, William Johnson wrote in his diary: "Where is the natural instinct that [Cartwright] has written so much about—oh whare [*sic*] did you come from." Hogan and Davis, *William Johnson's Natchez*, 392, July 11, 1842.

72. James O. Breeden, ed., *Advice among Masters: The Ideal in Slave Management in the Old South* (Westport, Conn.: Greenwood Press, 1980), 139.

73. Samuel A. Cartwright, "Diseases and Peculiarities of the Negro Race," *DeBow's Review* 11 (1851): 64–69, 184–89, 209–13, 331–37, 504–10, reprinted in DeBow, *Industrial Resources*, 2:315–27.

74. Ibid., 318–19, 325.

75. Ibid., 323.

76. Ibid.

77. Cartwright, "Negro Freedom an Impossibility," 650.

78. William Stanton, *The Leopard's Spots: Scientific Attitudes toward Race in America, 1815–1859* (Chicago: University of Chicago Press, 1960), vii.

79. See Cartwright, "Negro Freedom an Impossibility" (on identity of Negroes and serpents); Cartwright, "Unity of Human Race Disproved," *DeBow's Review* 29 (1860): 129–36; and the responses to it: "Dr. Cartwright on the Serpent, the Ape and the Negro," *DeBow's Review* 31 (1861): 507–16; "Dr. Cartwright Reviewed—The Negro, Ape and Serpent," *DeBow's Review* 32 (1861): 238–50; "Dr. Cartwright on the Negro, Reviewed," *DeBow's Review* 32 (1861): 54–62; "Dr. Cartwright on the Negro—Reviewed," *DeBow's Review* 33 (1861): 62–72.

80. See, e.g., A. P. Merrill, M.D., "Plantation Hygiene," *Southern Agriculturist* 1 (September 1851): 267–71; A. P. Merrill, M.D., "Distinctive Peculiarities and Diseases of the Negro Race," *Memphis Medical Recorder*, reprinted in *DeBow's Review* 28 (1860): 612–22; Dr. J. S. Wilson, "Peculiarities and Diseases of Negroes," *DeBow's Review* 28 (1860): 597–99, *DeBow's Review* 29 (1860): 112–15; Wilson, "Peculiarities and Diseases of Negroes," *American Cotton Planter and Soil of the South*, n.s., 4 (February, March, April, May, August, September, November, and December 1860): 79–80, 126–28, 173–76, 222–24, 366–68, 415–16, 510–12, 557–60, quoted in Breeden, *Advice*, 58–60, 111–13, 156–62; see generally Todd L. Savitt, *Medicine and Slavery: The Diseases and Health Care of Blacks in Antebellum Virginia* (Urbana: University of Illinois Press, 1978), 1–184 (citing numerous articles by Southerners on black medical distinctiveness).

81. See, e.g., *Dean v. Traylor*, Docket #549, Ga. Sup. Ct. Records, August 1849, GDAH ("negro consumption"), appeal reported in 8 Ga. 169 (1850); *Abbey v. Osborne*, Drawer 275 #52, April 1839, Adams Cir. Ct., Miss., HNF ("*Struma Africana* or *Cachexia* or what is sometimes known on the Virginia and Maryland plantations as *negro Poison*"); *Hill v. Winston*, Drawer 336 #25, May 1849, Adams Cir. Ct., Miss., HNF ("negro syphilis"); *Buckner v. Blackwell*, Drawer 353 #23, May 1857, Adams Cir. Ct., Miss., HNF ("cakescia affrina [*sic*] or negro consumption").

82. La. Civ. Code, bk. 3, tit. 7, chap. 6, §3, art. 2505.

83. "The slave shall be considered as being in the habit of running away, when he shall have absented himself from his master's house twice for several days, or once for more than a month." Ibid. The statutory rule was varied by case law when a slave was new to the state. See Schafer, *Slavery, Civil Law*, 136–44.

84. See, e.g., *Ward v. Reynolds*, Docket #4181, Book 221, Perry Cty. Cir. Ct., January 1858, Ala. Sup. Ct. Records, ADAH ("addictedness to running away"). Appeal reported in 32 Ala. 384 (1858); *Mizell v. Sims*, 39 Miss. 331, 333 (1860) ("not a runaway nor in the habit of running away" vs. "a habitual runaway"); *James v. Kirk*, Drawer 348 #55, May 1853, Adams Cty. Miss., HNF, appeal reported in 29 Miss. 206 (1855) ("the character of a runaway" and "the habit of running away"); *Tull v. Walker*, Drawer 70 #2744, 1830, Adams Cir. Ct., Miss., HNF ("his habits were very bad"); *Campbell v. Kinloch*, Charleston, Fall 1857, S.C. Sup. Ct. Records, SCDAH, appeal unreported ("his habits were very bad").

85. *Thomas v. Selser*, Minute Book 1840–45, Parish of West Feliciana, St. Francisville, La.; Docket #4774, New Orleans, March 1842, SCA-UNO. Appeal reported in 1 Rob. La. 425 (1842).

86. *Reynolds v. White*, Docket #3982, New Orleans, January 1849, SCA-UNO, unreported.

87. *Anderson v. Dacosta*, Docket #996, New Orleans, February 1849, SCA-UNO. Appeal reported in 4 La. An. 136 (1849).

88. *Collins v. Lester*, Docket #1349, May 1854, Ga. Sup. Ct. Records, GDAH. Appeal reported in 16 Ga. 410 (1854).

89. See, e.g., *Maury v. Coleman*, Docket #3063, Book 174 #4, January 1854, Ala. Sup. Ct., ADAH; *Farmer v. Fiske*, Docket #5248, December 1844, N.O., SCA-UNO. Appeal reported in 9 Rob. La. 351 (1845). At times, the possibility of a slave's dissatisfaction with the hire contract was written into the bargain. One case involved a hire contract that would end if the hired slave was displeased with his situation. *Compton v. Martin*, 5 Rich. 14 (S.C. 1851).

90. *Morton v. Bradley*, Docket #4175, Book 215, June 1857, Ala. Sup. Ct. Records, ADAH. Appeal reported in 30 Ala. 683 (1857).

91. *Mangham v. Cox & Waring*, Book 1856, Docket #2952, #32, Ala. Sup. Ct. Records, 1st Div., June Term 1856, ADAH, appeal reported in 29 Ala. 81 (1856); see also *Sessions v. Cartwright*, Drawer 340 #142, Adams Cir. Ct., Miss., November 1851, HNF.

92. *Cotton v. Rogolio*, Drawer 202 #143, October 1835, Adams Cir. Ct., Miss., HNF.

93. *Martin v. Bosley*, Drawer 49, Folder 3E, 1805, Adams Cty. Ct., Miss. Territ., HNF. Walter Johnson discusses similar cases in Louisiana. Johnson, *Soul by Soul*, 181.

94. *Winn v. Twogood*, Docket #2920, February 1836, N.O., SCA-UNO. Appeal reported in 9 La. 422 (1836).

95. Johnson, *Soul by Soul*, 163–66, 176–88.

96. *Bunch v. Smith*, 4 Rich. 581 (S.C. 1851).

97. *Atwood's Adm'r v. Wright*, 29 Ala. 346 (1856).

98. *Dunbar v. Skillman*, Docket #1575, March 1828, N.O., SCA-UNO, appeal reported in 6 Mart. N.S. 539 (La. 1828).

99. Slaves and buyers could collude in influencing the slave's sale price. In one case, a witness testified that he told a slave to "put up your stick and go halfbent, and if you don't bring much I'll buy you." *Carter v. Walker*, 2 Rich. 40, 42 (1845).

100. This seems to be an unusual twist on the perennial "rules vs. standards" debate—an instance where a rule gives more leeway than a standard. See Duncan Kennedy, "Form and Substance in Private Law Adjudication," *Harvard Law Review* 89 (1976): 1685–1778.

101. *Fortier v. LaBranche*, Docket #3289, New Orleans, June 1839, SCA-UNO. Appeal reported in 13 La. 355 (1839). Similarly, a slave buyer was denied rescission of the sale in *Smith v. McDowell* when the court found that the slave had only been returning (twice) to his former owner's plantation to see his wife. Docket #4431, New Orleans, January 1843, SCA-UNO. Appeal reported in 3 Rob. La. 430 (1843).

102. *Bocod v. Jacobs*, 2 La. 408, 410 (1831). Trial transcript is Docket #2101, November 1830, N.O., SCA-UNO.

103. *Nott v. Botts*, Docket #3123, N.O., March 1839, SCA-UNO. Appeal reported in 13 La. 202 (1839).

104. *Kirk v. James*, Drawer 348 #7049, Adams Cir. Ct., Miss., April 1855, HNF. Appeal reported in *James v. Kirk*, 29 Miss. 206 (1855). This was probably a case of a double legal fiction: a Mississippi sale disguised as a Louisiana sale to avoid the Mississippi ban on importation of slave merchandise, followed by the legal fiction of a Mississippi sale to allow the Adams Circuit Court to exercise jurisdiction. The complaint referred to a sale in "the Parish of Point Coupee, state of Louisiana, to wit, the County of Adams, state of Mississippi," a common-law fiction that allowed English courts to exercise jurisdiction over contracts entered into in Europe.

James' trading business had him in the courts often; he defended three suits for breach of warranty in the Adams County Circuit Court in 1851–52 alone. *Ayres v. James*, Drawer 338 #171, Adams Cir. Ct., Miss., May 1851, HNF; *Kirkland v. James*, Drawer 322 #191, Adams Cir. Ct., Miss., May 1852, HNF; *McCrain v. James*, Drawer 336 #136, Adams Cir. Ct., Miss., May 1852, HNF. See chap. 4 for a more detailed discussion of James' forays in court.

105. *Four juries* heard Kirk's suit. The first jury found for James, and Kirk was granted a new trial; two successive trials ended in mistrial. In 1853, the fourth jury found for Kirk, and Judge Stanhope Posey overruled James' motion for a new trial. James then lost his appeal to the Mississippi High Court of Errors and Appeals. Ibid.

106. 29 Miss. at 208.

107. Justice Handy was unmoved, affirming the lower court judgment. In this case, he ruled, the Louisiana rules were not mere evidentiary regulations unenforceable in Mississippi; they were express stipulations of the contract itself. Ibid. at 211.

108. *Trapier v. Avant*, Box 21, 1827, S.C. Sup. Ct. Records, SCDAH. Trapier's slaves drowned crossing in Avant's ferry; disputed facts included whether crossing in a paddleboat rather than a "flat" was contrary to custom, and whether Avant's ferryman had been negligent, or even present, at the time of the drowning.

109. Ibid.

110. Ibid.

111. For a useful discussion of the application of another tort liability rule to slaves, the fellow-servant rule, see Paul Finkelman, "Northern Labor Law and Southern Slave Law: The Application of the Fellow Servant Rule to Slaves," *National Black Law Journal* 11 (1989): 212–32. Finkelman argues that it was precisely because of the limits on slaves' agency—in this case, their inability to avoid dangerous work conditions—that Southern courts refused to apply this rule to slaves.

112. *Gorman v. Campbell*, Docket #1175, June 1853, Ga. Sup. Ct. Records, GDAH. Appeal reported in 14 Ga. 137 (1853).

113. Judge Lumpkin of the Georgia Supreme Court overturned the lower court verdict, finding for the slave owner. 14 Ga. 137 (1853); see Finkelman, "Northern Labor Law," 230; see also *Wilder v. Richardson*, Dudley 323, 324 (S.C. 1838)

("To run away is an act arising from the volition of the slave"); *Horlbeck v. Erickson*, 6 Rich. 154, 158 (S.C. 1852) ("The slave being a moral agent, and having volition, adventured from the impulses of his nature") (both hire cases).

114. I found no instances of parties in the courtroom explicitly comparing slaves to animals, although very occasionally a party cited cases involving unsound pigs or horses to bolster his legal argument. See, e.g., *Scarborough v. Reynolds*, 13 Rich. 98 (S.C. 1860) (plaintiff argued that a slave with a crooked arm was unsound, citing cases in which lame horses were ruled unsound); *Barnes v. Blair*, 16 Ala. 71, 72 (1849) (citing horse cases).

115. *Helton v. Caston*, 2 Bailey 95, 98 (S.C. 1831).

116. *Outlaw & McClellan v. Cook*, Minor 257, 257–58 (Ala. 1824); *Hogan v. Carr & Anderson*, 6 Ala. 471, 472 (1844). See also *Mayor & Council of Columbus v. Howard*, 6 Ga. 213, 219 (1849) ("If a man hires a horse, he is bound to ride it moderately"); John E. Stealey, "The Responsibilities and Liabilities of the Bailee of Slave Labor in Virginia," *American Journal of Legal History* 12 (1968): 336–53.

117. *Rand v. Oxford*, Docket #447, June 1859, Ala. Sup. Ct. Records, ADAH. Appeal reported in 24 Ala. 474 (1859).

118. Patricia J. Williams, *The Alchemy of Race and Rights: Diary of an African-American Law Professor* (Cambridge: Harvard University Press, 1991), 219.

CHAPTER FOUR
MASTERS' CHARACTER

1. See Johnson, *Soul by Soul*, 207–10.

2. Genovese, *Roll, Jordan, Roll*, 5. See also Tushnet, *American Law of Slavery*.

3. See generally Oakes, *The Ruling Race*; Fogel and Engerman, *Time on the Cross*; Fogel, *Without Consent or Contract*. For a discussion of the debate, see Peter J. Parish, *Slavery: History and Historians* (New York: Harper and Row, 1989), 50–61.

4. There is a growing body of literature on the historical "construction" of whiteness in American culture, and particularly in the law. See, e.g., David Roediger, *The Wages of Whiteness: Race and the Making of the American Working Class* (London: Verso, 1991); Alexander Saxton, *The Rise and Fall of the White Republic: Class Politics and Mass Culture in Nineteenth-Century America* (London: Verso, 1990); Noel Ignatiev, *How the Irish Became White* (New York: Routledge, 1995); Theodore W. Allen, *The Invention of the White Race* (London: Verso, 1994); Grace E. Hale, *Making Whiteness: The Culture of Segregation in the South, 1890–1940* (New York: Random House, Pantheon Books, 1998). For works specifically on law, see, e.g., Ian F. Haney-Lopez, *White by Law: The Legal Construction of Race* (New York: New York University Press, 1996); Cheryl Harris, "Whiteness as Property," *Harvard Law Review* 106 (1993): 1707–91; Richard Delgado and Jean Stefancic, eds., *Critical White Studies: Looking behind the Mirror* (Philadelphia: Temple University Press, 1997); Gross, "Litigating Whiteness."

5. Here I extend the argument James Oakes makes in *Slavery and Freedom* that slaves' "acts of resistance drove the decisive wedge" into the crack provided

by liberal legal institutions. Whereas, for Oakes, slave resistance takes on political significance only after the Fugitive Slave Act becomes a national political issue, I argue that slaves by running away shaped the politics among white Southerners because they shaped the public character of white men. The "crack" was provided not only by liberal institutions but by slaves themselves. See Oakes, *Slavery and Freedom*, 139.

6. The answer to this interrogatory was, "I thought him a good master and used to [*sic*] much limits towards them." (It is unclear whether this witness meant that the master used too much punishment, was too reserved in his punishment, or was accustomed to much punishment or accustomed to being reserved in his punishment.) *Caldwell & Bennett v. May*, Docket #2210, Book 21, pp. 108–30, January 1828, Ala. Sup. Ct. Records, ADAH. Appeal reported in 1 Stew. 425 (Ala. 1828).

7. *Herring v. James*, Drawer 329 #169, May 1847, Adams Cir. Ct., Miss., HNF. Appeal reported in *James v. Herring*, 12 S. & M. 336 (1849).

8. *Kiern v. Carson*, #12 Drawer 208, April 1835, Adams Cir. Ct., Miss., HNF.

9. *Townsend v. Miller*, Drawer 208 #12, April 1837, Adams Cir. Ct., Miss., HNF. The doctor in this case was none other than the infamous propagandist discussed in chap. 1, Samuel A. Cartwright.

10. *Alston v. Rose*, Drawer 112 #4, November 1822, Adams Cir. Ct., Miss., HNF.

11. *Strozier v. Carroll*, Docket #3409, June 1860, Ga. Sup. Ct. Records, GDAH. Appeal reported in 31 Ga. 557 (1860). "Paternalism" often meant white *women*'s caring for slaves: it was not uncommon to hear testimony such as that of Elizabeth Mayberry, who vouched for her knowledge of Burrell's health by explaining, "I had nearly the same opportunities that a mother would have to ascertain the bodily and mental condition of the boy Burrell having nursed him while young and up to the time I sold him in 1850 . . ." *Hill v. Elam*, Drawer 345 #83, November 1852, Adams Cir. Ct., Miss., HNF.

12. *Hagan v. Rist*, Docket #4503, New Orleans, June 1844, SCA-UNO. Appeal reported in *Rist v. Hagan*, 8 Rob. 106 (La. 1844); *Gatlin v. Kendig*, Docket #6894, New Orleans, February 1866, SCA-UNO. Appeal reported in 18 La. Ann. 118 (1866).

13. *Gatlin v. Kendig*.

14. *Blair v. Collins*, Docket #6449, New Orleans, December 1860, SCA-UNO. Appeal reported in 15 La. An. 683 (1860).

15. *Wyatt v. Greer*, Docket #1325, Book 35, June 1833, Ala. Sup. Ct. Records, ADAH.

16. *Sessions v. Cartwright*, Drawer 340 #142, November 1851, Adams Cir. Ct., Miss., HNF.

17. See Horwitz, *Transformation of American Law*, 58–62.

18. Genovese, *Roll, Jordan, Roll*. Mark Tushnet's study of the "law of slavery" builds on Genovese's work, arguing that "Southern slave law was constructed around the distinctions between regulation according to sentiment, ultimately grounded in the contradiction between bourgeois and slave relationships." Tushnet, *American Law of Slavery*, at 229. Tushnet analyzes Southern law in terms of a series of structural dichotomies: slave relations vs. market relations; law vs.

sentiment; interest vs. humanity. In his view, good judges sought to use the law to regulate only market relations, and to keep slave relations in the realm of sentiment. This approach ignores the way Southerners persistently conflated humanity and interest, and the way market relations permeated the culture of slavery.

19. See, e.g., Philip Scranton, *Proprietary Capitalism: The Textile Manufacture at Philadelphia, 1800–1885* (Philadelphia: Temple University Press, 1983) (discussing the "factory paternalism" of Philadelphia textile mill owners); Gerald D. Jaynes, *Branches without Roots: The Genesis of the Black Working Class in the American South, 1862–1882* (New York: Oxford University Press, 1986) (discussing the "paternalism of industrializing capitalism"); Shearer Davis Bowman, *Masters and Lords: Mid-Nineteenth Century U.S. Planters and Prussian Junkers* (New York: Oxford University Press, 1993), chap. 5, "Patriarchy and Paternalism" (discussing the literature on capitalist paternalism in Prussia and the U.S.).

See also Christopher Morris, "The Articulation of Two Worlds: The Master-Slave Relationship Reconsidered," *Journal of American History* 85 (December 1998): 982–1007 (proposing an alternative to the capitalism vs. paternalism debate by viewing American slave society, like modern peasantries, as two worlds— a capitalist and a noncapitalist one—in articulation).

20. Bowman, *Masters and Lords*, 166.

21. Tadman argues that "the vast bulk of the Old South's literary output on black 'character,' family, and 'amalgamation' ingeniously constructed a framework of fable whereby masters could both separate families whenever they wished and regard themselves as paternalists whenever they did." Tadman, *Speculators and Slaves*, 100–101, 210–12, 218.

Thomas Russell has shown one way in which "the law" operated to reinforce this Janus-faced approach to the slave trade: "[C]ourt-supervised slave sales comprised one-half of all slave sales . . . [s]lave sales by operation of law expressed social disregard for black families and slave humanity." Russell, "South Carolina's Largest Slave Auctioneering Firm," 1277–78. In other words, by allowing their slaves to be mortgaged and auctioned, or divided at estate sales, masters could profess paternalist concern for keeping families together while ignoring the real consequences of the system in which they participated.

22. This was sometimes a narrow line to walk. See chap. 2 above for a more detailed discussion of the preservation of honor in the marketplace.

23. *Hill v. Winston*, Drawer 336 #25, May 1849, Adams Cir. Ct., Miss., HNF.

24. Deposition of Nathaniel Glinn, *Herring v. James*, Drawer 329 #169, May 1847, Adams Cir. Ct., Miss., HNF.

25. Deposition of John Shepherd, *Mangham v. Cox & Waring*, Docket #2952, Book 1856, 1st Div. No. 32, June 1856, Ala. Sup. Ct. Records, ADAH. Appeal reported in 29 Ala. 81 (1865).

26. Benjamin Fort, agent of James Dean, *Dean v. Traylor*, Docket #549, August 1849, Ga. Sup. Ct. Records, GDAH. Appeal reported in 8 Ga. 169 (1849).

27. *Daniel v. Lance*, Box 21, January 1830, S.C. Sup. Ct. Records, SCDAH, appeal unreported.

28. *Sessions v. Cartwright*, Drawer 340 #142, November 1851, Adams Cir. Ct., Miss., HNF. For an interesting discussion of the increasing penetration of the marketplace into Southern culture during the antebellum period, see Christopher

Morris, "What's So Funny? Southern Humorists and the Market Revolution," in *Southern Writers and Their Worlds*, ed. Christopher Morris and Steven G. Reinhardt (College Station: Texas A&M University Press, 1996), 9–26. Morris discusses contests of character in the marketplace as recounted in Southern jokes, noting the growing emphasis not only on market savvy but on cash exchange.

29. See Bowman, *Masters and Lords*, 183 ("Southern planters had yet another and even more compelling reason to treat their slaves with at least a modicum of humane consideration—the huge capital investment embodied in plantation laborers . . ."); William K. Scarborough, "Slavery—The White Man's Burden," in *Perspectives and Irony in American Slavery*, ed. Harry P. Owens (Jackson: University Press of Mississippi, 1976), 105–8 (discussing "paternalistic mill villages of the New South" and "George Pullman's model town in Illinois"); Fogel and Engerman, *Time on the Cross*, 73 ("Paternalism is not intrinsically antagonistic to capitalist enterprise"). Unlike these authors, particularly Fogel and Engerman, I am making no claims here about the actual behavior of slaveholders.

30. M. W. Phillips, "The Best Means of Preserving Health on Plantations," *Southern Cultivator* 5 (1847): 142–43, quoted in Breeden, *Advice*, 39.

31. Ibid., 40.

32. P.T., "Judicious Management of the Plantation Force," *Southern Cultivator* 7 (1849): 69, quoted in Breeden, *Advice*, 40.

33. Quoted in Bowman, *Masters and Lords*, 183.

34. See, e.g., *Hogan v. Carr & Anderson*, 6 Ala. 471 (1844) (hire contract included implicit contract to "treat slave humanely, and provide for his necessary wants," including medical aid when sick); *Latimer v. Alexander*, 14 Ga. 259 (1853).

35. In Louisiana, the owner bore the risk of death, the hirer of illness or running away; in South Carolina, the risk was "apportioned" between hirer and owner in case of illness or running away; in Georgia, the hirer could not get the price abated unless the slave's illness existed, latent, at the time of hire. *Outlaw v. Cook*, Minor 257 (Ala. 1824); *Lennard v. Boynton*, 11 Ga. 109 (1852); *Wilder v. Richardson*, Rice—(S.C. 1838).

36. *Outlaw v. Cook*, Minor 257, 257–58 (Ala. 1824). But see *Lennard v. Boynton*, 11 Ga. 109 (1852) (hirer bears risk of death as well as illness, just as in Georgia full rent is due on house made untenantable by storm within lease term). Of course, owners could contract away the right to have hirers pay for time lost to illness. One pair of hirers refused to pay a note to the owner's estate, because they said that in return for their agreement to "deal tenderly with said negro," she had agreed "that the time which should be lost by said negro from labour on account of sickness was to be deducted from the amount of the [hire]." According to them, the slave had been sick for the entire year. *Caldwell & Bennett v. May*, Docket #2210, Book 21, pp. 108–130, January 1828, Greene Cir. Ct., Ala. Sup. Ct. Records, ADAH. Appeal reported in 1 Stew. 425 (Ala. 1828).

37. *Mayor and Council of Columbus v. Howard*, 6 Ga. 213, 219 (1849). Trial record is Docket #437, January 1849, Ga. Sup. Ct. Records, GDAH.

38. *Buhler v. McHatton*, Docket #3448, New Orleans, February 1854, SCA-UNO. Appeal reported in 9 La. An. 192 (1854).

39. *Sessions v. Cartwright*, Drawer 340 #142, November 1851, Adams Cir. Ct., Miss., HNF.

40. *Mosely v. Wilkinson*, Docket #2456, Book 118, February 1848, Ala. Sup. Ct. Records, ADAH. Appeals reported in 14 Ala. 812 (1848); 24 Ala. 411 (1854); 30 Ala. 562 (1857).

41. 30 Ala. at 575.

42. *Davis v. Wood*, Drawer 350 #40, May 1854, Adams Cir. Ct., Miss., HNF.

43. *Moran v. Davis*, Docket #1561, April 1855, Ga. Sup. Ct. Records, GDAH. Appeal reported in 18 Ga. 722 (1855).

44. *Kirk v. James*, Drawer 348 #7049, April 1855, Adams Cir. Ct., HNF. Appeal reported in *James v. Kirk*, 29 Miss. 206 (1855).

45. *McDermott v. Cannon*, Docket #5706, New Orleans, 1858, SCA-UNO. Appeal reported in 14 La. An. 313 (1859).

46. *Borum v. Garland*, Docket #3192, Book 79, January 1846, Macon Cty. Cir. Ct., Ala. Sup. Ct. Records, ADAH. Appeal reported in 9 Ala. 452 (1846).

47. *Maury v. Coleman*, Docket #3063, Book 174, January 1854 No. 4, Ala. Sup. Ct. Records, ADAH. Appeal reported in 24 Ala. 381 (1854) (Coleman had bought Phillips' note for the hire).

48. Kenneth S. Greenberg, *Masters and Statesmen: The Political Culture of American Slavery* (Baltimore: Johns Hopkins University Press, 1985), 20–21.

49. Ibid., 21. See also Genovese, *Roll, Jordan, Roll*, 75–86 ("A Duty and a Burden").

50. *Perkins v. Hundley*, Drawer 91 #25, May 1819, Adams Cir. Ct., Miss., HNF. Deposition of Nimrod Dorsey on part of Plaintiff.

51. Greenberg, *Masters and Statesmen*, 22.

52. See generally Patterson, *Slavery and Social Death*.

53. Strait Edge, "Plantation Regulations," *Soil of the South* 1 (February–May 1851): 20–21, quoted in Breeden, *Advice*, 41.

54. H. N. McTyeire, "Plantation Life—Duties and Responsibilities," *DeBow's Review* 29 (1860): 357–68, quoted in Breeden, *Advice*, 87.

55. Fisher, "Ideology and Imagery in the Law of Slavery," 1077. See also Oakes, *The Ruling Race*, 135–91.

56. *Gillian v. Senter*, 9 Ala. 379 (1846).

57. *Walker v. Cucullu*, Docket #326, New Orleans, La. Sup. Ct. Records, SCA-UNO. Appeal reported in 18 La. An. 246 (1866). See Johnson, *Soul by Soul*, 208–9, 212, for a brief discussion of this case.

58. The jury in the civil case accepted the witnesses' version and found for Cucullu. On appeal to the Louisiana Supreme Court, Walker's lawyer argued that evidence regarding Walker's slave management should have been excluded; the court rejected Walker's appeal, affirming the jury verdict.

For an example of language in an opinion disapproving a defendant's slave management, see *Caldwell v. Langford*, 1 McMullan 275, 275 (1841) ("flogging was without any excuse, and done in mere *wantonness of power*" [emphasis added]).

The judge's respect for a master's own code of laws, and assumption that a master who had such a code could be relied on to obey the law, has a modern counterpart in the Burger Court's approach to bureaucracies. As Mark Tushnet has shown, in the 1970s, the Court has distinguished between "self-contained bureaucracies governed by internal rules and internalized professional norms" and those, such as Southern prisons, that it views as haphazard and politicized. Mark Tushnet, "The Constitution of the Bureaucratic State," *West Virginia Law Review* 86 (1984): 1093–97.

59. See Breeden, *Advice*, 78–88 (chap. 6, "Discipline").

60. W. W. Gilmer, "Management of Servants," *Southern Planter* 12 (1852): 106, quoted in Breeden, *Advice*, 44.

61. Although in Louisiana, at least, allowing a slave such freedoms was not an *absolute* bar to recovery. *Boulin v. Maynard*, 15 La. Ann. 658 (1860).

62. *Anderson v. Dacosta*, Docket #996, February 1849, New Orleans, SCA-UNO. Appeal reported in 4 La. An. 136 (1849).

63. *Hill v. White*, Docket #4489, March 1856, New Orleans, SCA-UNO. Appeal reported in 11 La. An. 170 (1856).

64. *Barber v. Anderson*, Chester Cty. Ct., January 1830, S.C. Sup. Ct. Records, SCDAH. Appeal reported in 1 Bailey 358 (S.C. 1830).

65. *Ogden v. Michel*, Docket #5127, New Orleans, March 1843, SCA-UNO. Appeal reported in 4 Rob. 154 (La. 1843).

66. *Randolph v. Barnett*, Drawer 188 #38, November 1832, Adams Cir. Ct., Miss., HNF.

67. *Perkins v. Hundley*, Drawer 91 #25, May 1819, Adams Cir. Ct., Miss., HNF.

68. Fisher, "Ideology and Imagery in the Law of Slavery," 1077.

69. Of course, a finding of cruelty redounded to the benefit of the slave's owner, but not necessarily to the slave's benefit. For example, in *Jourdan v. Patton*, Docket #304, July 1818, N.O., SCA-UNO, appeal reported in 5 Mart. La. 615 (1818), Patton blinded Jourdan's slave. Jourdan won a full recovery of the value of the slave, but Patton, the abuser, got possession of the slave.

70. *Gillian v. Senter*, Docket #3234, Book 79, January 1846, Ala. Sup. Ct. Records, ADAH. Appeal reported in 9 Ala. 379 (1846).

71. Tapping Reeve, *The Law of Baron and Femme; or Parent and Child; or Guardian and Ward; or Master and Servant* (New Haven, Conn.: Oliver Steele, 1816), 286.

72. Ibid.

73. Ibid., 374. This right to chastise servants remained in Reeve's second edition (Burlington, Vt.: Chauncey Goodrich, 1846).

74. Scholarship on corporal punishment suggests that beating of children and servants was diminishing during this period; this cannot be said about slaves. See, e.g., Myra Glenn, "School Discipline and Punishment in Antebellum America," *Journal of the Early Republic* 1 (Winter 1981): 395–408. I am indebted to Leslie Harris for this reference.

75. *Moseley v. Gordon*, Docket #1392, Ga. Sup. Ct. Records, GDAH. Appeal reported in 16 Ga. 384 (1854).

76. Gordon's attorney, on cross-examination, tried to get Dr. Ridley to admit that he had never examined Daniel and hence was unqualified to discuss his disease; Ridley countered that "there were many diseases which a physician could

not understand properly without seeing them, and there were others which he could." Ibid.

77. See also *Hall v. Goodson*, 32 Ala. 277 (1858) (trial judge excluded testimony from owner's witness who "had owned and governed slaves, for the last forty years, and was well acquainted with the management of slaves, and knew what was reasonable and correct whipping for slaves," about whether the slave Simon had the appearance "such as a reasonable whipping would produce" after the hirer had whipped him with a cowhide, and "whether the use of a cowhide in punishing a slave, so as to produce wales on the arms two or three inches long and as large as his finger, which could be seen on him a year afterwards, was not an unusual and cruel punishment").

78. *Smith v. Meek*, Drawer 232 #76, April 1838, Adams Cir. Ct., Miss., HNF.

79. See also Judith K. Schafer, " 'Details Are of a Most Revolting Character': Cruelty to Slaves as Seen in Appeals to the Supreme Court of Louisiana," *Chicago-Kent Law Review* 68 (1993): 1283–1312 (looking at criminal prosecutions for cruelty and finding little protection for slaves).

80. La. Stat. January 2, 1834, §3.

81. *Hagan v. Rist*, Docket #4503, June 1844, N.O., SCA-UNO. Appeal reported in 8 Rob. La. 106 (1844).

82. La. Civ. Code, bk. 3, tit. 6, chap. 7, sec. 3, art. 2505 (1824).

83. *Gillian v. Senter*, Docket #3234, Book 79, pp. 303–7, January 1846, Cherokee Cty. Ct., Ala. Sup. Ct. Records, ADAH. The Supreme Court reversed on appeal, 9 Ala. 379 (1846), noting that it was "quite as well, perhaps better, that [the slave's] punishment should be admeasured by a domestic tribunal [rather than by the State]." See also *Dearing v. Moore*, Docket #4090, Book 186, January 1855, Ala. Sup. Ct. Records, ADAH. Appeal reported in 26 Ala. 586 (1855) (Moore found not guilty for shooting runaway slave Bob who "said he would die before he was taken").

84. See, e.g., *Fairchild v. Bell*, 2 Brevard 109 (S.C. 1807), in which a master beat his slave and then left him out to die; the doctor who took pity on the slave and cared for him then sued the owner for damages. The jury refused to give him damages, but the higher court overturned their verdict.

85. *Morton v. Bradley*, Docket #4175, Book 215, June 1857, No. 2, Pickens Cty. Ct., Ala. Sup. Ct. Records, ADAH. Appeal reported in 30 Ala. 683 (1857). The Alabama Supreme Court, in remanding the case for further testimony on the issue of whether Spencer had actually threatened Bradley, or had merely been fleeing, noted that "fleeing, even with a dangerous weapon in his hands, was not such resistance as authorized his shooting and killing."

86. *Moran v. Davis*, Docket #1561, April 1855, Ga. Sup. Ct. Records, GDAH. Appeal reported in 18 Ga. 722 (1855). See also *Cooley v. Joor*, Drawer 340 #36, Adams Cir. Ct., Miss., November 1852, HNF (in which owner wrote to hirer that "George appears to have run away from you and has been caught by the Negro Dogs and badly bitten and committed to the Jail of Woodville and now requires strict attention to make him able to attend business").

87. Perry County, Alabama 1850 Census, M432, roll 23.

88. *Nelson v. Bondurant*, Docket #4031, Book 186, January 1855, Ala. Sup. Ct. Records, ADAH. Appeal reported in 26 Ala. 341 (1855).

See also *Kemp v. Hutchinson*, Docket #452, July 1855, Monroe, SCA-UNO, appeal reported in 10 La. Ann. 494 (1855) (owner loses suit against overseer who drove an enslaved woman to commit suicide by his cruelty, because her death was the "voluntary act of the slave").

89. *Johnson v. Lovett*, Docket #3415, Ga. Sup. Ct. Records, GDAH. Appeal reported in 31 Ga. 187 (1860).

90. *McCoy v. McKowen*, Docket #6156, June 1851, MDAH, Record Group 32, Drawer 99. Appeal reported in 26 Miss. 487 (1853); Manuscript Population Schedules of the Seventh Census of the United States, Amite County, Mississippi, 1850. Household 53, Alexander McKowen; Household 114, Michael Forrest; no E. L. McCoy appeared in this census.

91. *Trotter v. McCall*, Docket #6301, November 1851, MDAH, Record Group 32, Drawer 100; 26 Miss. 410, 412 (1853); Manuscript Population Schedules of the Seventh and Eighth Censuses of the United States, Clarke County, Mississippi, 1850 and 1860, M432, Roll 370: Free Schedules; M433, Roll 384: Slave Schedules; M653, Roll 580: Free Schedule.

92. Manuscript Population Schedules of the Seventh Census of the United States, Hinds County, Mississippi, 1850, 187, Household 1938, George L. Potter; Plaintiff's brief, *Trotter v. McCall*; Clarke County Censuses. I was able to find in the censuses thirteen of the twenty-four jurors in the two trials of this case. See also *Lloyd v. Monpoey*, 2 Nott & McCord 446 (1820) (defendant kicked enslaved woman in the back, causing miscarriage; plaintiff includes the lost fetus in his calculation of damages).

But see *Thornton v. Towns*, Docket #3869, January 1865, Ga. Sup. Ct. Records, GDAH, appeal reported in 34 Ga. 1225 (1865). This case involved a number of slaves hired to work in construction—an eight- or nine-year-old boy, a man, and three women. The life-estate owner, Jesse Thornton, had taken possession of the slaves, charging the hirer Andrew Towns, a twenty-one-year old farmer with no slaves of his own, with cruelty and "inhuman" treatment. Towns tried to recover the slaves for the remainder of the hire term, and Thornton sued to enjoin him from doing so, alleging that Towns' cruelty justified his keeping the slaves. Towns had whipped and threatened to hang with a rope the young boy; forced one woman to work while ill, and refused to allow another time off for pregnancy and nursing her infant. Andrew Towns denied treating the slaves cruelly and explained that he put Chena back to work during her pregnancy only because "the doctor said she would improve if she got busy so he told her to get up and go to work"; that Chena then ran away and stayed in the woods for three or four weeks before returning to her original owner, Thornton. After that, Towns claimed that he let her "lay up" for several more weeks, and that he never "touched her a lick in his life." Towns explained his beating of the boy Golding as punishment for his having broken into the smokehouse; he asserted that he had told the boy only "in a gesting manner" that he would hang him, and that the "flogging was in [his] opinion more moderate than it should have been." The lower court refused Thornton's injunction, allowing Towns to recover the slaves, and the Georgia Supreme Court would not disturb the verdict.

93. Quoted in Charles S. Sydnor, *Slavery in Mississippi* (New York: D. Appleton-Century Co., 1933), 137.

94. On petition for rehearing, the steamboat captain argued that "[t]he slave being beaten, not violently but moderately, committed suicide . . . the suicide was not the consequence of the chastisement, but of the sullen and unmanageable temper of the slave." There is no record of whether he won on appeal. *McKinney v. "Yalla Busha,"* 3 La. Ann. xi, June 1848, N.O., SCA-UNO.

See also *McNeil v. Easley,* Misc. Ct. Cases, Briefs, Etc., 1820–73, Marengo Cty., Ala., SG 2803, Ala. Sup. Ct. Records, ADAH ("inhuman treatment" by a hirer justified owner's keeping a slave who escaped and returned to him).

95. *Townsend v. Jeffries' Adm'r,* Docket #3068, Book 174 #29, January 1854, Ala. Sup. Ct. Records, ADAH. Appeal reported in 24 Ala. 329 (1854).

96. Townsend's appeal rested on the attempt to exclude Dale's testimony because of the words "did see the said defendants *commit a trespass,*" which Townsend argued were impermissibly conclusory.

97. Manuscript Population Schedules of the Eighth Census of the United States, Madison County, Ala.: Free Schedule, M432, Roll 9. Household 92, John C. Townsend; Household 108, Willis Rout; Household 109, Daniel Curry; Household 111, Samuel Townsend, Jr.; Household 114, Samuel Townsend; Household 115, Edmond Townsend; Household 395, Mary Townsend. Slave Schedule, M432, Roll 21. Willis Rout, 50 slaves; Samuel Townsend, Jr., 20 slaves; Samuel Townsend, 85 slaves; Edmond Townsend, 143 slaves; M. Townsend, 34 slaves.

98. Madison Cty., Ala. 1860 Census. Jurors included: Lewis G. Malone, 26-year-old farmer in a household with 34 slaves; William S. Valiant, 42-year old brickmason with 10 slaves; John P. Trible, 39-year-old farmer with 350 acres and 1 slave; Richard Holding, 56-year-old farmer with 61,800 acres and 228 slaves; Archibald Rison, 47-year-old ginmaker with 4 slaves; Malkija Spragins, 26-year-old farmer with 5 slaves; John Scruggs, 33-year-old farmer in a household with 9 slaves; William Eldridge, 36-year-old farmer with 10 slaves; William Grimby, 25-year-old farmer; Josiah Springer, farmer with 6 slaves; Worley White, farmer with 10 slaves. I was unable to find Acker James in the census.

99. See, e.g., *Tillman v. Chadwick,* 37 Ala. 317 (1861) ("The hirer of a slave . . . is, for the [hire term], armed with the power of the owner").

CHAPTER FIVE
BODY AND MIND

1. *Blair v. Collins,* Docket #6449, December 1860, N.O., SCA-UNO. Appeal reported in 15 La. An. 683 (1861).

2. Of 1,200 appeals to the Supreme Court of Louisiana involving slaves, the most common type were warranties in the sale of slaves; of those, a majority litigated disease or death. Schafer, " 'Guaranteed against the Vices and Maladies Prescribed by Law,' " 307–14; in Adams County, 83 out of 177 civil trials involving slaves were warranty suits for illness or death (47 percent of all slave-related civil trials, and 83 percent of the warranty suits). See appendix.

3. By contrast, most of the defects noted in Louisiana sales documents were nonfatal diseases: a full one-quarter were hernias; one-fifth of the slaves involved were "cripples" or had other disabilities of the limbs; and 12 percent were blind or had eye problems. Presumably, it was not worth suing unless a slave had a

serious or fatal condition. Among estate inventories in the same period in Louisiana, a much larger number had serious illnesses. While one-quarter had hernias, and a significant number had physical disabilities, another quarter were listed as generally ill or with a specific, serious illness. The discrepancy between "defects" noted in sales documents and those that appear in probate inventories could reflect either the difficulty of selling "defective" slaves or sellers' efforts to conceal defects.

These figures come from Hall and Manning, *Slaves in Louisiana, 1735–1820* (data as of July 1995), which catalogs a voluminous number of documents and transactions involving slaves from Louisiana up to 1820. Out of nearly 50,000 records of sales and miscellaneous transactions in New Orleans during the American period, 1804–20, 1.8 percent recorded a defect in the slave sold. By contrast, 8.0 percent of slaves listed in 4,138 probate inventories from New Orleans during the same period had a defect recorded.

4. Eugenia Woodberry Autobiography, in Rawick, *American Slave*, vol. 3: South Carolina Narratives, pt. 4, p. 225.

5. Greenberg, *Honor and Slavery*, 37.

6. See Walter K. Johnson, "Masters and Slaves in the Market: Slavery and the New Orleans Trade, 1804–1864" (Ph.D. diss., Princeton University, 1995), 144.

7. Ibid., 81. See generally ibid., chap. 3, "Fantasy: The Semiotics of Slave Buying."

8. Prude notes that "fugitive notices were among the only widespread descriptions treating the 'lower sort' as central characters." Jonathan Prude, "To Look upon the 'Lower Sort,': Runaway Ads and the Appearance of Unfree Laborers in America, 1750–1800," *Journal of American History* 78 (June 1991): 134.

9. Interrogatories to David Middleton, *Powell v. Wells*, Drawer 348 #33, May Term 1855, Adams Cir. Ct., Miss., HNF.

10. Interrogatories to John Elbert, *Coffey v. Griffin*, Pullam & Co., Drawer 354 #42, November Term 1857, Adams Cir. Ct., Miss., HNF.

11. Testimony of Benjamin Fort, *Dean v. Traylor*, Docket #549, August 1849, Ga. Sup. Ct. Records, GDAH. Appeal reported in 8 Ga. 169 (1849).

12. *Drumwright v. Philpott*, Docket #1390, July 1854, Ga. Sup. Ct. Records, GDAH. Appeal reported in 16 Ga. 410 (1854).

13. Deposition of Dr. Joseph Guy, *Gillespie v. Simonton*, Drawer 112 #17, May Term 1819 / November Term 1822, Adams Cir. Ct., Miss., HNF.

14. Testimony of Madison Powell, *Powell v. Wells*, Drawer 348 #33, May Term 1855, Adams Cir. Ct., Miss., HNF.

15. *Tourny v. Kane*, Drawer 211 #238, April Term 1837, Adams Cir. Ct., Miss., HNF.

16. James Martin Autobiography, in Rawick, *American Slave*, vol. 5: Texas Narratives, 63; John Glover Autobiography, in Rawick, *American Slave*, vol. 2: South Carolina Narratives, pts. 1 and 2, p. 140.

17. *Durham v. Broddus*, Docket #2547, May 1858, Ga. Sup. Ct. Records, GDAH, appeal reported in 26 Ga. 524 (1854); see also *Campbell ads. Atchison*, Box 21, 1827, S.C. Sup. Ct. Records, SCDAH, appeal unreported ("Wiley was a mild looking fellow, and . . . his value was about $300").

18. See testimony of Louis Onnerling, *Walker v. Cucullu*, Docket #326, N.O., March 1866, SCA-UNO. Appeal reported in 18 La. An. 246 (1866).

19. Johnson, "Masters and Slaves in the Market," 11–12; Johnson, *Soul by Soul*, 18.

20. Johnson, "Masters and Slaves in the Market," 144.

21. Testimony of Madison Powell, Drawer 348 #33, *Powell v. Wells*, May 1855; see also testimony of William A. Pullum, *McCrain v. James*, Drawer 336 #136, May Term 1851 ("I do not think that Jim was a mulatto he was a full Blood negro of rather a light or chesnut cast of collor . . ."); testimony of James L. Caruthers, *Shields v. Lum*, Drawer 223 #258, October Term 1836 ("his Colour was that of a dark mulatto or Grief"); testimony of Zachariah Dorsey, *Lancashire v. Redman*, Drawer 184 #210, June Term 1834 ("rather slender, and a kind of pale black—not a yellow, nor a jet black").

22. *Stewart v. Saffron*, Drawer 238 #11, December Term 1835, Adams Cir. Ct., Miss., HNF.

23. *Hill v. Elam*, Drawer 345 #83, November 1852, Adams Cir. Ct., Miss., HNF.

24. Olmsted, *Cotton Kingdom*, 2:83.

25. Henry Banner Autobiography, in Rawick, *American Slave*, vol. 8: Arkansas Narratives, pts. 1 and 2, p. 105.

26. This detail contrasts with the runaway slave ads studied by Jonathan Prude, in which he found that descriptions were vague on height, weight, hair color, and age, offered more detail on black men than black women, and devoted the most detail to clothing, as a reliable identifier of a runaway slave. Prude, " 'To Look upon the Lower Sort,' " 142–43, 150; Prude found that clothing was noted in 76 percent of cases, "often in extraordinary detail." Ibid., 143. The only description of a slave in all the trial transcripts that included information on the slave's clothing was a copy of a runaway slave advertisement. While a slave ad's purpose was to alert the general public as to a man's or woman's distinguishing features, an aim that could be furthered by description of what he or she wore on the day of escape, trial description was identification of a different sort. The point was to indicate how well a witness knew the slave, how qualified he or she was to testify about the slave, and to assure that the parties were referring to the same person. Thus it made sense that clothing would not be mentioned, but physical descriptions were correspondingly more detailed. *Guice v. Holmes*, Drawer 347 #57, May Term 1854, Adams Cir. Ct., Miss., HNF.

27. Testimony of Dr. Washington Dorsey, John B. Righter, and Benjamin M. Osborne, *Abbey v. Osborne*, Drawer 275 #352, April 1839, Adams Cir. Ct., Miss., HNF. James H. Locke, an overseer, reported that Toney was "about five feet ten inches high, very dark tolerable stout built, since I have known him thin visage a part of his front teeth out he is much debilitated." *Feagin v. Beasley*, Docket #2126, April 1857, Ga. Sup. Ct. Records, GDAH, appeal reported in 23 Ga. 17 (1857).

28. See testimony of Samuel Spragg Joiner, plaintiff's witness, *Chretien v. Theard*, Docket #612, February 1822, N.O., SCA-UNO, appeal reported in 11 Mart. 11 (La. 1822) ("5 feet 5 or 6 inches high, large and red eyes, nose flat, upper lip large and covering the under one, stoop shouldered . . ."); testimony of Elizabeth Mayberry, *Hill v. Elam*, Drawer 345 #83, November 1852, Adams Cir.

Ct., Miss. ("I cannot give his height but he was inclined to be a chunky negro had a flat nose").

29. However, one adjective frequently recurring to describe women, but not men, was "good-looking" or "fine-looking." Isabella "was large well-proportioned and an unusually good looking woman and certainly as able as any woman of her age to perform field service." *Tourny v. Kane*, Drawer 211 #238, April 1837, Adams Cir. Ct., Miss. HNF. See also *Campbell ads. Atchison*, Box 21, 1827, S.C. Sup. Ct. Records, SCDAH, appeal unreported ("she was a pretty good looking old woman"); *Bennett ads. Carter*, Box 32, May 1836, S.C. Collection 139—Court of Appeals and Law, SCDAH, appeal reported in Riley 287 (S.C. 1837) ("the mother was a good looking woman"); *Dean v. Traylor*, Docket #549, August 1849, Ga. Sup. Ct. Records, GDAH, appeal reported in 8 Ga. 169 (1849). ("She was large and fine-looking").

30. *Bennett ads. Carter*, Box 32, May 1836, S.C. Collection 139—Ct. of Appeals and Law, SCDAH, appeal reported in Riley 287 (S.C. 1837); *Walton v. Jordan*, Docket #2099, March 1857, Ga. Sup. Ct. Records, GDAH, appeal reported in 23 Ga. 420 (1857); *Ramsey v. Blalock*, Docket #3500, August 1860, Ga. Sup. Ct. Records, GDAH, appeal reported in 32 Ga. 376 (1860).

31. *Hill v. Elam*, Drawer 345 #83, November 1852, Adams Cir. Ct., Miss., HNF; testimony of Dr. James C. Brandon, *James v. Griffin & Pullam*, Drawer 344, May 1854, Adams Cir. Ct., Miss., HNF.

32. *Farr v. Gist*, 1 Rich. 68, 72 (1844).

33. One historian has cited several of these cases as evidence of slave breeding. See White, *Ar'n't I a Woman?*, 101. Of the cases White discusses, three involve slaves with diseases of the womb that had been misinterpreted as pregnancy; in other words, the buyers claimed that the women were both *not pregnant* and *ill*. See *Tilman v. Stringer*, Docket #2486, April 1858, Ga. Sup. Ct. Case Files, GDAH, appeal reported in 26 Ga. 171 (1858); *Stevenson v. Reaves*, Docket #4043, Book 171, January 1854 Vol. 2 #8, Ala. Sup. Ct. Records, ADAH, appeal reported in 24 Ala. 425 (1854); *Hardin v. Brown*, December 1858, Bibb County Circuit Court Records, Macon, Ga., appeal reported in 27 Ga. 314 (1859). *Milton v. Rowland*, 11 Ala. 732 (1847), involved a death from gonorrhea; *Bennett v. Fail & Patterson*, June 1854, 2 Div. 4106, Ala. Sup. Ct. Records, ADAH, appeal reported in 26 Ala. 605 (1855), involved an umbilical hernia; *Atwood's Adm'r v. Wright*, 29 Ala. 346 (1856), involved a woman diseased "with a knot in her belly."

34. *Cotton v. Rogolio*, Drawer 202 #143, April 1837, Adams Cir. Ct., Miss., HNF (abortion); *King v. Hobbs*, Drawer 217 #69, April Term 1836/38, Adams Cir. Ct., Miss., HNF (pregnancy); *Oldenbrough v. Davis*, Drawer #99, May Term 1853, Adams Cir. Ct., Miss., HNF (menstruation).

35. *Levy v. Forrest*, Docket #607, N.O, January 1848, SCA-UNO, appeal reported in 3 La. Ann. xi (1848) (disease of womb and "venereal affection"); *George v. Bean*, Docket #7418, Drawer 105, 1855, Miss. HCEA Records, MDAH. Appeal reported in 30 Miss. 147 (1856).

36. *Tilman v. Stringer*, Docket #2486, April 1858, Ga. Sup. Ct. Records, GDAH ("change of life"); *Liles v. Bass*, Box 39, 1839, S.C. Sup. Ct. Records, SCDAH, appeal reported in *Lyles v. Bass*, Cheves 85 (S.C. 1840) ("female irregu-

larities which take place about 40 years of age"); *Woods v. Marshall*, Book 120 B, pp. 268–74, June 1849, Ala. Sup. Ct. Records, ADAH ("Amenorea").

37. Some historians have argued that the sexual demonization of blacks in white Southern racial ideology arose after the Civil War. Martha E. Hodes, *White Women, Black Men: Illicit Sex in the Nineteenth Century South* (New Haven: Yale University Press, 1997). See also Joel Williamson, *The Crucible of Race: Black/White Relations in the American South since Emancipation* (New York: Oxford University Press, 1984). While certainly the 1880s and 1890s saw a heightening of sexual fears and rape myths in the white South, one should not ignore the fact that under slavery part of the ideological justification for the lack of legal recognition of slave marriage, as well as for the "un-rapeability" of enslaved women, was that black women were sexually lascivious Jezebels. See Cobb, *Law of Negro Slavery*, 40–41, 99–100 ("The occurrence of [rape of a female slave] is almost unheard of; and the known lasciviousness of the negro, renders the possibility very remote," p. 100); Melton A. McLaurin, *Celia: A Slave* (Athens: University of Georgia Press, 1991); White, *Ar'n't I a Woman?*

38. Johnson, *Soul by Soul*, 113.

39. *Abbey v. Osborne*, Drawer 214, April Term 1838, Adams Cir. Ct., Miss., HNF.

40. *Powell v. Wells*, Drawer 348 #33, May Term 1855, Adams Cir. Ct., Miss. HNF; *Collins v. Hutchins*, Ga.; see also testimony of John B. Dupuy, *Moseley v. Gordon*, Docket #1392, July 1854, Ga. Sup. Ct. Records, GDAH, appeal reported in 16 Ga. 384 (1854) ("I am a planter and stay at home pretty closely, and saw him nearly every day. These are the opportunities I had of knowing his health").

41. *Watson v. Boatwright*, S.C. See *Gingles v. Caldwell*, Docket #3052, Book 156, June 1852, Ala. Sup. Ct. Records, ADAH, appeal reported in 21 Ala. 444 (1852) for a typical discussion of valuation of a slave's defect in order to calculate damages.

42. Greenberg, "The Nose, the Lie, and the Duel," 57; John W. Blassingame, ed., *Slave Testimony: Two Centuries of Letters, Speeches, Interviews, and Autobiographies* (Baton Rouge: Louisiana State University Press, 1977), 632 (scars on back as sign of "vicious temper"); Tadman, *Speculators and Slaves*, 187.

43. Solomon Northup, *Twelve Years a Slave* (reprint, Baton Rouge: Louisiana State University Press, 1968), 53; Johnson, *Soul by Soul*, 146 ("As they traced their fingers across the scars on the slaves' naked backs, buyers were looking for the causes rather than the consequences of bad behavior; they were looking for, as North Carolina planter William Pettigrew put it, 'deformity' of character").

44. Greenberg, *Honor and Slavery*, 15.

45. *Bruce v. Stone & Taylor*, Docket #2389, N.O., January 1832, SCA-UNO. Appeal reported in 5 La. 1 (1832).

46. See, e.g., *White v. Cumming*, Docket #357, Alexandria, October 1826, SCA-UNO ("there were marks where he had been bled repeatedly, old marks"); *McDaniel v. Strohecker*, Docket #1719, December 1855, Ga. Sup. Ct. Records, GDAH ("marks of medication upon the chest").

47. See, e.g., testimony of jailer J. D. Hamilton, Rusk County, Texas, about a slave who had been shot through the thigh, *Gatlin v. Kendig*, Docket #6894, February 1866, N.O., SCA-UNO. Appeal reported in 18 La. Ann. 118 (1866).

48. Deposition of James O'Conner, *Tull v. Walker*, Drawer 70, May 1830, Adams Cir. Ct., Miss., HNF.

49. I am indebted to Walter Johnson for this insight.

50. *Mangham v. Cox & Waring*, Docket #2592, Book 1856, 1st Div. No. 32, 1856, Ala. Sup. Ct. Records, ADAH. See also *Pilie v. Ferriere*, Docket. #1724, N.O., January 1829, SCA-UNO, appeal reported in 7 Mart. N.S. 648 (1829) ("she was marked with the blows of the whip and had blood on her clothes—that she appeared to have been whipt on the same day that Witness saw her and was in the opinion of witness too severely punished"); *McDaniel v. Strohecker*, Docket #1719, December 1855, Ga. Sup. Ct. Records, GDAH ("Plff was a negro dealer and stripped the girl down as witness pointed out to midway her breast and he witness saw [nothing] on her person except marks of the lash on her neck and that while stripping her . . . the girl took out a phial of cherry pectoral (which was labelled as good for a variety of complaints) and set it on the counter"); *Thornton v. Towns*, Docket #3869, January 1865, Ga. Sup. Ct. Records, GDAH ("Respondent gave him a moderate flogging to make him tell the truth as to what negro was with him . . . would not tell the truth . . . told him in a gesting manner that if he did not tell the truth he would hang him . . . Respondent says that no marks of the whip were left upon him and that the flogging was in Respondent's opinion more moderate than it should have been"); Deposition of Hugh M. Coffee, *Perkins v. Hundley*, Drawer 91 #25, May Term 1819 / January Term 1822, Adams Cir. Ct., Miss., HNF (". . . said negro Lawson was very much scarefied on his Back and Thighs in consequence of severe correction which appeared to have been given to him some years before as the wounds had become gristly"); testimony of Robert Montgomery, *Bruce v. Stone & Taylor*, Docket #2389, 1830?, N.O., SCA-UNO (Cross: "Had the negro man Charles, when shewn to you by Stone & Taylor or when you first saw him any Bruises or Contusions on his head or any part of the Body[?] The Deponent answered that he see none . . . Could you Judge from his appearance that he had been ill treated? Answer: That he saw no marks of it"); *Gholson v. Odom*, Drawer 169, November 1829, Adams Cir. Ct., Miss., HNF (Anthony was "badly whipped when Gholson purchased him," which Gholson claimed was related to the disease of which he later died).

51. Prude, "To Look upon the 'Lower Sort,' " 127.

52. Ibid., 137.

53. See generally Johnson, *Soul by Soul*.

54. Johnson, "Masters and Slaves in the Market," 128 (buyers and sellers sometimes paid doctors to oversee sales); Johnson, *Soul by Soul*, 119–20, 137.

55. *Smith v. Meek*, Drawer No. 232 #76, April Term 1838, Adams Cir. Ct., Miss., HNF.

56. Joel P. Eigen, *Witnessing Insanity: Madness and Mad-Doctors in the English Court* (New Haven: Yale University Press, 1995), 2; see also Catherine Crawford, "Legalizing Medicine: Early Modern Legal Systems and the Growth of Medico-Legal Knowledge," in *Legal Medicine in History*, ed. Michael Clark and Catherine Crawford (Cambridge: Cambridge University Press, 1994).

57. Theodric R. Beck, *Elements of Medical Jurisprudence* (Albany, N.Y.: Webster and Skinner, 1823). For a case citing Beck's *Medical Jurisprudence*, see *Buhler v. McHatton*, 9 La. Ann. 192 (1854). See James C. Mohr, *Doctors and the Law:*

Medical Jurisprudence in Nineteenth-Century America (New York: Oxford University Press, 1993).

58. Neither the medical jurisprudence treatises nor modern histories of medical practice mention slave cases. See Beck, *Medical Jurisprudence*; Mohr, *Doctors and the Law*; Savitt, *Medicine and Slavery*; Steven M. Stowe, "Seeing Themselves at Work: Physicians and the Case Narrative in the Mid-Nineteenth-Century American South," *American Historical Review* 101 (February 1996): 41–79.

59. Juriah Harriss, "What Constitutes Unsoundness in The Negro?" *Savannah Journal of Medicine* 1 (September 1858): 146.

60. Ibid., 147.

61. Cartwright, "Diseases and Peculiarities of the Negro Race," *reprinted in* DeBow, *Industrial Resources*, 2:320, 23.

62. Savitt, *Medicine and Slavery*, 10–11. John H. Warner suggests that "the notion that there must be a separate body of medical knowledge for the South was only one expression of the principle of specificity, a principle central to the belief system of American physicians of all regions. Medical treatment was not specific to disease . . . but did have to be sensitively matched to the specific characteristics of individual patients and the peculiarities of the environments in which they became ill and were treated." John H. Warner, "The Idea of Southern Medical Distinctiveness: Medical Knowledge and Practice in the Old South," 179, 185–86, in *Science and Medicine in the Old South*, ed. Ronald L. Numbers and Todd L. Savitt (Baton Rouge: Louisiana State University Press, 1989). See also Stowe, "Seeing Themselves at Work."

63. See Stowe, "Seeing Themselves at Work," 57, 71.

64. *Gasque v. Gadsden*, Box 42, S.C. Sup. Ct. Records, SCDAH. Appeal reported in *Gadsden v. Gasque*, 2 Strobhart 324 (S.C. 1848).

65. *Bennett ads. Carter*, Box 32, South Carolina Court of Appeals and Law, SCDAH, Opinions 1837. Appeal reported in Riley 287 (S.C. 1837).

66. *Hillier v. Hume*, Box 42, January 1856, S.C. Court of Appeals and Law Records, SCDAH. Appeal unreported.

67. *Bennet v. Fail*, Book 1854, No. 2, Div. 4106, June 1854, Ala. Sup. Ct. Records, ADAH, appeal reported in 26 Ala. 605 (1855). See also *Herries v. Botts*, Docket #3635, February 1840, N.O., SCA-UNO, appeal reported in 14 La. 432 (1840) (defendant argued that doctors confused jury); *Bertholi v. Deverges*, Docket #4521, May 1843, N.O., SCA-UNO, appeal reported in 4 Rob. La. 431 (1843) (judge notes that it is common knowledge that "doctors will differ"); *Dupre v. Desmaret*, 5 La. Ann. 591 (1850) (holding that redhibitory action cannot be based on "speculative opinions of physicians" based only on postmortem examinations); Mohr, *Doctors and the Law*, 100.

68. *Coffey v. Griffin Pullam & Co.*, Drawer 354 #42, November Term 1857, Adams Cir. Ct., Miss., HNF.

69. *Dinkins ads. Parkerson*, Box 34, Charleston City Ct., February 1839, South Carolina Court of Appeals and Law, SCDAH. Appeal reported in *Parkerson v. Dinkins*, Rice 185 (S.C. 1839).

70. "A morbid condition characterized by the accumulation of watery fluid in the serous cavities or connective tissue of the body," usually the heart. *OED*; see

William D. Postell, *The Health of Slaves on Southern Plantations* (Baton Rouge: Louisiana State University Press, 1951).

71. *Gantt ads. Venning*, City Court of Charleston, S.C., January 1840, South Carolina Court of Appeals and Law, SCDAH, appeal reported in *Venning v. Gantt*, Cheves 87 (S.C. 1840).

72. *Oldenbrough v. Davis*, Drawer 341 #99, May Term 1853, Adams Cir. Ct., Miss., HNF.

73. *Abbey v. Osborne*, Drawer 275 #52, April Term 1839, Adams Cir. Ct., Miss., HNF. Annual medical costs for one hundred slaves ranged from a high of $307 to a low of $49 on Hubard's plantation (Savitt, *Medicine and Slavery*, 19); average treatments from $1.30 to $2 on various plantations. Doctors usually charged $1–3 per medical visit. Planters made one of two kinds of arrangement: either an annual health-care contract (practice-by-the-year) or an agreement setting a fee for the treatment of a slave's particular disorder. Ibid., 199–200.

Most Natchez doctors were not particularly wealthy, with an average net worth of less than $35,000. Moore, *Cotton Kingdom*, 247. Only William Harper was worth as much as $110,000 in 1860. Ibid.

74. *Dean v. Traylor*, Docket #549, August 1849, Ga. Sup. Ct. Records, GDAH. For issues of heredity, see also testimony of John McLary, *Hill v. Elam*, Drawer 345 #83, November Term 1852, Adams Cir. Ct., Miss., HNF ("I am the son of Robert McLary and physician to his Family and am intimate with the Constitution of the Family of Negroes from which Burrell sprung and there is no predisposition to any Disease in that Family").

75. *Mosely v. Wilkinson*, Docket #2456, Book 118, February 1848, Ala. Sup. Ct. Records, ADAH; see also same case, Docket #4034, Book 171, Part 2, No. 6, January Term 1854, Ala. Sup. Ct. Records, ADAH.

76. *Davis v. Wood*, Drawer 348 #40, May Term 1854, Adams Cir. Ct., Miss., HNF.

77. Sharla M. Fett, "Body and Soul: African-American Healing in Southern Antebellum Plantation Communities, 1800–1860" (Ph.D diss., Rutgers University, 1995), chap. 4, "Danger, Distrust, and Deception," 27.

78. Ibid., 36–37.

79. See also Greenberg, *Honor and Slavery*, 39.

80. See, e.g., *Phillips v. Stewart*, 27 Ga. 402 (1859), *Watson v. Boatwright*, 1 Rich. 402 (S.C. 1845), *Gadsden v. Raysor*, Box 42, 1856, S.C. Sup. Ct. Records, SCDAH, appeal reported in 9 Rich. 276 (S.C. 1856); *Steppacher v. Reneau*, 25 Miss. 114 (1852), *Blair v. Collins*, Docket #6449, N.O. December 1860, SCA-UNO, appeal reported in 15 La. Ann. 683 (1861). For the holding that no post-mortem bars recovery, see *Fox v. Walsh*, 5 Rob. 222 (La. 1842); *Bloodgood v. Wilson*, 10 La. Ann. 302 (1855).

81. *James v. McCoy*, Drawer 344 #69, May 1854, Adams Cir. Ct., Miss., HNF; *Kiern v. Carson & Griffin*, Drawer 208 #12, April 1835, Adams Cir. Ct., Miss., HNF; *Adams v. Hughes*, Drawer 343 #138, November 1853, Adams Cir. Ct., Miss., HNF.

82. *Blair v. Collins*, Docket #6449, December 1860, N.O., SCA-UNO. Appeal reported in 15 La. An. 683 (1861).

83. *Nelson v. Bondurant*, Docket #4031, Book 186, 4th Div., No. 17, January Term 1855, Ala. Sup. Ct. Records, ADAH.

84. In one Natchez case, a subpoena was issued ordering the plaintiff's attorney to bring the slave Nancy to be displayed in the courtroom: "You are hereby notified to produce in open court on the trial of said cause the negro girl, named Nancy, charged and alleged to be unsound and for which unsoundness the above action was instituted by you, subject to examination before the jury upon the trial of said case." *Robson v. English*, Drawer 223 #62, December Term 1834, Adams Cir. Ct., Miss., HNF.

85. *Hardin v. Brown*, December 1858, Bibb County Court Records, Macon, Ga. Appeal reported in 27 Ga. 314 (1858).

86. Todd Savitt notes that medical "authors felt no compunction about presenting minute description of . . . those with personal body abnormalities, almost all of whom were black." Doctors preserved specimens from black patients for display and sometimes even put living black patients like Siamese twins on tour. Savitt, *Medicine and Slavery*, 304.

87. *Coffey v. Griffin Pullam & Co.*, Drawer 354 #42, November Term 1857, Adams Cir. Ct., Miss., HNF; *Blair v. Collins*, Docket #6449, December 1860, N.O., SCA-UNO. Appeal reported in 15 La. An. 683 (1861).

88. Fett, "Body and Soul," 38. See also Stowe, "Seeing Themselves at Work," 57.

89. *Hopkins v. Tilman*, Docket #2268, September 1857, Ga. Sup. Ct. Records, GDAH; appeal reported in 25 Ga. 212, 213 (1858). See also Letter from C. S. Rice to Joseph Shields, Box 2, Folder 4, Joseph D. Shields Papers, 1802–1842, LSU ("There has been some sickness on the place but not a great deal since I last wrote . . . Talking of Patience your brother William [a physician] prescribed cotton picking for a chronic attack of laziness under which she was suffering when he was at the Ridges").

90. Fett, "Body and Soul," 58–59.

91. Steven M. Stowe, "Obstetrics and the Work of Doctoring in the Mid-Nineteenth-Century American South," *Bulletin of the History of Medicine* 64 (1990): 540, 545. See also A. P. Merrill, "An Essay on Some of the Distinctive Peculiarities of the Negro Race," *Southern Medical and Surgical Journal* 12 (January 1856): 90 ("No class of people [other than Southern "negroes"] more urgently require, that the physician who attends them in their diseases, should rightly understand their mental characteristic . . .").

92. *Laurence v. McFarlane*, Docket #1722, July 1828, N.O., SCA-UNO. Appeal reported in 7 Mart. N.S. 558 (1828).

93. *Hopkins v. Tilman*, Docket #2268, September 1857, Ga. Sup. Ct. Records, GDAH. Appeal reported in 25 Ga. 212.

94. Henry Bibb, in Osofsky, *Puttin' On Ole Massa*, 122

95. Johnson, *Soul by Soul*, 210.

96. Fett, "Body and Soul," 53.

97. Samuel A. Cartwright, "Remarks on Dysentery among Negroes," *New Orleans Medical and Surgical Journal* (September 11, 1854): 162. Fett, "Body and Soul," 47. Fett notes that "[w]hite physicians, planters, and overseers frequently complained of the behavior of African Americans under medical treatment. Most

popular among these complaints was the failure of sick persons to follow health-related instructions. On this failure slaveholders blamed incidents of relapse, prolonged illness, and even death." Ibid., 50.

98. *Collins v. Hutchins*, Docket #1917, June 1856, Ga. Sup. Ct. Records, GDAH. Appeal reported in 21 Ga. 270 (1857).

99. *Stroud v. Mays*, Docket #483, September 1849, Ga. Sup. Ct. Records, GDAH, appeal reported in 7 Ga. 269 (1850) ("the boy Simon did not take such care of himself as he should have done").

100. Although medical historians recognize that "dirt eating" has been a recurrent problem among the impoverished of all races in the South, slaveholders associated it with "negroes," sometimes calling it "Cachexia Africana." William D. Postell, adopting the slaveholder's perspective to some extent (remarking that "[d]irt eating (Cachexia Africana) was the dread of every planter"), noted that slaveholders attributed many deaths to this practice, which they believed to be the result of hookworm infection: "Possibly because of the digestive disturbances associated with the infection, the slave found that the eating of bulky substances would for a time relieve him of his discomfort." Postell, *The Health of Slaves on Southern Plantations*, 82.

101. *Ramsey v. Blalock*, Docket #3500, August 1860, Ga. Sup. Ct. Records, GDAH, appeal reported in 32 Ga. 376 (1860). See also *Strozier v. Caroll*, Docket #3409, June 1860, Ga. Sup. Ct. Records, GDAH, appeal reported in 31 Ga. 557 (1860).

102. *Durham v. Broddus*, Docket #2547, May 1858, Ga. Sup. Ct. Records, GDAH. Appeal reported in 26 Ga. 524 (1858).

103. Fett, "Body and Soul," 53.

104. *Blair v. Collins*, Docket #6449, December 1860, N.O., SCA-UNO. Appeal reported in 15 La. An. 683 (1861); see also *Wells v. Spears*, 1 McCord 421 (S.C. 1821) (woman died from cold caught in swamp while runaway).

105. *Ails v. Bowman*, Docket #2062, January 1830, N.O., SCA-UNO, appeal reported in 2 la. 251 (1830); *McCay v. Chambliss*, Docket #4882, June 1857, N.O., SCA-UNO, appeal reported in 12 La. Ann. 412 (1857).

106. *Riggin v. Kendig*, Docket #4718, November 1856, N.O., SCA-UNO. Appeal reported in 12 La. Ann. 451 (1857).

107. See *Brocklebank v. Johnson*, Box 28, 1834, S.C. Sup. Ct. Records, SCDAH, appeal reported in *Johnson v. Brockelbank*, 2 Hill 353 (S.C. 1834) (bricklayer); *Campbell v. Kinloch*, Box 42, Fall 1857, Charleston, S.C. Sup. Ct. Records, SCDAH, appeal unreported (bread and cake baker); *Farmer v. Fiske*, Docket #5248, December 1844, N.O., SCA-UNO, appeal reported in 9 Rob. 351 (La. 1845) (female house servant).

108. See *Brocklebank*; *Carter v. Cooper*, Docket #2470, May 1833, N.O., SCA-UNO, appeal reported in 5 La. 446 (1833); *Randolph v. Barnett*, Drawer 188 Folder 2A #38, November Term 1832, Adams Cir. Ct., Miss., HNF (drowning while intoxicated).

109. Interrogatories to Edward Smith of Maryland, *Franklin v. Grissam*, Drawer 145 #74, May Term 1827, Adams Cir. Ct., Miss., HNF.

110. See Denise Herd, "The Paradox of Temperance: Blacks and the Alcohol Question in Nineteenth Century America," in *Drinking: Behavior and Belief in*

Modern History, ed. Susanna Barrows and Robin Room (Berkeley and Los Angeles: University of California Press, 1991), 354.

111. Richard W. Howland and Joe W. Howland, "Two Hundred Years of Drinking in the United States: Evolution of the Disease Concept," in *Drinking: Alcohol in American Society—Issues and Current Research,* ed. John A. Ewing and Beatrice A. Rouse (Chicago: Nelson-Hall, 1978).

112. Isaac Ray, *A Treatise on the Medical Jurisprudence of Insanity,* ed. Winfred Overholser (1835; reprint, Cambridge: Harvard University Press, 1962), secs. 317–20, pp. 302–5.

113. Sergeant S. Prentiss, *A Memoir of S. S. Prentiss* (New York: Charles Scribner, 1856), 1:130, note by editor, quoting Cartwright from *Boston Medical Journal* of 1853.

114. Herd, "The Paradox of Temperance," 357, 356.

115. Greenberg, *Honor and Slavery,* 141.

116. Douglass, *My Bondage and My Freedom,* 256.

117. Savitt, *Medicine and Slavery,* 248. Some writers on insanity did express the view that racial difference alone accounted for the low incidence of insanity among blacks. The editors of the *American Journal of Insanity* wrote, in an early issue, that "insanity is rare we believe among the Africans. Cinquez, and others of the Amistad Negroes, when in this country a few years since, visited the Retreat for the Insane at Hartford, Ct. and saw many of the patients there. They informed the writer of this article, that insanity was very rare in their native country." "Exemption of the Cherokee Indians and Africans from Insanity," *American Journal of Insanity* 1 (January 1845): 288.

118. John S. Hughes, "Labeling and Treating Black Mental Illness in Alabama, 1861–1910," *Journal of Southern History* 58 (August 1993): 436; postbellum commentators based their view of rising insanity among blacks on the 1840 census, which showed very low levels of insanity among enslaved blacks but high ones among Northern blacks. The census was shown to be flawed even by contemporaries. See ibid., 439, and Albert Deutsch, "The First U.S. Census of the Insane (1840) and Its Use as Pro-Slavery Propaganda," *Bulletin of the History of Medicine* 15 (May 1944): 469–82.

119. Hughes, "Black Mental Illness," 442; Gerald Grob, *The Mad among Us: A History of the Care of America's Mentally Ill* (New York: Free Press, 1994), 57–63.

120. *Stinson ads. Piper,* 3 McCord 251, 252–53 (1825).

121. Edward Jarvis, "Causes of Insanity," *Boston Medical and Surgical Journal* 45 (1851): 294; see also Grob, *The Mad among Us,* 60.

122. There were Southern asylums, such as the one at Williamsburg, Virginia, that admitted black patients, even slaves; however, they were a distinct minority. The English writer Harriet Martineau reported that when she found no slaves at the South Carolina Lunatic Asylum and asked where they were, a physician told her that "he had no doubt that they were kept in outhouses, chained to logs, to prevent their doing harm." Quoted in Peter McCandless, *Moonlight, Magnolias and Madness: Insanity in South Carolina from the Colonial Period to the Progressive Era* (Chapel Hill: University of North Carolina Press, 1996), 152.

123. Francis Wharton, *A Treatise on Mental Unsoundness Embracing a General View of Psychological Law* (Philadelphia: Kay & Bro., 1855), sec. 74, p. 60.

124. Ibid., secs. 174–221, pp. 142–87. As Susanna Blumenthal notes, Wharton had modified his view of moral insanity by 1873, when he warned against "psychological romanticism." Blumenthal, " 'The Duress of the Delusion': Mental Capacity and the Rules of Responsibility in Nineteenth-Century American Law" (paper presented at the American Society for Legal History Annual Meeting, Minneapolis, Minn., October, 1997), 14.

125. For cases in which "fits" were discussed as a physical illness, without reference to a male slave's morals or behavior, see *Mangham v. Cox & Waring*, Box 1856, 1st Div., No. 32, Docket #2952, June 1856, Ala. Sup. Ct. Records, ADAH; *Moss v. Davidson*, Docket #1875, January 1841, Miss. HCEA Records, MDAH, appeal reported in *Davidson v. Moss*, 5 How. Miss. 673 (1841); *McCrain v. James*, Drawer 336 #136, May 1851, Adams Cir. Ct., Miss., HNF; *Caton v. Donaldson & Wilburn*, Drawer 46 #13, July 1808, Adams Cty Ct., Miss. Territ., HNF. See *Nowell v. Gadsden*, Box 42, May Term 1848, Charleston, S.C. Sup. Ct. Records, SCDAH, appeal unreported, and *McCay v. Chambliss*, Docket #4882, April 1857, N.O., SCA-UNO, appeal reported in 12 La. Ann. 412 (1857), for cases involving epilepsy degenerating into "imbecility of mind."

126. See, e.g., Carroll Smith-Rosenberg, *Disorderly Conduct: Visions of Gender in Victorian America* (New York: Alfred A. Knopf, 1985); Elaine Showalter, *The Female Malady: Women, Madness and Culture in England, 1830–1980* (New York: Pantheon Books, 1985); Martha N. Evans, *Fits and Starts: A Genealogy of Hysteria in Modern France* (Ithaca: Cornell University Press, 1991).

127. *Icar v. Suares*, Docket #2649, N.O., January 1835, SCA-UNO. Appeal reported in 7 La. 517 (1835).

128. 7 La. at 518.

129. *Chapuis v. Schmelger*, Docket #2328, N.O., December 1851, SCA-UNO. Appeal unreported.

130. *Briant v. Marsh*, 19 La. 391, 392 (1841). See also *Nelson v. Biggers*, Docket #428, January 1849, Ga. Sup. Ct. Records, GDAH, appeal reported in 6 Ga. 205 (1849) (breach of warranty for "Betty, from imbecility of mind . . . a slave incapable of performing ordinary work and labor"). Witnesses for the buyer testified to the seller's having said that Betty "had not sense to raise her child and they took it from her and raised it in the house for she had overlaid her first one"; Osborn Unchurch, the buyer's overseer, "put her Betty to dropping corn and she could not do it for she had to be shown the place to drop and I put her to cover corn with manure and she did not have sense to do that . . ."; however, the seller's witness, James Heagans, testified that while Betty was not "as bright as some negroes," she was capable of the ordinary work of field hands. The lower court judge excluded this testimony; the buyer won. On appeal, the Georgia Supreme Court found error in the interpretation of the word "healthy" in the warranty as applying to "mind" as well as "body" and reversed.

131. *Buhler v. McHatton*, Docket #3448, E. Baton Rouge, March 1854, SCA-UNO. Appeal reported in 9 La. An. 192 (1854).

132. *Walker v. Hays*, Docket #6606, New Orleans, February 1860, SCA-UNO. Appeal reported in 15 La. An. 640 (1860).

133. Charles Cotesworth Pinckney listed among his slaves Old Sambo who "Pretends to be Crazy." McCandless, *Moonlight, Magnolias and Madness*, 154.

134. "The Medical Treatment of Insanity," *American Journal of Insanity* 3 (April 1847): 356–57. Both of these treatments were recommended by Dr. Benjamin Rush, who believed that madness was "as much an original disease of the blood-vessels, as any other state of fever," and that both bleeding and depletion by purge or emetics would draw blood from the head. Norman Dain, *Concepts of Insanity in the United States, 1789–1865* (New Brunswick, N.J.: Rutgers University Press, 1964), 18.

135. On moral treatment for whites, see David J. Rothman, *The Discovery of the Asylum: Social Order and Disorder in the New Republic* (Boston: Little, Brown, 1971), 137–46. On moral treatment for slaves, see McCandless, *Moonlight, Magnolias and Madness*, 154.

136. McCandless, *Moonlight, Magnolias and Madness*, 154.

137. Ibid., 157.

138. Fett, "Body and Soul," 60.

EPILOGUE

1. Davis, *Black Experience*, 146.

2. Ibid., 156–57.

3. *Huntington v. Brown*, 17 La. Ann. 48 (1865).

4. See, e.g., *Walker v. Cucullu, Gatlin v. Kendig*, 18 La. Ann. 118 (1866); *Chapman v. Matthews*, 18 La. Ann. 118 (1866); *Lynch & Weiman v. McRee*, 18 La. Ann. 650 (1866); *Trimble v. Isbell*, 51 Ala. 356 (1870); *Ala. & Fla. R.R. Co. v. Watson*, 42 Ala. 74 (1868); *Dozier v. Freeman*, Miss. 1873; *Barker v. Justice*, Miss. 1866; *Herndon v. Henderson*, Miss. 1868; *Dancey v. Sugg*, Miss. 1872.

In *McAffee v. Mulkey*, 40 Ga. 115 (1869), the plaintiff filed a petition in 1863 regarding an 1862 transaction; the case was heard in Lee Superior Court in 1869. The plaintiff raised the claims that a court could not enforce a debt for "slave consideration," and that enforcement of the debt violated the "Relief Act"; he then amended his complaint to raise typical soundness claims, on which grounds the case was decided. See also *Grier v. Wallace*, S.C. 1875 (in which the trial judge charged the jury that "the policy of the law or the decisions of the Courts overriding the Constitution and enforcing the collection of *negro bonds* was bad and unfortunate, and would not likely be the law long; but that the plaintiff . . . had a right to bring his action").

5. See, e.g., *Manufacturing Co. v. Dykes*, 36 Ga. 633 (1867); *Bailey v. Greenville & Columbia R.R. Co.* (S.C. 1870) (slave hire in 1864–65 must be paid for "whether the slaves were liberated by the emancipation proclamation of 1863 or not").

6. Andrew Kull, "Personal Liberty and Private Law: The Enforceability after Emancipation of Debts Contracted for the Purchase of Slaves," *Chicago-Kent Law Review* 70 (1994): 493–538.

7. Quoted in ibid., 519–20.

8. Ibid., 512.

9. *Hand v. Armstrong*, 34 Ga. 232 (1866) (upholding enforceability); *Bradford v. Jenkins*, 41 Miss. 328 (1867) (upholding enforceability); *Calhoun v. Calhoun*, 2 S.C. 283 (1870) (upholding enforceability); *Wainwright v. Bridges*, 19 La. Ann. 234 (1867) (denying enforcement); *Osborn v. Nicholson*, 80 U.S. (13 Wall.) 654 (1872) (upholding enforceability); *Palmer v. Marston*, 81 U.S. (14 Wall.) 10 (1872) (overturning Louisiana precedent).

10. See, e.g., *Bass v. Ware*, 34 Ga. 386 (1866).

11. Quoted in Kull, "Enforceability," 529. "James E. Martin, having re-purchased . . . loses the negro by freedom; and Riley the benefit of his mortgage taken from Durham. So that manumission is not only a *two-edged* sword, but rather like the flaming sword placed at the East of the garden of Eden, at Adam's expulsion, *turning every way towards the community*." *Riley v. Martin*, 35 Ga. 136 (1866).

12. Andrew Kull, "Enforcement of 'Slave Contracts' after Emancipation" (paper delivered at Stanford Law School, May 1994), 62.

13. See Dylan Penningroth, "Slavery, Freedom, and Social Claims to Property among African Americans in Liberty County, Georgia, 1850–1880," *Journal of American History* 84 (September 1997): 405–35.

14. Southern Claims Commission Records, RG 217, Allowed Claims—Adams County, Case File #17480, Henry Anderson (colored).

15. Ibid.

16. Claims Commission Records, Adams County, Case File #19728, John Holdman.

17. Claims Commission Records, Adams County, Case File #5757, Charles Smith (colored); testimony of William H. Lynch.

18. Claims Commission Records, Adams County, Case File #19537, William Hardin.

19. Claims Commission Records, Adams County, Case File #57521, Littleton Barber.

20. Claims Commission Records, Adams County, Case File #16373, Catherine Lucas, testimony of Vinson Brady; see also Claims Commission Records, Adams County, Case File #6616, Mrs. Jane Dent ("the Rebs threatened to hang me—because they said I furnished information to the Yankees"); Claims Commission Records, Adams County, Case File #10801, John Smith, testimony of Lewis Thompson ("He was taken out to be hanged once and his house was searched several times—he was suspicioned because he came from Kentucky and was a free man"); testimony of Rev. Randall Pollard ("Eight colored men were arrested and hanged about the same time for expressing their sympathies with the Yankees"). For details of the interrogations and hangings of Adams County slaves suspected of rebellion, see Jordan, *Tumult and Silence at Second Creek*.

21. Claims Commission Records, Adams County, Case File #7960, Katherine S. Minor. John Minor, Katherine's former husband, owned property in Adams County and Ascension Parish, Louisiana, valued at $555,600 in 1860. Although some of his wealth came from his father, the wealthy colonial planter Stephen

Minor, Katherine brought much of the wealth to the family from the Surget clan. James, *Antebellum Natchez*, 155.

22. Ibid.

23. Ibid. Katherine Minor's claim was allowed, although for a much lower sum than she had requested.

24. Records of the United States Court of Claims, RG 123, Sec. 22, Congressional Jurisdiction, Case File #1233, Andrew Brown, Folders 1 and 2.

BIBLIOGRAPHY

MANUSCRIPTS AND NEWSPAPERS

Court Records

ALABAMA DEPT. OF ARCHIVES AND HISTORY, MONTGOMERY, ALA. (ADAH), SG2803.
Alabama Supreme Court Records, 1822–61.
Misc. Court Cases, Briefs, Etc., 1820–73.

GEORGIA DEPT. OF ARCHIVES AND HISTORY, ATLANTA, GA. 92ɳI-I (GDAH)
Georgia Supreme Court Case Files, 1846–67.

UNIVERSITY OF NEW ORLEANS SPECIAL COLLECTIONS, ACCOUNT 106
Records of the Supreme Court of Louisiana, 1809–67 (SCA-UNO).

HISTORIC NATCHEZ FOUNDATION, NATCHEZ, MISS. (HNF)
Adams Circuit Court, Books of Judgment, 1822–1861.
Adams Circuit Court, Minute Books, 1822–61.
Adams Circuit Court Records, 1822–61.
Adams County Court Records, 1798–1822.
Appearance Docket, 1830.
Bar Issue Dockets, 1820–21, 1824–28, 1844–49.
Court Issue Dockets, 1837–41, 1850–61.
Indexes to Issue Dockets, 1837–40, 1844–49.
Issue Dockets, 1820–21, 1824–28, 1830, 1837–41, 1844–49.

MISSISSIPPI DEPT. OF ARCHIVES AND HISTORY (MDAH), RECORD GROUP 32
High Court of Errors and Appeals Records (HCEA), 1832–61.
Superior Court of Chancery, Western District [Natchez] Records, 1818–38.

SOUTH CAROLINA DEPT. OF ARCHIVES AND HISTORY (SCDAH)
Court of Appeals and Law Records, 1824–61.
Fairfield District Court of Common Pleas Judgment Rolls, 1813–24, 1848–51.
Laurens District Court of Common Pleas, Judgment Rolls, 1809–15.

Other Official Records

Land Deed Records, Adams County Courthouse, Natchez, Miss.
Land and Personal Assessment Rolls, Adams County, 1818–31; 1833–34; 1836; 1838–41; 1843; 1846–68; 1850; 1852–53; 1857–59; 1861–62.
Personal Tax Rolls, Mississippi Territory, Adams County, 1802; 1805; 1807–17.
Population Schedules of the Fifth, Sixth, Seventh, and Eighth Censuses of the United States, Adams County, Miss., M19 Reel 70, M704 Reel 213, MM432 Reel 368, 383 (1830–60); Abbeville District, S.C., M432 Reel 501 (1840); Edgefield District, S.C., M432 Reel 172 (1830); Perry County, Ala., M432 Reel 23 (1850); Madison County, Ala., M432 Reels 9, 21 (1860); Clarke County,

Miss., M432 Reel 370, M433 Reel 384, M653 Reel 580 (1850–60); Amite County, Miss. (1850); Hinds County, Miss. (1860).

Southern Claims Commission Records, RG 217, National Archives, Washington, D.C.

United States Court of Claims Records, RG 123, National Archives, Washington, D.C.

Wills, Adams County Courthouse, Natchez, Miss.

Newspapers and Periodicals

Ariel, 1825–29.
DeBow's Review, 1842–61.
Mississippi Free Trader and Natchez Gazette, 1855–56.
Mississippi Messenger, 1805–9.
Natchez Courier, 1834.
Natchez Daily Courier, 1852–54.
Natchez Semi-Weekly Courier, 1845–52.
Natchez Weekly Courier, 1854–61.

Manuscript Collections

HISTORIC NEW ORLEANS COLLECTION, NEW ORLEANS, LA.

Conner, Lemuel Park Papers, MS 20.
Helm, J. N.—Beverly Plantation Journal, MS 433.
Mississippi Bar Association Records, MS 25.
Slavery in Louisiana Collection, MS 44.

HOWARD-TILTON LIBRARY, TULANE UNIVERSITY

Colcock Family Papers, 1785–1917, Collection 520.
Kuntz Collection, F. Edward Turner Papers, Collection 600.
Mercer, William Newton Papers, Collection 64.
Weeks Family Papers, 1776–1979, Collection 198.

LOUISIANA STATE UNIVERSITY ARCHIVES, BATON ROUGE, LA. (LSU)

Britton, Audley Clark, and Family Papers.
Cartwright, Samuel A., Papers, 1826–50.
Conner, Lemuel P., Family Papers, 1810–1953.
Embree, Joseph, Papers.
Farrar, Alexander K., Papers, 1804–1931.
Liddell, Moses, and St. John Richardson Family Papers, 1813–1919.
McMurran, John T., Papers, 1836–75.
Merrill, A. P.—Aylett Buckner Papers, 1787–1870.
Quitman, John A., and Family Papers, 1823–72.
Reed, Thomas, Papers.
Shields, Joseph D., Papers, 1802–42.
Terry, William, Papers.
Vidal, Joseph, and Samuel A. Davis Family Papers, 1797–1869.
Walworth, Douglas, Family Papers.
Weeks, David, and Family Papers.

MISSISSIPPI DEPT. OF ARCHIVES AND HISTORY (MDAH), JACKSON, MISS.

Abbey, Richard, Subject File.
Adams, George, Subject File.
Boyd, Samuel S., Subject File.
Cartwright, Samuel A., Manuscripts.
Claiborne, J.F.H., Papers.
Coffey, Chesley Shelton, Subject File.
Gaines, Richard M., Subject File.
Harding, Lyman, Subject File.
Isler, Peter, Subject File.
Lewis, Seth, Memoirs.
Marschalk, Andrew, Subject File.
McMurran, John T., Subject File.
Quitman, John A., Subject File.
Reed, Thomas Buck, Subject File.
Sharkey, William L., Papers.
Shields, William B., Subject File.
Soria, Jacob, Subject File.
Turner, Edward, Subject File.
Vannerson, Judge William, Subject File.
Wailes, Benjamin L. C., Papers.
Winchester, George, Subject File.

SOUTHERN HISTORICAL COLLECTION, UNIVERSITY OF NORTH CAROLINA,
CHAPEL HILL, N.C.

Chotard, Elizabeth, Autobiography.
Quitman, John A., and Family Papers.

CENTER FOR AMERICAN HISTORY, UNIVERSITY OF TEXAS AT AUSTIN, TEXAS (CAH-UTA)

Natchez Trace Collection:
    Slaves and Slavery Collection.
    Tichenor, Gabriel, Papers.
    Winchester, George and Josiah, Papers, 1783–1902.
Southern Historical Archival Collection:
    Ellis, Powhatan, Papers.

Database

Hall, Gwendolyn Midlo, and Patrick Manning, coinvestigators. *Slaves in Louisiana, 1735–1820*. Collaborative Research Project of the National Endowment for the Humanities.

LEGAL CODES AND STATUTES

Alabama

Aikin, John D. *A Digest of the Laws of the State of Alabama*. 2d ed. Tuscaloosa: D. Woodruff, 1836.

Ormond, John J., Arthur P. Bagby, and George Goldthwaite. *The Code of Alabama*. Montgomery: Brittan and DeWolf, 1852.

Georgia

Cobb, Howell. *A Compilation of the General and Public Statutes of the State of Georgia*. New York: E. O. Jenkins, 1859.
Lamar, Lucius Q. C. *Laws of the State of Georgia*. Augusta: T. S. Hannon, 1821.
Prince, Oliver. *A Digest of the Laws of the State of Georgia*. 2d ed. Athens: Published by the Author, 1837.

Louisiana

Civil Code of the State of Louisiana. New Orleans: Published by a Citizen of Louisiana, 1825.
The Laws of the Territory of Louisiana. St. Louis: Joseph Charles, 1808.
Upton, Wheelock S., and Needler R. Jennings. *The Civil Code of the State of Louisiana, with Annotations*. New Orleans: E. Johns and Co., 1838.

Mississippi

Alden, T. J. Fox, and J. A. Van Hoesen. *A Digest of the Laws of Mississippi*. New York: Alexander S. Gould, 1839.
Code of the Ordinances of the City of Natchez, Now in Force. Natchez: Giles M. Hillyer, 1854.
Hutchinson, A. *Code of Mississippi, from 1798 to 1848*. Jackson: Price and Hall, 1848.
The Revised Code of the Statute Laws of the State of Mississippi. Jackson: E. Barksdale, 1857.
Statutes of the Mississippi Territory. Natchez: P. Isler, 1816.

South Carolina

Cooper, Thomas, and David J. McCord. *Statutes at Large of South Carolina*. 10 vols. Columbia: A. S. Johnston, 1836–41.

PUBLISHED PRIMARY SOURCES

Andrews, Garnett. *Reminiscences of An Old Georgia Lawyer*. Atlanta: Franklin Steam Printing House, 1870. Reprint, Atlanta: Cherokee Pub. Co.
Baldwin, Joseph. *The Flush Times of Alabama and Mississippi*. Reprint, New York: Sagamore Press, 1957.
Ball, Charles. *Fifty Years in Chains, or, The Life of An American Slave*. New York: H. Dayton, 1859. Reprint, Detroit, Mich.: Negro Universities Press, 1969.
Beck, Theodric R. *Elements of Medical Jurisprudence*. Albany, N.Y.: Webster and Skinner, 1823.
Blassingame, John W., ed. *Slave Testimony: Two Centuries of Letters, Speeches, Interviews, and Autobiographies*. Baton Rouge: Louisiana State University Press, 1977.
Breeden, James O., ed. *Advice among Masters: The Ideal in Slave Management in the Old South*. Westport, Conn.: Greenwood Press, 1980.

Brown, A. J. *History of Newton County, Mississippi from 1834 to 1894.* Jackson, Miss.: Clarion-Ledger Co., 1894.

Brown, John. *Slave Life in Georgia: A Narrative of the Life, Sufferings, and Escape of John Brown, Fugitive Slave.* Edited by F. N. Boney. Reprint, Savannah, Ga.: Beehive Press, 1972.

Cartwright, Samuel A. "Cartwright on Southern Medicine." *New Orleans Medical and Surgical Journal* 3 (1846): 259–72.

———. "Diseases and Peculiarities of the Negro Race." *DeBow's Review* 11 (1851): 64–69, 209–13, 331–37.

———. "Dr. Cartwright on the Caucasians and the Africans." *DeBow's Review* 25 (1858): 45–56.

———. "How to Save the Republic, and the Position of the South in the Union." *DeBow's Review* 11 (1851): 184–97.

———. "Negro Freedom an Impossibility under Nature's Laws." *DeBow's Review* 30 (1860): 648–59.

———. "Unity of the Human Race Disproved by the Hebrew Bible." *DeBow's Review* 29 (1860): 129–36.

Catterall, Helen. *Judicial Cases Concerning American Slavery and the Negro.* 5 vols. 1926. Reprint, New York: Octagon Books, 1968.

Cobb, Thomas R. R. *An Inquiry into the Law of Negro Slavery in the United States of America: To Which Is Prefixed, an Historical Sketch of Slavery.* 1858. Reprint, New York: Negro Universities Press, 1968.

Craft, William and Ellen. *Running a Thousand Miles for Freedom.* Reprint, New York: Arno Press, 1969.

Davis, Reuben. *Recollections of Mississippi and Mississippians.* Boston: Houghton, Mifflin, & Co., 1889.

DeBow, J.D.B. ed. *The Industrial Resources, Statistics, etc., of the United States, and More Particularly of the Southern and Western States.* Vol. 2. New York: D. Appleton & Co., 1854.

Donnan, Elizabeth, ed. *Documents Illustrative of the History of the Slave Trade to America.* Vol. 4. New York: Octagon Books, 1965.

Douglass, Frederick. *The Frederick Douglass Papers.* Edited by John W. Blassingame. 4 vols. New Haven: Yale University Press, 1979.

———. *My Bondage and My Freedom.* New York: Miller, Orton & Mulligan, 1855. Reprint, New York: Dover Publications, 1969.

Elliott, E. N. *Cotton Is King, and Pro-Slavery Arguments.* 1860. Reprint, New York: Negro Universities Press, 1969.

Foote, Henry S. *The Bench and Bar of the South and Southwest.* St. Louis: Soule, Thomas and Wentworth, 1876.

———. *Casket of Reminiscences.* Washington, D.C.: Chronicle Publishing Co., 1874.

Fulkerson, Horace S. *Random Recollections of Early Days in Mississippi.* Vicksburg: Commercial Herald Pub., 1888.

Gentry, North Todd. *Bench and Bar of Boone County, Missouri.* Self-published, 1916.

Goodell, William. *The American Slave Code in Theory and Practice.* New York: American and Foreign Antislavery Society, 1853.

Goodell, William. *Goodspeed's Biographical and Historical Memoirs of Mississippi.* Vol. 1. Chicago: The Goodspeed Publishing Co., 1891.

H. "Remarks on Overseers, and the Proper Treatment of Slaves." *Farmer's Register* 5 (1837): 302.

Harriss, Juriah. "What Constitutes Unsoundness in the Negro?" *Savannah Journal of Medicine* 1 (3) (September 1858): 145–52; 1 (4) (November 1858): 220–26; 1 (5) (January 1859): 289–95; 2 (1) (May 1859): 10–17.

Hogan, William R., and Edwin A. Davis. eds. *William Johnson's Natchez: The Diary of an Ante-bellum Free Negro.* Baton Rouge: Louisiana State University Press, 1973.

Hughes, Louis. *Thirty Years a Slave, from Bondage to Freedom.* 1897. Reprint, New York: Negro Universities Press, 1969.

Hurd, John Codman. "Implied Warranty on Sale of Personal Chattels." *American Jurist and Law Magazine* 12 (1834): 311–14.

Ingraham, Joseph. *The South-West by a Yankee.* 2 vols. New York: Harper & Brothers, 1835.

Jacobs, Harriet. *Incidents in the Life of A Slave Girl.* Reprint, New York: Oxford University Press, 1988.

Jarvis, Edward. "Causes of Insanity." *Boston Medical and Surgical Journal* 45 (1851).

The Law of Freedom and Bondage in the United States. 2 vols. Boston: Little, Brown, 1858.

Lynch, James D. *The Bench and Bar of Mississippi.* New York: E. J. Hale and Son, 1881.

"The Medical Treatment of Insanity." *American Journal of Insanity* 3 (April 1847): 356–57.

Merrill, A. P. "Distinctive Peculiarities and Diseases of the Negro Race." *DeBow's Review* 28 (1860): 612–22.

———. "An Essay on Some of the Distinctive Peculiarities of the Negro Race." *Southern Medical and Surgical Journal* 12 (January 1856).

Northup, Solomon. *Twelve Years a Slave.* Reprint, Baton Rouge: Louisiana State University Press, 1968.

Nott, Josiah C. "The Management of the Negro." *DeBow's Review* 10 (1850): 621–27.

Olmsted, Frederick Law. *Cotton Kingdom: A Traveler's Observations on Cotton and Slavery in the American Slave States.* 2 vols. New York: Mason Brothers, 1862.

———. *A Journey in the Seaboard Slave States, with Remarks on Their Economy.* New York: Dix & Edwards, 1856.

O'Neall, John Belton. *The Negro Law of South Carolina.* Columbia, S.C.: John G. Bowman, 1848.

Osofsky, Gilbert, ed. *Puttin' On Ole Massa: The Slave Narratives of Henry Bibb, William Wells Brown, and Solomon Northrup.* New York: Harper & Row, 1969.

Power, Steven. *The Memento: Old and New Natchez 1700 to 1897.* Natchez, Miss.: Published by the Author, 1897.

Prentiss, Sergeant S. *A Memoir of S. S. Prentiss*. New York: Charles Scribner, 1856.

Rawick, George P. *The American Slave: A Composite Autobiography*. Westport, Conn.: Greenwood Press, 1977.

Ray, Isaac. *A Treatise on the Medical Jurisprudence of Insanity*. 1835. Reprint, Cambridge: Harvard University Press, 1962.

Redpath, James. *The Roving Editor: or, Talks with Slaves in the Southern States*. New York: A. B. Burdick, 1859.

Reeve, Tapping. *The Law of Baron and Femme; or Parent and Child; or Guardian and Ward; or Master and Servant*. New Haven: Oliver Steele, 1816. 2d ed., Burlington, Vt.: Chauncey Goodrich, 1846.

"Report on the Diseases and Physical Peculiarities of the Negro Race." *New Orleans Medical and Surgical Journal* 8 (1851): 692–713.

Shippee, Lester B., ed. *Bishop Whipple's Southern Diary*. Reprint, Minneapolis: University of Minnesota Press, 1937.

Stroud, George M. *A Sketch of the Laws Relating to Slavery in the Several States of the United States of America*. 1827. Reprint, New York: Negro Universities Press, 1968.

Warren, Charles. *A History of the American Bar*. Boston: Little, Brown, 1911.

Wharton, Francis. *A Commentary on the Law of Evidence in Civil Issues*. 2 vols. 3d ed. Philadelphia: Kay & Bro., 1888.

———. *A Treatise on Mental Unsoundness Embracing a General View of Psychological Law*. Philadelphia: Kay and Bro., 1855.

Wheeler, Jacob D. *A Practical Treatise on the Law of Slavery*. 1837. Reprint, New York: Negro Universities Press, 1968.

Wilson, J. S. "Peculiarities and Diseases of Negroes." *DeBow's Review* 28 (1860): 112–15; 29 (1860): 597–99.

UNPUBLISHED DISSERTATIONS AND MASTER'S THESIS

Constant, Alan D. "The 1840 Presidential Election in the Natchez District, Mississippi." M.A. thesis, University of Texas at Austin, 1993.

Fett, Sharla M. "Body and Soul: African-American Healing in Antebellum Southern Plantation Communities, 1800–1860." Ph.D. diss., Rutgers University, 1995.

Johnson, Walter K. "Masters and Slaves in the Market: Slavery and the New Orleans Trade, 1804–1864." Ph.D diss., Princeton University, 1995.

Russell, Thomas D. "Sale Day in Antebellum South Carolina: Slavery, Law, Economy, and Court-Supervised Sales." Ph.D. diss., Stanford University, 1993.

UNPUBLISHED MANUSCRIPTS

Balleisen, Edward J. "Reconstructing the Law of Failure: The 1841 Federal Bankruptcy Act and the Culture of Debtor-Creditor Relations in America." Paper presented to the American Society for Legal History Annual Meeting, Seattle, Wash., October 1998. In possession of the author.

Blumenthal, Susanna. " 'The Duress of the Delusion': Mental Capacity and the Rules of Responsibility in Nineteenth-Century American Law." Paper presented at the American Society for Legal History Annual Meeting, Minneapolis, Minn., October 1997. In possession of the author.

Broussard-Hogan, Joyce. "The Career of John T. McMurran: From Yankee Lawyer to Planter Elite in the Natchez District, 1823–1866." Manuscript available at the Mississippi Dept. of Archives and History, Jackson, Miss.

Kull, Andrew. "Enforcement of 'Slave Contracts' after Emancipation." Paper delivered at Stanford Law School, May 1994. In possession of the author.

Miller, Mimi. "A History of African-Americans in Natchez, Mississippi." Manuscript available at the Historic Natchez Foundation, Natchez, Miss. January 12, 1992.

SECONDARY SOURCES

"Alabama's First Licensed Lawyers." *Alabama Historical Quarterly* 1 (Winter 1930): 367–69.

Alexander, Gregory. *Commodity and Propriety: Competing Visions of Property in American Legal Thought, 1776–1970*. Chicago: University of Chicago Press, 1997.

Alford, Terry. *Prince among Slaves*. New York: Harcourt Brace Jovanovich, 1977.

Allen, Theodore W. *The Invention of the White Race*. London: Verso, 1994.

Atiyah, Patrick S. *The Rise and Fall of Freedom of Contract*. Oxford: Oxford University Press, 1979.

Ayers, Edward L. *Vengeance and Justice: Crime and Punishment in the Nineteenth-Century American South*. New York: Oxford University Press, 1984.

Bancroft, Frederic. *Slave Trading in the Old South*. Baltimore: J. H. Furst Co., 1931.

Berlin, Ira. *Slaves without Masters: The Free Negro in the Antebellum South*. New York: Pantheon Books, 1974.

Berry, Mary Francis. "Judging Morality and Legal Consequences in the Late Nineteenth-Century South." *Journal of American History* 78 (1991): 835–56.

Binder, Guyora, and Robert Weisberg. "Cultural Criticism of Law." *Stanford Law Review* 49 (1997): 1149–1220.

Blassingame, John. *The Slave Community: Plantation Life in the Old South*. New York: Oxford University Press, 1972.

Bodenhamer, David J. "The Democratic Impulse and Legal Change in the Age of Jackson: The Example of Criminal Juries in Antebellum Indiana." *Historian* 45 (February 1983): 206–19.

Bodenhamer, David J., and James W. Ely Jr., eds. *Ambivalent Legacy: A Legal History of the South*. Jackson: University Press of Mississippi, 1984.

———. "Regionalism and American Legal History: The Southern Experience." *Vanderbilt Law Review* 39 (1986): 539–67.

Bowman, Shearer Davis. *Masters and Lords: Mid-Nineteenth Century U.S. Planters and Prussian Junkers*. New York: Oxford University Press, 1993.

Brown, Kathleen M. *Good Wives, Nasty Wenches, and Anxious Patriarchs: Gender, Race, and Power in Colonial Virginia.* Chapel Hill: University of North Carolina Press, 1996.

Burke, William Lewis, Jr. "A History of the Opening Statement from Barristers to Corporate Lawyers: A Case Study of South Carolina." *American Journal of Legal History* 37 (1993): 25–64.

Burnham, Margaret. "An Impossible Marriage: Slave Law and Family Law." *Law and Inequality* 5 (1987): 187–225.

Burton, Orville Vernon. *In My Father's House Are Many Mansions: Family and Community in Edgefield, South Carolina.* Chapel Hill: University of North Carolina Press, 1985.

Butler, Judith. *Bodies That Matter: On the Discursive Limits of "Sex."* New York: Routledge, 1993.

Campbell, Randolph B. "Research Note: Slave Hiring in Texas." *American Historical Review* 93 (1988): 107–14.

Cash, Wilbur J. *The Mind of the South.* New York: Doubleday, 1941.

Clark, Michael, and Catherine Crawford, eds. *Legal Medicine in History.* Cambridge: Cambridge University Press, 1994.

Clifford, James. *The Predicament of Culture: Twentieth-Century Ethnography, Literature, and Art.* Cambridge: Harvard University Press, 1988.

Collins, Winfield H. *The Domestic Slave Trade of the Southern States.* 1904. Reprint, Port Washington, N.Y.: Kennikat Press, 1969.

Comaroff, Jean. "Medicine, Colonialism and the Black Body." In *Ethnography and the Historical Imagination,* edited by John L. Comaroff and Jean Comaroff, 215–33. Boulder, Colo.: Westview Press, 1992.

Cotton, Gordon A. *The Old Courthouse.* Raymond, Miss.: Keith Printing Co., 1982.

Cottrol, Robert J. "Liberalism and Paternalism: Ideology, Economic Interest, and the Business Law of Slavery." *American Journal of Legal History* 31 (1987): 359–73.

Cover, Robert. *Justice Accused: Antislavery and the Judicial Process.* New Haven: Yale University Press, 1975.

Crenshaw, Kimberle. "Demarginalizing the Intersection of Race and Sex: A Black Feminist Critique of Antidiscrimination Doctrine, Feminist Theory and Antiracist Politics." *University of Chicago Legal Forum* (1989): 139–67.

Dain, Norman. *Concepts of Insanity in the United States, 1789–1865.* New Brunswick, N.J.: Rutgers University Press, 1964.

Davis, Ronald L. F. *The Black Experience in Natchez, 1720–1880.* Special Historical Study, Natchez National Historic Park, Miss. April 1993.

———. *Good and Faithful Labor: From Slavery to Sharecropping in the Natchez District, 1860–1890.* Westport, Conn.: Greenwood Press, 1982.

Delgado, Richard, and Jean Stefancic, eds. *Critical White Studies: Looking behind the Mirror.* Philadelphia: Temple University Press, 1997.

Deutsch, Albert. "The First U.S. Census of the Insane (1840) and Its Use as Pro-Slavery Propaganda." *Bulletin of the History of Medicine* 15 (May 1944): 469–82.

Diamond, Elin, ed. *Performance and Cultural Politics*. New York: Routledge, 1996.

Eigen, Joel P. *Witnessing Insanity: Madness and Mad-Doctors in the English Court*. New Haven: Yale University Press, 1995.

Escott, Paul. *Slavery Remembered: A Record of the Twentieth-Century Slave Narratives*. Chapel Hill: University of North Carolina Press, 1979.

Evans, Martha N. *Fits and Starts: A Genealogy of Hysteria in Modern France*. Ithaca: Cornell University Press, 1991.

Faust, Drew Gilpin. *A Sacred Circle: The Dilemma of the Intellectual in the Old South, 1840–1860*. Baltimore: Johns Hopkins University Press, 1977.

Fede, Andrew. "Legal Protection for Slave Buyers in the U.S. South: A Caveat Concerning *Caveat Emptor*." *American Journal of Legal History* 31 (1987): 322–58.

———. "Legitimized Violent Slave Abuse in the American South, 1619–1865: A Case Study of Law and Social Change in Six Southern States." *American Journal of Legal History* 29 (1985): 93–150.

——— *People without Rights: An Interpretation of the Fundamentals of the Law of Slavery in the U.S. South*. New York: Garland Publishing, 1992.

Fields, Barbara Jeanne. "Race and Ideology in American History." In *Region, Race and Reconstruction: Essays in Honor of C. Vann Woodward*, edited by J. Morgan Kousser and James M. McPherson, 143–77. New York: Oxford University Press, 1982.

Finkelman, Paul. "The Color of Law." *Northwestern University Law Review* 87 (1992–93): 937–91.

———. "The Crime of Color." *Tulane Law Review* 67 (1993): 2063–2112.

———. "Exploring Southern Legal History." *North Carolina Law Review* 64 (November 1985): 77–116.

———. *An Imperfect Union: Slavery, Federalism, and Comity*. Chapel Hill: University of North Carolina Press, 1981.

———. "Northern Labor Law and Southern Slave Law: The Application of the Fellow Servant Rule to Slaves." *National Black Law Journal* 11 (1989): 212–32.

———. "Slaves as Fellow Servants: Ideology, Law, and Industrialization." *American Journal of Legal History* 31 (October 1987): 269–305.

Finley, Moses I. *Ancient Slavery and Modern Ideology*. New York: Viking Press, 1980.

Fisher, William W., III. "Ideology and Imagery in the Law of Slavery." *Chicago-Kent Law Review* 68 (1993): 1051–86.

Flanigan, Daniel J. "Criminal Procedure in Slave Trials in the Antebellum South." *Journal of Southern History* 40 (November 1974): 537–64.

Fogel, Robert W. *Without Consent or Contract: The Rise and Fall of American Slavery*. New York: W. W. Norton, 1989.

Fogel, Robert W., and Stanley L. Engerman. *Time on the Cross: The Economics of American Negro Slavery*. 2 vols. New York: W. W. Norton, 1989.

Foster, Frances S. *Witnessing Slavery: The Development of Ante-Bellum Slave Narratives*. Madison: University of Wisconsin Press, 1979.

Fox, Richard Wightman, and T. J. Jackson Lears, eds. *The Power of Culture: Critical Essays on American History*. Chicago: University of Chicago Press, 1993.

Fox-Genovese, Elizabeth. *Within the Plantation Household: Black and White Women in the Old South*. Chapel Hill: University of North Carolina Press, 1988.

Fox-Genovese, Elizabeth, and Eugene D. Genovese. *Fruits of Merchant Capital: Slavery and Bourgeois Property in the Rise and Expansion of Capitalism*. New York: Oxford University Press, 1983.

———. "Slavery, Economic Development, and the Law: The Dilemma of the Southern Political Economists, 1800–1860." *Washington and Lee Law Review* 41 (Winter 1984): 1–29.

Franklin, John Hope. *The Militant South, 1800–1861*. Cambridge: Harvard University Press, 1956.

Fredrickson, George M. *The Arrogance of Race: Historical Perspectives on Slavery, Racism, and Social Inequality*. Middletown, Conn.: Wesleyan University Press, 1988.

———. *The Black Image in the White Mind: The Debate on Afro-American Character and Destiny, 1817–1914*. New York: Harper and Row, 1971.

Friedman, Lawrence M. *A History of American Law*. New York: Simon and Schuster, 1973.

Friedman, Lawrence M., and Jack Ladinsky. "Social Change and the Law of Industrial Accidents." *Columbia Law Review* 67 (1967): 50–82.

Gallagher, Catharine, and Thomas Laqueur, eds. *The Making of the Modern Body: Sexuality and Society in the Nineteenth Century*. Berkeley and Los Angeles: University of California Press, 1987.

Geertz, Clifford. *Local Knowledge: Further Essays in Interpretive Anthropology*. New York: Basic Books, 1983.

Genovese, Eugene D. *The Political Economy of Slavery: Studies in the Economy and Society of the Slave South*. New York: Vintage Books, 1967.

———. *Roll, Jordan, Roll: The World the Slaveholders Made*. New York: Vintage Books, 1976.

———. "Slavery in the Legal History of the South and the Nation." *Texas Law Review* 59 (1981): 969–98.

Gilman, Sander L. "Black Bodies, White Bodies: Toward an Iconography of Female Sexuality in Late Nineteenth-Century Art, Medicine, and Literature." In *Race, Writing, and Difference*, edited by Henry Louis Gates, Jr., 223–61. Chicago: University of Chicago Press, 1985.

———. *Difference and Pathology: Stereotypes of Sexuality, Race, and Madness*. Ithaca: Cornell University Press, 1989.

Glenn, Myra. "School Discipline and Punishment in Antebellum America." *Journal of the Early Republic* 1 (Winter 1981): 395–408.

Goldin, Claudia Dale. *Urban Slavery in the American South, 1820–1860*. Chicago: University of Chicago Press, 1976.

Gordon, Robert W. "Critical Legal Histories." *Stanford Law Review* 36 (1984): 57–125.

Gordon, Robert W. "Historicism in Legal Scholarship." *Yale Law Journal* 90 (1981): 1017–56.

Gotanda, Neil. "A Critique of 'Our Constitution Is Color-Blind.' " *Stanford Law Review* 44 (1991): 1–68.

Green, Thomas A. "A Retrospective on the Criminal Trial Jury, 1200–1800." In *Twelve Good Men and True: The Criminal Trial Jury in England, 1200–1800*, edited by J. S. Cockburn and Thomas A. Green, 358–99. Princeton: Princeton University Press, 1988.

———. *Verdict According to Conscience: Perspectives on the English Criminal Trial Jury, 1200–1800*. Chicago: University of Chicago Press, 1985.

Greenberg, Kenneth S. *Honor and Slavery: Lies, Duels, Noses, Masks, Dressing as a Woman, Gifts, Strangers, Death, Humanitarianism, Slave Rebellions, the Pro-Slavery Argument, Baseball, Hunting, and Gambling in the Old South*. Princeton: Princeton University Press, 1996.

———. *Masters and Statesmen: The Political Culture of American Slavery*. Baltimore: Johns Hopkins University Press, 1985.

———. "The Nose, the Lie, and the Duel in the Antebellum South." *American Historical Review* (1990) 95 (1): 57–74.

Grob, Gerald W. *Edward Jarvis and the Medical World of Nineteenth-Century America*. Knoxville: University of Tennessee Press, 1978.

———. *The Mad among Us: A History of the Care of America's Mentally Ill*. New York: Free Press, 1994.

Gross, Ariela J. "Litigating Whiteness: Trials of Racial Determination in the Nineteenth Century South." *Yale Law Journal* 108 (1998): 109–88.

Gutman, Herbert. *The Black Family in Slavery and Freedom, 1750–1925*. New York: Pantheon Books, 1976.

Haber, Samuel. *The Quest for Honor and Authority in the American Professions, 1750–1900*. Chicago: University of Chicago Press, 1991.

Hale, Grace E. *Making Whiteness: The Culture of Segregation in the South, 1890–1940*. New York: Random House, Pantheon Books, 1998.

Hall, Kermit L., and James W. Ely, Jr. *An Uncertain Tradition: Constitutionalism and the History of the South*. Athens: University of Georgia Press, 1989.

Haller, John S., Jr. "The Negroes and the Southern Physician." *Medical History* 16 (1972): 238—53.

Haney-Lopez, Ian F. "The Social Construction of Race: Some Observations on Illusion, Fabrication, and Choice." *Harvard Civil Rights-Civil Liberties Review* 29 (1984): 1–62.

———. *White by Law: The Legal Construction of Race*. New York: New York University Press, 1996.

Harris, Cheryl I. "Whiteness as Property." *Harvard Law Review* 106 (1993): 1707–91.

Harris, J. William. *Plain Folk and Gentry in a Slave Society: White Liberty and Black Slavery in Augusta's Hinterlands*. Middletown, Conn.: Wesleyan University Press, 1985.

Hay, Douglas, et al. *Albion's Fatal Tree: Crime and Society in Eighteenth-Century England*. New York: Pantheon Books, 1975.

Hellie, Richard. "Muscovite Slavery in Comparative Perspective." *Russian History/Histoire Russe* 6, pt. 2 (1979): 133–209.

Herd, Denise. "The Paradox of Temperance: Blacks and the Alcohol Question in Nineteenth Century America." In *Drinking: Behavior and Belief in Modern History*, edited by Susanna Barrows and Robin Room, 354–75. Berkeley and Los Angeles: University of California Press, 1991.

Higginbotham, A. Leon, Jr. *In the Matter of Color: Race and the American Legal Process: The Colonial Period*. New York: Oxford University Press, 1978.

Higginbotham, A. Leon, Jr., and Barbara K. Kopytoff. "Property First, Humanity Second: The Recognition of the Slave's Human Nature in Virginia Civil Law." *Ohio State Law Journal* 50 (1989): 511–40.

————. "Racial Purity and Interracial Sex in the Law of Colonial and Antebellum Virginia." *Georgetown Law Journal* 77 (1989): 1967–2029.

Higginbotham, Evelyn Brooks. "African-American Women's History and the Metalanguage of Race." *Signs* 17 (Winter 1992): 251–74.

Hindus, Michael S. *Prison and Plantation: Crime, Justice, and Authority in Massachusetts and South Carolina, 1767–1878*. Chapel Hill: University of North Carolina Press, 1980.

Hodes, Martha E. *White Women, Black Men: Illicit Sex in the Nineteenth Century South*. New Haven: Yale University Press, 1997.

Holifield, E. Brooks. *The Gentlemen Theologians: American Theology in Southern Culture*. Durham, N.C.: Duke University Press, 1978.

hooks, bell. *Black Looks: Race and Representation*. Boston: South End Press, 1992.

Horsman, Reginald. *Josiah Nott of Mobile: Southerner, Physician, and Racial Theorist*. Baton Rouge: Louisiana State University Press, 1987.

————. *Race and Manifest Destiny: The Origins of American Racial Anglo-Saxonism*. Cambridge: Harvard University Press, 1981.

Horwitz, Morton J. *The Transformation of American Law, 1780–1860*. Cambridge: Harvard University Press, 1977.

Howington, Arthur F. " 'Not in the Condition of a Horse or an Ox.' " *Tennessee Historical Quarterly* 34 (Fall 1975): 249–63.

————. *What Sayeth the Law: The Treatment of Slaves and Free Blacks in the State and Local Courts of Tennessee*. New York: Garland, 1986.

Howland, Richard W., and Joe W. Howland. "Two Hundred Years of Drinking in the United States: Evolution of the Disease Concept." In *Drinking: Alcohol in American Society—Issues and Current Research*, edited by John A. Ewing and Beatrice A. Rouse. Chicago: Nelson-Hall, 1978.

Hughes, John S. *In The Law's Darkness: Isaac Ray and the Medical Jurisprudence of Insanity in Nineteenth-Century America*. New York: Oceana Publications, 1986.

————. "Labeling and Treating Black Mental Illness in Alabama, 1860–1910." *Journal of Southern History* 58 (August 1993): 435–60.

Hunt, James L. "Note: Private Law and Public Policy: Negligence Law and Political Change in Nineteenth-Century North Carolina." *North Carolina Law Review* 66 (1988): 421–42.

Hunter, Tera W. *To 'Joy My Freedom: Southern Black Women's Lives and Labors after the Civil War.* Cambridge: Harvard University Press, 1997.

Ignatiev, Noel. *How the Irish Became White.* New York: Routledge, 1995.

Ingersoll, Thomas N. "Free Blacks in a Slave Society: New Orleans, 1718–1812." *William and Mary Quarterly* 48, no. 2 (1991): 173–200.

———. "Slave Codes and Judicial Practice in New Orleans, 1718–1807." *Law and History Review* 13 (Spring 1995): 23–62.

Isaac, Rhys. *The Transformation of Virginia, 1740–1790.* Chapel Hill: University of North Carolina Press, 1982.

James, D. Clayton. *Antebellum Natchez.* Baton Rouge: Louisiana State University Press, 1968.

Jaynes, Gerald D. *Branches without Roots: The Genesis of the Black Working Class in the American South, 1862–1882.* New York: Oxford University Press, 1986.

Johnson, Michael P., and James L. Roark. *Black Masters: A Free Family of Color in the Old South.* New York: Knopf, 1984.

Johnson, Walter. "Inconsistency, Contradiction, and Complete Confusion: The Everyday Life of the Law of Slavery." *Law and Social Inquiry* 22 (Spring 1997): 405–33.

———. *Soul by Soul: Life inside the Antebellum Slave Market.* Cambridge: Harvard University Press, 1999.

Jones, D. Marvin. "Darkness Made Visible: Law, Metaphor and the Racial Self." *Georgetown Law Journal* 82 (1993): 437–511.

Jones, Katharine M. *The Plantation South.* Indianapolis, Ind.: Bobbs-Merrill, 1957.

Jones, Norrece, Jr. *Born a Child of Freedom, yet a Slave: Mechanisms of Control and Strategies of Resistance in Antebellum South Carolina.* Middletown, Conn.: Wesleyan University Press, 1990.

Jordan, Winthrop D. *Tumult and Silence at Second Creek: An Inquiry into a Civil War Slave Conspiracy.* Baton Rouge: Louisiana State University Press, 1993.

———. *White over Black: American Attitudes toward the Negro, 1550–1812.* New York: W. W. Norton & Co., 1968.

Joyner, Charles. *Down by the Riverside: A South Carolina Slave Community.* Urbana.: University of Illinois Press, 1984.

Kairys, David, ed. *The Politics of Law: A Progressive Critique.* New York: Pantheon, 1982.

Kane, Harnett T. *Natchez on the Mississippi.* New York: William Morrow & Co., 1947.

Kennedy, Duncan. "Form and Substance in Private Law Adjudication." *Harvard Law Review* 89 (1976): 1685–1778.

Kiely, Terrance F. " 'The Hollow Words': An Experiment in Legal Historical Method as Applied to the Institution of Slavery." *DePaul Law Review* 25 (1976): 842–94.

Kilbourne, Richard H., Jr. *Debt, Investment, Slaves: Credit Relations in East Feliciana Parish, Louisiana, 1825–1885.* Tuscaloosa: University of Alabama Press, 1995.

Kolchin, Peter. *American Slavery, 1619–1877.* New York: Hill and Wang, 1993.

Kull, Andrew. "Personal Liberty and Private Law: The Enforceability after Emancipation of Debts Contracted for the Purchase of Slaves." *Chicago-Kent Law Review* 70 (1994): 493–538.

Landsman, Stephen. "The Civil Jury in America: Scenes from an Unappreciated History." *Hastings Law Journal* 44 (1993): 579–619.

Lazarus-Black, Mindie, and Susan F. Hirsch, eds. *Contested States: Law, Hegemony and Resistance.* New York: Routledge, 1994.

Lettow, Renee B. "New Trial for Verdict against Law: Judge-Jury Relations in Early Nineteenth-Century America." *Notre Dame Law Review* 71 (1996): 542–53.

Levine, Lawrence. *Black Culture and Black Consciousness: Afro-American Folk Thought from Slavery to Freedom.* New York: Oxford University Press, 1977.

Lichtenstein, Alex. " 'That Disposition to Theft, with Which They Have Been Branded': Moral Economy, Slave Management, and the Law." *Journal of Social History* 22, no. 3 (1988): 413–30.

Littlefield, Daniel C. *Rice and Slaves: Ethnicity and the Slave Trade in Colonial South Carolina.* Baton Rouge: Louisiana State University Press, 1981.

Mathews, Donald G. *Religion in the Old South.* Chicago: University of Chicago Press, 1977.

May, Robert E. *John A. Quitman: Old South Crusader.* Baton Rouge: Louisiana State University Press, 1985.

McCandless, Peter. *Moonlight, Magnolias and Madness: Insanity in South Carolina from the Colonial Period to the Progressive Era.* Chapel Hill: University of North Carolina Press, 1996.

McCash, William B. *Thomas R. R. Cobb (1823–1862): The Making of a Southern Nationalist.* Macon, Ga.: Mercer University Press, 1983.

McCurry, Stephanie. "The Two Faces of Republicanism: Gender and Proslavery Politics in Antebellum South Carolina." *Journal of American History* 78 (March 1992): 1245–64.

McIntosh, Wayne. "One Hundred and Fifty Years of Litigation and Dispute Settlement: A Court Tale." *Law and Society Review* 15 (1980–81): 823–48.

McLaurin, Melton A. *Celia: A Slave.* Athens: University of Georgia Press, 1991.

Mills, Frances Preston. *The History of the Descendants of the Jersey Settlers of Adams County, Mississippi.* 2 vols. Jackson, Miss.: 1981.

Mitnick, John Marshall. "From Neighbor-Witness to Judge of Proofs: The Transformation of the English Civil Juror." *American Journal of Legal History* 32 (1988): 201–35.

Mohr, James C. *Doctors and the Law: Medical Jurisprudence in Nineteenth-Century America.* New York: Oxford University Press, 1993.

Moore, John Hebron. *Andrew Brown and Cypress Lumbering in the Old South.* Baton Rouge: Lousiana State University Press, 1967.

———. *The Emergence of the Cotton Kingdom in the Old Southwest: Mississippi, 1770–1860.* Baton Rouge: Louisiana State University Press, 1988.

Morgan, Gwenda. "Law and Social Change in Colonial Virginia: The Role of the Grand Jury in Richmond County, 1692–1776." *Virginia Magazine of History and Biography* 95 (October 1987): 453–80.

Morris, Christopher. "The Articulation of Two Worlds: The Master-Slave Relationship Reconsidered." *Journal of American History* 85 (December 1998): 982–1007.

———. *Becoming Southern: The Evolution of a Way of Life, Warren County and Vicksburg, Mississippi, 1770–1860.* New York: Oxford University Press, 1995.

———. "What's So Funny? Southern Humorists and the Market Revolution." In *Southern Writers and Their Worlds,* edited by Christopher Morris and Steven G. Reinhardt, 9–26. College Station: Texas A&M University Press, 1996.

Morris, Thomas D. " 'As If the Injury Was Effected by the Natural Elements of Air or Fire': Slave Wrongs and the Liability of Masters." *Law and Society Review* 16 (1981–82): 569–99.

———. "Slaves and the Rules of Evidence in Criminal Trials." *Chicago-Kent Law Review* 68 (1993): 1209–40.

———. *Southern Slavery and the Law, 1619–1860.* Chapel Hill: University of North Carolina Press, 1996.

———. " 'Villeinage . . . as It Existed in England, Reflects but Little Light on Our Subject': The Problem of the Sources of Southern Slave Law." *American Journal of Legal History* 32 (1988): 95–137.

Nash, A. E. Keir. "Fairness and Formalism in the Trials of Blacks in the State Supreme Courts of the Old South." *Virginia Law Review* 56 (1970): 64–100.

———. "A More Equitable Past? Southern Supreme Courts and the Protection of the Antebellum Negro." *North Carolina Law Review* 48 (1970): 197–241.

———. "Negro Rights, Unionism, and Greatness on the South Carolina Court of Appeals: The Extraordinary Chief Justice John Belton O'Neall." *South Carolina Law Review* 21 (1969): 141–90.

Nelson, William. *The Americanization of the Common Law.* Cambridge: Harvard University Press, 1975.

Noll, Steven. *The Feeble-Minded in Our Midst: Institutions for the Mentally Retarded in the South, 1900–1940.* Chapel Hill: University of North Carolina Press, 1995.

Numbers, Ronald L., and Todd L. Savitt. *Science and Medicine in the Old South.* Baton Rouge: Louisiana State University Press, 1989.

Oakes, James. " 'The Compromising Expedient': Justifying a Proslavery Constitution." *Cardozo Law Review* 17 (1996): 2023–56.

———. "The Political Significance of Slave Resistance." *History Workshop Journal* 22 (1986): 89–107.

———. *The Ruling Race: A History of American Slaveholders.* New York: Alfred A. Knopf, 1982.

———. *Slavery and Freedom: An Interpretation of the Old South.* New York: Alfred A. Knopf, 1990.

Oliver, Nola N. *Natchez, Symbol of the Old South.* New York: Hastings House, 1940.

Omi, Michael, and Howard Winant. *Racial Formation in the United States: From the 1960s to the 1980s.* New York: Routledge, 1986.

Parish, Peter J. *Slavery: History and Historians.* New York: Harper and Row, 1989.

Patterson, Orlando. *Slavery and Social Death: A Comparative Study.* Cambridge: Harvard University Press, 1982.

Penningroth, Dylan. "Slavery, Freedom, and Social Claims to Property among African Americans in Liberty County, Georgia, 1850–1880." *Journal of American History* 84 (September 1997): 405–35.

Postell, William D. *The Health of Slaves on Southern Plantations.* Baton Rouge: Louisiana State University Press, 1951.

Prude, Jonathan. "To Look upon the 'Lower Sort': Runaway Ads and the Appearance of Unfree Laborers in America, 1750–1800." *Journal of American History* 78 (June 1991): 124–59.

Roeber, A. G. "Authority, Law, and Custom: The Rituals of Court Day in Tidewater Virginia, 1720 to 1750." *William and Mary Quarterly* 37 (January 1980): 29–52.

———. *Faithful Magistrates and Republican Lawyers: Creators of Virginia Legal Culture.* Chapel Hill: University of North Carolina Press, 1981.

Roediger, David. *Towards the Abolition of Whiteness.* London: Verso, 1994.

———. *The Wages of Whiteness: Race and the Making of the American Working Class.* London: Verso, 1991.

Rose, Willie Lee. *Slavery and Freedom.* Oxford: Oxford University Press, 1982.

Rosenberg, Charles E. *The Trial of the Assassin Guiteau: Psychiatry and Law in The Gilded Age.* Chicago: University of Chicago Press, 1968.

Rothman, David J. *The Discovery of the Asylum: Social Order and Disorder in the New Republic.* Boston: Little, Brown, 1971.

Rothstein, Morton. "The Natchez Nabobs: Kinship and Friendship in an Economic Elite." In *Toward a New View of America*, edited by Hans L. Trefousse, 97–112. New York: B. Franklin & Co., 1977.

Rowland, J. Dunbar. *Mississippi, the Heart of the South.* Vol. 1. New York: Southern Historical Publications Association, 1907.

Russell, Thomas D. "Articles Sell Best Singly: The Disruption of Slave Families at Court Sales." *Utah Law Review* (1996): 1161–1208.

———. "A New Image of the Slave Auction: An Empirical Look at the Role of Law in Slave Sales and a Conceptual Reevaluation of Slave Property." *Cardozo Law Review* 17 (1996): 473–524.

———. "South Carolina's Largest Slave Auctioneering Firm." *Chicago-Kent Law Review* 68 (1993): 1241–82.

Rutman, Darrett B., and Anita H. Rutman. *A Place in Time: Middlesex County, Virginia, 1650–1750.* New York: W. W. Norton, 1984.

Savitt, Todd L. *Medicine and Slavery: The Diseases and Health Care of Slaves in Antebellum Virginia.* Urbana: University of Illinois Press, 1978.

Saxton, Alexander. *The Rise and Fall of the White Republic: Class Politics and Mass Culture in Nineteenth-Century America.* London: Verso, 1990.

Scarborough, William K. "Lords or Capitalists? The Natchez Nabobs in Comparative Perspective." *Journal of Mississippi History* 54, no. 3 (1992): 239–67.

———. "Slavery—The White Man's Burden." In *Perspective and Irony in American Slavery*, edited by Harry P. Owens. Jackson: University Press of Mississippi.

Scarry, Elaine. *The Body in Pain: The Making and Unmaking of the World.* New York: Oxford University Press, 1985.

Schafer, Judith K. " 'Details Are of a Most Revolting Character': Cruelty to Slaves as Seen in Appeals to the Supreme Court of Louisiana." *Chicago-Kent Law Review* 68 (1993): 1283–1312.

———. " 'Guaranteed against the Vices and Maladies Prescribed by Law': Consumer Protection, the Law of Slave Sales, and the Supreme Court of Antebellum Louisiana." *American Journal of Legal History* 31 (1987): 306–22.

———. "The Long Arm of the Law: Slave Criminals and the Supreme Court in Antebellum Louisiana." *Tulane Law Review* 60 (1986): 1247–68.

———. *Slavery, Civil Law and the Supreme Court of Louisiana*. Baton Rouge: Louisiana State University Press, 1994.

Scheflin, Alan, and Jon Van Dyke. "Jury Nullification: The Contours of a Controversy." *Law and Contemporary Problems* 43 (Autumn 1980): 51–115.

Schultz, Marjorie S., ed. "Symposium: The American Jury." *Law and Contemporary Problems* 43 (Autumn 1980).

Schwarz, Philip J. *Twice Condemned: Slaves and the Criminal Laws of Virginia, 1705–1865*. Baton Rouge: Louisiana State University Press, 1988.

Schweninger, Loren. *Black Property Owners in the South, 1790–1915*. Urbana: University of Illinois Press, 1990.

———. "The Underside of Slavery: The Internal Economy, Self-Hire, and Quasi-Freedom in Virginia, 1780–1865." *Slavery and Abolition* 12 (September 1991): 1–22.

Scranton, Philip. *Proprietary Capitalism: The Textile Manufacture at Philadelphia, 1800–1885*. Philadelphia: Temple University Press, 1983.

Shapin, Steven. *A Social History of Truth: Civility and Science in Seventeenth-Century England*. Chicago: University of Chicago Press, 1994.

Shepard, E. Lee. "Breaking into the Profession: Establishing a Law Practice in Ante-bellum Virginia." *Journal of Southern History* 48 (August 1982): 393–410.

Showalter, Elaine. *The Female Malady: Women, Madness and Culture in England, 1830–1980*. New York: Pantheon Books, 1985.

Sicherman, Barbara. *The Quest for Mental Health in America, 1880–1917*. New York: Arno Press, 1980.

Simpson, A.W.B. *A History of the Common Law of Contract: The Rise of the Action of Assumpsit*. Oxford: Oxford University Press, 1975.

———. "The 'Horwitz Thesis' and the History of Contracts." *University of Chicago Law Review* 46 (1979): 533–601.

Smith, Roger. *Trial by Medicine: Insanity and Responsibility in Victorian Trials*. Edinburgh: Edinburgh University Press, 1981.

Smith-Rosenberg, Carroll. *Disorderly Conduct: Visions of Gender in Victorian America*. New York: Alfred A. Knopf, 1985.

Stampp, Kenneth. *The Peculiar Institution: Slavery in the Ante-bellum South*. New York: Vintage Books, 1965.

Stanley, Amy Dru. *From Bondage to Contract: Wage Labor, Marriage, and the Market in the Age of Slave Emancipation*. Cambridge: Cambridge University Press, 1998.

Stanton, William. *The Leopard's Spots: Scientific Attitudes toward Race in America, 1815–59*. Chicago: University of Chicago Press, 1960.

Stealey, John E. "The Responsibilities and Liabilities of the Bailee of Slave Labor in Virginia." *American Journal of Legal History* 12 (1968): 336–53.

Stephenson, Wendell. *Isaac Franklin, Slave Trader and Planter of the Old South*. 1938. Reprint, Baton Rouge: Louisiana State University Press, 1968.

Stevenson, Brenda E. *Life in Black and White: Family and Community in the Slave South*. New York: Oxford University Press, 1996.

Steinfeld, Robert J. *The Invention of Free Labor: The Employment Relation in English and American Law and Culture, 1350–1870*. Chapel Hill: University of North Carolina Press, 1991.

Stowe, Steven M. *Intimacy and Power in the Old South: Ritual in the Lives of the Planters*. Baltimore: Johns Hopkins University Press, 1987.

———. "Obstetrics and the Work of Doctoring in the Mid-Nineteenth-Century American South." *Bulletin of the History of Medicine* 64 (1990): 540–66.

———. "Seeing Themselves at Work: Physicians and the Case Narrative in the Mid-Nineteenth-Century American South." *American Historical Review* 101 (February 1996): 41–79.

Suggs, Jon-Christian. *Whispered Consolations: Law and Narrative in African American Life*. Ann Arbor: University of Michigan Press, 2000.

Sydnor, Charles S. *A Gentleman of the Old Natchez Region: Benjamin L. C. Wailes*. Durham, N.C.: Duke University Press, 1938.

———. *Slavery in Mississippi*. New York: D. Appleton-Century Co., 1933.

———. "The Southerner and the Laws." *Journal of Southern History* 6 (February 1940): 3–23.

"Symposium on the Legal History of the South." *Vanderbilt Law Review* 32 (January 1979).

Szasz, Thomas S. "The Sane Slave: A Historical Note on the Use of Medical Diagnosis as Justificatory Rhetoric." *American Journal of Psychotherapy* 25 (1971): 228–39.

Tadman, Michael. *Speculators and Slaves: Masters, Traders, and Slaves in the Old South*. Madison: University of Wisconsin Press, 1989.

Tansey, Richard Randall. "Bernard Kendig and the New Orleans Slave Trade."- *Louisiana History* 23 (1982): 159–78.

Taylor, William R., *Cavalier and Yankee: The Old South and American National Character*. New York: Harper & Row, 1961.

Thornton, J. Mills, III. *Politics and Power in a Slave Society: Alabama, 1800–1860*. Baton Rouge: Louisiana State University Press, 1978.

Tushnet, Mark. *The American Law of Slavery, 1810–1860: Considerations of Humanity and Interest*. Princeton: Princeton University Press, 1981.

———. "A Comment on the Critical Method in Legal History." *Cardozo Law Review* 6 (1985): 987–1011.

———. "The Constitution of the Bureaucratic State." *West Virginia Law Review* 86 (1984): 1077–1119.

Veeser, H. Aram, ed. *The New Historicism*. New York: Routledge, 1989.

Wahl, Jenny Bourne. *The Bondsman's Burden: An Economic Analysis of the Common Law of Southern Slavery*. New York: Cambridge University Press, 1998.

Wahl, Jenny Bourne. "The Bondsman's Burden: An Economic Analysis of the Jurisprudence of Slaves and Common Carriers." *Journal of Economic History* 53 (September 1993): 495–526.

Waldrep, Christopher. "Black Access to Law in Reconstruction: The Case of Warren County, Mississippi." *Chicago-Kent Law Review* 70 (1994): 583–621.

————. *Roots of Disorder: Race and Criminal Justice in the American South, 1817–80*. Urbana: University of Illinois Press, 1998.

————. "Substituting Law for the Lash: Emancipation and Legal Formalism in a Mississippi County Court." *Journal of American History* 82 (March 1996): 1425–51.

Watson, Alan. *Slave Law in the Americas*. Athens: University of Georgia Press, 1989.

Wayne, Michael. "An Old South Morality Play: Reconsidering the Social Underpinnings of the Proslavery Ideology." *Journal of American History* 77 (December 1990): 864–85.

————. *Reshaping Plantation Society: The Natchez District, 1860–1880*. Baton Rouge: Louisiana State University Press, 1983.

Wertheim, Frederick, "Note. Slavery and the Fellow Servant Rule: An Antebellum Dilemma." *New York University Law Review* 61 (1986): 1112–48.

White, Deborah Gray. *Ar'n't I a Woman? Female Slaves in the Plantation South*. New York: W. W. Norton & Co., 1985.

Wiecek, William M. *The Sources of Antislavery Constitutionalism in America, 1760–1848*. Ithaca: Cornell University Press, 1977.

Wiethoff, William E. *A Peculiar Humanism: The Judicial Advocacy of Slavery in High Courts of the Old South, 1820–1850*. Athens: University of Georgia Press, 1996.

Williams, Patricia J. *The Alchemy of Race and Rights: Diary of an African-American Law Professor*. Cambridge: Harvard University Press, 1991.

Williamson, Joel. *The Crucible of Race: Black/White Relations in the American South since Emancipation*. New York: Oxford University Press, 1984.

Wooster, Ralph A. *The People in Power: Courthouse and Statehouse in the Lower South, 1850–1860*. Knoxville: University of Tennessee Press, 1969.

Wren, J. Thomas. "A Two-Fold Character: The Slave as Person and Property." *Southern Studies* 24 (Winter 1985): 417–31.

Wright, Gavin. *Old South, New South: Revolutions in the Southern Economy since the Civil War*. New York: Basic Books, 1980.

————. *Political Economy of the Cotton South: Households, Markets, and Wealth in the Nineteenth Century*. New York: W. W. Norton, 1978.

Wyatt-Brown, Bertram. "Community, Class, and Snopesian Crime." In *Class, Conflict and Consensus: Antebellum Southern Community Studies*, edited by Orville V. Burton and Robert C. McMath, 171–206. Westport, Conn.: Greenwood Press, 1982.

————. "The Mask of Obedience: Male Slave Psychology in the Old South." *American Historical Review* 93 (December 1988): 1228–52.

————. *Southern Honor: Ethics and Behavior in the Old South*. New York: Oxford University Press, 1982.

————. *Yankee Saints and Southern Sinners*. Baton Rouge: Louisiana State University Press, 1985.

INDEX

mocratization of, 49; double character dichotomy of, 4; history of world's,
192nn.16 and 17; legal dispute application of, 53–57; Northern vs. Southern,
191n.3; public sexual intimacy with
slave violation of, 129; significance of
Deep South, 47–51; slave market and,
51–52; truth as central to, 49, 62;
Turner v. Ballard and, 58–61; warranty
suits as breach of, 54–55; whiteness and,
54, 98. *See also* slaves' dishonor; Southern culture
Hood, E. C., 140
Horlbeck, Dr., 136
Hughes, A. B., 104
Hughes, Mr., 137
Hundley, John, 111
Huntington, Eliza, 153, 154

Icar, Rose, 148, 149
idiocy, 123, 150
implied warranties. *See* warranties
importation of slaves, 30–32, 180n.51,
181n.58. *See also* slave trade
Incidents in the Life of a Slave Girl (Jacobs), 42
inferior courts, 182n.72
Ingraham, Joseph, 22, 28
Inquisition campaign (1841), 176n.27
insanity: drunkenness as first stage of, 144;
gender differences and, 147–51; medical
jurisprudence in identifying, 134; merging of moral/medical regarding, 146–52;
popular theories on, 146–47, 225nn.117
and 118; pretense as slaves' deceit, 66–
67; slave's character contributing to,
123; treatment for, 151–52, 227n.133.
See also slaves' diseases
insubordination, 148–50. *See also* insanity;
runaway slaves; slaves' agency
Isabella, 126

"Jack" stereotype, 74
Jacob, 119
Jacobs, Harriet, 42
Jacobs, Bocod v., 92
Jake, 35, 36, 41; See also *Brown v. Cox*
James, John D., 41, 57, 60, 93
James v. Kirk, 93
Jane, 150
Jeffries, William, 118
Jesse, 75

"Jezebel" stereotype, 74, 129
John, 85, 113–14
Johnson, Jonathan, 80, 81, 83
Johnson, Judge, 94
Johnson, Mr., 113
Johnson, Walter, 91, 124, 127, 141
Johnson, William, 26, 53, 62, 65
Johnson, Brocklebank v., 76–77
Johnson v. Wideman, 80–83, 146
Joor, Benjamin, 33
judges: appointment/election of, 29–30; instructions by, 38, 202nn.54 and 55; Limiting Act of 1822 and, 38
judicial system: of the Deep South, 6–7;
double character dichotomy of, 3–4. *See
also* legal cases cited; litigation
juries: in the *Brown v. Cox* case, 37–38;
civic participation on, 53–54; dissatisfac-
tion/satisfaction with, 40–41; judicial instructions to, 202nn.54 and 55; petit vs.
grand, 37, 54, 187n.96; records on,
186n.91
jurors: of *Brown v. Cox* case, 40; description of typical, 37, 188n.104; honor
manifested by, 53–54; media influence
on, 188n.105; selection of, 186n.92; as
slaveholding, 163t

Kate, 148–50
Kemble, Fanny, 152
Kendall, Dr., 137
Kenyon, Mr., 194n.43
King, William, 129
Kirk, Joseph J. B., 93
Kirk, James v., 93
Kitty, 74
Knott, Dr., 116
Kull, Andrew, 154
Kyle, Christopher, 63, 64

Lafortune, 77–78
Lalande, Pilie v., 74
Landier, Antoine, Sr., 107
Laurence v. McFarlane, 66
Laville, Jean, 77
the law: construction of race by, 96, 120,
208n.18; double character dichotomy in
context of, 8; economic development
and, 178n.44; on gaming and drinking,
145; honor culture and, 53–57; importance in Southern culture of, 23; power